Emerson's
Emergence

Emerson's Emergence

Self and Society in the Transformation of New England, 1800–1845

Mary Kupiec Cayton

The University of North Carolina Press

Chapel Hill and London

© 1989 The University of North Carolina Press

Library of Congress Cataloging-in-Publication Data

Cayton, Mary Kupiec.
    Emerson's emergence : self and society in the transformation of New
England, 1800–1845 / Mary Kupiec Cayton.
        p.   cm.
    Bibliography: p.
    Includes index.
    ISBN 0-8078-1870-4 (alk. paper)
    1. Emerson, Ralph Waldo, 1803–1882—Political and social views.
2. Capitalism—New England—History—19th century. 3. New England—
Social conditions. 4. New England—Intellectual life. 5. Social problems
in literature. 6. Self in literature. I. Title.
PS1642.S58C58   1989
814'.3–dc20   89-32663
                                                                  CIP

Portions of Chapter 2 were originally published as " 'Sympathy's Electric
Chain' and the American Democracy: Emerson's First Vocational Crisis,"
New England Quarterly 55 (1982): 3–24, and are reprinted here by permis-
sion of the *New England Quarterly*.

The paper in this book meets the guidelines for permanence and durability
of the Committee on Production Guidelines for Book Longevity of the
Council on Library Resources.

Design by April Leidig-Higgins

Printed in the United States of America

93 92 91 90 89   5 4 3 2 1

For Drew

Contents

Preface   ix

PART 1   Organicism

Chapter 1   An Education in Federalism   3
Chapter 2   The Socratic Response   33
Chapter 3   Spiritual Laws and Natural
Organicism   57

PART 2   Vocation

Chapter 4   The Armies of Zion   83
Chapter 5   The Idea of the Christian
Minister   112
Chapter 6   The Calling   137

PART 3   The Discovery of Self

Chapter 7   Uriel's Fall   163
Chapter 8   Concord Experiments   191
Chapter 9   Experience   218

Afterword: Emerson and the Culture
of Bourgeois Individualism   239

Notes   243

Bibliographic Essay   289

Index   299

A section of illustrations can be
found following page 118.

Preface

THIS BOOK has been ten years in the making. It began at a time when I had not heard of the "New Historicism" in literary criticism, and when historians were debating whether the intellectual history that examined figures such as Emerson was a dead endeavor.

When I began this study, my purpose was to synthesize the material available on the "New Social History" of early national New England and to reexamine Emerson's career in the context of that information. My impression was that most historians of Emerson had started by considering the individual in isolation (taking their cue from Emerson), and had added an historical, contextual overlay when it helped them to explain otherwise difficult problems. My intent was the opposite: to foreground the emerging urban, capitalist order of the Boston region, and to look at Emerson as a product of that particular time and place. I would start with New England and see how Emerson fit in.

In the years since the manuscript was completed, my point of view has changed somewhat. From 1982 through 1988, I worked as a temporary faculty member in an institution no better and no worse in its treatment of those on the margin than most in the country. During that period, when I accomplished little else besides teaching new and different courses in new and different ways, I became interested in what theory can teach us about the overarching assumptions of disciplines and modes of discourse. I found myself stuck for a while asking questions about the nature of intellectual discourse and about its value for those who do not engage in it formally. Mostly I wondered about its relation to a dominant social and economic order which it often purported to undermine, but which it ironically seemed to reinforce in very subtle ways. The central question of the study evolved over the years from "How can we put social history and literary criticism together?" to "How much do intellectuals have the power to act as transformative agents within society, and how much are they inevitably shaped by the circumstances of the age?"

Emerson's is a peculiarly important story in the development of American culture (which is to say, in the development of a social order molded and shaped by the necessities of a capitalist economy). Indeed, he has assumed mythic status as the firstborn American democratic philosopher and the advocate of the unlimited possibilities of the common man. He stands at the head of the traditional American literary canon. To examine his life and work is to think about the ways in which the hegemonic culture that plays an enormous role in structuring the major issues in our lives came to be made. Emerson, as one of the first American intellectuals to struggle self-consciously with the fruits of commercial capitalism, shows us how intellectuals make new meanings, how we unmake the old. Moreover, his story illustrates the ways in which we as makers of meaning are also made by the traditions of language and discourse we inherit. It is about the power of individuals and ideologies to transform the world, and about the inevitability that we ourselves will be transformed by our actions in the world in ways we cannot imagine. Although Emerson's story has been told hundreds of times from a variety of different perspectives, it has seemed to me in this new context a story worth telling again.

Antonio Gramsci's essay on "The Study of Philosophy" outlines the assumptions that have guided this study—although I happened upon it with a jolt of recognition when the study was well on its way toward completion. "One's conception of the world," writes Gramsci, "is a response to certain specific problems posed by reality, which are quite specific and 'original' in their immediate relevance." In this study, I have tried to explore some of the specific life circumstances that led Emerson to his peculiar philosophy of nature, individualism, and self-reliance. The assumption throughout is that the history of philosophy is more than the history of philosophers in dialogue with each other. It is rooted fundamentally in "the history of attempts made and ideological initiatives undertaken by a specific class of people to change, correct or perfect the concepts of the world that exist in any particular age and thus to change the norms of conduct that go with them; in other words, to change practical activity as a whole." The choice or construction of a philosophy is always implicitly a political act. Emerson's case is no different. In the emergence of a new culture, philosophers create a language that allows people to think coherently about the world in new ways, eventually restructuring their action as well as their thought. Emerson's task was to bring to conscious awareness new aspects of the social order and to name them for what they were.[1]

This story, then, is the tale of an Emerson who in fact was as influential as any of his age in articulating for his contemporaries a language by which to refer to the spiritual and emotional dilemmas of the new capitalist order. In so doing, he hoped to change profoundly the ways in which people thought about the business of living their lives. As people still living out the contradictions implicit in that order, we may yet find his a powerful voice, even if the limitations of his philosophy have become clearer to us over time.

Because I believe language to be so important in constructing the ways in which we think about and act in the world, I think it necessary to say a few words about the implicitly sexist language in the text which follows. Although I have felt disturbed about using the "generic" *he* or *mankind* in describing Emerson's world, I have also found it largely unavoidable. Emerson himself may have intended the use of the words to be generic, but the fact of the matter is that he was so willing to assume male experience to be the norm, that it is impossible in most instances to substitute "he and she" or "men and women." His is a male-centered philosophy that does not translate readily into a gender-neutral language, despite his best intentions. Where I have used masculine references in the manuscript, I have done so with the full knowledge that, although Emerson may have meant them inclusively, they in fact refer only to the experience of men in that time and place. Where women and men ought equally to be considered the subjects of a statement, I say so explicitly. I have retained original spelling in all quotations from primary source material.

As with any long-standing endeavor, I have incurred a number of intellectual debts I am grateful to have the opportunity finally to acknowledge. John L. Thomas gave me his example, encouragement, and support, and believed in this project perhaps more than I did. I am deeply grateful to him for bearing with me. Gordon S. Wood also contributed greatly to this project. Although I have come to disagree with him on certain issues, he has stimulated me to think deeply and critically through his own scholarship.

The late Hyatt Waggoner offered the kind of incisive advice that could only have come from a person with a long and distinguished career, even though he had doubts that anything new might be said on the subject. Patricia Caldwell, Barton St. Armand, and Donald Scott gave me valuable readings of the manuscript, as did Dale Bauer, Philip Gura, Amy Shrager Lang, and Peter Williams. Lewis Perry's NEH Summer Seminar for College Teachers on "Democratic Culture in America" helped me to clarify my thinking on a number of issues. Anne C. Rose on a few crucial occasions provided me with the benefit of her companionship and experience, and Judith Fryer gave me encouragement and financial support at important times. Susan Amussen, Steve Bullock, Paul Gilje, Shank Gilkeson, Don Spaeth, Dan Jones, and David Williams helped clarify my ideas and suggested possible source materials. Lois Simmons's and Julie Schlicter's help in manuscript preparation was invaluable.

I thank the University Professors Program at Boston University for the time and financial support that allowed me to follow out questions raised by some of the earlier readings of the manuscript and the College of Arts and Science, Miami University, for financial help in the preparation of the final manuscript. I am also grateful to the staffs of the Houghton Library and the Harvard University Archives of Harvard University, the John Hay Library of Brown University, the Massachusetts Historical Society, the Boston Athenaeum, the Congregational Library of Boston, and Doug Baker of the First Parish in Concord for their assistance. Emerson's manuscript sermons and various manuscript letters from the Emerson Family Papers are quoted by permission of the Houghton Library. Salem Street Church's records are quoted courtesy of the Massachusetts Historical Society, and those of Second Church, Boston, by permission of the First and Second Church. Permission to quote from the manuscript examining records of the Park Street Church has been granted by the Congregational Library, Boston, on behalf of the Park Street Church.

My students at the School of Interdisciplinary Studies (Western College Program) have never been interested in Emerson, and this manuscript probably would have been done long ago were it not for them. Nevertheless, they kept me honest. Because they never stopped asking what is at stake when we teach and write, I never could either. For their willingness to challenge what others accept as a matter of course, I thank them.

I am most deeply indebted to my family, whose presence and support sustain me. Henry and Claire Kupiec, Robert and Vivian Cayton, Lee and Irene Pelley, and Rita Carroll provided various kinds of support, both financial and emotional, during the course of this project. Elizabeth Renanne Cayton has gladly suffered both of her parents' spending substantial amounts of time writing about "dead people"—and dead men, at that. She has even had the great good grace to pretend to be interested in stories about Ralph Waldo Emerson or the Northwest Territory. Hannah Kupiec Cayton gladdened the final work on the manuscript by arriving in the world midway through revisions on Chapter 8, and by waking up only on her father's nights on duty. Andrew Cayton has read the entire manuscript and given me a helpful outside perspective when I have most needed it. He has kept faith in me and in this project during some times when it has been difficult to do so. For his companionship I am profoundly grateful. Because he has lived it with me for so long, this book—in love and deepest gratitude—is for him.

PART I

Organicism

CHAPTER I

An Education
in Federalism

It is a singular fact that we cannot present to the imagination a longer space than just so much of the world as is bounded by the visible horizon; so that even in this stretching of thought to comprehend the broad path lengthening itself & widening to receive the rolling Universe stern necessity bounds us to a little extent of a few miles only. . . . But what matters it[?] We can talk & write & think it out.—Journals and Miscellaneous Notebooks, *January 1820*

ON 25 MAY 1803, Ralph Waldo Emerson was born in Boston, Massachusetts. The Reverend William Emerson, pastor of Boston's First Church, was not at home to witness his son's birth. He had been attending the annual Election Day sermon with the other assembled luminaries of the commonwealth. As he made his way home to the parsonage on Summer Street to learn of the birth of his son, he would have been able to take in the sights of spring in a city with which few modern Bostonians would be familiar. He would have passed cows and sheep on the Common and perhaps even seen a few pigs roaming the streets, for the public grazing land was yet to be fenced in and the hog pens were still to be built. He might have been stung by a stiff sea breeze and would have detected the unmistakable tang of salt in the air, for Boston was still nearly surrounded by sea. It was connected to the mainland only by a narrow neck of land on its south side, and by a bridge over the river Charles on its northwest. Docks and warehouses rimmed the peninsula, evidence of the international trade that had made Boston prosperous in recent years. Such trade was transforming it from a provincial town to a center of regional activity. Where there were no docks, there were shallow inlets, bays, and marshlands. If William Emerson looked up, he could have identified the three mountains on which Boston had been built, mountains which lent Tremont Street its name. Beacon Hill, the most prominent of the three, had not yet been leveled to provide the landfill now known as Back Bay. Then the Back Bay was in fact a body of water that lay behind the older part of the city. Emerson's father also would have passed gardens, fields, and orchards on his walk. Indeed, his own parsonage sat in the middle of an acre of land; in spring, the delicate scent of the fruit trees just outside his window mixed with the smell of the sea and the stench of animals.

Despite these pastoral scenes, Boston in 1803 was no longer the rural outpost established nearly two centuries before by those sent on an errand into a real wilderness; with a population of some twenty-five thousand souls, it was one of the principal cities in America, the metropolis of New England. This bustling entrepôt for the New England hinterlands was obviously undergoing a rapid expansion. As recently as 1780, Boston had contained only about ten thousand people, but with the end of the Revolution and the subsequent upsurge in international trade, it had grown, attracting laborers and manufacturers from the back country.[1] If William Emerson had wanted to walk as far as the old North End of the city, he would have seen the narrow, crowded streets that had been settled for decades. Closer to the new end of town where he lived, there were the distilleries and the ropewalks, the cabinetmakers and glassblowers and tallow chandlers who had become fixtures of this new, commercial Boston. If his journey had taken him further west, he would also have walked along new streets, straight and wide and planned, that ran between the new brick homes of the well-to-do, with their carefully tended gardens. Public buildings sprouted on the more remote lots of the city.

Although Boston was undergoing radical changes that would profoundly affect the life of Ralph Waldo Emerson, they probably did not disturb his father as much as they might have disoriented a resident of long standing in the city. William Emerson had only recently arrived in Boston. He had been born in Concord, Massachusetts, a provincial village some twenty miles northwest of Boston, where his ancestors has resided for a century and a half. The Emersons had long been clergymen. His father, also named William, had been minister at Concord prior to his death in 1776. A chaplain to Continental army troops, the elder William Emerson had died while on a march to Fort Ticonderoga. His wife, Phebe Bliss Emerson, was left with a babe in arms, and promptly married Ezra Ripley, her husband's successor in the pulpit at Concord. It was the stern Ripley who acted as father to William Emerson.

Like most aspirants to the ministry in Massachusetts, William was schooled at Harvard College. After serving a year as a country schoolmaster, he received a call to the church in the village of Harvard in Worcester County in 1792. The young minister—bright, sophisticated, and bookish—found life in the out-of-the-way town barely tolerable and yearned for the more stimulating atmosphere of cosmopolitan Boston. The town failed to provide its minister adequate support, and when the young pastor decided to take a wife in 1796, he began to look for opportunities to leave. When the First Church in Boston issued its call, William Emerson was ready to interpret it as the voice of God. Installed as pastor there in 1799, he became by virtue of his position a permanent and important part of the powerful Boston establishment.

Ruth Haskins Emerson was the woman William Emerson married during the lean years in the rural countryside. He met her in Malden when both were visiting relatives, and they married in 1796 despite William's financial situation. Unlike her husband, she knew Boston well, having been born there in 1768. Her father, John Haskins, was a rising merchant in the West India trade; originally a cooper, he had been taken into partnership by his stepfather and had developed a large shipping and distilling business. In status-conscious colonial Boston, Haskins's social standing was high enough to earn him a captaincy in the Boston Regiment, an organization that like most prerevolutionary institutions awarded leadership positions on the basis of social rank and wealth. Early in the Revolution, Haskins had been a Son of Liberty; as time wore on, however, he had fallen out with the more radical, working class elements of Boston led by Samuel Adams, and for most of the war he remained a moderate royalist. In politics he favored government by the best men; in religion he was an Anglican. As a child, Ruth Haskins had been given the choice of espousing the Congregationalism of her mother or the Anglicanism of her father. She had chosen Anglicanism. Both her parents, like most well-to-do Bostonians of their era, were tolerant liberals in matters of religion despite their apparent sectarian differences. Since William Emerson too was a religious liberal, the superficial differences in their religious affiliations posed no great barrier to their marriage. Indeed, Mary Moody Emerson— sister to William and more Calvinist than any other Emerson— pronounced her future sister-in-law "virtues self."[2]

When Boston called, Ruth Haskins Emerson was not as eager as her husband to move back to the city of her birth. "Truly in one view," she wrote her sister, "a removal is not likely much to advance my own private happiness and ease. My partiality for retirement and rural scenes is great, and my aversion is great to the useless ceremony, parade, and pomp, that almost necessarily are attached to a town life." As small a city as Boston was in 1799, urban life there presented a sharp contrast to the life of the surrounding villages. Nevertheless, she continued, the annoyances of town life were surely "outweighed by the prospect of means for Mr. Emerson's greater improvement in the profession in which he most delights." Like many another ambitious young man, William Emerson traveled to Boston to seek fame, honor, and greater financial security.[3]

I

William Emerson had been at the annual Election Day sermon on the afternoon of his son's birth because, as a member of the established clergy, he was among the elite of Boston and wielded considerable power. Though ministers did not usually possess the wealth requisite for entry into the Massachusetts gentry, their spiritual position and learning compensated for what they lacked in material possessions. Liberal ministers like William Emerson were instrumental in preserving the values that the notables of New England held dear. They were the caretakers of learning and culture. In the era during which William Emerson came to live in Boston, they were in the process of establishing a variety of institutions designed to perpetuate the religious and secular knowledge they believed necessary to insure a stable, orderly society. William Emerson himself was a founder of the Massachusetts Historical Society and the Boston Atheneum, editor of a religious and literary periodical, the *Monthly Anthology*, chaplain to the state senate, and an overseer of Harvard College. He was well off enough to employ a kitchen maid and important enough to be asked to deliver the annual Fourth of July oration for the town of Boston in 1802. Like Caleb Strong, inaugurated governor that Election Day, William Emerson was dedicated to the principles of Federalism, an ideology that idealized communal virtue, harmony, and consensus. It had taken firm root in Massachusetts in the tumultuous years following the Revolution, and though it lent its name to a political party, it implied a good deal more than just politics. It encompassed, in fact, an entire worldview.[4]

As the dominant ideology of Massachusetts in the late eighteenth and early nineteenth centuries, Federalism represented the value system of a hegemonic order of merchants and propertied elite. In language that invoked the legacy of the Revolution, Federalists claimed to define patriotism and civic virtue in ways appropriate for all groups of the region. Federalism as an articulated ideology took its name from those individuals who supported the establishment of a strong federal government as an antidote to the various excesses to which state governments had presumably given license in the period following the Revolution. Noting a variety of manifestations of social disarray, Federalists lamented "the atmosphere of mistrust, the breakdown of authority, the increase of debt, the depravity of manners, and the decline of virtue" prevalent in contemporary society in the wake of the Revolution.[5] They believed in a government that entrusted power to a natural aristocracy dedicated to the common interest of the people as a whole, rather than to a democratically defined body representing differing interests of differing groups.[6]

The "democratization" of the political and economic spheres was understood by Federalists as social disintegration, or, in the jeremiadic language often utilized in this period by Election Day sermonizers, declension. For the most part, the class of individuals who coalesced under the banner of Federalism had not intended a democratic transformation of the social order by means of the Revolution. As the propertied and privileged of colonial society, their own aim had been to eliminate the corruption of a parasitic class of royal placemen and administrators. During the 1780s and 1790s, they came to believe that the chief threat to the republic was "democracy," by which they meant the unbridled pursuit of self-interest at the expense of the common good. The culprits were new men in public life who were unwilling to adopt the values and behaviors of the natural aristocracy.[7]

Like groups of all sorts at this time, Federalists appealed to the notion of republicanism to define the unique identity and mission of the new American nation-state. In theory, the health of the new republic would be insured by individuals who, by maintaining independence of means through ownership of property, would remain beyond corruption or the blandishment of demagogues. How republicanism was best to be understood in practice continued to be contested terrain for decades, however. Some in the American republic, represented in the political sphere by the Jeffersonian Republicans, saw liberalism as the practical working out of republicanism. Linking the private pursuit of happiness and the concomitant expansion of the market with the enhancement of the public welfare, this liberal version of republicanism (as Joyce Appleby has called it) undercut Federalist paternalism by finding the common good in innovation and full participation in the economic sphere. Thus, it opened the way for the participation of new men in the social order. The liberal Republicans drew on a rhetoric of individual rights, appealed to in the Revolution as justification for revolt against the Crown, in order to transform individuals formerly outside the political arena into new political subjects. The Federalists, in contrast, believed such a social order lent itself to chaos and potential disaster.[8]

Gentlemen were to govern—not gentlemen artificially made by patronage or heredity, as in prerevolutionary Massachusetts, but gentlemen nevertheless. They would naturally rise to the leadership positions in society, demonstrating their worthiness to lead by their learning, virtue, and accomplishments. A natural aristocracy of talent and ability—"the Union of wisdom with goodness[,] a nobility founded by the Author of the universe," as Boston orator William Sullivan put it on the Fourth of July, 1802—would lead the republic.[9] Democracy, as opposed to the sort of republicanism that the Federalists professed, was popular rule. For men of principle who espoused the rule of law and virtue, democracy was potentially no better than mob rule. Popular rule undermined government by principle, for principles were determined by reason and by reason's God, not by popular fiat. Democracy always posed the danger that individuals would assert private self-interest in the face of public good. "God preserve us," William Emerson himself would write his sister Mary Moody Emerson in 1807, "in this howling and tempestuous world! . . . One might almost as well be amidst the . . . billows of the ocean, as to be over whelmed by the floods of democracy."[10] In the high-mindedness of the people as a whole, the Federalists had little trust. With proper leadership, however, they might live in peace and prosperity and develop their own capacities for virtuous action.

The gentry who led this Federalist society advocated a pattern of social relations that appealed to many people whose social position was not as prominent as that of William Emerson. What legitimized this social vision, at least implicitly, for the skilled artisans, laborers, and small farmers whom it presumably excluded from political power and moral decision making? The answer lies in part in the fact that, for a while at least, Federalism provided a coherent language through which to understand and talk about significant social change in the region. Although Federalism was an ideology manifestly designed to salvage the idealized hierarchical and deferential world of colonial Massachusetts, a world in which control by an elite was assured, it also represented an attempt to preserve the personal social relations that had characterized most of the cities and towns of eastern Massachusetts prior to the Revolution. Believing that homogeneity and social integration were the best ways to insure social stability in a relatively self-sufficient milieu, Federalist ideology captured a precapitalist ethos threatened by the rapid growth of commerce and increase in mobility in the years following the Revolution. In such an environment, the stability that Federalism seemed to offer proved appealing to many. The towns and villages of New England had been close-knit, personally oriented societies that placed a premium on consensus and condemned conflict as self-seeking and self-aggrandizing. Federalism promised to banish the conflicts that were inevitable as the market encroached. It offered a way of explaining and coping with the discomfort experienced by people caught in a transition to a new way of life.[11]

To enter into the world of the Federalists in a concrete way, we need only look at the Election Day sermon to which William Emerson had been listening on the day of his son's birth. It had been delivered by Emerson's houseguest, the Reverend Reuben Puffer, and followed a pattern of election sermons familiar to its audience. Such annual jeremiads had been delivered in the same way for over a hundred years in Boston. Chastising the people for their collective transgressions against God, Puffer also exhorted his listeners to recall that God had chosen them for a sacred mission if they would but keep their part of the covenant.[12] Despite the formal similarities to previous election sermons, however, there was in Reuben Puffer's jeremiad a message that his forefathers would not have delivered. That message hinged on Federalist conceptions of order, harmony, and community in a republic. To be sure, in the vision of society that Puffer outlined for his audience, one could readily trace the Puritan family resemblance. Nevertheless, the familiar inheritance had been subtly but permanently transformed in the wake of the Revolution.

Puffer began his speech before the elders of Massachusetts by calling attention to "the origin, progress, decline, and final subversion of civil states"—"a most interesting subject of contemplation."[13] As his audience no doubt expected, he proceeded to establish the traditional connection between New England and Israel. Since the Revolution, that comparison had usually reflected the liberal and rational tendencies of religion in Boston rather than the strict Biblical comparisons of orthodox Calvinism. Thus it was that day that Puffer examined the Jewish nation as a particularly interesting illustration of the law of the rise and fall of nations.

As a Federalist, Puffer was intent on explaining for his audience the laws by which nations, especially republics, survived and flourished. The life of nations was as precarious as that of individuals. Anyone studying the histories of the ancient republics of Greece and Rome, as Federalists were wont to do, could observe that history took a cyclical course of rise and decline. Thus, the Federalists, who valued the corporate community as the highest and best, indeed the God-given, form of social expression, were interested in discovering the laws that would insure the survival of their own republic. This concern with law by no means indicated an indifference to traditional religious concerns. The Federalists knew that God still visited his judgment on nations for their collective sins. But an enlightened age could trace out the pattern of a rational God in a lawful universe.[14]

Puffer urged New Englanders to see themselves once again as a chosen race and a city set upon a hill. By 1803, however, it was no longer the fact of the migration to a new world that guaranteed New England's claim to prominence. Rather, it was the experiment in communal virtue spawned by the Revolution that merited the world's attention. All nations had a share in this republican vision, Puffer asserted: "The experiment is here making, whether, human guilt and depravity considered, mankind are capable of preserving the spirit, and supporting the form of a free, republican government." The rest of the world looked to the new republic to see whether human beings could voluntarily subdue their passions— govern themselves in a personal sense—to create a lasting and virtuous social order.[15]

Like all good jeremiads, however, Puffer's contained not only visions of the glorious future within the grasp of his listeners, but also warnings that God's chosen people had begun to sin against him and against their own destiny. If Puffer's exhortations to virtue and honor revealed the hopes of William Emerson's class for New England, his monitions revealed their fears. "Whenever there shall be a general departure from the principles, which give support and permanency to our national institutions," Puffer warned, "they will crumble to atoms." He was compelled by concern for his listeners' moral welfare to enumerate for them their transgressions. Among the chief of their sins was the political and social dissension that divided them into competing factions. They were "agitated by party and rent by internal dissensions"; they selfishly neglected the "true interests" of the community, for they had become "more intent upon carrying some favourite point, or in mortifying an opponent, than in doing what the substantial interests of the community rendered necessary."[16]

The people's interests, Reuben Puffer told his Election Day audience, were to be determined coolly and dispassionately, watchfully and circumspectly, by those with the best information about what was "most conductive to the general benefit." In divisive manipulation of citizens for the private and selfish ends of party or faction, Puffer asserted, "the work of mischief begins"—"hence originates that rage for innovation, which like a resistless torrent, sweeps away all the defenses of public liberty erected by wisdom and foresight, and in its course demolishes the stablest pillars of social order and happiness."[17]

Puffer warned too against the lust for wealth. The achievement of the Revolution, in which the rule of government had been wrested from the hands of men corrupted by power and wealth and restored to the people, was no guarantee that the republic would survive. That issue hung on the virtue of its citizenry, its willingness to choose good over gain. Hence, Bostonians throughout the Federalist era heard variations on Puffer's jeremiad, some secular and some sacred. For example, Joseph Stevens Buckminster, the foremost preacher of William Emerson's day, preached against the "inordinate pursuit of pleasure, or what is, with great significance, called in modern times, dissipation." William Ellery Channing, normally a sanguine preacher, from time to time echoed Buckminster's fear that the "tendency of the present state of things" was "to self-indulgence." The self-indulgence and the growing dissipation of the times posed a danger not only to the individual's soul, but to the welfare of the community. Without the necessary practice of self-restraint and republican virtue, the entire social fabric was likely to unravel.[18]

This Federalist ideology of virtue and principle, harmony and consensus, order and stability, was the ideology of the Boston of William Emerson, the Boston into which Ralph Waldo Emerson was born. Although the elder Emerson died in 1811 when his son was barely old enough to remember him, the worldview of William Emerson's class predominated in Boston for a good while longer. The city would grow and its social structure would change drastically, but the conservative social organicism of Federalism would retain a hold on Boston's elite. Its values would continually be placed before Bostonians in patriotic speeches and political rhetoric. In the midst of this philosophy, patently at odds with the reality of life in the rapidly changing city of Boston, Ralph Waldo Emerson grew to maturity.

II

As the sons of William Emerson and Ruth Haskins Emerson grew up in Boston, they received the Federalist education proper to the sons of the professional classes in the city. There were five Emerson boys: William, Ralph Waldo, Charles Chauncy, Edward Bliss, and Robert Bulkeley. (John Clarke Emerson died when his brother Ralph was four, Phebe Ripley Emerson before Ralph was born; another sister, Mary Caroline Emerson, died in 1814 in her third year.) In 1812, at the age of nine, Ralph Waldo Emerson entered the Boston Latin School, where he was to receive the rudiments of the classical education that would prepare him for college. By reading the histories of the ancient republics, Greece and Rome, the young republicans learned the political vocabulary of their fathers: in the Athenian democracy or the Roman republic, they found historical models of heroic civic virtue and communal solidarity, which they were taught to emulate. This sort of an education, as the *New England Quarterly Magazine* for September 1802 claimed, would inculcate the moral virtue necessary in the rising leadership class of society: "The best ages of Rome afford the purest models of virtue that are anywhere to be met with. Mankind are too apt to lose sight of all that is heroic, magnanimous and public spirited. . . . Left to ourselves, we are apt to sink into effeminacy and apathy."[19]

As the rising leaders of society (for the Boston Latin School was attended only by those preparing for college), these young men would also practice the techniques of oratory that they would need to debate the course of community affairs with other talented, learned, and virtuous men. They had to learn the arts of persuasion not in order to obtain some personal or partial good for themselves, but in order to head off the demagogues who would manipulate the passions of the crowd. In 1806, Harvard College itself acknowledged the importance of oratorical skills in a republic by establishing the Boylston Professorship of Rhetoric and Oratory. Youngsters did not need to wait until they reached Harvard to practice their oratory, however. Every Boston schoolboy knew well David Everett's recitation piece, "Lines Spoken at a School-exhibition, by a Little Boy Seven Years Old," for nearly all of them had declaimed it in front of an audience at that tender age.[20] Saturday was the usual day for declamation at the Latin School, when the boys were called upon to practice the arts of eloquence before their peers and their schoolmaster. So important was public speaking skill deemed for these rising leaders of society that public exhibitions were held regularly and medals given to the most impressive orator of each class. Like others of his class, Emerson was to be a highly visible figure in a highly public community.

In order to emphasize the primacy of the community and the role that individuals were to play in it, the Boston of Emerson's youth organized a great many public ceremonies. It was over such occasions that the schoolboy orators were preparing to preside. On these occasions, Boston's citizenry experienced through iconography and ritual the intricate hierarchy of social station at the heart of the Federalist ideology. Every summer, for example, Harvard held its annual commencement, a pageant that Boston considered its own. In its spectacles and exhibitions, the town's fledgling leaders exhibited their persons and talents to the crowd. The day was a state holiday, for Harvard was not seen as the educator of privileged young men, but as the training ground for those who would be responsible for the society and culture of the community. Or again, the Washington Benevolent Society, a charitable Federalist club with strong political overtones, held a public celebration each April

30, the date of Washington's inauguration. The processions, banners, orations, and exercises in the Old South Church were typical of the public events organized by many such semipublic organizations. Emerson may well have marched in their "company of schoolboy Federalists . . . dressed uniformly in blue and white, with Washington's Farewell Address, in red morocco, hanging round their necks, and with his gorget, which he had worn in the old French War, attached to their banner" like some saint's relic.[21] Militia exercises also took place on the Common and attracted large crowds.

In such ceremonies, everything from the dress of the participants to the symbols they carried and the order in which they marched in the procession was designed to submerge the individuality of the participants in the ethos of an organic community acting together. If the Federalists preached an attitude of public responsibility toward the community as a whole, ceremonies such as these reinforced in a visible way for both participants and spectators a sense of the ties they shared. Such iconology offered them a visible symbol of the town's structure, values, and ideals as seen by the dominant social order.

Despite the young Emerson's immersion in such a culture, however, he seems to have had some of the uneasiness about received cultural values common to the young. For example, although he frequently wrote poetry in the heroic tradition of the Roman epics, a style that demanded high and noble subjects, he handled his attempts at lofty and patriotic poetry with some ambivalence. On the one hand, he seemed to respect the traditional forms and rituals of Federalist republicanism as worthy of imitation; on the other, he also felt impelled to deflate those traditions, mocking them in overt parody and in farcical uses of heroic forms. Here, for example, in the mock-heroic lines he wrote to his brother Edward when the latter left home to attend school at Andover, he parodies the sententious heroism his elders have taught him:

> And now arrives the chariot of state
> That bears with regal pomp Ned, Bliss the great
> See from afar arise a dusty cloud
> And see approaching fast the gathering crowd
> See yonder rank of learned sages come
> Like reverend fathers of majestic Rome
> Down from their aged heads their hats they bend

On either hand the bowing lines extend
While thro' the midst with elevated mein [*sic*]
Stalks "Edward Emerson the great" between
Hark the loud clangor of the sounding bell
To Andoveria's college hails thee well[22]

In his early letters, Emerson appears to be trying to assimilate the high notions of his class about honor and rank, but he does so in a way perhaps a bit more irreverent than some of his contemporaries. He jokingly protests, for example, his brother William's violation of protocol in writing first to his brother Charles, "omitting to write to me the 'Man of the House' 'Generalissimo' &c. &c." From time to time he half-seriously played with deferential forms of polite address, writing to Edward as "your honor" and closing "I have the honor to be your excellency's most obedient and faithful Servant." William, too serious about his own rank and reputation as far as his younger brother was concerned, is ridiculed as "his Deaconship." As the eldest surviving brother, it seems to have been William who took his education in Federalism most seriously.[23]

One reason why Emerson may have been ambivalent about the elitist values of Federalist Boston was the latent but important conflict between his ascribed social station and the material circumstances of his life. Because he was the son of one of Boston's most prominent and learned men, it was expected that he would receive the education and training that would allow him to assume a position of public leadership. He did receive such an education, but sometimes it must have seemed at odds with the genteel poverty in which he and his family lived after the death of the elder William Emerson in 1811. Although Emerson could remember little of his father's death but "the stateliness of the funeral, at which the Ancient and Honorable Artillery escourted to the grave the body of their late chaplain," the financial cataclysm that followed would affect his own life for many years.[24] The Society of the First Church allowed the Emerson family to remain in the parsonage on Summer Street for a year, and for another, the family lodged in the Haskins family home in Boston. After that, the widow Emerson and her five sons had to scramble to make ends meet. The boys were frequently sent for extended periods of time to relatives who would help with their support. Ralph and Charles both spent time with the Ripleys in Concord. Bulkeley lived for many years with an aunt in Waterford, Maine. Several of the boys lived for weeks or months with another of their aunts, Mary Moody Emerson, who herself sometimes lodged with her sister-in-law in Boston. The frequent removals from relative to relative and boarding house to boarding house prompted the fifteen-year-old Ralph to write his brother William, "It appears to me the happiest earthly moment my most sanguine hopes can picture, if it should ever arrive to have a home, comfortable & pleasant, to offer to mother." In fact, this hope was one of the reasons that decided young Emerson to "study divinity & keep school at the same time"; he would "try to be a minister & have a house."[25] William Emerson had similar plans.

Although they would meet in twos and threes for a few months at a time, the five Emerson brothers would never enjoy a common home for any length of time after 1811. Ruth Emerson took in boarders during most of her son Waldo's adolescence. Her son Edward reported to his aunt Mary Moody Emerson that his mother was "so much engaged with her work" that she was "obliged to sit up until about midnight every night."[26] Though Emerson's lack of a home and a stable family life was no doubt difficult for him, it was not an unusual state of affairs in nineteenth-century New England for adolescent sons to be intentionally separated from their families. Although the practice was no longer frequent among the members of Emerson's social caste, sons of the less well-to-do—mobile artisans and tradesmen—were still apprenticed out to other families at an early age. It would be these middling orders who in a few years would begin to question the premises of Federalist social organicism. Emerson's later willingness to break with his own social class would grow in part out of an experience that in some ways resembled theirs. Because of his upper-class education, however, the premises of his own social order that he questioned would prove different from those to which the middling orders would object.

Yet Emerson's personal circumstances alone do not explain his adolescent disaffection. Although Emerson's own early experiences seem to have exacerbated his feelings, others too sensed after the Treaty of Ghent in 1814 that things were not quite right in Boston. What some historians have called the Era of Good Feelings seems to have been an era of acute dissatisfaction and apprehension for many Bostonians, especially those of Emerson's generation. In order to understand why, it is necessary to look briefly at the changes the city of Boston itself was undergoing in the early nineteenth century. If Emerson's own adolescence was a disorienting one, the city of his birth was also weathering a difficult time.

III

Despite the Federalist rhetoric that glorified an older way of life, Boston during Emerson's youth stood on the verge of major transformations in nearly every aspect of its corporate existence. As population grew and transportation and communication improved, its patterns of social interaction altered substantially. Charles Francis Adams, the son of one of Boston's more prominent families, remarked a generation later, "Men of a former generation . . . found themselves puzzled. They saw change going on, and they mistook it for decay."[27] Changes occurred in the quality as well as in the scope of relationships among individuals living in the area, changes that accompanied the rise of merchant capitalism on a large scale in eastern Massachusetts and the urban culture supporting it. Commercialization, with its tendency to break down older webs of relationships as individuals entered a more abstract, impersonal market, threatened the disruption of a social order based on the ideal of self-sufficient, well-integrated communities.[28]

The underpinnings of a commercial, urban social order had developed in Boston even before the Revolution, with a mercantile elite controlling most town offices as well as a sizable and growing segment of propertyless men.[29] Nevertheless, despite its population of just under thirty-five thousand in 1810, Bostonians persisted in thinking of themselves as inhabitants of an overgrown small town. Problems were still discussed by the whole community in the town meeting, although as in other towns, selectmen were caretakers for the bulk of business. Church membership in Boston was based on voluntary affiliation rather than on geography, as in rural areas, but individuals were expected to belong to a church and pay taxes for its support all the same. Despite the fact that the city was already becoming too large a place to depend on consensual government in the form of town meetings, which were appropriate to the intimacy of smaller communities, it clung both to the institutions of small town life and to the mores that underlay them.

Fortunately for the communal orientation of Federalism, the population of both Massachusetts as a whole and Boston in particular retained a high degree of homogeneity during the early part of the nineteenth century. Despite its size, Boston remained a peculiarly provincial city capable of sustaining such a civil and moral code for a long time. Timothy Dwight, a visitor to Boston in 1810, noted how strikingly the city had maintained its personal atmosphere, one in which individual characters could be known and scrutinized by others: "Here a man is not as in London, lost in an immense crowd of people, and thus hidden from the inspection of his fellowmen; but is known, and is conscious that he is known. His virtues, and his vices, his wisdom and his folly, excite here, much the same attention, and are examined in much the same manner, as in a country village. A strong sense of the public approbation, or disapprobation, therefore, cannot fail to reach every man, who is not stupid."[30] Although there were already a few men in Boston, far from stupid, whom the public disapprobation of the city's elite no longer bothered, those who really counted in society were still apt to know each other and to be influenced by the personal behavior of society's notables.

Even before Boston's rapid expansion, however, the city had seemed to many country folk a sinkhole of iniquity and unorthodox opinion. Joseph Buckminster, a minister at Portsmouth, New Hampshire (itself no village), feared for the spiritual safety of his son, Joseph Stevens Buckminster, when the latter expressed his wish to reside in Boston in 1803. The senior Buckminster thought his son too young and inexperienced to wrestle with the spiritual temptations that cosmopolitan life there would offer. In time, even natives and longtime residents of Boston began to express some misgivings about the possibility of living a virtuous and satisfying life in such a maelstrom of persons and opinions. "Boston Babylon," Emerson himself would call the city by 1822. As time went on, people like the prominent Bostonian William Sullivan would become disturbed as they watched the cozy little universe they had known invaded by faces they did not recognize. As Sullivan walked through the business section of the city, it seemed curious to him to see among the crowd "ten of the number whose persons I never saw—and some of the ten whose names I never before read." Unlike the Boston of personal acquaintance that Dwight had observed eighteen years before, the city upon which Sullivan gazed had become unsettlingly less manageable, less within the scope of his own personal venue.[31]

As the city grew and diversified, the public and communal character of life on which Federalism depended was steadily eroding. Beginning in 1801, the bylaws of Boston began to spell out in great detail proper modes of behavior in the new and impersonal urban environment. Society had been small enough so that most standards of conduct could be enforced personally—by the approval or disapproval of one's peers or betters, or in the most extreme cases, by the intervention of the powerful or of the church. With the increase in population, however, it became increasingly unrealistic to rely on personal ties of influence, or even the public influence of the church, to maintain public order. In a city as large as Boston, the ties that had held people together in smaller communities were becoming brittle. Hence, protocol was codified for all to observe upon pain of impersonal legal enforcement. No person, for example, was to be allowed "to dig or break up the streets," after 22 May 1801.[32] The bylaws also dealt with the responsibilities of vendors to their customers. Once Bostonians had assumed that the produce in their marketplace would be sold by the farmers who grew it and could guarantee its quality. Now, however, individuals could sell their produce to middlemen, who could and would defraud them. In 1813, a new bylaw was passed to prevent such practices, requiring that "no person not offering for Sale the produce of his own farm, shall be permitted to occupy that part of the ancient market which is called Dock Square."[33]

Controversies in Boston in the 1810s over Sabbath violations further illustrate the failure of the old public mores to stand up, at least among certain segments of the population. The oldest Massachusetts law respecting the Sabbath had been passed in 1792, requiring that no person labor or be present at a public diversion on the Sabbath. That statute also forbade traveling and prohibited tavern keepers from entertaining merchants of their own town on the Lord's Day, and it kept individuals from unnecessarily absenting themselves from Sabbath worship. Obviously, such customs had long been a part of New England life, but they had been enforced without recourse to commonwealth statute until 1792. And indeed, the law seems to have been effective, for in 1809 traveler Elias Boudinot of New Jersey found that he had to "in Justice to the

People of Boston, acknowledge that the Lords day is more apparently honoured than with us." Despite Boudinot's admission, however, those who knew Boston better were beginning to observe a rising tide of Sabbath violations. At first the problem was that "great numbers of Children & young Men, have lately adopted the practice of going into Water on the Lord Days [sic]." A newspaper advertisement authorized by the selectmen requested "all Parents and Guardians . . . to prevent this practice in the Youth under their care."[34]

By 1814, however, the complaints about the "rude and indecent conduct of boys" in one of the neighborhoods on the Sabbath betrayed more serious breaches of social order. During this period reaction to Sabbath breaking became more strident. Naturally, more statutes were passed, defining in even greater detail the nature of a Sabbath violation for those perverse citizens willing to abide only by the letter of the law. An 1817 Boston ordinance, for example, defined precisely which sorts of places were to be considered taverns, permitted to provide food and lodging to out-of-towners on the Sabbath, and which were not. In addition, conscientious citizens such as the Reverend Charles Lowell complained to the selectmen that the Boston *Intelligencer* was being published on Sunday. Eventually, enough such complaints about corporate Sabbath breaking in defiance of the usage of the town and the state would prompt the formation by concerned citizens of Sabbatarian societies, bent on suppressing such flagrant violations of the Lord's own ordinances.[35]

The problem of private citizens' disregard for the Sabbath also demanded attention. Many of these profligates appear to have been young men, probably migrants to Boston from rural New England. Having moved into large urban boarding houses rather than surrogate households, they were determined to raise a ruckus on their day off instead of attending the traditional duties of worship.[36] In the increasingly amorphous city, these youths found themselves released from a social network in which the responsibilities and expectations of each member of the family vis-à-vis the community were clearly defined and stringently enforced. In the debates over religious disestablishment taking place in Massachusetts in the 1810s and 1820s, the newcomers became a strong argument for the retention of a formal religious establishment. Harvard Professor Levi Frisbie remarked that their mobility and indifference to religious concerns posed a threat to standing institutions. "Strangers are continually coming to reside within the precincts of different parishes, young men are coming forward into life," he wrote. These young men were likely to "delay attaching themselves to the religious society, till they begin to doubt whether it were necessary to do it at all."[37] In Boston, where it was easy to put off joining the church, where in fact it had become impossible to determine who among the city's hordes had joined, Frisbie's fears were apparently realized. The young and mobile neglected joining the church for so long and with so little retribution that they began to doubt its necessity.

Moreover, these unchurched classes of the city, especially the poorer elements, seemed to be responsible for Sabbath disturbances. Churches had to take responsibility for part of the problem, for Boston churches had made no accommodations for those members of the community who could not or would not pay the pew rents. Small towns had been able to avoid the problem of the unchurched poor, since in the country, individuals belonged to the established parishes. They were warned to meeting unless they elected to sign off in favor of a dissenting sect. Those neglecting public worship were identified by the community and forced to belong to a church of some sort. In the Boston that was emerging in the early years of the nineteenth century, however, these individuals fell by the wayside. "Look into our principal houses of worship," Levi Frisbie admonished his Unitarian brethren. "Where is that well-dressed assemblage of the poorer mechanics, laborers and apprentices, who usually appear in the galleries of country churches?" If they were "warned to parish meetings, called upon to vote in the settlement of ministers, erection of meeting houses," he mused, "would they not feel themselves to be members of a religious community, and instead of wasting their sabbaths in idleness or in low dissipation, be found worshippers in the temples of God?"[38] The Boston Society for the Moral and Religious Instruction of the Poor, founded in 1816 to dispense Bibles and conduct Sunday schools among the poor, acknowledged that "some of our churches have no places set apart for the poor, and in most of them, but very few can find seats." The churches of Boston attempted to remedy the oversight by opening Sunday schools, intended to channel the energies of the riotous and unchurched poor into a religious and improving channel. "Many of our youth . . . who would otherwise have been neglected and have been nuisances to the community," the Boston *Recorder* reported, "have manifested a disposition to avail themselves of the privilege gratuitously afforded them." The benefits of such schools were immediate. One local gentleman who had had "60 panes of glass broken on *one Sabbath* by boys in the neighborhood" "witnessed no disturbances nor depredations upon the Sabbath" after the opening of the local Sabbath school.[39]

But Sabbath violations and disregard for religion seemed only part of a larger pattern of communal disintegration. By 1815, drunkenness had become a large enough problem to provoke concerned citizens to establish a Massachusetts Society for Suppressing Intemperance. Pauperism, prostitution, vagabondage, assault and battery all seemed to be on the increase.[40] Each of these offenses was more likely to occur in a community where strangers could enter and leave at will. The anonymity afforded by a large city permitted transgressions against the public order that would have been more easily controlled in towns. If parts of Boston had come to seem dens of vice, full of "vagabonds, boys, beggars, and drunkards, who, under pretence of gaining a livelihood, [learn] the habits of begging, stealing, or gambling," it came naturally to Bostonians to blame this corruption on the personal vice of the city's inhabitants.[41] The town was disintegrating because of spreading moral turpitude.

To add to the horror of what they took to be social disintegration, many of the descendants of the Puritans had begun to fear that religion itself had become infected with the factionalism and degeneracy of Boston. A true church would have been able to restrain the sinful tendencies of a people, many believed, but they only needed to look around them to see a city full of sin. The church had proven an unfaithful shepherd. In 1804, orthodox Calvinists, led by the Reverend Jedediah Morse of Charlestown's First Church, made the symbolic gesture of protesting the appointment of Henry Ware, Sr., as Hollis Professor of Divinity at Harvard. Ware was a liberal religionist, and his appointment as chief educator of the Massachusetts ministry provoked cries of protest from the orthodox faithful who had been uneasy for some time with the increasingly liberal tendencies of the city's clergy. Those tendencies, they suspected, had been productive of the sort of moral disorder that Boston and its environs was experiencing. Though the orthodox protest failed to keep Ware from his chair, it did provoke an open split in the ranks of Massachusetts Congregationalism between the orthodox and the liberals. In a society dedicated, at least rhetorically, to the preservation of communal solidarity, such an admission was disturbing, to say the least. Nevertheless, the orthodox felt that virtue itself was in peril in the chaotic city, and if the liberals could not maintain moral order there, the orthodox were perfectly justified in breaking with them.

Morse, heartened to find that others felt as he did about the issue of Unitarianism, as the Arminian creed was increasingly being called, stepped up his campaign against liberal religion. In 1805 he founded a periodical, the *Panoplist*, to continue to battle the Unitarian menace. Over the seventeen years of its existence, Morse's *Panoplist* plunged vigorously into controversy. Indeed, its editor took righteous delight in taking to task the Unitarian publication, the *Monthly Anthology*, and its successor, the *Christian Disciple*. In 1815, the exchange between the two forms of Congregationalism in Massachusetts became particularly heated as Morse published in pamphlet form one chapter of Thomas Belsham's London-published biography of Theophilus Lindsey. The pamphlet was reviewed in the *Panoplist* by Morse's friend, Jeremiah Evarts, in an article titled provocatively, "Are You of the Boston Religion or of the Christian Religion?" His attack set off a year-long pamphlet war between William Ellery Channing and the Reverend Samuel Worcester of Salem, who took up arms in Morse's cause.

Nor was Morse's the only voice raised in protest against Unitarianism. In 1809, John Codman, ordained the year before as pastor of Dorchester's Second Church, had refused to exchange pulpits with the Unitarian ministry of the Boston Association. Such exchanges had been practiced routinely for years as a way of exposing congregations to different preachers and of cutting down on the number of sermons that a minister needed to write each month. But Codman had doubts over "the various and heterogeneous sentiments" held by his colleagues in the Boston Association and therefore refused to expose his flock to the dangers of theological heterodoxy which he feared would encourage them to take lightly the revealed law of the Lord. His parish, however, felt that Codman was unnecessarily solicitous for their welfare, and a parish meeting was called in April 1810 to remove him. By October 1811, the parish was publishing articles against the immovable Codman, claiming, "You have, in our opinion, gone . . . to such an improper and unwarrantable extreme, as in effect to make us a separate religious society; cutting us off from that intercourse with the greater part of those Christian societies (and of our own denomination) with which we have been on terms of friendship and communion." In a society that professed to value unity as the highest social virtue, Codman's parishioners wondered if any circumstances could justify a break with the churches of the rest of the community. The issue went to a ministerial council for arbitration, but the council came to an impasse over whether Codman should be censured. A second council meeting in May 1812 voted five to four to vindicate Codman, but Codman's parish did not concur with their decision, and they voted in November to dismiss him. Codman arrived in the meeting house the following Sunday to find his pulpit occupied by someone else. Undaunted, he preached from the stairs below the pulpit until the usurper was forced to retire from the field in confusion.[42]

The Codman situation eventually resolved itself happily when liberal religionists, finally persuaded that Codman would not be moved, left Second Church to the orthodox and founded a new Unitarian parish in Dorchester. Nevertheless, the Codman controversy signaled the heightening of religious tension in the community and convinced the orthodox to take defensive measures. In 1811, the orthodox ministers founded their own ministerial association, thus obviating the need for exchanges with the heterodox. In addition, in 1809, evangelically inclined members of Boston's Old South Church covenanted together to form a haven for the city's orthodox in Park Street Church. Dedicated to "Evangelical principles," the Park Street congregation, though slighted by most of the city's other parishes as a source of dissension, became the center of orthodox evangelical activity in Boston.[43]

Although Bostonians had begun to take sides in the religious warfare being waged in print and pulpit during the 1810s, Ruth Emerson's family tried as best they could to ignore it, insisting that Christians might differ doctrinally, but all were Christians. Edward Bliss Emerson even attended the orthodox school at Andover despite the fact that his father had been among the most liberal of Boston's ministers. The Haskins family tradition of toleration for all Christian creeds may have helped Ruth Emerson's children to ignore the distinctions between Christians during this period. Whatever the reason, only Mary Moody Emerson had some misgivings concerning liberal religion. She had grown up in the country, and when she came to the city to assist her sister-in-law with the care of her family, she had hated what she saw there and insisted that the place stank of irreligion. Nor did another of Emerson's aunts, Elizabeth Haskins Ladd of Newton, approve of Ralph's preparing to enter Harvard College in the fall of 1817. It was the stronghold of liberal religion, and she was "very much grieved" at the news that he intended to study there. She urged on him the virtues of Brown University in Providence. Brown was Baptist, but it was at least orthodox and not lax in its support of morality.[44]

Amid these first rumblings occasioned by the decay of an older social order, Ralph Waldo Emerson left Boston Latin School for Harvard College in October 1817. He was fourteen years old—younger than most of the freshmen, hopeful about his future, and desirous of doing deeds that might leave a mark on the world. But in the Boston of 1817, it was not as clear as it had seemed in 1803 how one might achieve permanent glory. The Federalist worldview seemed to provide few satisfying answers. Despite its exhortations to the citizens of Boston to remain virtuous and communally oriented, the town seemed set on a straight path to anarchy. At the age of fourteen, however, Emerson was too young to ponder the problem. "I hope going to *Cambridge* will not prevent some future time my being as good a minister as if I came all *Andovered* from *Providence*," he thought, knowing that in the current religious climate, his alma mater might make a difference.[45] What he could not know was that the conflicts besetting his native city would gradually increase in intensity, and would shape not only the course of his ministry, but the course of his life as well.

IV

By 1817 the Federalist party had already entered its long decline as a political force to be reckoned with in Massachusetts, but the social organicism that it preached still maintained a strong hold on the sensibilities of many Bostonians. Nowhere were the ideas of that ideology more prominently espoused than at Harvard College of the University at Cambridge. Harvard's role for almost two centuries had been to train the future leaders of Massachusetts, not only in academic subjects, but in the paths of righteousness as well. The various conferences and exercises given at Harvard exhibitions during Emerson's attendance there reveal the continuing concern of the seminary with moral issues, especially the connections between the various branches of learning and civic virtue.[46] The students conferred on "Wealth, Power, and Knowledge, as contributing to individual happiness," declaimed on "the connexion between the poetry of a people, and their civil freedom and moral character," and disputed "whether republican institutions be favourable to learning."[47] The key questions with which they were expected to come to terms during their matriculation were questions of morals and of human character. The college was presided over by the genial James Thornton Kirkland. Kirkland had been minister at Boston's New South Church for sixteen years before assuming his Harvard post, and he was thoroughly a part of the liberal Boston establishment. His republicanism, however, was not as backward-looking as that of many others in his class. Indeed, the Federalism of the liberal Christians had softened to a toleration of freedom of thought, research, and expression, so long as the activity seemed to spring from a desire to find truth rather than to aggrandize self. As a liberal Christian, Kirkland shared in the Enlightenment optimism of his coreligionists, a faith in the lawfulness of religion and of nature. He had come to believe that a community of sentiment was best achieved through a discovery of the laws that united individuals, the laws of nature and of nature's God. Knowledge of these laws would teach individuals how to cultivate the virtue that held social institutions together.[48]

At Harvard College in 1817, students were subject to stringent laws, regulations, and fines designed to govern their behavior and mold them into conscientious citizens. Dress was prescribed; chapel was mandatory; courses consisted mainly of a continuation of the classical curriculum of the Latin School and of studies in the various branches of moral philosophy. Somewhat constrained by the rigid course of study and regulations, Harvardians formed student clubs in which issues that the curriculum ignored were ostensibly discussed. Phi Beta Kappa and the Speaking Club were formed in the late eighteenth century to encourage friendship and literary improvement. In the Hasty Pudding Club, founded in 1795, students frequently debated questions of literature, morality, and politics. Much of importance in Emerson's own education took place outside the classroom in such quasi-educational clubs. He belonged to the Pythologian Club, a society designed to "qualify men for usefulness in active life," by encouraging practice in the public arts of speaking and writing. As an antidote to the overemphasis on the classics at

Harvard, Emerson himself helped organize a book club that made available periodicals and popular novels to members and provided them with opportunities to discuss them.[49]

Despite the best efforts of the Boston elite to train its sons in the way they should go, the "corruption" that was becoming evident in the city across the Charles had infected its seminary of higher learning. Timothy Dwight on his visit to Boston noted the concern of the people of the region with the morals of the young men at the college. Since the West Boston Bridge had opened in 1809 and reduced the distance between the school and the city to three miles, university officials observed that "the allurements of this Metropolis have often become too powerfully seductive to be resisted by the gay and sometimes even by the grave youths, who assemble here for their education." The "bustle and splendour of a large commercial town" were undermining their morals.[50] Students were drinking and carousing, spending their time going to the theater and engaging in other immoral activities. University officials tried to handle the situation by assessing fines and imposing new disciplinary restrictions, but to no avail.

Although the college had a history of student disturbances, Emerson's years there seem to have been tumultuous ones in the university's history. From the testimony of participants, it is difficult to know exactly why rebellions rose in number and intensity during this time. George Ticknor, Smith Professor of the French and Spanish Languages and Literature, and Professor of Belles Lettres, thought that it was the unchallenging curriculum that was responsible for student restiveness. "We are neither an University—which we call ourselves—nor a respectable high school,—which we ought to be," he charged in 1821 as he proposed curricular reform. Because students were not challenged, he insisted, "the morals of great numbers of the young men who come to us are corrupted."[51] As Harvard students' reputations for carousing and immorality spread, potential scholars were frightened away and tutors were forced to spend most of their time in police action.

In mid-July of 1818, Emerson noted that the seniors remained in Cambridge, moping about. Two days after he remarked on the mood there, a fight broke out between students and townspeople, an altercation involving some seventy persons and "a great deal of noise swearing &c." In November 1818, Emerson's own class was involved in a food riot in which students protested the poor quality of their meals by throwing food and breaking windows in the Commons. College authorities suspended five of the ringleaders. They considered such insubordination undesirable but not unusual: such riots had occurred periodically at Harvard for a long time, for meals in the Commons were traditionally inferior. The disturbance escalated into a full scale rebellion, however, as members of Emerson's class protested the unjust suspensions (as they believed) of their fellows. Josiah Quincy, a member of Emerson's class and the son of Boston's former congressman and its soon-to-be mayor, recalled the march of the assembled sophomore class to the "Rebellion Tree." There they swore to boycott all college exercises. "Resistance to tyrants is obedience to God," the young Quincy wrote in his journal for the day, as members of the class tore twigs from the tree and wore them in their bosoms as signs of solidarity in rebellion.[52]

Even after the disturbances were quelled, some of the class kept the memory of the rebellion alive by establishing the Conventicle Club, another drinking and dining organization, but one in which memories of the rebellion held a prominent place. Although Emerson himself tended to be quiet and unobtrusive during his years at college, he joined the club and wrote its drinking song. Like most drinking songs, its principal purpose was to promote camaraderie and conviviality; nevertheless, the extent to which such jovial fellowship was based in an unmistakably angry and righteous rebellion is striking:

> You may say what you please of the current rebellion
> Tonight the Conventicle drink to a real one
> The annals of ages have blazoned its fame
> And Paeans are chanted to hallow its name.
> > Derry Down.
>
> Alas for the windows the Sophs have demolished,
> Alas for the Laws that they are not abolished,
> And that *Dawes* could abide the warm battle's brunt
> And the Government's vote it was Gay Lee & Blunt
> > Derry Down
>
> But this shock of the Universe who could control
> Aghast in despair was each Sophomore soul
> Save one who alone in his might could stand forth
> To grapple with elements—Mr Danforth

Let the Earth & the Nations to havoc go soon
And the World tumble upward to mix with the moon
Old Harvard shall smile at the rare conflagration
The conventicle standing her pledge of salvation.
                    Derry Down.[53]

Nor was the rebellion of Emerson's own class the last of the faculty's troubles during the period from 1817 to 1821. The class of 1823
was even more reckless than Emerson's own. In 1820, they escalated
a food throwing battle in the Commons to something resembling a
guerrilla war against college authorities. It lasted the better part of
three years and resulted in suspensions, bonfires, riots, protests,
"intoxication, . . . gross indecency, and insult." The most notable of
these protests occurred in November of Emerson's senior year when
the whole sophomore class left the town en masse in protest over
new government disciplinary measures. So great was the disorder in
the Cambridge school that in 1821 one observer wrote to George
Ticknor that "dissipated pleasures prevail amongst the young men
at Cambridge, in a greater degree than at any former period within
my knowledge." The college could be saved from "utter ruin" only
by the severest of disciplinary measures.[54]

As was the case in Boston, where the social order also seemed to
be in danger of disintegrating, the faculty reacted to campus disorder by pointing to the intemperance and intractability of the students—defects of character. Although some faculty members like
George Ticknor suggested that such behavior could also be laid at
the door of Harvard itself and undertook curriculum reform in 1823,
the principal solution to such problems, most agreed, was the further tightening of discipline. For their part, students justified their
rebellion using the rhetoric of revolution. To be sure, such justifica-
tions were made in personal and particularistic terms—a popular
student had been unjustly suspended by the government, for example, or individual pedantic tutors had made unreasonable demands
on their charges. Although no sweeping demands were made and no
elaborate ideological apologies given for the uprisings, the language
the students borrowed suggested that something more than sheer
boredom or youthful exuberance lay at the heart of the commotion.

Perhaps Ticknor was on the right track when he pointed to the
curriculum as a culprit: Harvard's continual exhortations to self-
control and moral virtue must have seemed like empty nostrums

to these young men born in a period of disorienting social change in New England. The old appeals to the common good no longer seemed credible in a world where increasingly no one seemed to have the common good in mind. The official Harvard education of Emerson and his classmates taught them concepts and roles that were at odds with the demands of a society in flux. But from the perspective of the tutors, faculty, and officers of Harvard—representatives of the Massachusetts gentry and their older way of life—the students' behavior must have seemed particularly disturbing. As far as they could tell, society's future leaders were becoming as corrupt as the society they were supposed to lead.[55]

Emerson did not stand out as unusual in the chaotic atmosphere of Harvard during the middle years of the Kirkland administration. As far as anyone in his class could tell, Ralph Waldo Emerson (or Waldo, as he had taken to calling himself) was a serious and reserved young man with a penchant for storytelling and pretensions as a poet. He continued to be a mediocre scholar, as he insisted on studying what interested him rather than what Harvard taught. He indulged a taste for modern literature and philosophy when he had a chance, but because he was so poor, he was obliged to earn his tuition as a waiter to President Kirkland when classes were in session, as part-time schoolteacher when they were not. The tall young man with the piercing eyes and prominent nose also had responsibilities at home in Boston. His older brother William had taken a teaching position in Kennebunk, Maine, leaving Waldo as the mainstay of his mother. Thus, the younger brother divided his time between Cambridge and Boston, remaining something of an enigma to most of his classmates. He participated in some of their activities, but even more frequently was forced to observe them from a distance, studying, reflecting, and analyzing.

Although Emerson seems to have had little comment on the rebellions of his class beyond what he wrote in the Conventicle's drinking anthem, it is clear from his journal entries during his college years that he regarded the tendencies of his age with some dismay. In the middle of his junior year, Emerson began keeping a journal that served as a repository for his musings, his class notes, and his attempts at poetry. He would keep such journals for most of the rest of his life. His mood as it is conveyed in the journals for his junior and senior years was not overly optimistic. "I find myself often idle, vagrant, stupid, & hollow," he observed. He found his disaffected state "somewhat appalling" and resolved to "discipline [him]self with diligent care" lest he fail to achieve anything in life. Nevertheless, he was troubled by an indolence for which he could find no explanation but his own weakness of character. At times, this dissatisfaction emerged as an indictment of life itself. "In fact it is an excessively paltry humbug of a world," he wrote during his senior year, "—and every circumstance of human comfort is a triumph of human ingenuity."[56]

In his attempts at literature, young Emerson's disenchantment with the character of his times comes through equally strongly. His poems imitated those of Gray and Thomson, Collins and Goldsmith, all written in the post-Augustan twilight of a world losing its faith in the power of virtuous human action to sustain a social world. From the neoclassical tradition these poems borrowed their denunciations of a society gone to seed, but unlike the biting, satirical Augustans, these poets born between two worlds lamented the passing of the older vision wistfully, nostalgically, and with little hope of its recovery. This point of view seemed to appeal to Emerson, but at times his poetry took the more strident and satiric tone of those republican poets who held out some hope that denunciation of folly in the social sphere might bring about its purification. Emerson assumes such a stance in this 1820 portion of a long epic, in which he ridicules those who court popular tastes in the arts:

> They seek the favor of the uncourtly throng
> As men whose independent minds are strong
> With judgement weak they find some childish bard
> Who rhymes & writes because the times are hard
> With blind applause they welcome all his verse
> Proclaim the better & defend the worse
>
> While wisdom weeps, & wits may wisely laugh
> Like Jews they bow before a homemade calf [57]

At other times, however, he seems to write a kind of Graveyard School republicanism, lamenting the passing of the ancient republics as Goldsmith lamented the passing of his deserted village:

There was a little city of the world
Where former times saw Grecian banners furl'd
Free as the winds that swept its mountain rock
Stern time in vain renewed his frequent shock

Nature in strength had built its little walls
And Freedom built his altar in the halls
Fast by Albanias giant mountain stood
The fathers breasting the Ionian flood.[58]

Emerson ended the poem here, never explicitly tracing the downfall of the Athenian city-state. Nevertheless, the tone and the subject matter suggest an elegy mourning the passing of an heroic age in a city that republican orators were fond of comparing to the American republic.

Throughout the young Emerson's education, this elegiac feeling of living in the latter days dominated his first awkward attempts at self-expression. In his disaffection with the temper of life he was not alone. Not only was he used to the jeremiadic traditions of the Boston orators, both sacred and secular; among his own peers he could trace a discontent with the way things were that the ideology of their fathers could not explain satisfactorily. When Emerson looked around his native town, it must have seemed to him that something was amiss. At first he felt dissatisfaction with the course of his own life; his failings were personal. Only later would it occur to him that there might be a social or a cultural dimension to his malaise. In the latter days of Federalism in New England, this son of old Boston watched the town of his birth transformed beyond anything his father could have imagined. The tumults of Boston in 1820 made the warnings of Election Day 1803 seem very tame indeed.

CHAPTER 2

The Socratic

Response

While the thronged city shook with clamor rude
The Angry minstrel sighed for Solitude.
—Journals and Miscellaneous Notebooks, *1820*

IN AUGUST 1821, Emerson graduated from Harvard and returned to Boston to teach in his brother William's school for young ladies. Though he had "not much cause, I sometimes think, to wish my Alma Mater well personally," he wrote in February 1822—for he had not been "highly flattered by success, and was every day mortified by my own ill fate or ill conduct"—he was beginning to feel nostalgic for college life. Schoolteaching was an unrewarding profession, the enclave of preprofessional students desirous of making money enough to allow them to continue in their studies. It was an apprenticeship in which many of Emerson's class were engaged and against which many of them balked. "I am (I wish I was otherwise) keeping a school & assisting my venerable brother lift the truncheon against the fair-haired daughters of this raw city," he wrote a classmate six months after their graduation. "It is but fair that those condemned to the 'delightful task,' should have free leave to waste their wits, if they will, in decrying & abominating the same."[1]

In the stagnant backwaters of the Boston classroom, Emerson imagined that his former classmates were doing far better than he in advancing their lives and fortunes. They, no doubt, were getting on with the business of preparing for professional lives. For himself, however, "my sole answer & apology to those who inquire about my studies is—I keep school.—I study neither law, medicine, or divinity, and write neither poetry nor prose."[2] He felt lazy and apathetic. The external achievements of this period of Emerson's life might lead us to judge it as notably lackluster, but a good bit was going on internally. During the period prior to his entry into the ministry in 1826, Emerson came to formulate a philosophy of life and a sense of mission using the Federalist materials he had inherited from the past. His was not merely a revival of an increasingly anachronistic ideology, however. In these years, Emerson struggled to adapt the inherited language of his fathers to new times and new circumstances.

I

For a number of Bostonians—including Emerson—the reorganization of the town government in 1822 occasioned serious reflection on the precariousness of the times. In that year, a controversial movement for civic restructuring led to the incorporation of Boston as a city and the adoption of a form of government designed to accommodate the rapid changes taking place there. A group of citizens had insisted for some years that their interests were not being met under the old regime, and by 1820 they had acquired enough power to challenge the town's elite for its control. As they overtly advocated the pursuit of self-interest in government, they crystallized for many of Emerson's class the vague sense that something was wrong. Boston seemed sick with the disease of competitive factionalism. A shift in Boston's form of government was self-consciously designed as a partial cure.

By 1820 Boston's population exceeded forty-three thousand. Obviously, that number, including seven thousand qualified voters, could not fit into Faneuil Hall, a structure built to accommodate the town meeting when Boston numbered fewer than fifteen thousand citizens. In fact, Bostonians had not been attending the meetings in large numbers for years. When routine business was on the agenda, town meetings usually consisted of the selectmen, the town officers, and thirty or forty inhabitants who presumably acted on behalf of the whole. Unfortunately for those who found rule by this elite acceptable, some of an increasingly self-conscious middle class began to express openly the belief that government ought to represent the various interests of the town, not some vague conception of the common good. In 1820, dissident elements of mechanics and tradesmen proposed electing to the United States House of Representatives "a *practical commercial* man," tapping an individual familiar with the "*Merchants, Mechanics,* and others dependent on *Commerce.*" The lawyers who had traditionally filled political office, they argued, were not familiar with the peculiar needs of commerce and trade. These upstarts nominated Samuel A. Wells, a respectable merchant. Federalists nominated Benjamin Gorham, a patrician lawyer, for the seat, claiming as usual that "this district ought to be represented in the first place, by a man of *talents,* by one who has liberal and practical views not only on commercial, but upon all subjects." Wells's candidacy did surprisingly well, sounding a warning note for the Federalist ideology of the whole in politics. A substantial number of people had begun to argue quite openly that interest should be one of the prime considerations in the election of public officials.[3]

Disturbed at the turn politics were taking in Boston, Federalists took a closer look at the town meeting. They had long been opposed to the incorporation of Boston as a city, ostensibly on the grounds that such a move would promote democratic factionalism, a condition that flourished when relationships were defined in anything other than a personal and "natural" way. There had been periodic agitation since 1784, but a proposal for incorporation had failed as recently as 1815.[4] Those who favored change in the form of town government contended that the large, unmanageable town meeting was itself becoming no better than mobocracy. "If all the inhabitants of such town assemble," the 1815 committee charged with investigating the possibility of change in town government reported, "it is obvious that business cannot be well transacted by so numerous a body, liable as it always must be, to be swayed by local views, party feeling, or the interests of designing men." Federalists like Josiah Quincy perceived in the meeting the rise of interests with increasing political strength, and experienced as never before the impracticality of government in its accustomed form. The constitution of the town government had resulted in "an irresponsibility irreconcilable with a wise and efficient conduct of its affairs." Hence, in the interest of maintaining elite control of public affairs, Federalists like Quincy embarked on a program of governmental reform.[5]

In drawing up the city charter, the same sorts of dissident elements who had supported Wells's congressional candidacy demanded further concessions to guarantee representation by interests within city government. Rather than having city aldermen from each of Boston's twelve wards elected at a general meeting in Faneuil Hall, "a party was strenuous that each ward should elect its own alderman" in its own ward. "We can step in with our leathern aprons on," they believed, "[and] choose a man of our own sentiments— one who we know." No longer accepting as legitimate the premise that any single group of people, however talented or knowledgeable, could speak for the whole, these dissidents took a major step toward government by interest. Federalists for their part feared that ward voting would accomplish exactly what they had been trying to avoid. It would turn "the wards into petty democracies," and of course "no one wants to live in a wild furious democracy, and so go to despotism." Ultimately, however, ward voting triumphed, although by less than 500 votes out of 4,800 cast. All officials of the city and commonwealth henceforward were to be elected in neighborhoods rather than at the meeting of the whole.[6]

Naturally enough the rise of such overt advocacy of self-interest in Boston disturbed those who believed in the old tenets of Federalism. Emerson's reaction to the events surrounding the establishment of the city government reveals just how much faith he still had in the old rhetoric of social organicism. In a series of letters to John Boynton Hill, a fellow member of the Conventicle and the correspondent to whom he bemoaned the fate that had assigned him to schoolmastering, he provided a running commentary on the events in his city in 1822 and 1823. Although his remarks were couched in a lightly satiric tone and he claimed to have no serious interest in "our city-politics" (it was only "by way of trying my pen," he wrote, that he bothered to comment on such matters at all), Emerson clearly felt some dismay at what he saw happening around him.[7] When these letters are coupled with the more private and philosophical reactions recorded in his journals for the same period, the role Boston played in spurring Emerson to think deeply about the relationship between individual and social virtue emerges clearly.

Despite his disclaimers, the account Emerson gave Hill of the recent city reorganization was by no means without serious commentary. "The inhabitants divide themselves here, as every where else, into three great classes," he noted. "First, the aristocracy of wealth & talents; next, the great multitude of mechanics & merchants and the good sort of people who are for the most part content to be governed without aspiring to have a share of power; lastly, the lowest order of day labourers & outcasts of every description, including schoolmasters." Significantly, these "orders" did not seem to Emerson to be different economic groups with interests plainly divergent from each other. Rather, they were different social castes of people who, if all things worked together as they ought, should have a common interest at heart. There was, of course, a new group of people, those not integrated into "the great multitude" or "the good sort of people," and that number, Emerson commented facetiously, included schoolmasters. A dangerous class of people, marginal and dependent, they had little interest in the common good, because they had nothing at stake there. Also significant was Emerson's acknowledgment of the better class of the city as an aristocracy of wealth and talent. They were the ones who governed, and rightly so, Emerson implied, for the "good sort of people" were "content to be governed" by them.[8]

At the election of President Monroe, Emerson continued, parties seemed for a time to wither. "There was no division of factions, except the giant ones of Federalist & Democrat," he wrote; "but when these died away, the town became so tiresomely quiet, peaceful, & prosperous that it became necessary at once, for decent variety, to introduce some semblance of discord. A parcel of demagogues, ambitious, I suppose, of being known, or hoping for places as *partisans* which they could never attain as citizens—set themselves down to devise mischief."[9] Although the offhanded tone appears to undercut Emerson's commentary, the Federalist distinction between partisan and citizen comes through clearly. The partisan is the party adherent who tries to effect private ends by fomenting civil discord and demagoguery; the citizen is recognized and elevated to positions of responsibility by his fellows on the basis of talent and virtue. The partisan thrives on discord and community disorder, while the citizen seeks to eliminate them.

In accusing the governing elite of partisan politics, partisans had begun to work on the emotions of good citizens, Emerson claimed.

Hence it has followed that, within a twelvemonth the words "Aristocracy," "Nabob," &c have begun to be muttered. The very natural circumstance, that the very best men should be uniformly chosen to represent them in the legislature, is begun to be called a formal conspiracy to deprive them of their rights & to keep the power entirely in the hands of a few. Lately, this band of murmurers have actually become an organized party calling themselves "The Middling Interest," & have made themselves conspicuous by two or three troublesome ebullitions of a bad spirit at the town meetings.

Disturbed, Emerson observed in a letter to Hill that this party openly acknowledged itself as an "Interest." Its adherents believed firmly in the conflict of interests within society. They branded the talented who governed an "Aristocracy," implying that those who claimed to have the common good of society at heart were, like themselves, out only after the main chance. As evidence of this faction's intentions of disturbing the peace of good citizens, Emerson told Hill that the upstarts had passed a measure in town meeting calling for the publication of a book in which "every man's property & tax" was recorded. Such a listing aimed to make individuals conscious of the differences in wealth and social standing among them.[10]

More disturbing still "was the vote that the Selectmen be directed to instruct the Representatives to obtain from the Legislature leave to erect Wooden Buildings." For years, the erection of such buildings had been outlawed in Boston because closely clustered wooden structures posed a fire hazard to the entire town. The buildings of brick or stone with tile roofs that the law required proved a greater expense to the rising bourgeoisie, who often could not easily afford them. To the Federalist way of thinking, however, such expenditures were necessary to preserve the safety of the whole, and Emerson seemed to concur. Six months later, Emerson would reaffirm to Hill his opinion that these people were up to no good with their wooden building ordinance. In fact, the clamor over wooden buildings was "a mere watchword" designed to unite a particular group of people to pursue their own particular interest. So far as Emerson could tell, "this party only unites the old Democratic party under a new name."[11]

The transition from town to city symbolized to many Bostonians a crucial stage in the decay of the corporate communal ideal. "Sicut Patribus sit Deus nobis"—"Let God be to us as to our Fathers"— they wrote hopefully on their city seal in 1822, but it was clear that Boston was setting out on a new course. However, it was not the change from town to city that in itself disturbed Emerson. Rather, it was the overt and unapologetic pursuit of a private good that nettled, an attitude that seemed to be spreading in the city. Recalling the histories of the nations that he had been reading since childhood, Emerson feared that disregard for honor and virtue would prove the first step on the road to social chaos. He told Hill as much in a letter written the day before the Fourth of July 1822: "In this merry time, & with real substantial happiness above any known nation, I think we Yankees have marched on since the Revolution, to strength, to honour, & at last to ennui. It is most true that the people (of the City, at least,) are actually tired of hearing Aristides called the just—& it demonstrates a sad caprice, when they hesitate about putting on their vote, such names as, Daniel Webster, & [William] Sullivan, & Prescott & only distinguish them by a small majority over bad and doubtful men." Emerson feared that whatever the pretensions of the dying Federalist order, the people in rejecting it were rejecting the rule of virtue and the ideal of a principled consensus. It was the democracy whose advent William Emerson had so feared. Emerson found events in Boston "a dismal foreboding" and added, "Will it not be dreadful to discover that the experiment made by America, to ascertain if men can govern themselves—does not succeed? that too much knowledge & too much liberty makes them mad."[12]

Even as he related in letters to Hill the changes taking place in Boston in the spring and summer of 1822, Emerson ruminated in his journals on their deeper significance. "It is matter of great doubt to me whether or not the *populace* of all ages is essentially the same in character," he wrote in April. Were all persons necessarily selfish and corrupt? "Will vulgar blood always rebel and rail against honourable, virtuous, and opulent members of the same society? Will the good always be in peril from the misdeeds & menaces of the bad?" These days he tended to answer such questions in the affirmative. If so, however, the question remained whether republican institutions could do anything to restrain those impulses, or whether they too were bound to be corrupted. In his journals for April and May 1822, Emerson turned over the problem in his mind. One "solitary individual" might, "by the native force of intellect," set to work "numerous & mighty engines in the midst of intelligent society," that would transform it, he mused. Such a person would work "upon the passions & interests of many men, . . . inducing them to do what but yesterday appeared contrary to their views & profits." Such an individual would be adept at "managing a whole community as the Architect controuls his builders so that each, solely bent on doing his own part, is yet subservient to a harmonious whole." The way to handle the apparent chaos that surrounded him, he concluded, was to systematically discover the laws that governed human behavior and human society and to apply them. At the end of April and the beginning of May, then, Emerson began to review the history of the nations to see if he could not abstract the factors that determined the balance between good and evil in societies. Through an accurate understanding of the ethical laws of hu-

man societies, he could,like the master Architect, divert the course
of an entire community.[13]

II

Emerson's philosophical and ethical approach to social problems in
the spring of 1822 was not necessarily new, nor was it uniquely his
own. Even "the lowest orders of the people" now hotly debated
questions of morality, he observed in an essay written during his
senior year in college. Like many who searched "to know the principles of ethical science," the young Emerson believed that people
might find the true and immutable foundation of their relationship
to one another and with the universe around them. Laws of nature
and of God lay beneath the surface of men's daily lives; as the human intellect discovered these laws, individuals and societies might
use them to advance in knowledge and wisdom. At Harvard the
young Emerson had resolved to "survey the political condition of
the world as Ethics[;] discover the Lex legum on which legislation is
to proceed."[14]

It was the Athenian philosopher Socrates and his desire to discover the laws governing men's actions that in particular inspired
Emerson to take a philosophical approach to the problems of his
age. In his 1820 Bowdoin Prize essay on "The Character of Socrates," he had outlined the life of the first of his representative men. It
is easy to see in the essay strong parallels between Socrates' situation and Emerson's own. The young man's description of the times
in which Socrates lived would have struck a familiar chord in most
Bostonians. When Socrates was born, "there was freshness of glory
diffused over his country which no after times equalled," he wrote.
Great achievements, within the memory of Socrates, marked Athens's golden age—an age that Federalist orators had many times
paralleled to Emerson's own. Sadly, Emerson claimed, continuing
the parallel implicitly, "the Athenians, beholding their strength,
acquired a fearlessness of contending interests about them, and of
the consequences of their own actions, which was imparted from
the political community as a whole to each separate state, and from
the state to each individual." Such laxity had its natural and unavoidable consequences. Socrates "lived to see them degenerate,

and crouch to the despotism of the Thirty to submit to defeat abroad, and to faction at home."[15]

Now Socrates was not, like his countrymen, "the sport of circumstances." Rather, "by the persevering habits of forebearance and self-denial he had acquired that control over his whole being" that left him unscathed amid changes in fortune and condition. Like all good men, he wanted to help his country. Seeing Athens "embarrassed and plunging without help in the abyss of moral degradation," Socrates felt called upon to do something. He desired to lead his countrymen, but "he would not treacherously descend to flatter them" as a demagogue would. He lived in a society in which "the inducements to virtue were weak and few, but to vice numberless and strong." In Athens, "degenerate republicans" did not pursue fame "by toilsome struggles for pre-eminence in purity, by discipline and austere virtue." Rather, they resorted to "squandered wealth, profligacy, and flattery of the corrupt populace." What could a young man, determined to speak out on virtue's behalf, expect from such a community?[16] Here was Emerson's dilemma precisely.

According to Emerson, Socrates decided that Athens needed a new philosophy of virtue, directed especially toward the young. The "patriotic philosopher" had determined to devote his life to drawing up practical rules of life for the many: "To the inquisitive he unfolded his system, and the laws and dependencies of morals."[17] Individuals were to be taught the laws governing the regulations of the universe, and they would come to know why they should live virtuously, as well as how to do so. Socrates, the man of principle in an age gone rotten, could thus play a decisive role in strengthening the moral fiber of the declining republic. By spreading the good news that human life followed ethical laws of nature that could be known and adhered to by all individuals, Socrates could reform the city-state from the ground up.

Emerson saw himself, in the image of Socrates, as an ethical philosopher, and set out to discover for himself the ethical base of the "great moral bond" of which he dreamed. This bond would "[overleap] the little local boundaries of mountain or stream, of colour or dress," and would "[compass] with its ample arch a thousand centres of civilization and government." Natural law itself became the way of understanding, explaining, and potentially transforming the raucous social order in which he lived. If life around him seemed to be disintegrating and the official exhortations to virtue proved no remedy, Emerson determined to discover for himself the preordained moral economy by which a lasting virtue and an harmonious social order might be achieved.[18]

Affirming that man is a social animal, Emerson first noted "the disproportionate influence which the social feelings exercise upon the mind." "What are the springs of action, which incite any one man to do noble and praiseworthy deeds?" he asked. To him, the answer was clear: "Patriotism, Love, Emulation. And where were these begotten?—in Heaven? in unreal and fictitious scenes? in the silent groves, and the solitary hut of the ascetic? No; these form the atmosphere and the bond of union to *social*, cultivated, and active Man. . . . Great actions, from their nature, are not done in a closet; they are performed in the face of the sun, and in behalf of the world." Institutions led the faculties "to their fullest development," for something believed in and felt by many banded together had infinitely more strength than something felt by "solitary minds in distant quarters." The "moral economy" of the universe demanded that men educate each other. No one could fathom the human race who considered it in any other but its social character.[19]

This does not sound like the Emerson of his mature period, the Emerson of "Self-Reliance" and of "Circles"; indeed, Emerson's understanding of the social character of human nature shifted over the course of the years. Nonetheless, he never abandoned his belief that a social affinity was an ineradicable part of human nature, and his later disenchantment with society never totally obscured his admission that men were social beings for good reason. The task he set himself was to imagine "the advantages and condition of that state of society which would result from an entire harmony and cooperation of its parts." As time went on, he would become more greatly preoccupied "to shew why this [harmony] has not, & cannot be brought about; hence to deduce legitimate rules of conduct for the rational philanthropist."[20] But in his early twenties, Emerson remained dedicated to an ideal of social transformation through an understanding of the moral economy of the universe.

III

As if in response to the trends he detected in the city around him, Emerson in May 1823 moved to Roxbury, a country district on the outskirts of Boston. In 1823, the forces transforming Boston had just begun to reach the suburban village of narrow streets and small farms. Two new churches had been built in 1821; Roxbury Street would be paved and brick sidewalks laid in 1824, and in 1825 the town would become big enough to decide that the rest of its streets needed official names. Despite the changes that were beginning to transform life there, however, Roxbury's green fields presented a sharp contrast to the city into which it would soon become absorbed.

Emerson lived with his mother in a small cottage off the Dedham Turnpike, some two miles from where the road left the city. He continued to teach in his brother William's school for young ladies in the mornings, fleeing in the afternoons to the "wild blossoms & branches" of the Canterbury district of Roxbury. There, he confessed to his correspondent Hill, he hoped to resume his poetic endeavors and to take a more serious attitude toward his studies.[21] The quiet countryside of Roxbury failed to improve Emerson's poetic abilities greatly, but it seems to have been decidedly helpful in stimulating his interior, intellectual growth. From the summer of 1823 through midwinter of 1825, his journals show a thoughtful and methodical concern with moral and ethical issues. He advanced his professional aspirations during this time as well, deciding to commit himself to the formal study of the ministry and beginning informal studies with William Ellery Channing of the Federal Street Church, Boston.

Throughout his period of country meditation, the issue that continued to haunt Emerson was the one that would distress him throughout his ministry: how one could establish and maintain a virtuous life in the face of what seemed to be a degenerate—or at the very least, a morally indifferent—social order? At first he used the familiar terms of Federalism to bewail the moral perversity of society and to mourn the inefficacy of his own life. "Aristocracy is a good sign," he asserted, for it had been "the hue & cry in every community where there has been anything good, any society worth associating with, since men met in cities." Likewise, Emerson affirmed the new and somewhat desperate patrician contention "that you regulate men's conduct, whether you can affect their principles or no." Nevertheless, during his sojourn in Roxbury, Emerson began to change his mind about how social harmony was best to be achieved.[22]

"Sympathy's 'electric chain' wherewith we are darkly bound" was the invaluable gift of a divine providence. This law of nature meant that no "marked character should anywhere arise without sending its strong contagion to an indefinite extent." Thus, the virtuous private citizen exerted an infinite effect on the whole of society. More ominously, however, it occurred to Emerson that vice might also be communicated from person to person with the ease of a contagious disease. Anyone could be polluted unknowingly by contact with a corrupt society, and the more corrupt society seemed to Emerson, the more he recalled to mind that duty of nature "to guard the purity of the social bonds, to abstain from vile & to affect virtuous conversation." Men were naturally to be swayed by the example of others, and this law of nature could prove in the worst of times to be a hindrance to the exercise of virtue.[23]

Emerson's ruminations on human nature began to take on a decidely pessimistic tone. It seemed to him that "the influences of sympathy are so strong that man never was or can be insulated in his feelings in the midst of society, can never present an absolute contrast to those who surround him." Evil as well as good resulted from the social bond. Emerson believed this "moral evil [to be] . . . almost inseparable from the high advantages of social life." It was what made the individuals of his age follow "superficial modes & customs," what distracted them "from the deepseated sentiments and sources of action" that produced virtuous behavior. The social sympathies could turn individuals from "the strong self application of the notion of personal accountability & personal immortality to an idolatrous regard for forms and opinions, to a slavish love of bodily pleasure, in the pursuit of which the only things worth living for diminish in our distempered judgments till they wear a fantastic visionary form and at last cease to disturb our fatal lethargy." Emerson's moralistic language spoke of a loss of personal accountability, of a mass declension from earlier moral standards, caused by the too strong influence of the powers of sympathy.[24]

For Emerson the dilemma was plain: how was one to take advantage of society's benefits while avoiding its temptations to a slavish conformity to the opinions of others—opinions that were apt to be immoral? Emerson's relative isolation in Roxbury suggested to him an answer: the individual had to make a concerted effort to control the influences of sympathy. One way to do so was to seek solitude— "not the solitude of place" (although this had been the kind that Emerson himself had recently enjoyed), "but the solitude of soul." Solitude gave the individual "a breathing space, a leisure, out of the influence of dazzling delusions, the pomp, & vanity of this wicked world." In quarantining himself from the infectious attitudes of a corrupt society, the individual would be able to follow the inner voice of conscience and of principle. "I commend no absurd sacrifices," he cautioned; "I praise no wolfish misanthropy that retreats to thickets from cheerful towns and scrapes the ground for roots and acorns either out of a grovelling soul or a hunger for glory that has mistaken grimace for philosophy." Rather, he urged individuals to escape only from "the deceptive judgements of other men." "It is not that you should avoid men," Emerson advised, simply "that you should not be hurt by them." The kind of solitude he described was designed "not to break the brotherhood of the race but to enable you to contribute to it a greater good."[25]

In making such an argument, Emerson thought he was only extending an old Federalist tenet: principle was not to be determined by consulting the opinions of others but by consulting one's own conscience. In a society ruled by morally upright men, the social order might check the passions of people; in a social order ruled by men on the make, however, the individual was left to preserve his own integrity as best he could. Although the language retains the conservative rhetorical overtones of Federalism, the implications of Emerson's discovery are powerful: the rise of economic individualism, which is to say the overt pursuit of material self-interest among the population of Boston, was not necessarily accompanied by a rise in moral individualism—independence of judgment about moral matters. In fact, Emerson noted quite the opposite. The more individuals proclaimed themselves free to seek out their own interests in the market or in the political arena, the less likely they were to be able to transcend the boundaries of individual economic interest to imagine a common good or the common welfare. Emerson had come to articulate for himself in a crude way one of the fundamental dilemmas of the new social order: How was moral independence to be achieved in a culture that increasingly drew individuals into an economic process that left them blind to all but a self-defeating, very narrowly defined self-interest? Independent as actors in the market, they lacked the vision to exercise control over the impersonal, self-perpetuating social process that in the end controlled them.[26]

On his last night in Roxbury before he joined the middle class of the Harvard Divinity School in 1825, Emerson reflected on all that had happened to him since he had left college in 1821. "I have inverted my inquiries two or three times on myself, and have learned what a sinner & a saint I am." His cardinal sin was idleness—a "sinful strolling from book to book"—but his time had not been entirely wasted. "I have grown older and have seen something of the vanity & something of the value of existence," he wrote, "[and I] have seen what shallow things men are & how independent of external circumstances may be the states of mind called good & ill."[27] Although in a public sense he had done nothing noteworthy during these years of restless seclusion, he had not wasted them. He had found the keynote of his ministry.

IV

By 1825 the population of Boston had passed the fifty-thousand mark. Greedy for land to accommodate its exploding population, Bostonians began to expand their peninsula by creating land where there was none. They filled in the shallow marshes that lay on either side of the neck, so that by 1824, Beacon Hill had been leveled to its present height. The town grew by the addition of the streets and lots the landfill provided. In addition, Bostonians increased their commercial access to the hinterlands by building bridges to surrounding towns. In addition to the Charles River Bridge, the bridge to Dorchester Neck, and Cragie's Bridge (which spanned the Charles at the city's West End), a bridge joining West Boston with Cambridgeport and another to South Boston were completed in the 1820s. The construction of these bridges opened up all of the adjoining towns to receive the spillover of Boston's swelling population. With arteries to the outside world in place, communication between Boston and its contiguous towns rendered these suburbs virtually a part of the metropolis. So intimately linked with the city did these towns become that Boston would annex several of them within fifty years.

Such expansion could not help but accelerate the already well-established trend toward factionalism and interest group politics in the expanding city. Dissenting factions had begun increasingly to voice a view of politics that violated the cardinal tenets of the Federalist brand of republicanism. "Fear not party zeal," Boston orator Charles Sprague told his Fourth of July audience in 1825; "—it is the salt of your existence." Stalwart Federalist merchants such as Thomas Handasyd Perkins were beginning to feel that Federalists who were popular with the people, politicians such as Josiah Quincy, were also selling the interests of the community down the river in the service of their own ambition. "Quincy has thrown himself into the hands of the 'Midling or Medling Interest,'" Perkins lamented to Harrison Gray Otis resentfully. For their own part, a new breed of Federalists that included men such as Quincy—men who were persuaded to take some of the dissident demands seriously—saw themselves not as a part of the rising tide of self-interest in politics, but rather as leaders who would stem that tide by a few well-chosen concessions to the Middling Interest.[28]

Nevertheless, despite Quincy's alliance on some issues with Boston's bourgeoisie, he too was disturbed at their conduct. "There can be no surer sign that the liberties of a people are hastening to a dissolution," he told them, "than their countenancing those who form parties on men and not upon principles." He could go so far as to concede that the interests of different groups could differ, but he could not under any circumstances condone the selfish pursuit of private and personal good. And in the Jackson party, which arose in the later 1820s, many found evidence of precisely the kind of party Quincy feared. Organized around an individual's personality, that of Andrew Jackson, Jacksonians seemed to their opponents to have no regard for principle. Federalists accused them of being "rather a miserable concern . . . composed of such as want office and the disaffected of all parties." In fact, David Henshaw, the Boston druggist who headed the Massachusetts Jacksonians, seems to have been precisely the sort of office-seeking man-on-the-make whom the elite feared. His sole interest in entering politics appears to have been securing patronage.[29]

Between 1825 and 1830, no election drew 30 percent of adult white males to the polls in Massachusetts, despite the increasingly shrill pitch of the rhetoric. With the beginning of the century's fourth decade, however, the pace of politics began to pick up. The scurrilous and ignorant General, the leader of the party of "envy" and "the low idle," had been elected to the presidency in 1828, and Emerson was disturbed by a citizenry capable of electing such a man.[30] Even more alarming, additional parties were beginning to coalesce based on self-interest. The Massachusetts Antimasonic party, formed in convention in Faneuil Hall in December 1829, clearly opposed the elite establishment, claiming that Masonry (which counted nearly half of the delegates to the Massachusetts General Court as members) was inimical to the interests of the whole. Implicit in their stand was a new idea of politics based on class and interest. In addition, groups of mechanics and workers banded together in western Massachusetts in the late 1820s, demanding attention to their interests. Believing that "mechanics in no part of the world stand in a situation equal to that, which their usefulness demands," the union known as the Workingmen's party hoped to advance the interests of "the WORKING CLASS," neglected by the parasitic capitalists who enjoyed the fruits of their labor. The movement spread to Boston in 1830, when the New England Association of Farmers, Mechanics, and Other Workingmen was formed in September 1832. An entrenched elite, confident of their own wisdom in determining what was good and for whom, saw this new form of "concentrated action" as an attempt "to lead the poor to wage a civil war against the rich."[31]

Clearly such a philosophy of conflicting interests ran counter to the official consensual grain of paternalist politics in Boston. "All are the parts of one whole," Edward Everett frantically reminded the Workingmen's party in 1830; "between those parts, as there is but one interest, so there should be but one feeling." As long as it was intended to advance the interests of all who worked (which was to say, all the virtuous and respectable members of the community), the Workingmen's party was laudable and praiseworthy. Everett suggested that the party exclude partisans, "all bad men," habitual drunkards, "men who take advantage of the law to subserve their own selfish and malignant passions," "idlers," and "busy-bodies." All others who worked shared a common interest and should be pressed to the bosom of this new organization. Thus Everett willfully misread the aims of the party in order to eradicate from it any taint of economically based conflict. William Lloyd Garrison, a young man of old Federalist principles from the town of Newburyport, commented in the first issue of the *Liberator* on the attempt afoot "to inflame the minds of our working classes against the more opulent, and to persuade them that they are oppressed by a wealthy aristocracy." Garrison acknowledged as "unquestionably true" the fact that private grievances existed. Nevertheless, he clung to the belief that individuals in the city shared a common interest and ought to devote themselves to the good of the whole. The ills of the present were "not confined to any one class of society," and "every profession" was "interested in their removal—the rich as well as the poor." To incite mechanics to violence over wrongs blown out of proportion was, Garrison believed, "in the highest degree criminal."[32]

As even the semblance of consensus disappeared in Boston, adherents of the older way of doing things despaired. "If you leave the tents of your fathers," a Boston orator despaired in a jeremiad on the day Andrew Jackson was inaugurated as president, "where will you go?" Where, he asked, "would you seek shelter for your republican principles"? Did his listeners want to live "where public spirit is swallowed up in cabal, and party sinks into faction; where, after having been tost about among the shifting eddies of interest, and made dizzy with a wild rotation of opinions, you are prepared to become a mere free-thinker in politics, ready to propagate any doctrine that stands highest in the price-current of the day?" Apparently many did. By 1834, Josiah Quincy would observe the "almost total change in the relations of society" in the preceding twenty-five years. "A race of politicians" had sprung up who "steer the ship of state by the winds of popular favor, before which they run, which they never seek to stem, which they dare not resist." Government, like society itself, seemed no longer concerned with principle. Self-interest, ambition, and expediency ruled the day.[33]

V

Emerson entered the ministry during this period of growth and overt discord in Boston's history. In 1825 and 1826, he suffered through various diseases of the eyes, lungs, and limbs, and was even forced to journey to the south for a few months during the winter of 1826–27 to restore his precarious health. Nevertheless, the young man was finally approbated to preach in 1826. From 1827 to 1829 he engaged in occasional preaching in New England pulpits, substituting for settled ministers while waiting for his own broken body to mend. He was called to the pastorate of Boston's Second Church in 1829, and shortly thereafter he married Ellen Louisa Tucker of Concord, New Hampshire. From the time he was approbated to preach until his resignation from his pastorate in October 1832, he preached 164 sermons. In these sermons, which substitute in large part for journal entries during this period, Emerson took note of the decline of faith in the common good, in principle, and in virtue in his native Boston. He feared that his congregation had come to the point he anticipated in 1825 where the good life seemed utopian fantasy. During his time in the ministry, he preached the importance of virtue in the life of the community as well as in the lives of individuals. To the old Federalist emphasis on consensus and harmony, however, he added the twist he had formulated in Roxbury: one ought to aspire to such oneness of mind only with other principled individuals. As for the majority of unprincipled individuals, persons who aspired to virtue were bound to keep their moral distance from them in order to preserve their own integrity.

Emerson as pastor called upon his congregants in the best tradition of the New England jeremiad to leave off their selfishness and concern themselves with the public good. The God of New England civil religion, the author of principle, harmony, and goodness, guaranteed the community peace if individuals would only adhere to a virtuous course. The salvation Emerson and his Unitarian brethren promised was as much communal as it was personal and individual. Although he continued to exhort his congregation not to "despair of the commonwealth of man," he could not ignore the ominous decay in virtue, both public and private, that others were bewailing. Conflicts of interest, political animosity, fraud, sensuality, slander and licentiousness in the press, strong self-interest, election of self-seeking men to public office—all of these caught Emerson's attention in the late 1820s and early 1830s.[34] In an 1831 sermon, he accounted for the spread of evil in the country by placing the blame squarely on the shoulders of a self-seeking citizenry. "But how should it happen that in this virtuous nation such evil things should be done?" he asked. The answer was clear: "[I]t is because every man is no better than he is." The selfish and grasping individuals of Boston were getting the kind of community and the kind of government they deserved: contentious and unprincipled, a creature of the lust for power and of public opinion.[35]

Politics was the stage on which the self-interestedness of citizens played itself out, Emerson believed. To his congregation on Massachusetts's annual Fast Day in 1831, he warned of evil signs of the times, including "the ferocity of party spirit which sees no crime but political interest," "the increasing habit of regarding power as a prize instead of a trust," and "the absence of stern uncompromising men of principles from the helm of power." The treatment of the Cherokee Indians, whom the United States government was in the process of removing from their tribal lands in Georgia in 1831, exemplified in yet another way the decline of government by principle. "A barefaced trespass of power upon weakness," the action appeared "a most alarming symptom how obtuse is the moral sense of the people." For such "indifference to a wrong as long as it does not touch ourselves" was "one of the most certain marks of moral corruption."[36]

One of the principal reasons that such corruption in government was spreading was the attitude of material self-interestedness that a majority of the people were beginning to take. "Riches are a Trust," Emerson admonished his congregation, as even the elite began to look to its wealth as a way of insuring private happiness for themselves and their families. "The whole world runs now after power" as an end in itself instead of "being received as a trust" or an opportunity to do the community good, Emerson noted. Elective office, "a great lottery prize," was going to "the servant of public opinion, or what is commonly so called, but which is the private opinion of the hour or the party." "Thoroughly selfish" men had worked for the election of Andrew Jackson, who advocated the interests of the many rather than the good of the whole. His was "the Bad party in the country," a party of pawns whose "whole aim ever is to *get the hurra on our side.*" Even after his departure from the active ministry, Emerson would preach to lecture audiences that Jacksonian Democrats not only sanctioned the pursuit of self-interest in the community, but also promoted it.[37]

It was becoming clear to Emerson that in a country full of grasping materialists, what was good for the whole could not be ascertained by polling individual citizens. "Public opinion," Emerson regretfully reported, "will bear a great deal of nonsense. There is scarce any absurdity so gross whether in religion, politics, science, or manners, which it will not bear."[38] Citizens could no longer be counted upon to choose what was good—if, indeed, they ever could have been counted upon to do so. These were times, Emerson told his listeners on Fast Day (traditionally an occasion for stocktaking and jeremiads), when people were content to cast the pearls of virtue and honor before the swine of popular approbation. "The deep & solid foundations of a great character which always must be laid in much solitude, in austere thought, and in a religious habit" were neglected. Instead of building on solid foundations of virtue, "we rather rush into the crowd & take part with the successful & sacrifice the holiest principles to any popular cry, & thence comes it that these atrocities which have been wrought in different sections of the country by mobs—Yes—we must blush to say it even in New England the soil of the Forefathers a spirit which invades the houses of legislation and it has come to be a familiar sound to hear the Will of the people proclaimed as a reason why something should be done contrary to law to equity & to faith."[39]

Emerson's republicanism took on a twist that the changes in social conditions in Boston rendered inevitable. He continually reminded individuals that however private their lives had come to seem—and no one could deny that at times the community as a whole might seem a vague and irrelevant concept—their pursuit of individual personal virtue rather than individual economic self-interest was the foundation of a healthy social order. Though persons might see their own material interests as distinct from those of individuals around them now, all shared the duty and responsibility of pursuing the dictates of morality, for civic reasons as well as for personal ones. "You have a public duty built on the private virtues," Emerson asserted. "You have been wholly mistaken in the belief that your actions in their good or evil consequences terminated in yourself & provided you were willing to encounter the risque of a breach of law you were accountable to none but the lawgiver & on none but you could any displeasure fall. You did not only sin for yourself—. Such a sin cannot be committed in the universe. It is not an event consistent with the nature of social life. You sinned to the injury of your brother, your neighbour."[40] Any individual transgression wreaked havoc on communal order and virtue. The common standard was what was acceptable or successful rather than what was right. Respectability rather than virtue had come to be the measure of moral behavior.

The result was disastrous—"a deformed society which confessedly does not aim at an ideal integrity, no longer believes it possible, and only aims by the aid of falsehoods at keeping down universal uproar, at keeping men from each other's throats." No one claimed responsibility for the directions events were taking; no one imagined that he was "anything more than fringes and tassels to the institutions into which [he was] born." Human society was an amoral monster, out of control, headed God only knew where. Presumably free and moral individuals acted as if they were part of "a Routine which no man made and for whose abuses no man holds himself accountable." In this "community composed of a thousand different interests[,] a thousand various societies filled with competition in the arts, in trade, in politics, in private life," the moral center was missing. On the Fourth of July 1829, Emerson warned his listeners against believing that public duty consisted of "a simple sympathy." "Our sympathies are very cheap, easily excited," he told them. "It is easier to shout with a crowd than to forebear on any stirring occasion." When the individual surrendered his conscience to others, "their opinion begins to look to us like truth, & their act like virtue." The only way to a moral and humane society for the easily influenced citizens of Boston was to remain independent of the powerful machine of popular opinion.[41]

Although Emerson drew on the language of Federalism for his vocabulary during the years of his ministry, there is a subtle difference evident in his pastoral admonitions. Whereas traditional Federalist discourse emphasized the "common good" in its description of the values appropriate to a healthy republican social order, Emerson began to focus on the generalized laws that produced that common good. In so doing, he envisioned a new way of perceiving social relationships. A widespread lack of agreement on the nature of the "common good" made the simple intent to pursue it insufficient. It was not enough to rely on the moral protestations of any group that they had the good of the whole at heart. Rather, in an atmosphere of contention and self-seeking, the ability to understand in the abstract the laws governing and determining the common good became all-important. Only those best aware of objective (which was to say universal) ways of defining the common good had the right to exercise social leadership in the name of the whole. In reformulating the criteria for moral leadership within society, the young Emerson, although not yet clear on its implications, began to articulate a powerful conception of the intellectual's role in an urban, commercial social order. Where relationships between individuals were based on impersonal criteria of commodity or labor exchange that isolated them from each other and produced diverging economic interests, intellectuals exerted extraordinary moral leadership. In their pursuit of knowledge of the "objective" laws of nature, they provided a model of the civic virtue that could release individuals from the grasp of popular opinion.

It would be oversimplifying to characterize this attempted shift in perspective as either nostalgic or progressive. To the extent that Emerson utilized the language available to him, he was in part confined in his ability to see as natural anything other than the experience of the groups to which he belonged. Undeniably, those with the power to define the social values of Emerson's culture—the "natural aristocracy" already schooled and practiced in thinking in certain ways about religion, commerce, and nature—were those most likely to lay claim to defining the modes of rationality that determined which were appropriate "universal" laws and which were not. Nevertheless, to the extent that the different groups contesting for power in Boston—lesser commercial people, artisans, laborers, and a self-designated working class—were able on a wider and wider scale to make the language of Federalism a problematic one, Emerson had available to him opportunities to question and to transform both the language he had inherited and its way of constructing social values. Potentially, his rereading of the meaning of "common good" left the door open to dissident individuals and groups to propose other ways of divining the laws of human nature.

Only with time would Emerson become aware of the implications of the change in perspective he proposed, however. During most of his ministry, neither Emerson nor his listeners seemed to be conscious of the radical potential inherent in his message. Only around another issue entirely, that of the Lord's Supper, would its incipient threat to established ways of doing things become clearer. Before that issue arose, his appeal to the laws of nature seemed more reassuring than otherwise to a congregation in search of security in troubled times. The laws of nature—God's laws—would provide a safeguard for the individual within the shifting fortunes of the modern world. Duty, to be deduced from the laws of human nature, would be "the principle of equipose & stability in the soul." It would give persons incontestable and abstract guidelines to living their lives, and its tenets could not, like the giddy social whirlpool around them, change at a moment's notice. If one could no longer rely on the permanence of the persons or things surrounding one, the eternal laws of nature would always be a rock upon which to build one's house.[42]

Even as Emerson was denouncing the city's communal falling off from virtue, many Bostonians had begun to express strong fears that the best of their history was behind them. "This age of commemoration," Edward Everett called it in 1828, observing the tendency of his generation to dwell, perhaps overfondly, on the exploits of the past. William Powell Mason also noted in his 1827 Fourth of July oration for the city of Boston that the United States was destined for greatness, but he warned the present generation that they would be held accountable if the country should fall short of its destiny. "Let us turn from the contemplating of the deeds and virtues of our ancestors," he pleaded, "and endeavor to expose, whilst we may yet avoid them, some of the rocks and precipices which lay in our path, and which are not the less dangerous because they are decked with flowers." Certainly Boston's celebration of the fiftieth year of independence provoked many of the nostalgic orations that Emerson would later resent as self-congratulatory. But most of these celebrations of revolutionary patriotism carried along with their filiopietism an implicit warning to true believers: unless citizens kept carefully to the path of public and private virtue, the Revolution might well mark the high point of American development.[43]

In the period from 1827 to 1831, Emerson too noted the social changes that wracked the city of his birth. He had come to believe that if society itself could not produce the happy existence possible only for the virtuous individual, the individual would have to discover the laws that governed good and evil, virtue and vice, on his own. In the manner of Socrates, citizens would have to cultivate in themselves a new philosophy of virtue, a philosophy to short-circuit their sympathy with the tendencies of a society that had become increasingly unprincipled and immoral. Emerson knew that "the America of the selfish & ambitious man" was "no more fair or noble" than any other nation of the world, even if some of his contemporaries were intent on celebrating their Fourth of July holidays as if nothing were wrong. If individuals did not rededicate themselves to the virtue and principle that republicanism represented, they might as well have been born in the most despotic country on earth—for their own country would soon come to resemble such despotisms. Their patriotic bluster would be just so many incantations against an approaching ruin.[44] During his ministry, Emerson was determined as best he could to keep the prophecies of these latter day Jeremiahs from coming to pass. While his city slid downhill, he diligently sought ways of halting the decline. In Nature he was to find, as he thought, a solution.

CHAPTER 3

Spiritual Laws and Natural Organicism

What work of God is so beautiful as this fellowship he has established among his creatures—this natural relation of man to man. We speak and are understood heart to heart, & find our attachments strengthened precisely in proportion to the measure of virtue.—Sermon, [The heaven of a common life], 23 May 1829

DESPITE THE STRONG ECHOES of Federalist organicism in Emerson's sermons, there was a dimension to them that would have disturbed Reuben Puffer or William Emerson had either still been alive to hear him. In preaching moral reform and communal virtue to Boston's Second Church, the younger Emerson was not consciously doing anything more radical than adapting the ways of his fathers to changing times. If his fathers had preached virtue as the basis of a stable social order, he was determined to do so as well. If they had valued the individual who held himself aloof from popular opinion, then so would he. By urging the individual to come to a judgment of the good and the true independent of the community, Emerson believed he was salvaging the individual's ability to be virtuous in a corrupt social order.

In fact, however, Emerson the pastor propounded a moral philosophy that would speed the demise of that social order. His sermons contained many of the elements of other civic-minded republican discourses, but as time went on they increasingly began to rely on a new and more personal philosophy of adherence to nature. How Emerson arrived at a natural organicism that rejected the very customs, ceremonies, and ethos of social organicism that held Federalist society together is the story of his interior response to the perception of decline in consensus in Boston during the 1820s. It is also the story of a conversion experience that would have pleased his old Calvinist aunt, Mary Moody Emerson, had its tendencies been reversed. In the mid-1820s, the young ministerial candidate was converted from despair in the evil of man to faith in his possibilities, from doubt in a distant God to faith in an immanent one. If society seemed noxious, Emerson found a restorative for virtue in the God he discovered in nature.

I

The young Emerson found nature orderly, religious, and inspirational, but it was not at first in the physical landscape that he discovered these qualities. In fact, the pleasures of nature had no power over this young man so anxious to make his place in society. In 1823, for instance, during a "Walk to the Connecticutt" with his brother, he commented in his journal on the monotony and uniformity of the landscape. So uncongenial did the countryside seem to him at the age of twenty that it "elevated the Tavern to a high rank among [his] pleasures." "Cambridge," he confessed in a letter to Aunt Mary, "would be a better place to study than the woodlands." Though he admitted to experiencing "a little of that *intoxication* which you have spoken of," the exhilaration for young Emerson was more physical than spiritual. While Mary Moody Emerson, in her peculiar blend of eighteenth-century rationalism and Calvinist enthusiasm, recommended nature as a means of "contemplating the Author of nature & revelation" rather than as an end in itself, her nephew found there only "a soft animal luxury."[1]

Nevertheless, in nature taken abstractly, as the collection of laws set in motion by a Great Clockmaker of a God, Emerson took some interest. Contemplation of the laws by which the universe operated could teach humankind something about its place in a larger scheme of things. And if in 1822 and 1823 he failed to appreciate the power of the landscape to inspire, he did ponder with fascination "the general silent course of the Divine Government, manifested in the tendencies of human institutions and the human mind." During these years, Emerson focused philosophically on a nature that reflected a God who imposed a pattern on events, "an Omniscient Governor" who gave the otherwise meaningless mass of facts a soul. Things that before seemed unconnected and meaningless now followed a pattern, even if that pattern was not fully known to individuals. "The march of events which was loose and fortuitous, becomes dignified & divine," Emerson wrote, "the commerce of minds and the advancement of your own—things of which the importance was doubtful, call out your wonder as soon as you begin to discern the perfections of God walking amid these events and his Omniscient mind communicating with yours."[2]

One of the laws Emerson found written in the fabric of human nature—an important aspect of the larger pattern that he was determined to study—was the moral law. He believed the virtue that republican orators urged on their contemporaries to be merely "a conformity to the law of conscience," a natural law of the human constitution. That law, wrote Emerson in 1822, consisted of "the sovereign necessity which commands every mind to abide by one mode of conduct, & to reject another. Its divine origin is fully shewn by its superiority to all the other principles of our nature. It seems to be more essential to our constitution, than any other feeling whatever. It dwells so deeply in the human nature that we feel it to be implied in consciousness." As God had orchestrated the physical universe by laws that held all things together in a harmonious process, so had he infused into the human psyche a principle that would maintain order and virtue in society if it were only obeyed.[3]

Emerson's discovery of such natural laws of man and society in nature was neither arbitrary nor idiosyncratic. New England in the early nineteenth century was still aglow in the light of eighteenth-century rationalism, the religion inspired by Newton and resting on a study of the book of nature as well as the book of revelation. The material universe was a text to be scanned as minutely for evidences of a sovereign Creator-God as were the Sacred Scriptures. At Harvard, the citadel of Unitarianism, Henry Ware, Sr., from 1805 to 1838 lectured on natural and revealed religion and drew heavily on the natural theology of Archdeacon William Paley and Bishop Joseph Butler. These natural theologians contended that rational evidence could be found in nature not only for God's existence, but for each of his attributes. Paley's *Natural Theology* (1802) was the best known work of the time on the relationship of nature to religion. Used by Ware at Harvard beginning in 1812, it treated natural facts "as the conscious contrivances of a benign Providence." Levi Frisbie, first Alford Professor of Natural Religion, Moral Philosophy, and Civil Polity at Harvard (1817–1822) was entrusted with delineating for his charges the relationship between natural religion and the constitutions of men's minds. Emerson studied under both these proponents of the Unitarian philosophy, a philosophy that prided itself on its reasonableness according to nature.[4]

The Unitarians found that the study of nature for the purpose of detecting the operation of divine laws was a beneficial exercise. They did not expect to revel in the sensual or sentimental side of nature. That would be "as if one were to love and study the bible as a book of entertaining stories. No, he that would read nature to his profit, must go deeper." The contemplation of the spheres, the seasons, and the various orders of life were to suggest to the religious individual a "unity in the midst of variety." According to the *Monthly Anthology*, the periodical of the Boston Unitarian literati edited for a time by Emerson's father, nature was to be beheld not for its own sake but in order to learn better the divine laws of order and harmony writ large in the physical universe. The Christian "looks round on the changing scenery, and in every leaf of the forest, every blade of grass, every hill, every valley and every cloud of heaven" discovers "the traces of *divine benevolence*." Nature communicated symbolic nuances of the imperishable. Not the symbol itself but the immutable moral truth symbolized was to be cherished. Moreover, the configuration of the whole, rather than the individual parts, was important—an argument that carried as much weight in the metaphysical sphere as it did in the area of republican political philosophy.[5]

Just as Emerson's early reflections on the lawfulness of nature were derived from a well-established Unitarian perspective, so did his elaborate definitions of the moral sense grow out of what he had learned from Frisbie at Harvard. The Unitarians posited the existence of an innate moral sense in the individual. This sense could intuit the difference between good and evil. Such a moral sense was both judgmental and motivational in character: it knew the difference between right and wrong and was innately drawn toward the right if the individual kept his passions from overwhelming it. All individuals possessed this common moral sense, although by exercise some might develop it to a finer level of discrimination than others. Thus had a good God enabled them to know the laws that ought to regulate their own conduct.

The Harvard moral philosophy was both an extension of and a reaction to John Locke's philosophy of sensationalism. Locke had contended that the mind operated by laws as uniform and discernible as those of physical nature. The understanding combined sensations into ideas in an orderly fashion. Man operated as part of the cosmos, itself orderly and regulated by the Divine Mind. On the face of it, such a philosophy would seem a perfect bulwark of the Federalist universe of law and harmony. Nevertheless, Lockean sensationalism had been assaulted during the eighteenth century from two camps, both of which argued positions that promised to upset traditional notions of morality and conscience. The skeptic David Hume had charged that sensationalism was really only the portrait of a mind composed of sensations having no verifiable connection with any larger reality outside the mind. The laws that the mind imputed to physical creation could not be verified as real. Therefore, the existence of truth or morality in any metaphysical or transcendent sense could not be proven; it had merely to be assumed.[6] From a somewhat different perspective, the idealist George Berkeley had also argued, like Hume, that no necessary connection existed between sensations and ideas. Nevertheless, the benevolent Governor of the Universe had decreed that the laws of the mind in different individuals should correspond to one another. Hence, the "true" or "objective" condition of external reality was irrelevant; what mattered was the mental attribute given to physical reality by the human psyche, which fortunately acted in a uniform way, since it had been willed to do so by the Mind of God.

The philosophy that Harvard Unitarians accepted was one formulated in response to these attacks on the notion of an objective morality and the Lockean doctrine. Thomas Reid and his disciples in the Scottish Common Sense School, George Campbell, James Beattie, and Dugald Stewart, maintained that consciousness contained some principles independent of experience, principles that ordered the data gained thereby. Certain things were self-evident to the mind, one of which was morality. Emerson in his 1821 Bowdoin Prize essay had applauded Reid's attempt to refute Hume and Berkeley. He had studied Locke's *Essay on the Human Understanding* at Harvard, as well as the Scottish modifications of Lockeanism of Dugald Stewart and Thomas Brown. At this early stage in the growth of his thought, he echoed the "official" Harvard moral philosophy as the most persuasive and coherent system of philosophical inquiry. According to one of his students, Emerson delighted to hear his students praise Dugald Stewart's philosophy, which "he had lately read and which was one of the few metaphysical works he liked." Among the most appealing aspects of the Scottish philosophy was its insistence on the innate capacity of humans to know the good and the moral. Stewart, like Reid, proposed the existence in individuals of a moral sense. Moral obligations were potentially knowable to all, since the mind had a natural capacity for sensing right and wrong, good and evil, much as the eye was naturally fitted to receive the light. Emerson not only studied the common sense philosophy while at Harvard, he also read Scottish periodicals such as the *Edinburgh Review*, the *Quarterly Review*, and *Blackwood's Edinburgh Magazine*, all of which propounded the Scottish philosophy. Thus, Emerson came easily by his belief that nature had endowed man with innate moral capacities. Nature gave the individual the ability to make correct moral choices. If he was not making the correct choices, it was because he was failing to attend to the voice of his own nature.[7]

The theology of nature and the Scottish common sense philosophy both complemented the Federalist emphasis on order and harmony within society. The physical universe operated according to certain laws, and these laws published the unity and harmony that the mind of the Deity had conferred on creation. Virtue represented adherence to the course that nature and nature's God had laid down for the human personality, vice its violation. Corruption was the willful disruption of the harmony of the whole, accomplished when private and personal ends, beneficial only in the particular and unusual case, were substituted for the general ends decreed by nature. In the worldview that Emerson inherited, virtue could be defined in natural terms.

Despite the lessons that nature might teach individuals about the lawfulness and order God had built into humans and into the universe, nature was not spirit. The universe was dualistic. "There are two natures in man, flesh and spirit," Emerson wrote, echoing the accepted philosophy in 1822. Their tendencies were "wide as the universe asunder." Even William Ellery Channing, the most liberal minister in Boston and something of a Platonist, acknowledged that fact. "I heard Dr. Channing deliver a discourse upon Revelation as standing in comparison with Nature," Emerson wrote on a Sunday in October 1823. "He considered God's word to be the only expounder of his works, & that Nature had always been found insufficient to teach men the great doctrines which Revelation inculcated. . . . An universe of matter in which Deity would display his power & greatness must be of infinite extent & complicate relations and of course too vast to be measured by the eye & understanding of man. Hence errors. . . . Dr. C. regarded Revelation as much a part of the order of things as any other event." Emerson noted in approval, "It would have been wise to have made an abstract of the Discourse immediately."[8]

Thus God had created "an Order," "a System," which was "a harmonious whole, combined & overruled by a sublime Necessity, which embraces in its mighty circle the freedom of the individuals, and without subtracting from any, directs all to their appropriate ends."[9] Individuals were to be ruled by the laws of this universal order if they would allow themselves to be. By seeking to follow the rule implanted in his own nature by God, the individual would not only be cooperating with God's plan, but he would also be helping to bring about the unity and the harmony built into the universe by a benevolent Deity.

In their insistence that powerful laws of the human psyche could produce social unity just as natural laws produced a unity in nature, Unitarians buttressed the notion of social organicism with a justification taken from nature. Men were to cooperate in a harmonious social order because their natures demanded that they do so. Social organicism and natural organicism were meant to be complementary. Despite its location of an innate sense of good and evil within the individual, such a common sense philosophy was not intended to be antinomian. In fact, its practical effect, at least in Emerson's time, was to restrain democratic tendencies in the moral sphere. As Emerson had hinted in his Bowdoin Prize essay, the common sense philosophy indeed lacked a certain "neatness and conclusiveness," for it had no logical justification for the correspondence it drew between objective and subjective reality. It merely asserted that such a correspondence exited. In its treatment of morality, it also asserted a good many other things on specious grounds, for instance, that some faculty for knowing an objective good or evil "must" exist, and that the individual must "naturally" recognize good and evil. The natural morality that they insisted to be objective truth tended rather to be the established morality of the day. Instead of releasing individuals to follow a good that their own minds discovered, common sense as it played out in the "official" philosophy of Boston's educated elite insisted that they dutifully follow the pattern of morality written in their hearts by nature. Since the local interpreters of the common sense philosophers themselves defined what natural was, there was seldom much room left for innovation. In a culture in which traditional morality could not be preserved by the personal enforcement of communal mores, the version of the common sense philosophy in vogue in Boston in the 1820s implied that individuals could still be expected to adhere to the old moral codes. The assumption was that all individuals carried within their bosoms an imprint of the traditional morality.[10]

As long as visible groups and factions refrained from disputing the character of natural impulses and natural morality, social organicism and natural organicism complemented each other. In the early 1820s, Emerson, like most Unitarians, still believed the two to be complementary. "There is a great community of minds whom their Maker has formed to depend much and constantly upon each other," he wrote in his journal. They were "linked & leagued together by external & indissoluble bonds."[11] As rents in the social fabric became apparent, the relationship between the two constructs in time became more problematic. Gradually over the course of the late 1820s and early 1830s, natural organicism would for Emerson begin to take precedence over the social organicism it had earlier reinforced.

II

Had the young Emerson been of a different religious background, he might have been a prime candidate for the conversion experience that revivalists such as Lyman Beecher were preaching in Boston. He was a young man without a career; he lived in an urban environment in which none of the old rules seemed to hold. His life was unsettled. It is not surprising that such a person might find in the nature set in motion by the Great Clockmaker little personal consolation. The Emerson who could write that life consisted merely of "a few dark hours poisoned by evil, and clouded by anxiety" saw in nature the sign and seal of his own mortality. "In the external & enchanting variety of sky & season, amid the softness of the first vernal airs," he apprehended only "a melancholy voice which makes itself heard, teaching the vanity of joy, the neighbourhood of remorse; saying that Nature acts the part of a deceiver, when in this scene of human danger & fate, she wears so gay & gorgeous apparel." There he only saw a mirror of what disturbed him so greatly elsewhere: "a tendency in all things human to decay."[12]

Although nature had the tendency to bring "new life" out of "the ruins of society," that was no comfort to one condemned to dwell among the ruins. From time to time Emerson manifested the morbidity that typically preceded conversion among young persons. In this vision in an 1822 journal passage, he clearly echoed some of the apocalyptic strains of his own culture and created an unintentional parody of Byronic despair. Nevertheless, the tone and imagery of the vision communicate a disturbed state of mind:

> A cry in the wilderness! the shriek and sudden sound of desolation! howl for him that comes riding on darkness through the midnight; that puts his hand forth to darken the moon, and quenches all the stars. . . . Lo! he stands up in the Universe and with his hands he parts the firmament ascended from side to side. And as he trode upon the dragons I saw the moon which burned underneath—Wake, oh wake, ye who keep watch in the Universe! Time, Space, Eternity, ye Energies that live, for his name is DESTRUCTION!—who keep the *Sceptre* of its eternal order, for He hath reached unto your treasuries, & he feeleth after your Sceptre to break it in pieces. Another cry went up like the crash of broken spheres, the voice of dying worlds. It is night.

It is impossible to tell whether the young man's vision was a response to the fearful chaos of his own life or a thinly veiled desire to introduce destruction and chaos on a society that was ignoring him. Whatever the stimulus that produced such a violent and foreboding fantasy, however, it is clear that Emerson had come upon difficult times emotionally. In the winter of 1822, he translated his mood into verse:

> I stand amid the wilderness. Disdain
> Hath marked her victim; Hunger, Cold,
> Misfortune shake their shrivelled hands at me
> And gird me in their hideous company.

He felt separated from others and unable to see how he fit into society. "Men are only alike in infancy," he observed in 1823; afterwards they go their own separate and unfathomable ways, "and every step separates him further from all the rest." Although he continued to take the Unitarian view that nature and society were united and harmonious, its cosmic optimism seems to have provided him with little personal assurance.[13]

Emerson seems to have come to an "experimental" understanding of natural religion sometime during the summer of 1825. He had entered the Harvard Divinity School in February 1825, but his eyes began to trouble him shortly after he had begun studying there. His illness forced him to suspend his studies briefly, and he recuperated at his uncle Ladd's farm in Newton. One day while working in the field Emerson struck up a conversation with a Methodist field hand. When the ministerial candidate remarked on his difficulty in praying, his democratic oracle told him, "You pray all the time, and all your prayers are answered." At first he was not sure what the remark had meant, although he was intrigued by it. How was it that one could pray all the time? As he thought about it, however, he discovered the Methodist's meaning. In his first sermon, "Pray Without Ceasing," Emerson explicated that meaning for his listeners. In the course of his ministry, he would preach the sermon twelve times, for he believed he had found a way to make the demands of morality and the lawfulness of nature real to an age that too easily ignored them.[14]

The moral degeneracy Emerson saw around him he had always attributed to the tendency of his contemporaries to think the physical divorced from the spiritual. "What is the secret sorcery that has bewitched men's souls?" he asked in the spring of 1823. "I will tell you. It is because men are blindly[,] madly attached to the present moment, and hazard the infinite future rather than forego the gross and inconsiderable joys which are soliciting their appetites today." Individuals were distracted by the superficialities of the natural life and failed to attend to the "unspeakable conceptions of the Cause and Design." One of the reasons they so freely disregarded the claims of their spiritual nature was that they did not perceive the immediate effect of violating spiritual laws. In the natural sphere cause and effect were obvious; in the moral sphere they were more covert. "It were a sermon much wanted, much more than flippant essays on perfectibility, that which should bring home the probability of the constant presence & moral action of Deity, tho' the thunder does not strike transgression," Emerson decided in early 1825. "For it is the want of visible tokens of judgment that generates all skepticism." "Pray Without Ceasing" was that sermon. In it Emerson attempted to illustrate for his listeners that spiritual laws of cause and effect operated in just the same way that natural laws did.[15]

"Pray Without Ceasing" had several points to make. One was that virtue meant a habitual uprightness of character rather than isolated benevolent acts. Another was that violations of the moral laws had real and observable effects in society. What was newest in Emerson's sermon, however, was the implication that natural laws and spiritual laws were so intimately related as to be almost indistinguishable. The innovation was not so radical that it discouraged the committee of ministers from the Boston Association from approbating him to preach on the basis of the sermon. Nevertheless, it did point the way to a greater identification of natural and spiritual law than had been the case in Unitarianism. It also prepared the way for Emerson's advocacy of obedience to natural law—the law of man's nature—regardless of the potential short-run social consequences as a type of spiritual law.

"It ought to be distinctly felt by us that we stand in the midst of two worlds, the world of matter and the world of spirit," Emerson told his listeners at the beginning of the sermon. Although an audience not privy to Emerson's internal speculations prior to the sermon's composition might have thought he was reemphasizing the dualism between matter and spirit, he was in fact taking their dualism as a given. Instead he meant to emphasize their equal importance in the life of the individual. Spirit (or mind) was just as real, just as observable in its effects, as matter. "It has been one of the best uses of the Christian religion to teach that the world of spirits is more certain and stable than the material universe," he continued. Thought and feeling were the most real and profound influences on human affairs. Nevertheless, the mass of men persisted in thinking that material cause and effect constituted the only true reality, that their thoughts had no bearing on anyone or anything unless translated into overt physical action. It was time to realize, Emerson told them, "that thoughts and passions, even those to which no language is ever given, are not fugitive undefined shadows, born in a moment, and in a moment blotted from the soul, but are so many integral parts of the imperishable universe of morals." Individuals needed to be "taught that they do not think alone." Mind was more real than matter, spiritual law more significant than material law.[16]

As a concrete example of what he meant, Emerson turned in his sermon to the truth uttered by his Methodist field hand the previous summer: "You pray all the time, and all your prayers are answered." Prayer was not a formal, liturgical act; it was a predisposition or a state of mind. "Every secret wish is a prayer," Emerson told them; "every house is a church, the corner of every street is a closet of devotion." Spiritual acts were natural acts, and natural acts were spiritual. Every state of mind, every natural inclination was in some way moral, indicating a predisposition to act in a moral or immoral way. *"Every desire of the human mind is a prayer uttered to God and registered in heaven,"* he insisted. Every thought set in motion spiritual laws of cause and effect, and the individual "received" what he desired. Did he secretly want to be rich? All his thoughts and actions would be directed to that end, either consciously or unconsciously. Did he want to be virtuous? If so, by the same token, he would be rewarded with the tranquility that was the fruit of a spiritual life. Character was a sort of action, for it was the motivating force that produced virtuous or vicious action automatically.

Emerson's discovery of an analogy between natural and spiritual laws began subtly to change his attitude toward the nature of individual and social virtue. With his newfound confidence that the individual could actively, by an internal effort of will, dedicate himself to the laws that controlled both nature and society, Emerson came to the conclusion that happiness depended not on external circumstances but on the individual's ability to come to an inner equilibrium based on an understanding of spiritual laws and their natural consequences. "Let it be felt that the mind is all, & then it will follow in irresistible logic as it does in actual truth that the only reasonable efforts to increase human happiness must be aimed at the mind & not the body," he averred in September 1828. He asserted forcefully that the moral person need give no heed to the practical effects of his actions, for a lawful God would bring them to a happy result. Truth says, "Give yourself no manner of anxiety about events, about the consequences of actions," he wrote; "they are really of no importance to us. They have another Director, controller, guide. The whole object of the Universe to us is the formation of Character." Faithfulness to one's own nature superceded faithfulness to social mores.[17] Emerson's reliance on the laws of nature rather than on those of society gave him a confidence in himself that he had heretofore lacked. Though a majority of individuals might disapprove of his actions because of their orientation to material laws only, he had the confidence that "in squaring [his] conduct" with these spiritual laws of his being, he was "backed by the Universe of beings." "In a degree [the individual] is always affected by the nation, age, family, profession, friendship he falls upon," he preached, but a man had in him an active and assertive will that could affect others as well. The good man "exerts influence as well as receives it." The better the person, the greater his influence for the good on others.[18]

But was not this encouragement to the individual to trust the lights of his own nature an invitation to anarchy? The answer is yes, if—and only if—one assumes that sincere persons may differ in moral judgments. Emerson's notion of the objective existence of moral laws that all sincere persons could know meant that sincere persons would always agree. It was through a reliance on nature, Emerson believed, that a virtuous consensus might be restored to a community at each other's throats. The philosophy of nature was an attempt to circumvent a social process already well underway, not a conscious attempt to accelerate it. "All men on whose souls the light of God's revelation truly shineth, with whatever apparent differences, are substantially of one mind, work together, whether consciously or not, for one and the same Good," Emerson told the congregation gathered at the ordination of the Reverend Hersey Bradford Goodwin as colleague pastor of Ezra Ripley at Concord in 1830. In another sermon, Emerson advised his listeners, "Consider that every good man, every good thing, every good action, word, & thought that you love, is only a *fragment of the divine Nature.*" By very definition, divine Nature was order and harmony. Had not such order and harmony been the aim of social organicism? "God is the substratum of all souls," Emerson believed. "Is not that the solution of the riddle of sympathy?"[19]

III

As Emerson's ministry progressed, he became increasingly convinced that obedience to the laws within was the key to virtue, the way to keep the powers of sympathy from drawing the individual into a life of conformity to the dictates of fashion. "Smother no dictate of your soul, but indulge it," he wrote in 1830, for goodness had been built into the soul's nature by God. "Do not stifle your moral faculty & force it to call what it thinks evil, good." In order to make the spiritual laws of their own natures intelligible to a congregation who refused to see their power, Emerson persisted in explaining the laws of spirit as psychological processes embedded in the mind rather than as principles alien to the everyday life of individuals. Morality was something as tangible in their own lives as the causes and effects of physical laws. It was something people could understand immediately and intuitively. By 1830, even the distant and omniscient Governor of the Universe had become something that the individual might understand in some small way by referring to the processes of his own mind, for the mind was made in God's likeness. "What is God?" Emerson asked. "The most elevated conception of character that can be formed in the mind. It is the individual's own soul carried out to perfection. For no other Deity can he conceive. He is infinite, as I am finite: He is sinless as I am sinful; He is all wise as I am all ignorant. He is strong as I am weak." He was, in other words, the most perfect expression of Mind and its spiritual laws that could be imagined. He was an "experimental" version of natural religion. The individual could know God because he could feel God within himself.[20]

Throughout his ministry Emerson moved closer to reconciling the division between spirit and nature, trying to make the laws of morality in some way tangible and the claims of spirit real. In 1830 he found assistance in European romanticism, a philosophical point of view that promised to eliminate the gap between spirit and nature altogether. Spirit's laws were not different in kind from those of nature; they merely transcended or subsumed them. Although Emerson's discovery of such philosophers as Samuel Taylor Coleridge and Marie Joseph de Gérando did not change his moral opinions materially, it did offer him a philosophical justification for his claims that nature and spirit were related. They were, the romantic philosophy told him, only two different ways of looking at the same thing.

The Lockean philosophy, even in its Scottish reincarnation, had remained concerned mainly with external sensations. It had conceived of the human mind as passive and dependent on its environment for its sustenance. Inevitably, the "noble doubt" raised by Berkeley intruded itself: How could one know that objective and subjective reality corresponded? The common sense realists handled the problem merely by asserting that they did, but Emerson was troubled by a latent dualism that threatened to divorce the material and the spiritual, the subjective and the objective.

The Neoplatonic romanticism that arose in response to Stewart and the common sense philosophers, the romanticism Emerson discovered in 1830, seemed to him to bind the universe into a unity that would not, like the Scottish school, threaten to unravel at the seams. Neoplatonists inched back toward a Berkeleyan idealism, asserting the primacy of the spiritual (or mental) over the physical. The mind determined the nature of reality by imposing order on the sensations it received. The physical sensations in and of themselves were unimportant; they had no intrinsic meaning. Echoing Berkeley, these romantics claimed that the ideas of the mind that gave order to physical nature were mirrors of the abstract spiritual laws of the Divine Mind that had created the universe and sustained it. Such romanticism also differed from Lockean sensationalism and its common sense offshoot in its notion of how moral laws were perceived. The common sense thinkers had posited the existence of a "common sense"—a faculty that functioned in the same way as any other sense would, in passively receiving data from the external world. As the eye would immediately recognize light, so the moral sense would immediately be able to discern good and evil as a reflex action. The trained conscience could become more accomplished at discernment, just as the trained eye could focus on more subtle physical details. Nevertheless, the response of this conscience was more or less automatic unless the individual willingly allowed his passions to gain dominion over it. The mind that the idealists envisioned, in contrast, was a more active instrument in determining morality. It did not make reflex judgments, as the common moral sense did; rather, it intuited the spiritual laws that governed the universe directly, for it was an image of the Mind that created the universe. It came to know truth not by virtue of an accumulation of physical sensations (for truth was not something that could be received from without), but as the mind of God knew it—abstractly and with the ability to discern how individual laws were related to a larger spiritual whole. For example, the moral sense could know that honesty was a moral virtue; it could judge right from wrong in both particular and general instances. The nineteenth-century Platonists claimed for the mind the ability to intuit not only that honesty was a moral trait, but the higher spiritual laws that governed the universe and determined why honesty should be moral. They not only could know that the law existed; they also might know why it existed.

Thus, the mind was not merely an assembler of random sensations, but an active producer of the ideas that were reality. The romantic who possessed such a mind did not merely recognize through an interior sense the dictates of a traditional morality; he was free, he thought, to discover the underlying laws that governed even morality. His intuition of these laws, as it turned out, might prove traditional moral codes or responses wrong. Such a philosophy was intended to be organic on a most basic level, for it was to reflect the most fundamental laws of relationship within the universe conceived as a unity. Instead, however, by allowing the individual to discover such laws on his own, romanticism would destroy the kind of organicism based in social consensus. Such an individual would transcend the limits of geographical fellowship, claiming a community with Nature itself.

Emerson synthesized his own romanticism from at least three different sources. The Cambridge Platonists, represented chiefly by Ralph Cudworth, emphasized the objective existence of moral laws that the mind could know directly. In his *True Intellectual System of the Universe* and in his *Treatise Concerning Eternal and Immutable Morality*, Cudworth defended the existence of a spiritual universe in which virtue and good had an objective existence. This was a view Frisbie had adopted in his courses at Harvard, and it was indeed "an emphatic departure from the empirical theory of the sensuous philosophy,—the philosophy founded on the experience of the senses, as the antithesis of the intuitions of the soul, . . . in which the followers of Locke and Paley had found a placid repose." It is interesting to note that Cudworth's own advocacy of the good life took place in response to a seventeenth century in which he believed that corruption, materialism, and debauchery were rife. No wonder, then, that in Cudworth, Emerson found a kindred soul.[21]

In addition, Emerson's acquaintance with de Gérando, the French Neoplatonist, whetted his interest in the Pythagorean School of Platonism. The Pythagoreans, as interpreted by de Gérando, offered to Emerson a metaphysical theory that assumed the unity of the universe. Emphasis was on the spiritual integration of all parts, as Neoplatonists felt no need to explain away a gap between exterior and interior that troubled the Lockean common sense philosophers. The diversity of life of which the senses constantly reminded man dissolved into the unity of an abstract, spiritual truth that the mind intuited directly. Here was a philosophy that confirmed and systematized Emerson's own intuitions about the unity of mind and matter under the aegis of spirit.[22]

The third and most important source of Emerson's Neoplatonism was Samuel Taylor Coleridge. Coleridge's influence was significant, since it was he who passed on to Emerson much of the philosophy of Kant and the German transcendentalists. The human mind, not external reality, might prove the source of order in the universe. Drawing on Schelling's Kant-inspired *Naturphilosophie*, Coleridge stressed the power of human intuition to discover these spiritual laws. By asserting that the intellect mirrored the mind of God and thus not only could know that nature was lawful, but also could discover the laws that governed it, the transcendentalist philosophers maintained that the ideal and the spiritual were reality. They also insisted that the best way for the individual to discover this spiritual reality was in the sanctity of his own conscience. Mind could know the ideal without reference to external facts or persons. The individual needed only to examine his own conscience to know truth. Emerson's exposure to the visionary philosophy began with his readings of Coleridge, Madame de Staël, and Wordsworth in his teens, but he was not strongly impressed with any of these at the time. At the Harvard Divinity School, he began to read the prose of Coleridge, beginning with Coleridge's proposed reconstruction of Christian theology in 1826. The *Edinburgh Review*, an important periodical among the educated of Emerson's Boston, carried occasional articles on German literature during the 1820s that piqued Emerson's curiosity, but it was with his discovery of Coleridge's *The Friend* and his *Aids to Reflection* in 1830 that Emerson finally immersed himself in the romantic alternative to sensationalism.[23]

Coleridge conveyed to his eager reader in *Aids to Reflection* a Kantian distinction between the Reason and the Understanding. Reason focused on the unity of phenomena, Understanding on their differences. Coleridge saw Reason as "the knowledge of the laws of the WHOLE considered as ONE: and as such it is contradistinguished from the Understanding, which concerns itself exclusively with the quantities, qualities, and relations of *particulars* in time and space." This Reason was a spiritual faculty; it did not derive from the sense, since senses by their nature only apprehended the particular and the material. Nor was Reason merely a logically derived catalogue of cause-and-effect rules of the physical universe. That reasoning, however abstract, remained a part of the world of sense. Rather, this faculty of the human mind was "an *intuition* or *immediate* Beholding accompanied by a conviction of the necessity and universality of the truth so beheld." Anything apprehended only by the senses could change; Reason was the "sole principle of permanence amid endless change." Reason evidenced a real unity in the world, for reason was the law that bound disparate entities together. Religion was the contemplation of the universal that Reason revealed, and its purpose was to guide men to a recognition of the principles that governed the universe.[24]

Why should Emerson have been drawn to such a philosophy? It is apparent that the idealism of romantic Platonism satisfied for him a philosophical lack in Lockean sensationalism. Beyond mere intellectual curiosity, however, the universe of the Neoplatonists promised an individual acutely troubled by the apparent contentiousness of his society a way of drawing unity, harmony, and order out of apparent chaos. Underneath the surface of nature lay abstract, spiritual laws that rationalized and bound all together. Behind the fragmentation of the increasing size and diversity of urban Boston, the promise of a lasting interrelationship between individuals lay at the heart of man's own nature, would he but recognize it. Emerson found in nature the order and stability lacking in human affairs. "Give me a place to stand on," he had quoted Archimedes' famous maxim in his mid-twenties, "and I will move the earth."[25] Nature, interpreted in its romantic sense as a system of spiritual laws rather than as a collection of material objects, as process rather than as matter, was his place to stand amidst the kaleidoscopic shifting of human affairs. Moreover, such a philosophy sanctioned his own inclination to rely on his own judgment rather than on communal mores. He now had a philosophical justification for rejecting what others valued, if what they valued seemed to him to be based on Understanding rather than Reason. Finally, Reason taught that nature, if obeyed systematically, reconciled all differences on a spiritual level. For Emerson, nature considered as a romantic whole seemed to provide a substitute for the lost organicism of the social sphere. It was cosmic organicism. Between 1830 and 1834, Emerson gradually became such a romantic idealist.

IV

If there was any lesson taught by nature, the physical mirror of spiritual laws, it was that unity resulted from the harmonious relationships of the parts to the whole. "Every thing good is universal nature," Emerson asserted in 1830. "Wrong is particular. Right is universal." The individual, the particular, the idiosyncratic disrupted the unity of the whole, throwing all into disarray. Only by following the universal law did all things work together for the good. "I am thrilled with delight by the choral harmony of the whole," Emerson celebrated, as he extolled the virtues of taking the larger view. "Design! It is all design. It is all beauty. It is all astonishment." In 1834, Emerson recalled for his journal a moment of epiphany from his boyhood, an experience in which the material world had bodied forth this spiritual insight. Walking on the beach as a boy, he became enchanted with the colors and shapes of the shells he found there. He put some of them in his pocket, thinking to carry home with him the beauty he had observed. However, "when I got home," he remembered, "I could find nothing that I gathered—nothing but some dry ugly mussel & snail shells." Separated from the shore where they lay "wet & social by the sea & under the sky," the shells might as well have been in a cabinet of natural history for all the inspiration they afforded Emerson. Apart from the entire landscape of which they formed a part, they held no beauty.[26]

What held true in the material sphere Emerson inevitably found equally true in the interior or spiritual sphere as well. The individual fulfilled the dictates of his nature only as part of a larger whole. The tendency in those about him to value the particular and to see personality, profession, and social class as the principal determinants of identity disturbed Emerson: "The vast majority of men though by nature all related to and having access to the world of thought, yet live and act mainly in quite another region, that is, in the apparent world of the senses, acting with simple reference to their actual relations, that is, as mortals, as fathers, as tradesmen, as householders." The "tendency in the mind to separate particulars & in magnifying them to lose sight of the connexion of the object with the Whole" had led to the formation of parties, cabals, and sects. Individuals concerned only with appearances neglected "that universal nature which obliterates all ranks, all evils, all individualities." Emerson saw it clearly to be man's duty to bring himself back into consonance with the rest of nature which he alone disrupted via the corruption of self-interest. "Man is powerful only by the multitude of his affinities, or, because his life is intertwined with the whole chain of organic and inorganic being," Emerson would tell Bostonians in 1836.[27]

To "separate my individual nature and deeds and possessions from the rest, to withdraw my interests from the common soul and confine it to my person and property" led to dire results for the community as well as for the individual. Adherence to the divine plan of nature meant abandoning one's own private interests and dedicating oneself to the common good. Although this common good was defined by Nature and Nature's God now rather than by the consensus of a community, the Emersonian individual was to be mindful always of "the unity, the community of men," the fruit of the "strictly identical nature of which all the individuals are organs." In fact, the rapid disintegration of the New England he knew seemed to Emerson symptomatic of the violation of the inner laws of human nature that held society together. "My neighbor feels the wrong that my self-interest produces," Emerson believed, "feels that here is appropriation, here is not love, and shrinks from me as far as I have shrunk from him. His eyes no longer seek mine on the streets; we look diverse ways." Like Boston's temperance and Sabbatarian reformers, Emerson attributed the disorganization and disaffection of urban, commercial Boston to flaws in the moral outlook of individuals.[28]

God had not made man's nature evil. "Error, vice and disease have their seat in the superficial or individual nature," Emerson proclaimed, the nature to which the "idea of Man" acted as antidote. The idea of Man comprehended man in the abstract and what he might be were he to follow the laws of his nature. Emerson saw this generic man as a knower of the laws of Reason, constituted the same in all: "It is in all men, even in the worst, & constitutes them men. In bad men it is dormant; in the good, efficient. But it is perfect and identical in all, underneath the peculiarities, the vices, & the errors of the individual. A man feels that his fortune, friendships, opinions, yea, all the parts of his individual existence, are merely superficial to the principle of Right. Compared with the self existence of the laws of Truth and Right whereof he is conscious, his personality is a parasitic deciduous atom." The unity of man's nature insured that all moral judgments would be identical if pursued by the light of nature. Education ideally ought to aim to "sink what is individual or personal in us, to stimulate what is torpid of the human nature, and so to swell the individual to the outline of this Universal Man and bring out his original and majestic proportions."[29]

In emphasizing the personalities of individuals over their general and common nature, Emerson believed, men had not only lost sight of the connections between the part and the whole; they had also conjured up a faulty notion of God. God could not be a person, Emerson believed, for a person was necessarily finite and unconnected with other creatures when seen as personality. "The *personality* of God" must be seen as a contradiction, for "a person is finite personality, is finiteness." Rather, God was implicated in the universe as the principle that gave unity to nature. He was the apotheosis of the Reason, or spiritual law, the source of the abstract principles and laws that pervaded creation and gave it unity. "The pure intellect is God," Emerson asserted. Hence, the soul that became aware of its own nature also came to know God, for God was the law of nature that produced man's own particular nature. No longer the Great Clockmaker who set the world in motion and presided over it aloofly, Emerson's God pervaded the universe as the spiritual principle that kept it from flying apart into a welter of unrelated phenomena.[30]

Such an "experimental" discovery of the God in one's own soul made "all things lose at once their solitary, independent value." Thenceforward they were to be "regarded in a new light as parts of God[']s agency—nothing is insignificant, for every thing is a part of the mighty whole." Emerson believed, in the tradition of eighteenth-century rationalism, that such a God "does not operate always for the immediate shortsighted good of the individual." Salvation was not "definite partial good." Rather, salvation for Emerson became the immediate perception of the relation between the individual and the whole, a realization that redeemed the individual because it obliterated him, except as a manifestation of God.[31]

Nature so conceived destroyed any notion of a unique self-importance in individuals. But in exchange for what it took away, it recompensed a hundredfold the individual who believed. To the question the young Emerson had asked himself in 1827, "What is certain? What is probable?" he had found his answer: Nature. Emerson believed he had now found the unshakable source of "the peace of mind which dwells with unblemished virtue" that he had longed for in his youth. In a world in which everything seemed to be changing too quickly and for the worse, Nature offered asylum to the troubled individual. Through a grasp of the concept of nature, "the spirit learns to discern stability at the heart of agitation and Law riding sure through wild and prodigious motion." In the context of nature, man could feel at home. There he could find eternal answers to eternal questions. Amid the turmoil of social and political systems in transition, Emerson took refuge in a surety "which is not, like Religion or Politics, bound around with so many traditions & on which he may exhaust his whole love of truth,—his heart & his mind." In a society apt to pervert the moral perceptions, Emerson observed, "few are free." Nature was the key that unlocked the individual from the prisonhouse of conformity and appearance.[32]

Nature, then, became the remedy for all human ills, although in a somewhat paradoxical way. As natural law, it was the essence of man's social being, for it provided (in Georg Lukacs's words) an " 'ordered,' calculable, formal, and abstract" way of viewing human behavior, a way that seemed to transcend petty self-interest.[33] The rule behind the merely phenomenal, it held within it the principles that rationalized all human action. At the same time, however, nature enabled men to move beyond their enmeshment in social sympathies and freed them to consult their individual consciences in the judgment of moral behavior. The way to social harmony led directly through radical individualism, and a true valuation of human beings through a willingness to ignore their particular circumstances. Emerson's reliance on generalized, abstract laws of nature as a way to morality and human happiness mirrored, although in a way that seems not to have been apparent to him, the new economic order's increasing reliance on generalized, abstract laws of exchange and commodity as ways of ordering human relationships. Uncomfortable with the contentious character of urban, commercial Boston, Emerson resisted it. And in so doing, he constructed a moral order that both implicitly recognized and completed the processes at work around him.

Eventually Emerson's spiritual philosophy of nature would lead him to embrace the landscape that had so bored him at the age of twenty. In his thirty-first year, he would leave Boston for the country town of Concord, convinced that the world of commerce, self-interest, competition, and factionalism in the city made it nearly impossible for the individual to heed the voice of his own nature. In the Concord countryside, Nature would become "the beautiful asylum to which we look in all the years of striving and conflict as the assured resource when we shall be driven out of society by ennui or chagrin or persecution or defect of character."[34] What convinced Emerson that it was nearly impossible to be virtuous in Boston was not his detached observations of "corruption" there or his innate attraction to the country landscape. Rather, Emerson fled to Concord and to nature because of a painful personal discovery that Bostonians cared little for virtue and much for forms. In a church in Boston's old North End, Emerson would come to the conclusion that adherence to spiritual laws had become impossible in Boston, even in her churches.

PART 2

Vocation

CHAPTER 4

The Armies of Zion

The city is recruited from the country. . . . The city would have died out, rotted and exploded, long ago, but that it was reinforced from the fields. It is only country which came to town day before yesterday that is city and court today.—"Manners," Essays: Second Series, October 1844

FROM 1826 TO 1832, two churches located at opposite ends of Hanover Street competed for the immortal souls and theological loyalties of the residents of Boston's North End. One was Unitarian, the other orthodox Congregationalist. The Unitarian church, a fixture in the neighborhood since its foundations as Boston's Second Church in 1650, was presided over by Henry Ware, Jr., the mild-mannered, warm, but dignified son of Harvard's Hollis Professor of Divinity. The Reverend Mr. Ware represented the best the Unitarian establishment had to offer. Concerned for his people, liberal and intellectually tolerant, learned and eloquent, the precocious young clergyman was well loved. He had taken charge of the smallest and least opulent Unitarian congregation in Boston, a strictly middle class parish, in 1817. Under his able pastoral guidance, the Old North, as it was commonly called, grew in size and devotion.[1]

Ware, however, was plagued by the weak lungs endemic to the Boston ministry in the early nineteenth century, and in 1828 reluctantly begged his congregation to dismiss him for reasons of health. A grateful church and society could not bear to see their pastor of eleven years depart, and they proposed to take on the added financial burden of a colleague pastor to assist him in his duties. During one of Ware's bouts with illness, they had heard the son of the late minister of the First Church in Boston preach, and he was much to their liking. In 1829, Second Church issued its call to Ralph Waldo Emerson to take up the duties of colleague pastor. Troubled by his own ill health, Emerson accepted the call reluctantly.

If my own feelings could have been consulted, I should have desired to postpone, at least, for several months, my entrance into this solemn office. I do not now approach it with any sanguine confidence in my abilities, or in my prospects. I come to you in weakness, and not in strength. In a short life, I have yet had abundant experience of the uncertainty of human hopes. I have learned the lesson of my utter dependency; and it is in a devout reliance upon other strength than my own, in a humble trust in God to sustain me, that I put forth my hand to this great work.[2]

On 11 March 1829, Emerson formally assumed his pastoral duties. Immediately afterwards, an exhausted Ware departed for Europe in an effort to restore his wasted body. He returned in the summer of 1830, only to resign his pulpit permanently in October to accept the new Hollis Professorship of Pulpit Eloquence and Pastoral Care at Harvard. Seventy-four of the eighty-three members of Second Church voted to call their colleague pastor to full responsibility for the church in Hanover Street. By the end of 1830, the spiritual welfare of the North End's Unitarians lay in Emerson's hands.

At the other end of Hanover Street lay a church more recently gathered. In the summer of 1825, evangelical Christians decided that it was time to spread the message of unadulterated Calvinism by colonizing a church based on old-time principles. Twenty-six members of Boston's existing orthodox Congregational churches, including fifteen from Park Street, six from Old South, and five from Union Church, covenanted together to form the new Hanover Street Church. As their first pastor, the infant congregation called the firebrand revivalist from Connecticut, Lyman Beecher. A short, square, impulsive man, Beecher was so full of nervous energy that he kept a sand pile in his basement and shoveled it furiously whenever he felt restless. Blessed with a magnetic personality and a riveting power of oratory, Beecher came to Boston to declare war on just such "heretics" as Ware, Emerson, and the Second Church. He wanted to stand at the head of "a united and simultaneous effort to rescue from perversion the doctrines and institutions of our fathers." That perversion was Unitarianism.[3]

If Emerson filled his own ministry with warnings against contention, controversy, and self-interest among his congregation, he did so in response to more than political divisions arising within "Boston Babylon." Like the politicians who urged party spirit on the inhabitants of the city, evangelicals such as Lyman Beecher advocated an exclusivity in religious affairs completely at odds with the

Boston elite's notion of social organicism. Beecher played on the increasingly salient divisions of the people of Boston to bring the long simmering religious controversy there to a boil. Thus Emerson's ministry at Second Church developed in large part in response to Beecher's at Hanover Street.

I

Theologically, the Unitarians and the evangelicals differed on only a few important doctrinal issues. Although these certainly were significant, they were often argued to rarefied extremes. Whether God was Trinity or Unity, whether the church ought to include the few or the many, and whether power or reason was God's chief attribute were the sticking points in the controversy. Yet the theological issues themselves fail to explain sufficiently why the dominance of Unitarianism in Boston in the 1820s outraged persons such as Beecher and the thousands of followers he attracted during his six years there. "It was as fire in my bones," Beecher said of Unitarianism; "my mind was all the time heating—heating—heating." He waited for the day, the revivalist wrote a fellow Massachusetts clergyman, when Unitarianism would "cease to darken and pollute the land." It is difficult to imagine how the gentle Ware or the solemn Emerson could provoke such heated reactions. Yet obviously Beecher, as well as the churches who called him to Boston, perceived hidden in the Unitarian theology a serious threat to the good, the true, and the holy.[4]

By 1820, the split between the orthodox and the Unitarians in Massachusetts had become so serious and so widespread that the courts were forced to intervene. How was church property to be disposed of when the established parish split into two parishes, one orthodox and one Unitarian, in response to sectarian differences? In the Dedham decision of 1820, the Supreme Judicial Court of Massachusetts ruled that the society (members of the parish precinct) was to determine the disposal of church property rather than the church itself (those admitted to full membership). The Dedham decision led to the formal Unitarianization of over a hundred parishes, as societies opted in favor of liberal Christianity despite church predilections. The decision raised the barriers between the two groups even higher than they had been in Jedediah Morse's heyday. By 1825,

Unitarians were forced to acknowledge what had long been the case: there existed a breach between Congregationalism in its two different forms that would not be healed soon. In that year, liberal religionists banded together to form the American Unitarian Association.[5]

It was also in 1825 that the man determined to make sure Unitarians were no longer mistaken for Christians arrived in Boston. Lyman Beecher had preached fiery conversion at a series of revival meetings in Old South Church in the spring of 1823. Writing to his colleague Nathaniel Taylor in Connecticut in May 1823, he claimed the revival effort in Boston "the most important charge, for the moment, in these United States."[6] Hanover Street Church, born of Beecher's revival activity in Boston, remained under Beecher's leadership the center of an aggressive evangelicalism during Emerson's pastorate at Second Church. Beecher had been pastor of a rural Connecticut parish when the call from Hanover Street came. Carefully considering the spiritual power to transform New England that would be his in the metropolis, he determined that Hanover Street spoke the will of God for him. As he would later explain to his son Edward when the latter was called to the Park Street pulpit in 1826, "It is here that New England is to be regenerated, the enemy driven out of the temple they have usurped and polluted, the college to be rescued, the public sentiment to be revolutionized and restored to evangelical tone. And all this with reference to the resurrection of New England to an undivided and renovated effort for the extension of religious and moral influence throughout the land, and through the world."[7] Here, a stone's throw away from the young Emerson's first pastorate, Lyman Beecher was preparing to reform the world and to usher in the millennium. Among the targets of his denunciations were "the Unitarian ministers here . . . young men, and most of them feeble men. They have not the confidence and control of the population nominally under them as their predecessors had"—a description (although Beecher seems not to have known him) of Emerson himself during this period.[8]

The renewed emphasis on orthodoxy that Beecher preached played on themes that had been prominent in Boston evangelicalism since Jedediah Morse had first raised them back in 1804. Religion was weak and people were indifferent to the laws of God. Therefore, the town of Boston, the region of New England, indeed, the country as a whole, were in moral disarray. "You can form no adequate idea of the strength of Satan's kingdom in this town and its vicinity," Edward Griffin lamented on his arrival in Boston in 1810 to assume the pastorate of Park Street Church.[9] The evangelicals insisted that religious declension meant moral declension. If the times of the fathers had been better, it must have been because they had adhered to a truer religion than the one the current generation espoused.

At first these evangelicals had been apt to blame the declension on the nonchalance of the Christian community without naming names. If all those "who profess a friendly regard to the cause of Christ" would "put forth their utmost exertions to save a sinking world, as they would do to save themselves from a shipwreck, their friends from a pestilence, or a populous city from a general conflagration," the *Panoplist* urged, "the consequences would be inconceivably joyful and glorious." A Christian city would willingly obey the law, stop drinking, keep the Sabbath, and teach the young the ways of their fathers. But eventually it had become painfully obvious that Boston, indeed New England as a whole, was not a Christian Sparta. The culprit, the evangelicals came to believe, was Unitarianism. "Unitarians Indifferent to Truth," ran the headline of an 1822 article in the evangelical *Boston Recorder*. The reason for their indifference, the *Recorder* implied elsewhere, was that Unitarianism was an upper class religion. Echoing the Middling Interest's accusations that the Boston elite was merely another interest out for its own good, the evangelicals challenged, "Shew us the poor family which it has elevated—shew us the poor family which it warms." The truth was, the *Recorder* continued, that "any man of common sense and common observation" knew Unitarianism as "a system of religion which the rich, the fashionable, and the learned embrace, and that it never was, and never can be adapted to the great mass of society." Unitarians concerned themselves with social appearances, the orthodox believed, but to truth and righteousness they were indifferent.[10]

Along with Unitarians, the orthodox agreed that as a rule, dissension was to be avoided by good Christians. By the 1820s, however, they believed that the extent of error and vice around them justified controversy. Concerned evangelicals no longer defined controversy as a disruption of communal peace and stability. After all, they insisted, the Unitarian indifference to the true basis of morality had already accomplished that. When Beecher came to Boston, the *Recorder* began to defend its disputatious attitude as a way of making

known the truth that would restore peace and stability. "In a controversy of this kind, the friends of truth have nothing to fear," the
Recorder boldly replied to Unitarian charges that evangelicals were
disrupting the peace of the commonwealth. Controversy would promote piety, not destroy it. The assertion was a mirror image of the
brash political contention that partisanship would improve the
city's condition, not undermine it.[11]

And if anyone came to Boston bringing not peace but the sword, it
was Beecher. "The faith delivered to the saints produced a stricter
morality than any contemporaneous system," Beecher had proclaimed in 1823. If the tree were to be known by its fruit, then
Unitarianism was rotten, root and branch. It was of the utmost
importance for this true son of the Pilgrims to restore the faith of
the fathers to a place of honor and respect in New England: "All the
great designs which God has to answer by planting our fathers here
in this nation and world depend, as I believe, on the efforts of this
generation to rescue their institutions from perversion, and restore
them to their native purity and glory." If the faith could be restored,
God's purpose in bringing Christians to the American continent and
preserving them through the baptism of the Revolution would be
answered. They would take their place among the nations as the
New Israel. Otherwise, they would plunge into the depravity that
all other nations of the world had known. Looking around him and
seeing the times to be critical, Beecher concluded, "Now is the time
to strike for all New England and the United States." Although
Beecher's jeremiads sounded strikingly like Reuben Puffer's, between them lay a crucial difference over how New England's redemption from depravity was to be achieved.[12]

During Beecher's years in Boston, Unitarian views on theology
and church polity were closer to those of Emerson's father's generation than evangelical views were. They reflected a concern that the
church should consist of all the faithful residing in a particular area,
not just the elect few. Unitarians drew little distinction between the
church and the society or parish. The records of Emerson's Second
Church, for example, indicate a casual distinction at best between
the two bodies. The church and the society nearly always met and
voted in common. The church called a ministerial candidate to the
pulpit, but the society paid his salary, thereby effectively canceling
out any independent action on the part of the church. The Unitarians generally followed the Half-Way Covenant, baptizing children

if one of their parents was a member of the church. But in 1828, the First Church of Boston dispensed with even that minimal requirement. Thereafter, not only could anyone be baptized, but anyone expressing a desire to join into fellowship might be considered a member of the church. Moreover, the Unitarian position on the Lord's Supper was in the Stoddardean tradition. Anyone, whether regenerate or not, could partake of the ordinance as an aid to spiritual growth. Evidently many parishioners retained scruples about participating in the sacred ordinance, giving rise to periodic sermons extolling the value of the rite as "peculiarly significant of our discipleship, and especially expressive of fidelity and attachment."[13]

Unitarian theology, as the very name given the Arminians implied, emphasized not only the unity of the social order but the unity of God as well. To teach that Christ was God undermined *"the Unity of God,"* Channing preached in 1822. God was one, a model for nature and for mankind. "Unitarianism is in accordance with nature," he claimed in a New York sermon in 1826. "It teaches one Father, and so does creation, the more it is explored. Philosophy, in proportion as it extends its views of the universe, sees in it, more and more, a sublime and beautiful unity, and multiplies proofs that all things have sprung from one intelligence, one power, one love. The whole outward creation proclaims to the Unitarian the truth in which he delights. So does his own soul. . . . Nature is no Trinitarian." For Unitarians, God was one, nature was one, man was one. The orthodox doctrines of necessary atonement and utter depravity effectively separated individuals into two groups, the saved and the damned. The Unitarians categorically denied any such division. "Is Christ Divided?" Nathaniel Frothingham asked in an 1829 sermon to First Church preached on 1 Corinthians 1.13. The answer was a resounding no.[14]

As ministers as far back as John Codman had suspected, Unitarianism had become home to a variety of doctrinal opinions. The growth of the city had encouraged the growth of this heterogeneity of sentiment. The Unitarian pulpit met this potential threat to church unity by avoiding doctrinal issues entirely. Instead, Unitarian ministers preached only ethics from the pulpit, for on ethics all religious persons might presumably agree. William Sprague's collection of testimonials to Boston's Unitarian clergymen gives us a good idea of what a broad cross section of the Unitarian clergy were talking about—and even more significantly, what they left out. The Reverend John Pierce remembered of John Eliot, pastor of New North Church from 1779 through 1813, "He rarely, if ever, introduced controversy in the pulpit. . . . Indeed, he was so averse to religious controversy, even in private, that I have known him sometimes abruptly leave a circle in which it had been introduced." Of John Lathrop, Emerson's predecessor at Second Church from 1768 to 1816, Pierce remarked that his preaching "was rather practical than doctrinal." James Freeman, the first self-proclaimed Unitarian in Boston as pastor of King's Chapel from 1782 to 1835, preached sermons that "were seldom doctrinal, less frequently controversial," almost always acceptable to "Christians of any communion." John Thornton Kirkland, while pastor of New South Church, generally spoke "ethical dissertations." Joseph Tuckerman, pastor of the Bulfinch-Street Chapel for the Poor and director of the Ministry-at-Large to the Poor of Boston from 1826 to 1840, thought "but little" of "speculative questions in theology," preferring to talk about "certain elementary principles of religion, which have all the force of axioms." As pastor of the Second Church from 1829 to 1832, Ralph Waldo Emerson departed little from the ethical, practical preaching then current in Unitarian circles. His sermons were, if anything, even more practical and less scriptural than those of his colleagues in the ministry.[15] The preachers shared in common a belief that "religion is the highest law of our being." They therefore proceeded in their sermons to discuss the law of our being, not the more technical question of theology, which was apt to produce disagreement among their listeners.[16] As Theodore Parker recalled of his parents, good Unitarians both, "They made a careful distinction between a man's character and his creed, and in my hearing never spoke a bigoted or irreverent world."[17]

The Unitarian emphasis on character and ethics underscored the unity of all men despite their apparent differences. This is not to say that the unity so insistently preached in fact existed. Rather, Unitarian insistence upon unity, as well as its reaction to the perceived threat to unity that Beecher posed, suggests exactly the opposite. In a city rapidly disintegrating into sects and parties, classes and factions, Unitarian rhetoric represented an effort to put the brakes on a process already well underway. If the city's population was already diversifying and congregations were taking on a more heterogeneous character, liberal Christians chose not to disturb the precarious peace existing in those congregations. They avoided subjects of controversy in the hopes that diverse opinions could coexist as long as persons kept a higher good in sight. The violence with which Unitarians would respond to evangelicalism stemmed from the liberal belief that the orthodox were not in fact men of good will. Their willingness to engage in controversy bore witness to that fact.

On the most obvious level, Emerson's opinions on church doctrine and polity did not differ significantly from those of other Unitarians. A sect was the same thing as a party, he asserted, and both were unthinkable, for they encouraged the individual to live his life according to the opinions of others rather than by the dictates of virtue. "A Sect or Party is an elegant incognito devised to save a man from the vexation of thinking," he wrote in his journal for 1831. Moreover, sectarianism encouraged the believer to erect false barriers between himself and others. If we were wise, Emerson told his church in 1827, "we should escape that strange delusion of valuing ourselves above our neighbor because our religious opinions were more exclusive & our faith more orthodox. . . . If we were wise we sh[oul]d discover how pitiful was the angry altercation about words & creeds and exchange this sinful emulation of human passions, miscalled religion, for that high & genuine emulation wherein the angels & archangels of God are partakers, the emulation of good deeds." The law of God and the Gospel condemned "the exclusion spirit of party, the jealousies of nations, & joins all men together as the family of God." Such controversy substituted animosity for good will. Its "strong tendency to make us dislike and denounce our neighbor, if he does not think as we do" leads us to "forfeit the blessings of the Christian religion," Emerson told his congregation. Hence, sectarian feeling was directly opposed to the Christianity it purported to represent.[18]

As far as Unitarians were concerned, people like Beecher were promoting division and factionalism in the church of Christ itself. To Beecher's way of thinking, however, Unitarian doctrine was not only wrongheaded; it was also a dangerous policy on which to organize the church polity. The Unitarians were attempting nothing less than the effacement of "the distinction between the regenerate and the unregenerate," their aim being to "enlarge the circle of Church fellowship to include the whole congregation."[19] If just anyone were allowed into church fellowship, all lost sight of the obligations church fellowship entailed. The spiritual laws of God were trampled upon, the moral laws of Christian responsibility forgotten. Beecher saw precisely this situation as he gazed on the rapidly changing city that the fathers had intended as a New Jerusalem. Since in Boston Unitarianism the unregenerate society hired the minister, the New England ministry was a flock of hirelings, its congregations a gathering of worldly vipers. No wonder, then, that the city was polluted by the moral disorder that sin produced. The churches of New England stood for nothing, Beecher told Hanover Street Church.

To restore the moral tone that the fathers had envisioned, Beecher advocated a return to the Bible as "a Code of Laws." "The law of the Lord is perfect," Beecher thundered, "adapted to the exigencies of a lost world." Unlike the Unitarian philosophy of liberal-minded tolerance, it "produces a fear of the Lord, which endures forever." Such liberty as the Unitarians granted people to do what they would was no liberty at all, Beecher believed. "Freedom for everyone to do as he chooses" was "anarchy, and not liberty." Liberty was the ability of the people to pass moral and Christian laws, "full of puritanical precision," that would act as bars to "irreligion and profligacy." It seemed to Beecher that Unitarians had taken the teeth out of such moral and Christian laws as were already on the books by refusing to enforce them. Hence, Sabbath violators, drunks, and blasphemers ran loose on city streets—all because the Unitarian establishment was so oblivious to the commands of God that sin was a matter of indifference to it. Heretical rationalists had forgotten "that men by nature do not love God supremely, and their neighbor as themselves." Because irreligion in the persons of the Unitarians was assuming a position of power not only in Boston but in the United States as a whole, the situation was grave. "We boast of our liberties, and rejoice in our prospective instrumentality in disenthralling the world," Beecher warned; "but our own foundations rest on the heaving sides of a burning mountain, through which, in thousands of places, the fire has burst out, and is blazing around us. If it cannot be extinguished, we are undone; our sun is fast setting, and the darkness of an endless night is closing in upon us."[20]

In a spirit of righteous polemicism, on his arrival in Boston Beecher founded a periodical that was to publish the truths of the faith once delivered to the saints. The Spirit of the Pilgrims, the voice of evangelicalism, first appeared in January 1828, proclaiming that "controversy has always been the great instrument of recovering individuals and communities from the dominion of errors." Of course, he asserted, controversy for selfish or sectarian gain was to be avoided at all costs, for Beecher still believed in the supreme values of communal order and harmony on which the Unitarians themselves placed so much emphasis. But before one could settle down to Christian harmony among the brethren, it was necessary to engage in brutal spiritual warfare against the pagan influences that were the real source of social unrest. When individuals had come back to the Church of Christ, there would be time enough to think about living in Christian peace. Then would New England see again "the exemplary practice of those duties, which so honorably distinguished the first settlers of New England." This filiopietistic restoration of the communal order and harmony of a sacred past was, for Beecher, to harbinger the millennium. The only roadblock was the irreligion that Unitarianism represented.[21]

The Unitarians, for their part, did not respond kindly to the attacks of Beecher and the evangelicals. Beecher, they responded, was a bigot. He was, in fact, reviving the poisonous dissension of party spirit in Boston. Indeed, until 1822, Unitarians refused to label themselves as such, fearing to create thereby the impression that they considered themselves a separate and exclusive sect. Joseph Stevens Buckminster had claimed early in the controversy that they certainly did not see themselves as a select group. "The most exclusive spirit of Calvinism" branded "*heterodox*" in an uncharitable, ungodly spirit everything that was "*unorthodox*." The orthodox were trying to provoke divisions among the people for their own peculiar benefit, just as political partisans were trying to do. Happily, Mr. Buckminster, as his memorialist reports in words of glowing praise, "was not a sectarian in feeling, nor a controversialist in practice."[22] Rather, he was content to concentrate on the important moral and ethical truths that bound people together. The Unitarians throughout the controversy would think it best to emphasize the sources of union rather than of division. For Unitarian social organicism in matters both theological and political remained a reflection of an upper class tradition of paternalism. The community was one family, and every effort ought to be made to keep it so, despite minor fraternal squabbles.

The orthodox for their part thought that the Unitarian unwillingness to engage in doctrinal controversy meant that they had something to hide. For in the eyes of the *Spirit of the Pilgrims*, Unitarians had formed a conspiracy of rich and powerful heretics—a group of self-interested men—who meant to hoodwink the godfearing part of the population into complicity with their self-aggrandizing schemes. Beecher praised the *Panoplist* for flushing out the Unitarians, "compelling [them] to leave the concealment by which they had been so long gaining influence, and . . . in which lay the far greater proportion of their strength." Unitarian footdragging implied that these men knew that they were doing wrong and were concealing it. The *Spirit of the Pilgrims* meant to carry on the noble work of the *Panoplist*. By exposing to the light of day the beliefs of the Unitarians, which they themselves "have generally been very slow and reluctant" to express, the orthodox would break their power and win the city back to Christ.²³

II

Indeed, there was some truth in what Beecher had to say about Unitarian reticence. The well-educated Unitarian clergy had avoided doctrinal controversy, feeling not only that such issues as the divinity of Christ would divide their congregations, but also that their congregations were ill-equipped to handle such esoteric speculation. Their paternalistic assumptions led them to feed their congregations spiritual milk, thinking the people unable to digest the meat of doctrinal speculation. Beecher was also right in assuming that once people learned of the Unitarian theology, some would have misgivings about it.

Beecher was right again in pointing out that Unitarian assumptions about the nature of church membership were not working. By avoiding issues that might generate controversy, Unitarians found themselves left with a religion that seemed devoid of content. The church became a place where neighbors were to gather and listen to lessons on ethics. The premium was on getting on well together. This state of affairs could easily degenerate into a desire merely to get by, and as the orthodox never hesitated to point out, it in fact often did. Unitarians were "gentlemen who have *no religion at all* but an unconquerable thirst for popularity," the *Boston Recorder and Telegraph*, an evangelical periodical, charged. The "corpse-cold" religion, as Emerson would later call it, reaped the harvest of its emphasis on the practical over the controversial or the ideal. Hence, one visitor from Scotland observed of Boston Unitarianism, "Talk to [a New Englander] of what is high, generous, and noble, and he will look on you with a vacant countenance. But tell him of what is just, proper, and essential to his own well-being or that of his family, and he is all ear."²⁴ It seems that many individuals read the Unitarian emphasis on practical morality as a justification for whatever behavior conformed to common public standards. Emerson's frequent sermons to his own parishioners on the importance of personal judgment in ethical affairs indicates that he, for one, was aware of the problem. The desire to preserve harmony among the congregations at all costs had produced what seemed to many vapid and meaningless unity indeed. No wonder the orthodox saw Unitarianism varying "according to the state of public sentiment."²⁵

Moreover, despite the Unitarian attempts to mute controversy, the unity and harmony they prized so highly seemed to be slipping through their fingers. They in fact had little more in common than their weekly meeting in the same church, and many were no longer bothering to come together even that frequently. Henry Ware, Jr., tried to remedy the situation during his tenure at Second Church by proposing ways of getting parishioners together to talk more seriously about religious matters. Early in his pastorate he set up religious societies that met regularly to discuss religious subjects. Believing that "there are advantages to be derived from familiar conversation on religious subjects, which cannot be derived from public preaching," Ware organized a series of "private services." Such meetings were apparently not successful enough, so in 1824 Ware reasserted that "the great principle on which the prosperity and edification of the Church must depend, . . . the principle of association, union, sympathy, cooperation," had eluded the church in recent years. This trend was to be seen not only in Second Church, but also "in the general habits of all the Churches with which we are connected." The church had as its very reason for being the extension of "the influence of religion by mutual counsel and cooperation." But as he looked around him, the minister who had once accused his own father of "cold sermonizing" found little to praise in his church. If the church were to forget its sacred mission, "and instead of a constant union in worship and action, Christians only meet infrequently at the table of the Lord," then surely would religion die out in Boston. For this reason, Ware concluded, it seemed

"adviseable [sic] that this Church should adopt measures for promoting a greater unity of feeling and action among its members."
Ware, like Beecher, found a disquieting lack of fervor in Boston's
churches.[26]

As a result of his own observations, and at least partially because
revivalists such as Beecher made defensive action necessary, Ware
proposed a series of quarterly meetings to inquire into the state of
religion in the church. Here the Unitarians would conduct their
own revivals of religion, not under the bigoted principles of a Beecher, but under the auspices of the rational warmth of Ware. Such
meetings would "draw more closely the bond of union and sympathy between the members."[27] Although the meetings lapsed during
Ware's period of incapacitation, his new colleague pastor revived
them upon his arrival. In February 1830, the meetings took on an
even greater importance. It was then resolved that they no longer
be limited to church members and that they be held monthly. Emerson attempted to bring his wayward sheep back into the fold
through a society for mutual spiritual improvement, and in doing so
he participated in the Unitarian movement back to experimental
religion.[28]

In addition, it was also resolved when Ware had initially raised
the question in 1824 "that the Church . . . be regarded henceforward
as an association, actually and actively united for the accomplish-
ment of religious and benevolent purposes."[29] This revised definition of the church's nature reflects the beginning of a marked departure from a long-held ideal. It meant that the church would no
longer be the spiritual manifestation of the community. Rather, it
was to be a voluntary organization, formed of those with self-ex-
pressed common interests. In order to rekindle piety in the Unitarian churches, Ware found it necessary to emphasize their separate-
ness from the community at large. Unitarian pietists thus set out on
a road that would end with the self-conscious separation of the
religious sphere from the secular sphere in Boston—the very sin
they had long tried to avoid.

Ware's definition of the Second Church as a voluntary organization
was itself prompted by more than the waning piety within the
church's walls. In fact Second Church's measures to renew religious
fervor were to a large extent attempts to combat the flow of North
Enders to Lyman Beecher's doors.[30] Beecher appealed most strongly

to the type of people moving into Boston's highly mobile North End. Country folk suffering from culture shock in the loosely integrated metropolis that so many saw as Babylon, these young and single veterans of several moves found a home in the familiar atmosphere of orthodoxy that Beecher's Hanover Street provided. Second Church's status as the church of the community was being threatened more because the demographic composition of the community was changing than because its spiritual ardor was lacking. The new residents of Boston were seeking something that the Unitarian establishment could not provide, and evangelical Christianity stepped in to fill the gap.[31]

What the heterogeneous congregations of the Unitarians failed to provide these new Bostonians was a sense of inclusion within a personal community. Unitarian churches were, by their very nature, mirrors of Boston during the late 1820s—loosely organized, loosely integrated, and presided over by an entrenched elite. One became a member of a Unitarian society by paying the pew tax that entitled one to a voice in the affairs of the congregation. During the first decades of the nineteenth century, little provision was made for those unwilling or unable to pay the tax. As long as those outside the church accepted reasonably peacefully the cultural hegemony of the social organicist ideal that Unitarianism represented, it mattered little whether they formally professed communion with the church. With the political and religious turmoils of the early 1820s, however, these disaffected elements of society became a force to contend with.[32]

Boston's crisis over the legitimacy of interest politics during the city government reorganization of 1821–22 was one signal that those outside the pale of the city's traditional institutions were no longer content with a standing order that seemed to ignore them. In the religious sphere some of these discontented elements declared their independence of an established elite by rejecting Unitarianism. Boston's Park Street Church, organized in 1808 by dissidents within existing congregations, established the prototype of the church organization that was to provide an alternative to Unitarianism. In the years immediately preceding Emerson's tenure at Second Church, Park Street's model would be adopted by the Union Church (1822), the Phillips Church in South Boston (1823), the Green Street Church (1823), Beecher's own Hanover Street Church (1825), the Salem Street Church (1827), and the Pine Street Church (1827). Park

Street was the first Congregational church in Boston to require adherence to a particular dogmatic creed. Boston's other Congregational churches only asked a pledge of "repentance towards God and faith in our Lord Jesus Christ" as a criterion for membership. In addition, the church drew up a trust deed to establish the right of "successive male members of the church" to elect the minister and control the affairs of the church, thus stripping from unregenerate pewholders the control they exercised in Unitarian affairs. The Park Street brethren also refused baptism to children unless one parent was a member in full communion. These moves were intended to insure that the new congregation might remain untainted by the stain of "heterodoxy." This church would consist only of the orthodox—those in complete agreement on doctrinal questions. Thus Park Street would be an island of purity, or spiritual homogeneity, within the sea of Unitarian heterogeneity.[33]

To insure that communicants clung to the spiritual orthodoxy that prompted them to enter the church, Park Street adopted a stringent regimen of church discipline copied by the evangelical churches that were its progeny. In 1814 the church voted to establish a standing committee "to inquire into the moral character of applicants for admission, . . . without however diminishing the right or responsibility of other members to make similar inquiries."[34] In the records of the Examining Committee of Park Street, the names of the friends or acquaintances of the candidate for admission who were already within the congregation were carefully noted. The church meant to insure that only those of spotless moral character were welcomed.[35]

All members were to be well acquainted with the lives of all others. Nor did becoming a member exempt one from the close moral scrutiny of one's fellows. Members who absented themselves from church for an extended period of time were investigated. Members were also encouraged to report cases of lapses from Christian morality to a church committee charged with investigation. This committee would bring the defendant to trial, and if found guilty, the culprit would be excommunicated. In Unitarian churches, excommunication tended to be a measure of last resort, taken rarely and only if the offender's continued membership might prove a scandal to the community at large. It was assumed that the community itself could ordinarily enforce moral laws. The orthodox evangelicals had no such faith in the community's power. They did not hesitate to excommunicate; whether the crime was public or private made no difference. From 1809 to 1834 twenty-five members were excommunicated from Park Street; during the same period no excommunications were recorded at Boston's First and Second churches (Unitarian), although a few persons were suspended for "immoral" acts.[36] Significantly, the largest number of cases investigated in any single period in Park Street's history occurred between July and December 1829. Fourteen persons were brought to trial there under the stern eye of the Reverend Edward Beecher, son of the Hanover Street revivalist. Among the sins prompting the trials were drunkenness, dishonesty, theft, fornication, lying, assault, profanity, Sabbath breaking, worldliness, apostasy, adultery, and wife desertion.[37] The churches intended to control by their own legal and judicial systems what the civil law and the civil judiciary could not. They would assume functions that formerly belonged to the community as a whole.

Thus the evangelical churches of Boston undertook the task of "building up a Church on principles entirely superior, and even opposed to those of selfish society." If the community could no longer produce order and morality, then the church would assume that function as an agency outside of and opposed to society. Within the church one might feel the "vital union among all hearts" that seemed lacking elsewhere. There, Lyman Beecher reported, "the congregation is full and solemn, and seems to be amalgamated into a homogeneous mass of belief and solemnity by the power of truth." As far as the evangelicals were concerned, the evangelical churches of the city would provide the "fraternal unanimity and Christian public spirit" otherwise lacking in the city. There would the church become "a distinct and well defined company" with common beliefs and goals, rather than the meaningless gathering of the unregenerate that was Unitarianism.[38]

To whom did this vision principally appeal? Occupationally one can speculate that it drew to it the same sorts of people who were agitating for government by interest in Boston in 1822—mechanics, artisans, and tradesmen, the petit bourgeoisie who had styled themselves the "Middling Interest," whom Beecher would later call "the working classes." No exhaustive analysis of the occupational breakdown of evangelical Christians in Boston has been undertaken. Nevertheless, evidence from Rochester, New York, during the same period indicates that shopkeepers and skilled workmen predominated in the first wave of evangelical Christians, followed as their influence spread downward by less skilled laborers and workmen. A study of temperance attitudes in Boston during the 1830s also suggests that among temperance advocates, who tended disproportionately to be members of evangelical congregations, shopkeepers and skilled manual laborers predominated.[39] Beecher mentions to his son William his 1826 visits "among the middle class and the poor," and says of his congregation at Hanover Street, "There was a flock of young people of the middle classes."[40] These were people broken out of the traditional patriarchal mold. No longer tied intimately by personal or occupational connections to the elite who governed the city, such groups felt impelled to take matters into their own hands where the elite had failed.

Moreover, as Beecher observed, the new communicants tended to be young and to come from the country. Although Beecher's Hanover Street Examining Committee records were lost in the fire that consumed his church in 1830, the records of Park Street Church and Salem Street Church reveal some interesting tendencies among those seeking admission to the church. Salem Street Church in the North End was formed of a Beecherian revival and ministered to by Beecher himself after the conflagration of his own church. Of the first one hundred members, two-thirds were female. Seventy of the hundred mention in their conversion narratives having been born in or having lived in a place other than Boston for a substantial period of time. The place other than Boston was usually a small town in Maine, New Hampshire, Massachusetts, Vermont, or New York. Twenty-nine mention having been in the city for less than four years, nineteen for less than two years. Nor did those who came to the city during this period necessarily stay put. Many moved into Boston only to return to the country for some years before again returning to Boston. In Park Street as well, the members of the congregation had a tendency to move. Of the 831 people received into Park Street Church from 1809 to 1834, during Edward Beecher's tenure as pastor, nearly half (403) were dismissed from the church to join some other within fifteen years of the date that they were received.[41] The older part of the city that was the center of the revival movement had traditionally been the home of that portion of Boston's population that was most mobile, and the evangelicals were appealing to this element, not to native Unitarian urban dwellers.[42]

The conversion narratives of these prospective communicants

suggest why they chose evangelicalism over Unitarianism upon their move to the city. For some, the orthodox religion of the evangelical churches resembled more closely the orthodox religion of their country youth than did liberal, cosmopolitan Unitarianism. Many had been touched by revivals at home, so they felt at home with them.[43] For many others, however, the shock of the city and the breaking of the social ties that they had known occasioned the conversion. Joseph Johnson of Middlebury, Vermont, for example, moved to Boston in March 1827. "When he came to Boston," Johnson's Examining Committee reported, he "was immediately convinced of the importance of becoming religious—of being a real Christian—but endeavoured to postpone the subject, and did for a considerable time." One can imagine that life in the big city for the young man from Middlebury was disconcerting, however, and he became "distressed" by October. By January 1828, Johnson was petitioning the Salem Street Church for admission. Similarly, Mary Blood, a native of Pepperell, Massachusetts, expressed a desire to the Park Street Examining Committee "to join the people of God in order to have some one to watch over her." At a revival in her home town she had resisted conversion, but upon her arrival in Boston in April 1828, "her impressions were deepened." In October, she begged admission to the church.[44]

To such as these, "persons probably who, since they came to the city, [had] formed as yet no connection with any church," the attempt to recreate a sense of intimacy and community through the rigors of church discipline must have been reassuring.[45] The evangelical fulminations against the evils rampant in the city, coupled with Beecher's fulsome praise of the virtues of the agrarian life, must also have sounded convincing. Many of these young and highly mobile people were unmarried and frequently lived in boarding houses or with families other than their own. The church provided a substitute kinship network of "brothers" and "sisters" who eased the jolting transition to the urban metropolis. Furthermore, it reassured them that the sense of discomfort that they experienced in the urban environment was a function of the evils there rather than any shortcoming in themselves.[46] Hence, the narratives frequently contained a new twist on the old conversion story. Not only does the new convert profess love for God and a willingness to serve him; frequently she mentions explicitly her newfound love for the Christian community that she formerly shunned. Mrs. Elizabeth

Greenwood voiced the formula that became standard in the narratives of the late 1820s and early 1830s: "Loves secret prayer. Loves the people of God."[47]

III

To this conversion formula a third ingredient was frequently added: "Feels interested in benevolent objects, and in the salvation of others."[48] The evangelical churches' determination to erect a community of doctrinal purity outside the confines of the existing social order did not mean that each individual community needed to be isolated. Rather, it was possible to form a network of orthodox communities whose concerted action might transform the face of the entire nation. Orthodox benevolent organizations having a transcongregational appeal were not entirely new in this era. At least two missionary societies had arisen in Massachusetts prior to 1800: the Society for Propagating the Gospel among the Indians and Others in North America (1787) and the Massachusetts Missionary Society (1799). Nevertheless, with the rise of the evangelical protest against "heterodoxy," such voluntary organizations were transformed in purpose. Unitarian charitable and benevolent organizations had always been geared toward assisting the destitute in the local community or toward fostering the growth of rational piety in the abstract, and they continued to do so during this period. Benevolent Unitarians such as Henry Ware, Jr., were involved in crusades for temperance when Boston seemed to be becoming intemperate, crusades for peace when war threatened Boston, and crusades for education when Boston's population seemed to be becoming particularly intractable. Certainly this limited benevolent effort may have simply resulted from the fact that Unitarianism happened to be a creed largely confined to the neighborhood of Boston. Nevertheless, if Unitarians no longer confined their efforts to particular towns or congregations, they continued to think of the geographical region as the town writ large. Societies arose to handle communal problems; the community simply happened to be a little larger than it used to be.

The evangelicals, in contrast, saw their reform efforts as ways to affect the destiny of the entire world. If the church was the spiritual convocation of the pure in heart, standing outside the secular order, the voluntary benevolent associations represented the attempt of evangelicals to change society through a practical, secular arm. Through the evangelical reform societies, like-minded Christians of all congregations might band together to Christianize the nation through the force of their faith. Cleora in the *Panoplist* commented on the efforts of "all holy beings [to] unite their voluntary and cheerful exertions" to bring on the millennium. Their purpose, according to Beecher, would be "to effect the moral renovation of the world." The American Society for Educating Pious Youth for the Gospel Ministry, for example, was established in 1815 to fund poor but orthodox youth from throughout the state in their study for the ministry. In a similar manner, the heavily evangelical American Temperance Society, formed in 1826 by several evangelical churches in the Boston area, drew on the sentiments of Christians everywhere who believed that there was "somewhere a mighty energy of evil at work in the production of intemperance." Evangelicals also committed large amounts of energy and money to missionary efforts both at home and abroad, hoping to enlarge the number of the saved.[49]

The difference between Unitarian and evangelical approaches to the unchurched provides a good example of the ways in which Unitarian and evangelical benevolence differed. The Unitarian Ministry-at-Large, headed by former Chelsea pastor Joseph Tuckerman, arose in 1826 to deal with the problem of relieving the distress of the ever-increasing numbers of the poor in Boston. During Tuckerman's pastorate in the village of Chelsea, "the rich and the poor . . . met on terms of equality before the church door on Sunday, [and] interchanged expressions of friendly greeting." Such an ideal of social organicism seemed to be crumbling in the metropolis across the river as the rich no longer cared about the poor and the poor absented themselves without excuse from the meeting house on Sundays. The Ministry saw as its task the eradication of the class feeling that urbanization had exacerbated. The Reverend Cyrus Bartol, Tuckerman's colleague in the Ministry, described it as "a bond of union of vital power to unite all." Its purpose was "to destroy all caste."[50] The principal trouble of the poor was not a lack of material goods, the Unitarian establishment believed. Rather, it was "this estrangement of men from one another, of class from class," William Ellery Channing mused in 1841, that led to the formation of "different communities"; the tragedy lay in the existence of "two nations" separated from one another by more than geography. Eventually Channing would decide that material adjustments would have to be made if the chasm between the two classes was ever to be bridged, and Emerson in time would follow suit. But in the late 1820s and early 1830s, the time of Emerson's involvement in the Unitarian establishment, the goal remained the reintegration of the poor into the great family that was Boston, a family over which an elite dutifully and paternalistically presided. Many people would be surprised to find out how many paupers lived near their doors, the Ministry's 1835 Semi-Annual Report observed. These people should ask themselves, "What benefit can I confer upon these fellow creatures of mine? Can I not connect myself with them?" What the poor needed and wanted, the Ministry believed, was a restoration of the ties of mutual obligation that deferential society had provided: "They may not need our money; they may seldom require any temporal aid; but they need our sympathy, our interest, all the assistance we can give them through our counsel, our advice, and our example, the words of our lips and the light of our lives." What they did not need was preaching that emphasized their differences from others, whether class or sectarian. "Avoiding party measures and narrow purposes," the classic Unitarian rhetoric pronounced, "their pastor should labor to unite them to each other, and to the other classes of society, in the bonds of peace and good will."[51]

The evangelicals for their part were concerned with emphasizing the differences between people—between the moral and the immoral at the very least. The kind of sectarian preaching that the Unitarians were condemning was the very sort in which the evangelicals were engaging. Beecher's expressed purpose was to erect among the orthodox "a phalanx terrible as an army with banners," including a political association formed with the purpose of overthrowing the Unitarian establishment.[52] The evangelicals, however, were not merely concerned with drawing Boston's unchurched into their terrible phalanx. When the cornerstone was laid at the Hanover Street Church, the Reverend Samuel Green proclaimed that in "raising the standard of the cross in Bengal, Ceylon, the Isles of the Pacific, and our western wilderness with one hand,—with the other ... repairing the waste places of our American Zion, distributing the word of life, erecting temples, redeeming this goodly heritage of our pious forefathers from error and death," the orthodox intended to unite the pious everywhere into a powerful reforming army. The evangelical concern with spreading the uniform culture of Christianity eventually blossomed into a concerted effort to dominate the development of culture in the newly settled Mississippi Valley. Such an atmosphere led William Lloyd Garrison to use as inscription for the first issue of the *Liberator*, published in 1831, "Our Country is the World—Our Countrymen are Mankind."53

Unitarians such as William Ellery Channing responded vehemently to the evangelical campaign. In his "Remarks on Associations," Channing outlined Unitarian objections to the evangelical associations. Although such associations could be the source of much good, they held an even greater potential for evil, for in them "the concentration of great numbers on a single point—is now placed within the reach of all parties and sects." Here the demagoguery of political democracy could be duplicated in the religious sphere. "A few leaders" might dictate to vast groups of people what ought to be believed and what ought to be done. "A kind of irregular government" was already developing that was determined through democratic means to keep the just man from following his own conscience: "Public opinion may be so combined, and inflamed, and brought to bear on odious individuals or opinions, that it will be as perilous to think and speak with manly freedom as if an inquisition were open before us. It is now discovered that the way to rule in this country is by an array of numbers which a prudent man will not like to face. Of consequence, all associations aiming or tending to establish sway by numbers ought to be opposed. They create tyrants as effectively as standing armies." Evangelical benevolence ignored the "unbounded diversities" unfolded in "our common nature." Rather than teaching men of diverse conditions to live together harmoniously, such organizations dogmatically set up a monolithic standard of conduct, "making narrowness a matter of conscience."54

Like Channing, with whom Emerson had studied for the Unitarian ministry, Emerson too was disconcerted with the exclusive spirit that reigned in benevolent organizations. They too seemed to arise out of a party spirit that valued achievement of partisan ends over true charity. "It is not true that the different charitable societies are rivals," he asserted in 1827. He preferred to think them "rather members of one body." Nor was it accurate for any one group to suppose that it possessed a monopoly on the truth. For this reason, Emerson objected to evangelical missionary efforts abroad. It took a smugness akin to "that Judaical spirit of exclusion" to fail to credit the pagans with virtue of some sort. True charity made all individuals aware of the similarities in the human constitution rather than the differences. An emphasis on a single point of view stood in the way of the ends of true human benevolence. And true charity for Emerson, as for most Unitarians, began at home. "When religion was sent to the Post office [and] was made to travel in newspapers through all lands & over all seas," Emerson noted, "she began to relinquish her duties in the closet at home." The echo would appear ten years after Emerson left the ministry in his description of the abolitionist in "Self-Reliance": "If an angry bigot assumes this bountiful cause of Abolitionists, and comes to me with his last news from Barbadoes, why should I not say to him, 'Go love thy infant; love thy woodchopper: be good-natured and modest: have that grace; and never varnish your hard, uncharitable ambition with this incredible tenderness for black folk a thousand miles off. Thy love afar is spite at home.' "⁵⁵

True charity did not mean converting all to a single point of view; rather, it meant establishing a bond of connection between oneself and others. Charity in itself had an "intrinsic excellence," for "the soul of man was made to act for others as much as his body was made to breathe the air." Benevolence improved both the giver and the recipient by reminding them that they ought to consider themselves attached to one another. Envisioning Boston "a city ramparted around with great charities," Emerson praised benevolence rightly conceived as "a great sentiment of brotherly love embodied," and he felt confident that the estranged "hearts of men will warm to each other when they behold it." Hence, most of the charity efforts of Emerson's Second Church, like those of most of the other Unitarian churches, were geared toward relieving the distress of those in the parish or those in the surrounding community. The collection of the charitable Evangelical Treasury of the church for 1828–29, for example, was used to support the sick, the indigent, and the destitute of the parish, the church's own Sabbath school, and its library. Only fifty dollars out of an annual expenditure of about two hundred dollars was directed outside the immediate community, with that money being given to the "society of Christians in New York" to aid them in building a house of public worship.⁵⁶

Moreover, in response to evangelical claims, Emerson insisted that reformers erred when they looked on themselves as instruments for single-handedly eradicating evil from the world. He believed that such people were interested more in achieving social control of the unregenerate than in spurring the individual on to develop the virtuous character that would enable him to police himself. Their religion was false religion; it "attempted to alleviate suffering by mending the circumstances of the sufferer[,] his character remaining the same." True religion, in contrast, "proposed to change his character without any alteration to ye circumstances."[57] The individual who appointed himself "to guard one province of the moral creation from ruin" was apt to be caught up in causes and thereby to neglect the true bases of charity. Emerson frequently held up to his congregation the example of the man who gave food or clothing to wretches in the street, "perhaps from reasons of expediency or from the same reason you would strengthen the police," but who felt "no obligation to love [his] fellow man." This man, like the better part of the community, would be perfectly willing to prosecute anyone because of a difference in religious or political opinion. Members of the Society for Suppressing Intemperance, the Peace Society, the Howard Benevolent Society, the Bible Society, and the Missionary Society all came in for such criticism by name. They were too apt to forget the benevolence of the heart.[58]

IV

Yet who was responsible for the unchristian divisiveness that troubled the city? Emerson was not as willing as Channing to assume the label Unitarian, for the answer to that question was not as clear cut for him as it had been for Channing. The Unitarians, it appeared to Emerson, were just as responsible for the falling out among Boston's Christians as the so-called evangelicals. They were being just as narrow-minded as the orthodox by engaging in the spiritual warfare to which the evangelicals had invited them, and they were giving themselves over just as blithely to sectarianism. Individuals were too anxious to be identified as members of a particular party; they were overwhelmed by the desire to belong to a sect. "Now if a man is wise," Emerson asserted, "he will not profess himself to be a Unitarian, but he will say to himself, I am not a member of that or of any party. I am God's child[,] a disciple of Christ or in the eye of God a fellow disciple with Christ." A person with this attitude would be able to recognize the true and the good in any religious creed. "Now let a man get into a stage coach with this distinct understanding of himself divorcing himself in his heart from every party & let him meet with religious men of every different sect," Emerson preached, "& he will find scarce any proposition uttered by them to which he does not assent—."⁵⁹

Emerson saw different theologies as different ways of talking about the laws of human nature. The very fact that all religions arose from the moral part of man's nature meant that they all communicated a part of the truth. If one would but take a "humble attitude of inquiry," one would discover "a wonderful tendency to unanimity in human opinions." The liberals emphasized the human capacity for virtue, the orthodox the liability to sin, but both approaches were based on accurate observations of the laws of the human condition. All persons could do good; all also did evil. In order to hear the truth of what the sectaries were saying, it was necessary only to convert their theological statements into statements about human nature. Although the evangelicals would have branded Emerson's approach to theology heretical, Emerson, in the best Unitarian tradition, was willing to overlook what he took to be minor differences in language. What was important was that the evangelicals were religious and that they were Christian. All religious points of view merged at some point into a higher unity, Emerson believed; why scruple over fine points?⁶⁰

The Unitarian's hotheadedness had made them as contentious and as narrow-minded as they accused the evangelicals of being, Emerson concluded. In a blanket condemnation, he expressed his misgivings that the "people will be such zealous Baptists or such zealous Unitarians or such zealous Calvinists that they will not be zealous Christians." Indeed, as a result of "unchrist[ian] differences," contributions to the fund to maintain the widows and orphans of Congregational ministers had fallen off, as many feared that their contributions would be used to support beneficiaries of the wrong sect. When Beecher's Hanover Street Church burned to the ground in 1830, the cheers of Unitarian spectators deeply disturbed Emerson. You should teach your children that "if a fire consume a church that is not of your communion or name . . . that your Christian sympathy is commanded by the event," he berated his congregation the following Sunday. In his view, Unitarians had become so involved in controversy that they had forgotten the most basic of Christian feelings. People were letting themselves be pushed into taking sides: "You are understood by the multitude, and are in the greatest danger to be understood by yourself, as branding the other opinion, and excluding yourself from the peculiar good fruits of it."[61]

To his added dismay, Emerson recognized that the evangelicals had several good points to make that Unitarians might do well to heed. The orthodox charge "what is called the Unitarian Church with giving something like the privilege of sanctuary to reprobates of every sect," and perhaps that was not too far from the truth. There was evidence that Unitarians took their religion much too lightly. Methodists, whatever their faults, felt religion to be real; Unitarians, in contrast, were obsessed with form and traditional usage. Revivals, despite the fact that they neglected human reason, were based on unimpeachable spiritual principles once the sectarian rhetoric was stripped away. In these meetings persons sought the Holy Spirit, "which, in common language, means, earnest desire of becoming better." Lukewarm Unitarians could take note of the fervor of these revivals.[62]

That Unitarians had become lukewarm in their practice of late Emerson could not deny, nor would he, even if such an admission should lend evidence to evangelical claims. Again and again he urged on his congregation the necessity of what Lyman Beecher and his colleagues were preaching—"experimental religion." Fearing that his congregation had fallen into thoughtless worship, Emerson admonished them that they "not come up hither to sleep, . . . not come with torpid souls." And the only true experimental religion was a religion of conscience, clung to because the believer knew it to be true, not because it might be fashionable or productive of social order. "Very good men incline to a certain diffidence & separation of their religious views from common feelings & the cheerful common speech of men," Emerson observed. In this much he could agree with the evangelical indictment of Unitarianism. Sadly, however, although something vital was lacking in the liberal religion of his Unitarian parishioners, neither the Calvinists nor the Unitarians were doing much about it. "One usurps the Christian name to consecrate the rancour of bigotry," Emerson asserted, while the other "turns the liberty wherewith the gospel has made him free into a cloak of licentiousness." Nothing of love remained in them. "These great religious shows" had degenerated into so much sham.[63]

Thoroughly disgusted with both sides in the religious controversy, Emerson mounted his pulpit to teach his congregation the true object of religion: "*by exhibiting a true account of the soul & its relations to induce it to act in a manner agreeable to its whole nature.*"[64] If Calvinists meant to destroy the brotherhood of man by their unnatural and intolerant exclusivity, Emerson would preach the unity of mankind. If the Unitarian controversialists meant to make of religion a mere show, or worse, to ignore their own faults in the interest of partisan advantage, then Emerson would urge his listeners to forget sectarianism and listen to the complaints of evangelicals. Emerson could see the justice of the claims on both sides. He could see that the state of religion, and as a consequence, the state of society in Boston, was fast degenerating. The demand for rigid adherence to a single creed was not the answer, however. In heterogeneous Boston it had become only too obvious that a diversity of persons and opinions existed. One could not wish them away.[65] Nonetheless, the well meaning tolerance of Unitarianism was not the answer either. It had produced only confusion and indifference to the higher laws of morality. The evangelical-Unitarian controversy had been a disaster for all persons of good will. It divided the community. It led those caught up in it to espouse a partial and distorted view of human nature. It destroyed true Christianity.

Thus for Emerson the religious controversy was not only a theological discussion conducted in periodicals. The revivals and sectarian activity that Unitarians feared as a threat to their way of life were occurring at his own doorstep. The church—both Unitarian and orthodox—was corrupt, Emerson concluded. Christians, unsure "what their duty demand[ed]," wallowed in uncertainty while clerics and partisans traded uncharitable jibes. The good people of Boston were neglecting their religious duties because they had lost sight of the tenets of true religion. "Not keeping the eye fixed solely on the principle but turning now to what custom reputed good sanctions, & now to principle & vainly attempting to reconcile them they cannot arrive at any settled conclusion," Emerson told his people.[66] He for one would play the part of good shepherd to his flock. He would preach the truths of man's moral nature on which no sect had a monopoly. Once his people heard the truth, they would know it, and the truth would make them free. Emerson would free them

from the shackles of sectarianism, teach them about what constituted the true bonds of unity. The Christian fervor of holy fellowship would be revived, but without evangelical bigotry. True religion might return to Boston. So Emerson hoped during his ministry
at Second Church, until a recalcitrant church dashed his hopes in
September 1832. His stand on the Lord's Supper would separate the
Christians from the Unitarian sectaries, he believed. Second Church
proved to be Unitarian at heart.

CHAPTER 5

The Idea of the Christian Minister

Exhortations & examples are better than psalms & sermons.—Journals and Miscellaneous Notebooks, 13 October 1832

EMERSONS HAD BEEN CALLED to the ministry in New England for the better part of two centuries. The first Emerson in America, Thomas Emerson of Ipswich, farmed the land. But his son Joseph was settled as minister of Mendon, Massachusetts, in 1667. He married Elizabeth, the daughter of the Reverend Edward Bulkeley. The Reverend Mr. Bulkeley had succeeded his own father, Peter Bulkeley, as minister of Concord, Massachusetts. None of Elizabeth and Joseph Emerson's three sons was drawn to the ministry, but their grandson Joseph married another minister's daughter and was called to the pulpit of Malden, Massachusetts. Three of this younger Joseph's sons entered the ministry, including William Emerson. William married Phebe, the daughter of the Reverend Daniel Bliss of Concord and succeeded to his father-in-law's pulpit in 1776. William, Jr., born in 1769, was left an orphan in 1776 when his father died on a march with Continental Army troops in Vermont, but he soon had a new stepfather. The Reverend Ezra Ripley married William's mother and succeeded to William Emerson, Sr.'s pulpit in Concord. Family legend had it that the younger William Emerson "had no predilection for the ministry, but yielded upon hearing Dr. Ripley pray that his mother's strong desire that he should be a minister might be fulfilled."[1] Thus it was that William was called to the ministry in 1799. At a time when sons were still apt to follow occupationally in the footsteps of their fathers, the family ministerial tradition was bound to weigh heavily in the career choices of William Jr.'s own sons. That Ralph Waldo Emerson, second son of William Jr. and great-great-great-grandson of the first Joseph, should have decided in 1824 to enter upon the study of divinity surprised almost no one.

The clergy of Boston were frequent topics of interest and gossip among the four Emerson brothers. As admired public figures in the city and as family intimates, their comings and goings were frequently chronicled in letters from one brother to another during periods of separation.[2] Perhaps with an eye to their future profession, William's sons looked with great interest on the professional community of which their father had been a part until his death in 1811. William Emerson's sister, Mary Moody Emerson, frequently reminded her nephews of the high estate to which the family had traditionally been called. "Those who point the path to the attainment of moral perfection are the guardian Angels," she wrote Ralph Waldo Emerson in 1818.[3] When William III, the eldest of the Emerson brothers, disappointed his family by deciding against divinity, the mantle fell onto the shoulders of his brother Waldo. William had determined during a year of study following college in the heady transcendental air of Germany that the modern ministry choked the intellectual and spiritual life out of a man. It was a point of view that in time his younger brother would come to share. But for a decade, the path away from the ministry for Emerson first led through it.[4]

I

The wise and good of New England had been called to the ministry since the founding of Harvard College in 1636. Fearing the devastating social and spiritual effects of an ignorant ministry, the Massachusetts clergy established the institution as a place of training for New England's ministerial candidates. The clergyman saw it as his responsibility to lead others, and his learning as much as his spiritual office gave him license to do so. His worldly wealth did not usually qualify him for inclusion among the august of the town, but the clergyman was entitled to a place among the town's elite as its instructor, father, and moral guide.[5] Ezra Ripley, Emerson's stepgrandfather, remained a minister in the traditional New England mold. "Like Moses in the wilderness, a shepherd and judge of the people" who assumed an "unquestionable right to know about their temporal and spiritual affairs," the Concord divine was among the last of a dying breed of pastors who saw themselves as settled for life over a flock for whom they were pastor and father, prophet and judge. For such men as these, the ministry was not a profession; it was a life.[6]

Emerson's father's ministry had taken a different shape from that of Ezra Ripley, however, although William Emerson had not intended it that way from the first. He was part of a new cohort of urban ministers who differed in two respects from the ministerial ideal that Ezra Ripley represented. First, they were somewhat less likely to settle in one parish for life. As a result, they were far more likely to feel responsible for spreading learning and wisdom in the abstract than for ministering to particular local communities. The Ezra Ripleys of Massachusetts saw themselves primarily as pastors. William Emerson and his brethren in the Unitarian ministry in Boston saw themselves primarily as scholars. As the century wore on, the rift between the two facets of the traditional ministerial role would widen, creating conflicts for the sons of William Emerson's generation.

For William Emerson there were compelling reasons why he should depart from the path of his fathers. Tradition dictated that the Reverend Mr. Emerson, once settled in the country hamlet of Harvard, would grow old in the service of his flock there. As the country folk's willingness and ability to support a minister dwindled in the years following the Revolution, however, Emerson, settled in 1792, found himself by 1796 falling behind financially as his parish refused to appropriate a salary sufficient for his maintenance. He had endured "the life of a monk," he wrote his stepfather, because he could not remedy it. But he wanted to marry now and could wait no longer for the parish to do its duty by him. In March 1796 he met with the elders and deacons of his church and with the selectmen and treasurer of the town to have the matter out. A depreciating currency no longer bought in 1796 what it had in 1792, he explained to them. He requested that his salary be adjusted for inflation and that his salary in arrears be paid after such an adjustment had been made. The town meeting chose a committee to consider the question, but William Emerson had little optimism concerning the outcome:

From the various sects of religionists, that have been nurtured amid the caves and wilds of this town, there is a number of apostates, who worship they know not what, and who, to my great infelicity, bear a small proportion in the payment of my salary. They are seldom, or never, seen, except at the annual meeting . . . , when they come forth from the abodes of sloth and unrighteousness, with an unprincipled and obstinate determination to oppose the raising of a single cent of money for the purposes of literature and religion.

Emerson's pessimism was justified. Harvard never made good its debt to him.[7]

But if Harvard could not support Emerson, Boston could. That "paradise of [the ministerial] order" had found itself short of ministers since the end of the Revolution and filled its lack with young country ministers. Boston's First Church, enchanted by the learned and cosmopolitan young Emerson, wanted Harvard's minister. He in turn was anxious to go where his support would be assured and where he would not feel the want of intellectual stimulation. First Church cast its appeal to Harvard to release its minister from his pastoral bonds in altruistic language.

> The Alarming attacks that are made on our holy religion by the Learned, the Witty and the Wicked, especially in populous and Sea Port Towns, calls aloud on professing Christians to invite and support in places of the most eminence, such Spiritual Workmen, as are endowed with Talents to convince or confound the Wicked by their arguments and to allure them by their Amiable Behavior; such a person will do good everywhere, but will he not do most good in a place where Infidelity and Vice acquire Strength by that Liberty which should only nourish true religion and good Order?

Here was an impeccable spiritual argument for the move: a witty minister to convert the witty, an amiable pastor to fit the needs of an amiable flock. Unsatisfied with First Church's argument, Harvard demanded some compensation for the pastor Boston would steal. After several rounds of bargaining, First Church agreed to remit to the Congregational church of Harvard the sum of $1000— the price of one minister. When the affluent First Church moved from Washington Street to Summer Street in 1808, the incident was not forgotten. It gave rise among wags to the following derisive rhyme:

> Farewell, Old Brick,—Old Brick, farewell:
> You bought your minister and sold your bell.[8]

The situation was still new enough in 1799 to be unusual, but it marked the beginning of a long-term trend. Young ministers, responding to market forces, began to be hired into relatively lucrative pulpits by Boston congregations, and with the expectation that they would be learned men and entertaining preachers rather than dedicated pastors. The minister began to be seen by many, although most were not yet ready to admit it, as a dispenser of professional services, hired to be the chief ornament of a community. Particular ministers, such as the young and eloquent Joseph Stevens Buckminster, attracted popular followings through their powers of oratory. Buckminster had not even been a public professor of religion while in college, yet within a very few years this "youthful prodigy of pulpit eloquence" had large audiences hanging on his every word.[9] Thus the urban pulpit began to provide the stage on which the young and learned could display their talents, influence the community, and win fame and renown. The average age of settled ministers in Boston dropped as congregations seemed to crave the innovation and the excitement that a younger voice might provide. By 1818 Henry Ware, Jr., observed that the average Boston minister was only thirty-two years old.[10]

As congregations continued to place a premium on oratorical ability, they tended to become more critical of the speaker's rhetorical talents. Buckminster himself, in a sermon entitled "Take Heed How Ye Hear," complained that "we will hardly consent to learn our duty, except from a particular mouth." "Time was," the *Christian Examiner* wailed in 1825, "when the good people of this land retired silently from the sanctuary, saying little of the sermon, and more of the duty of improving it." But no longer. Now "there is much discussion about the preachers, in a style and manner as if the benefit to be derived from them mainly depended, not on the matter, but on the man,—not upon what is said, but upon how it is said." Ruth Haskins Emerson commented in 1818 on the "performances" of the participants at John Gorham Palfrey's installation at Brattle Street Church. In such an atmosphere, with such rising expectations on the part of their congregations, it is not surprising that the Boston clergy devoted itself to improving its learning and its oratorical talents. Those ministers settled at the beginning of the century had to cut back on pastoral visitation in order to prepare themselves for the pulpit on Sundays. "If they would render their sermons such as would satisfy themselves, and such as their societies demanded,"

Buckminster's memorialist recorded, "they must give up the enjoyment of the almost daily hospitality of some kind parishioner." Occasionally such intense and solitary study backfired as the minister, "in consequence of the distance between his own mind and the minds of his hearers," led his listeners up dark alleyways of abstruse reasoning. Yet on the whole, such intellectual cultivation seemed to pay off as congregations ravenously consumed pulpit oratory and preaching became a popular topic of discussion and appreciation.[11]

If the new breed of minister was apt to neglect some of the traditional pastoral duties of the New England clergy, it still prized its leadership role in society as a whole. Since the Unitarian ministry generally allied itself by birth and by marriage as well as by learning with the powerful merchants and lawyers who dominated Boston, it took upon itself a portion of the responsibility for setting the tone of the community. The Unitarian ministers of William Emerson's generation founded benevolent societies, edited journals dedicated to the promotion of belles lettres, and conceived the first American historical and learned societies. William Emerson was "never weary in contriving and encouraging plans for the improvement of the moral and literary character of the community," according to his memorialist, a brother minister and a fellow founding member of the Massachusetts Historical Society. He was "graceful and dignified, though seldom impassioned" in speech; his sermons were "remarkably chaste and regular in their structure, correct and harmonious in their style." He was first and foremost a scholar and a man of letters dedicated to raising the moral level of the community through learning. This was his role as pastor of First Church in Boston from 1799 to 1811, and although it was a departure from tradition, it quickly became the urban norm.[12]

Boston Unitarians came to require of their pastors one thing more in addition to eloquence and scholarship before Ralph Waldo Emerson entered the ministry in 1824. They wanted close personal contact with him; they wanted his friendship. The "intimate connexion with his people" that Bostonians came to expect of a minister might seem at first glance an effort to reconstitute the traditional pastoral relation. Yet the new pastoral relation was in fact marked by subtle differences. The new pastor was to be "our friend, our guide, an inmate in our families"—but not necessarily leader and judge. Among the generally well-to-do Unitarian congregations of urban Boston, the minister was no longer the only educated member of the congregation. Where "the press preaches incomparably more than the pulpit," preaching was no longer the principal source of teaching and of information in the community. Hence, the pastor frequently found himself in a new relation to the congregation, a relation for which he was by training unprepared. People no longer wanted in a sermon basic moral instruction that they could not get elsewhere; rather they wanted to be moved by the minister's artful performance and delivery. They no longer looked to him for leadership, at least not in the old ways; congregations now turned to the minister for the care of their psychic well being. He would no longer take responsibility for the spiritual health of a community of souls, for less and less could either the Unitarian congregation or the city of which it was a part be called a cohesive community. Now he would aim to touch individually each member of his congregation.[13]

Some, like William Ellery Channing, came in time to welcome the new egalitarian character of the ministry. "The ministry need not continue what it has been," he conceded, "and the time is coming when it will be found to be the most effectual mode of getting near to our fellow-creatures." Others, like Henry Ware, Jr., feared that ministers were yielding up too readily the dignity of their office. The "tendency in the state of society to destroy the distinction between clergy and people" must be resisted, he believed. By 1826 the new trend in the ministry had become so pronounced that clergy officially recognized it by establishing a new professorship of pastoral theology at the Harvard Divinity School. Although the chair was filled only after Emerson's ministerial apprenticeship, what was taught there under the rubric of pastoral theology in the early 1830s illustrates the changing expectations of the Unitarian ministry. Henry Ware, Jr., Emerson's senior colleague at Second Church, was called to fill the vacancy. Until this time ministerial training consisted of the general intellectual education that college provided along with specialized postgraduate study in theology. Ware's new job was to train aspiring ministerial candidates in a new area—"the eloquence demanded for the pulpit, and the prudence and affections that must guide in the parish walk." Ware defined pastoral care as "that duty toward individuals and families, which consists in personal acquaintance and intercourse for the purpose of knowing the character and condition of the flock." Merely making the traditional parish visitations no longer sufficed. The minister

*Southeast prospect from an eminence near the Common, Boston.
Lithograph drawn and engraved by S. Hall (1790).
Boston Athenaeum.*

*Staffordshire plate showing the State House and Boston Common
in the foreground (1805).
Boston Athenaeum.*

Sketches by Ralph Waldo Emerson in the leaves of his college journal.
By permission of the Ralph Waldo Emerson Memorial Association and of the Houghton Library, Harvard University.

*Emerson in clerical garb.
Photogravure, from a
miniature painting in
1844, by Mrs. Richard
Hildreth.
By permission of the
Ralph Waldo Emerson
Memorial Association
and of the Houghton
Library, Harvard
University.*

*Boston from the South Boston Bridge (ca. 1825). Lithograph by
Deroy, after a drawing by J. Milbert, published by Imp. Lithog.
de Henry Gaugain.
Boston Athenaeum.*

Lyman Beecher (1775–1863), by Chester Harding (ca. 1830).
Yale University Art Gallery. Gift of W. T. R. Marvin.

Hanover Church.
Boston Athenaeum.

Ezra Ripley.
First Parish in Concord.

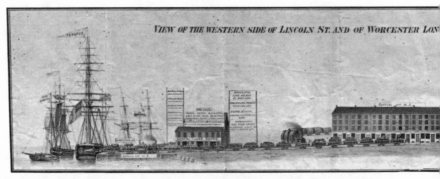

VIEW OF THE WESTERN SIDE OF LINCOLN ST. AND OF WORCESTER LON

Projected South Cove development. A promoter's dream of the 1830s. Lithograph. Boston Athenaeum.

The commercialization of Boston: the Old State House as a mercantile building. Mid-nineteenth-century lithograph by Tappan & Bradford. Boston Athenaeum.

Boston (ca. 1850). Lithograph by G. Matter.
Boston Athenaeum.

Concord Center (1840). Drawing by J. W. Barber.
Concord Free Public Library.

Lidian Emerson
with son Waldo.
By permission of the
Ralph Waldo Emerson
Memorial Association
and of the Houghton
Library, Harvard
University.

Bush, the Emerson home in Concord.
Concord Free Public Library.

Margaret Fuller. En-
graving by Henry
Bryan Hall, Jr.
National Portrait Gal-
lery, Smithsonian In-
stitution, Washington,
D.C.

Waldo Emerson. By permission of the Ralph Waldo Emerson Memorial Association and of the Houghton Library, Harvard University.

Emerson in lecture costume. Concord Free Public Library.

was now to use whatever means necessary to influence the characters of the "promiscuous assembly" that was his parish. For the first time the *Christian Examiner*, the Unitarian periodical, advocated that ministers learn "what is comprehended under the common name of *Psychology*," for it would make him "acquainted with the operations continually going on in the internal world of thought and feeling."[14]

Here, then, was the career that Emerson stood on the verge of entering in his twenty-first year. The Unitarian ministry, a profession in transition, raised a set of confusing, often contradictory expectations in its incumbents. An older ministerial tradition told ministers to look upon themselves as community leaders; changes in the community and the nature of leadership there, however, made the old ideal of patriarchal leadership superannuated. Trained to look on themselves as scholars and teachers, the clergy encountered increasing pressure from their congregations to view themselves first and foremost as emotional counselors. Sermons were no longer to be judged by the marrow of spiritual truth they contained, but by their power to move the audience and keep its attention. Nor was the minister any longer to view himself as head of a parish that was often synonymous with the community as a whole; rather, he was to be the personal friend and counselor of each individual soul under his care. No longer was it necessary for him to feel tied for life to a particular assembly, for his mission was to influence individual souls, who had only a marginal spiritual interest in their parish communities. Whether the minister was to be a public man in the public sphere of the larger community or whether he was to be the knower of the private and intimate truths of the human heart was as yet unclear. In 1824 he was both, and he was neither. Emerson's time in the Unitarian ministry would be spent trying to clarify for himself just what a true minister was called to do. To whom was he responsible, and why?[15]

II

On 18 April 1824, when Ralph Waldo Emerson declared, "I deliberately dedicate my time, my talents, & my hopes to the Church," the thorny issues of his pastoral responsibility lay before him. During the period between his college graduation and his entrance upon the study of divinity, having outgrown his youthful lust for fame, Emerson set about defining for himself what he wanted from life. "Shall I embroil my short life with a vain desire of perpetuating its memory when I am dead & gone in this dirty planet?" he mused in March 1824. The answer this time was no. He would begin to live in an ideal realm, pleasing God rather than man, and that would be his contribution to the age. The literary endeavors that he had before contemplated as a means of increasing his own renown he would put to a moral use in the ministry. He had found a place where he might "be better remembered than in Courts or Camps, in the Marts of business or the halls of learning"—that is, "in the poor man's prayer."[16]

This newly humbled Emerson had from the beginning some doubts about his ability to do justice to his sacred calling. He found his reasoning faculty "proportionately weak." Perceiving a new strain in the ministry, however, a strain represented by such men as William Ellery Channing, Emerson rallied. Although he lacked the logical mind of the scholar, his "strong imagination & . . . keen relish for the beauties of poetry" led him to "the highest species of reasoning upon divine subjects," which was "rather the fruit of a sort of moral imagination, than of the 'Reasoning Machines' such as Locke & Clarke & David Hume." The new vogue in preaching depended on talents such as Emerson possessed. He had inherited from his father "a passionate love for the strains of eloquence." In his better hours, he believed himself "the possessor of those powers which command the reason & passions of the multitude." Hence, preaching for him would not be a problem. He was a born orator if nothing else.[17]

Yet the ministry possessed a second component about which young Emerson had doubts. The clergyman's duty of "private influence" over the characters entrusted to him troubled Emerson. He felt "a sore uneasiness in the company of most men & women, a frigid fear of offending & jealousy of disrespect, an inability to lead & an unwillingness to follow the current conversation," which cut him off from people. He felt comfortable in assuming the public role of teacher to his people, but meeting their private and personal needs after he stepped down from the rostrum was another matter. "What is called a warm heart, I have not," he moaned. His extreme lack of self-confidence in the private sphere combined with a temperamental shyness to undermine his ability to deal with people individually: "In my frequent humiliation, even before women & children I am compelled to remember the poor boy who cried, 'I told you, father, they would find me out.' " If what his congregation expected was a man of personal warmth rather than an exemplar of public, pastoral leadership, then Emerson was lost. "It may be I shall write *dupe* a long time to come," Emerson wrote with some misgivings as he made his final determination. However, he fervently hoped that this would not be the case. Perhaps the ministry could transform his natural diffidence into virtue. Perhaps it would be the "regeneration of mind, manners, inward & outward estate" that he desired. In any case, he had done enough complaining about the evils of the age. It was now time to do something about them. "I have hoped," he wrote in 1824, "to put on eloquence as a robe, and by goodness and zeal and the awfulness of virtue to press & prevail over the false judgments, the rebel passions & corrupt habits of men."[18] With sober but resolute determination, Emerson ascended the platform of the ministry, determined to remake the world in the image of virtue and morality.

Emerson always looked on the ministry as a means for accomplishing these larger ends rather than as an end in itself. Although he continued to doubt his ability to serve as a moral exemplar for his people, he saw the ministry as an opportunity to begin a new sort of vocation—"a career of thought & action" extending forward into "distant & dazzling infinity," in which the moral principles inherent in human life might be made plain.[19] His would be an old-fashioned ministry through which the power of principle would be revealed through the word rather than by the force of an amiable personality. In Emerson's vocation, the moral leader, the impassioned scholar, and the "friend and aider of the life of the soul" were to merge in one public man who, as moral teacher, would reveal to his age the secrets of the inner life of man. "To open to ourselves—to open to others these laws—is it not worth living for?—to make the soul, aforetime the servant of the senses, acquainted with the secret of its own power; to teach man that by self-renouncement a heaven of which he had no conception, begins at once in his heart"—was this not vocation enough for any man? By 1829 Emerson had fashioned for himself this idea of the Christian minister. He was "a man who is separated from men in all the rough courses where defilement can hardly be escaped; & who mixes with men only for the purposes that make himself & them better; aloof from

the storm of passion, from political hatred, from the jealousy &
intrigue of gain, from the contracting influence of low company &
little arts." He added hopefully, "And shall not he get strength of
virtue & light & love who is set apart to the office of walking between God and man[?]"[20]

For Emerson, the minister was primarily a preacher. Time and again
during his pastorate he mused both silently and aloud on the nature
of his "gift-public."[21] Since ministers were "the objects of fashionable interest & criticism," they enjoyed an unusual opportunity to
influence public opinion, and it behooved them to think well on
what they were to say and how to say it. Against much modern
preaching Emerson leveled the charge that, in harping on "a few and
ancient strings" of theology, the sermon too frequently did not "apply itself to all the good and evil that is in the human bosom." As
antidote to the straitened circumstance in which pulpit oratory too
frequently found itself, Emerson proposed for the preacher a greater
freedom in the choice and treatment of subject so that he would no
longer limit himself to discussion of Biblical texts or rehearse for
his listeners the tired theological and moral treatises to which they
were accustomed. The inspired preacher would speak of nothing
less than human nature itself. The true foundations of eloquence
lay not in delineating the individual's responsibilities as merchant,
mechanic, lawyer, or fishmonger, or even those of citizen and patriot. Rather, the pulpit orator was to appeal to the "common
ground" of his listeners. He was, said Emerson, "simply to hunt out
& to exhibit the analogies between moral & material nature in such
a manner as to have a bearing upon practice."[22]

Whatever the mode of speech it took to get across the message of
common humanity and true morality was the one the conscientious
minister ought to adopt. If that meant mentioning the Gospel explicitly less frequently in the course of the sermon, then so be it. To
do so was good if individuals were thereby taught the Gospel message in a more understandable way. Emerson was determined to try
out new forms of sacred address, and he made his intention clear
early in his ministry: "I shall not be so much afraid of innovation as
to scruple about introducing new forms of address, new modes of
illustration, and varied allusions into the pulpit, when I believe that
they can be introduced with advantage. I shall not certainly reject
them simply because they are new. I must not be crippled in the

exercise of my profession." So cavalier was Emerson's neglect of Scripture in his sermons during the first year at Second Church that his efforts met with a gentle rebuke from senior pastor Henry Ware, who hinted that the junior minister ran in danger of exceeding the bounds of clerical propriety in the breadth of his sermons. Yet Emerson, with a polite nod to Ware's experience, continued to believe that a preacher, to be "equal to the demands of the times and to the hope of the times," must be "manly and flexible and free beyond all the example of the times before us." He persisted in his determination to teach morals in a language understandable in his time and place, in a style designed to bring him into a "closer *rapport* with his hearers."[23]

Nor could he count it any reproach if he were "reminded that my subjects have little variety." In the ideal of the ministry that Emerson had envisioned for himself, there was but one topic, the Reason of Man, and but one style, absolute simplicity. Sin sprang from prejudices about the nature of man; the preacher's duty was to clear the cobwebs from the eyes of the faithful. Since all men shared a common nature, the speaker need not embellish in order to grab his listeners' attention. "The voice of Reason common to him and you and all men" spoke through the man who allowed it to, and it spoke with irresistible eloquence. "I am always made uneasy when the conversation turns in my presence upon popular ignorance & the duty of adapting our public harangues & writings to the minds of the people," Emerson confessed. "Men know truth as quick as they see it." Emerson's sermons never told his listeners what to believe. Instead, they hinged on the assumption that if people were given the opportunity to direct their thoughts to the truths of human nature, Reason itself would convince. The sermons are thus replete with phrases such as "I only wish to call your attention to the fact" and "I propose to offer to your attention."[24]

Emerson's inclination in the ministry was to welcome many of the changes that brought the roles of clergy and laity closer together. Although he wished to maintain a certain elevation of social status as teacher, he saw his teaching as bringing out in individuals knowledge already latent in them. The contemporary minister "comes as a friend to provoke his brother to good works," he told his parishioners. "He no longer dictates doctrine. He now solicits your attention to truths which engage him & therefore should engage you. He drops all shadow of a claim of authority over you." Preaching, after all, was no longer the instruction of the ignorant masses; rather, it was "only an exposition of our human nature" to the ear that had grown callous or the heart obstructed by passion. Sometimes the knowledge that the flock, in gaining a friend and equal, had lost a shepherd saddened both minister and people: "It may sometimes seem," Emerson reflected, "that he has lost something of useful influence in the loss of the accidental & traditional respect which attached to him & that one restraint more so taken away from a community whose love of freedom is prone to degenerate into licentiousness." But such respect had flourished on the assumption that the shepherd alone could communicate the revealed truths of redemption to his flock. If rational religion consisted in sensitivity to universal truths of human nature, however, the preacher could no longer claim for himself the voice of authority. He was more nearly akin to the voice of conscience than the voice of Jehovah.[25]

But as the pressures and perquisites of acting the patriarch were removed from the minister, the preacher to the heart of man had new burdens and anxieties to shoulder. The minister who spoke on his own authority as human being rather than as agent and messenger of God lost the traditional guarantees of the validity of his message. The evidence for the truth he communicated increasingly became his own life. The teachers of oratory during the early nineteenth century laid heavy emphasis on sincerity as the prime prerequisite for effective oratory. If, as Hugh Blair argued in his rhetoric textbook in use at Harvard during Emerson's years there, no man could be "truly eloquent, . . . who does not speak the language of his own conviction, and his own feelings," this was doubly true in the case of the minister. "The Preacher himself, in order to be successful, must be a good man," Blair asserted. Edward Tyrrel Channing, brother of William Ellery Channing and Boylston Professor of Rhetoric and Oratory at Harvard, pronounced in a lecture that Emerson probably attended, "It is his virtues, his consistency, his unquestioned sincerity that must get the orator attention and confidence now. And, according to a foreign visitor to Boston in 1827, the point was probably well taken. The Unitarian minister's hold over the minds of his listeners seemed to be "derived mainly from their reliance on his sincerity, whatever some of them might have thought of his doctrines." The personality in fact became as convincing as the sermon, if not more so.[26]

The bright lights of the new pietistic strain of Unitarianism quickly picked up this theme as they trained their new charges in pastoral responsibilities. Joseph Tuckerman, the new Minister-at-Large in Boston, advised a Mr. Green of Lynn at his ordination to "shew in your *preaching* what [Chris]tianity is that you may shew also in *your whole life* what it is to be a [Chris]tian." This charge meant that the minister ought to undertake an intensive self-scrutiny in order to experience first hand the sentiments about which he preached: "Let it be your first care, to look deeply into your heart; to *know yourself*. Understand distinctly what are your own principles, & springs of actions." William Ellery Channing, Emerson's model of the good minister, believed that good preaching was "the natural movement of a sincere, ardent, independent mind"; hence, he asserted that the minister's "whole life and influence should have one tendency." Henry Ware echoed the same themes. The minister preached by example as well as by word. Indeed, he who preached "by life as well as by doctrine, preaches better also in the pulpit; for then, his voice is not that of a public orator, but of a friend and brother."[27]

Frequently the effect of this advice was to torture young ministers with the inadequacy of their own virtue and sincerity. Ezra Stiles Gannett, later Channing's colleague pastor at Federal Street Church, had a somewhat extreme but not atypical reaction to the added pressures on the clergyman to practice the moral perfection that he preached: "I am very well in body, but am ready to scream, who is sufficient for these things? I am sufficient in no way. What shall I do? When I have neither talents nor virtues proper for such a place, ought I not quit it directly? . . . I would give or do anything, if I could cherish that spirit of devotion without which a minister sins every time he is forced to pray, and this I do day after day, and it is registered against me. Ought I not be miserable? Can I help inquiring what I shall do?" Young ministers, in order to become good preachers, were constantly to examine their own sincerity. "What we say however trifling must have its roots in ourselves or it will not move others," Emerson asserted firmly in 1832. The ministerial emphasis on sincerity and the congregational expectation of a life of perfection from its pastor would take as heavy a toll on Emerson as it did on the distraught Gannett. But for a few years, sincerity and devotion within the structure of the ministry seemed a genuine possibility for Emerson.[28]

Or it would have been a possibility if only his parish had left him a few minutes to himself to think. But unfortunately, as Emerson rapidly found out, the dual roles of the ministerial office—preacher and pastor—were "often in some measure incompatible." The preacher found himself under constant pressure to compose new inspirational sermons. A Boston minister was expected to preach two written sermons per Sabbath and to deliver two or three evening lectures during the week. To compose a sincere and moving sermon, the minister needed time to think and to feel; to compose a learned discourse, he needed time to study. Too often he found that he had time for neither. Because such a schedule could take a terrible toll on the young minister, many waited until they had built up a repertoire of sermons before they assumed a permanent pastorate. Emerson himself refused the call of three different congregations before settling at Second Church. "Myself and some of mine advisers exhort me to wait a great while—2 or 3 years—for sound head & wind & limb & sermonbarrelfull before I settle," he explained to his brother William. The example of Henry Ware's invalidism provided Emerson a warning of what might happen to the overextended young preacher. The preparation of so many sermons weighed heavily on Emerson's mind even after he accepted the post at Second Church. "The prospect of one each week, for an indefinite time to come is almost terrifick," he wrote his grandfather.[29]

If his preaching and writing schedule were not strenuous enough, the young minister had an exhausting round of pastoral duties to contend with. "I have made somewhat more than fifty pastoral visits," he lamented during his first year on the job, "and am yet but in the ends & frontiers of my society."[30] Also among Emerson's responsibilities as pastor were discourses to raise money for the local philanthropies of the liberal churches, baccalaureate addresses at schools, talks at the Orphan Asylum and at the House of Corrections, Great and Thursday Lectures, attendance at ordination councils, baptisms, marriages, funerals, visitation of the sick, organization of meetings to attract the unchurched, the chaplaincy of the state senate, the supervision of church financial affairs, and participation on the city school board.[31] Second Church in particular laid a heavy burden of activity on its pastor since Emerson's predecessor in the pulpit there had initiated many new pastoral programs on which Emerson was obliged to follow up. "The untried and difficult task of applying religion as a vital and active principle to the whole sphere and scene of life,—to every thing that a man does,—

to every thing that a man thinks and feels and purposes," ate away at the young minister's health as well as his time and energy. Whereas in the previous century ministers had a reputation for being long-lived, in Emerson's Boston they were dying young, of sheer exhaustion.[32] Emerson's familial delicacy of constitution did not bode well for him in his chosen vocation. Far more devastating, however, was the psychological disability that he had noted when weighing his decision to enter the ministry. His temperamental discomfort with others would not be so easily cured as his strained eyes or debilitated lungs. In the day-to-day performance of his pastoral duties, Emerson's congenital uneasiness caused him much embarrassment. Dr. Chandler Robbins, Emerson's successor at Second Church, recounts the story of the experienced-hardened veteran of the Revolutionary War who called Emerson to his deathbed for some words of consolation to speed him heavenward. Emerson, as was frequently the case, felt awkward and at a loss for words. Upon seeing the young minister hesitate, the old man arose in great wrath and ordered Emerson from the room. "Young man," he barked, "if you don't know your business you had better go home."[33]

Ambiguity about the ministerial role, the strenuous demands of being preacher and pastor, the intensive self-scrutiny that the ministry bred, as well as the temperamental defect of character—any one of these factors might have caused Emerson to doubt his ministerial calling. The combined weight of all of them hastened the day when he would admit to himself that it was "the best part of the man . . . that revolts most against his being the minister."[34] There was yet another factor entering into the crisis of conscience that Emerson would face in 1832 over the celebration of the Lord's Supper, however. Around him swirled a religious controversy that as Unitarian pastor in a city stormed by the shock troops of revivalism he could not avoid. Finding himself forced to take sides in the dispute between the Unitarians and the evangelicals, Emerson the sincere minister faced a crisis of conscience that would eventually propel him out of the the Unitarian ministry and into a career unlike any other of his age.

III

The heated Unitarian-evangelical dispute, the visible sign of Boston's polarization, forced Emerson to take up the implications of the religious controversy in Boston with his congregation. Feeling his parishioners being swept up into the contention, Emerson grew adamant against adherence to belief or creed based on anything other than personal faith—even Unitarianism. Both Unitarians and evangelicals were corrupting true religion, Emerson came to believe, because they deferred to tradition or to the opinions of others rather than to the sacred voice of Nature. They accepted belief unquestioningly. Such an attitude resulted in the rise of parties and sects based only on tradition rather than on true virtue. "Calvin thinks for thousands; and Wesley for thousands," Emerson contended, "and that office of thinking or believing which cannot be done for another is done in appearance, & the worst consequences follow." The dire consequences included the spectacle of "the distracted, bleeding, I had almost said,—the hating church of Christ." Christians now "magnify one anothers faults," Emerson told his congregation; "they misrepresent each other's faith. They organize the means & institutions of recrimination . . . until this horrible profanation—I can call it by no better name—of the gift of God has got to be so familiar to the eye that it causes no surprize & men that are called good engage in the warfare themselves." Such behavior could never result when individuals consulted the promptings of their nature. Faith could not be held on opinion, for if it were, "it cannot be strange if the practice grows worse." There was only one remedy for any Christian, Unitarian or evangelical. "It is time to forsake the interpreters, & go back against the book itself," Emerson declared. "Hast thou faith?" he asked his parishioners, echoing St. Paul's question to the Romans: "Have it to thyself before God."[35]

It was wrong to assume that God saved or damned groups of men. Such an opinion sprang from too literal an interpretation of Biblical symbolism. God saved or damned the individual only as the individual discovered the truths of his moral nature (salvation) or failed to discover them (damnation). Fortunately, Emerson believed, "a revolution of religious opinion" had begun; individuals were beginning to look to themselves for answers; they were no longer content to accept blanket judgments of religious demagogues. "What is my relation to Almighty God? What is *my* relation to my fellow man?

What am I designed for? What are my duties? What is my destiny?" they began to ask.[36] Here was a good omen for the future of religion. When people asked these questions of themselves, they were sure to come back to a religion based on principle. Religious formalism would die a natural death.

Among the formal structures of religion was the celebration of the Lord's Supper. One of the oldest of Christian rites, it had been passed down in the church for centuries as a commemoration of the death of Christ. Although there had always been controversy among New England churches about who should be entitled to participate in the service, the question had come up with some frequency of late, perhaps as a result of evangelical exclusion of Unitarians from the rite. Early in his ministry, Emerson had little objection to the celebration of the Supper. Indeed, as late as May 1831 he defended the use of the forms of religion in a sermon to his congregation. In this imperfect world, we need forms, he told them, for "the form is the vehicle through which spiritual things address themselves to the senses, & through the senses to the soul." As long as men understood that the symbol stood for something internal, it might prove of benefit to them. In fact, because different individuals were of different minds, it was inevitable that the symbolic ceremony should be interpreted differently by different people. Well-intentioned individuals were not to be excluded from the celebration of the Supper on any account, since the sole end of the ordinance was "*to make those who partake of it better.*" "All who named the Lord's name" should be welcomed. Anything less made what was intended as an instrument of grace an end in itself. It most decidedly did not intimate, as many sectaries implied, "that a line runs through the world, dividing men into saints and sinners, that you have stood on one side and now stand on the other."[37]

As time went on, however, Emerson began to have doubts about the value of the rite. It was too often serving as a symbol of division rather than as a symbol of union. The question of religious exclusivity was an issue that the controversy between the evangelicals and the Unitarians had already brought to the fore. Here was the issue on which Emerson chose to make a stand. Through it he would try to give his people concrete evidence of what formalism in religion meant and how it ought to be dealt with. The value of the ceremony was already in doubt in the minds of several of Emerson's contemporaries in the ministry. As Emerson would later explain in a sermon to Second Church detailing his rationale for his stand, the form seemed remote from modern practice. Ministers had had their quarrels with the rite before and had remained in the ministry. It was not unusual that Emerson should have chosen to oppose the rite. It was unusual, however, for the minister to resign his charge because of it.

Sobered by four frustrating years in the ministry, Emerson, many say, was simply looking for a way out, and the Lord's Supper provided a convenient excuse. He had never overcome his temperamental aloofness. When his wife Ellen died in 1831, one version of the story goes, Emerson no longer felt pressure to remain in a profession for which he had always felt much distaste. He expected a sizable inheritance from his wife's estate that would provide him a living—why not leave?[38] Herein lies a part of the story, surely, but not the whole of it. Emerson never had as many doubts about the ministry as this critique suggests. He knew what he intended to do with his life by the time he entered the ministry and felt for a long time that the ministry was the place to accomplish it. William Ellery Channing possessed a cold and formal temperament, but he remained in the profession without scruple and continued to function as Emerson's ideal of the clergyman. Moreover, Emerson's son tells us, his father had little doubt that most of the church members would go along with him. Certainly many of the church's younger members agreed with Emerson's theological reasoning.[39] "I had hoped to carry them with me, but I failed," Emerson himself recalled in his old age.[40] If he merely wanted to leave, why pick an issue on which he might have carried the day? Others such as Edward Everett had quietly left the active ministry for other callings. What was to have prevented Emerson from doing the same?

The answer is that Emerson wanted much more than a way out. The Lord's Supper had become a symbol of the formalism in religion that so offended him as well as of the artificial distinctions between creeds that ten years of theological warfare had produced. Indeed, religious formalism had been the product of the religious controversy in which a premium was placed on deriving one's spiritual— even secular—identity from membership within a particular sect. It was important in such an atmosphere of spiritual and social controversy to identify oneself in a visible way as Unitarian. By insisting on the value of dogma and forms, on the importance of such theological issues as the nature of miracles and the proper character of the Lord's Supper, Emerson saw the Unitarians descending to the level of the evangelicals, who choked the spirit by adhering to the letter of the law. People were content, even eager, to revel in ceremonies and theologies that bore little relevance to their daily lives if only they could identify themselves with a particular sect. But if religion belonged to a world apart, Emerson believed, it was useless. By bringing to the attention of his parishioners the discrepancy between their religious attitudes and the important facts of their daily lives, Emerson tried to act the conscientious pastor to his people. He hoped to solidify their faith. What will you leave your children? he challenged them. "Will you leave them a declining church, a decaying public morality, public worship falling into contempt . . . ?"[41] His stand on the Lord's Supper was an effort to insure that they did not.

For Emerson, moreover, the issue involved a modern conception of the ministry as a place where a man might give himself over to conscience. The pastor had to be sincere in order to be an affecting preacher, yet religious controversy was pushing him into a corner. Partisan-minded parishioners were beginning to expect a defense of Unitarian theology and practice as they came under attack by evangelicals. As early as 1825, Emerson's brother William gave up the study of the ministry, warning him that "every candid theologian after careful study will find himself wide from the traditionary opinions of the bulk of his parishioners. Have you yet settled the question, whether he shall sacrifice his influence or his conscience?" For Emerson increasing pressures to say what was expected clashed with his responsibility as a virtuous individual to be true to what his conscience told him. It was particularly incumbent upon the pastor as one "who would win [his people] to a life of purity" to show them "the shining example of his own." If the pastor expected his parishioners to be true to the inner voice of reason, he must set the example. "I know very well that it is a bad sign in a man to be too conscientious, & stick at gnats," Emerson wrote in his journal. "Without accommodation society is impracticable." But the Lord's Supper was esteemed "the most sacred of religious institutions." Emerson found that he could not "go habitually to an institution which they esteem holiest with indifference & dislike."[42]

Emerson's resolution to force the issue began to take shape in the summer of 1832. "I have sometimes thought that in order to be a good minister it was necessary to leave the ministry," he mused on 2 June; "The profession is antiquated." Shortly thereafter the pastor called some of his church members to a meeting in which he stated his views on the Lord's Supper. Second Church's records sum up the pastor's argument: "It was the pastor's belief, that the eating of the bread & the drinking of the wine are rather tolerated than approved by us; that to some, they were an impediment to devotion; perhaps to none an aid. This incongruity between the act & the sentiment was his own main objection to the rite." Influenced by opinion rather than by religious feeling, many participated in the Supper simply because it was expected of them, he believed. Emerson suggested in its stead "a mode of commemoration which might secure the undoubted advantages of the Lords Supper without the objectionable features." A committee was appointed to consider the subject. They returned to their pastor the answer that they wanted the rite maintained, but they expressed continued esteem for him. They praised his adherence to conscience as being in the best Protestant tradition.[43]

In July Emerson fled to the mountains of New Hampshire to think about what to do next. He was upset over the church's answer and his attitude comes through clearly in his journal entries. "Here among the mountains" he hoped to "see the errors of men from a calmer height of love & wisdom." He needed to deliver a message to his people, and if his course of action in the future remained unclear to him, what he needed to tell his people was not: "Religion in the mind is not credulity & in the practice is not form. It is a life. It is the order & soundness of a man. It is not something else *to be got*[,] to be *added*[,] but is a new life of those faculties you have. It is to do right. It is to love, it is to serve, it is to think, it is to be humble."[44]

As Emerson roamed the mountains searching for answers, his brother Charles worried over Waldo's future. "I think enough has now been done, (perhaps too much) for the expression of individual opinion," he told his brother William. He hoped that Waldo might "be brought to the persuasion that it is his duty to stay where he is & preach & pray as he has done & administer the ordinance as nearly as he conscientiously can, in accordance with the faith & wishes of his pious parishioners." But Waldo would not. By 24 July Charles knew that his brother meant to bring the issue to a head. Emerson intended to present his dilemma to his entire congregation and would probably ask a dismission. "This will bring things to a legal *issue*," Charles wrote William. The society would have to decide whether they agreed with the church's decision or whether they would follow their pastor. On 9 September 1832, Emerson set forth his objections to the rite in a sermon based on a text from St. Paul's letter to the Romans: "The Kingdom of God is not meat and drink; but righteousness, and peace, and joy in the Holy Ghost."[45]

Interestingly, John McAleer notes, Emerson never wrote anything that he repudiated so strongly after the fact—although the reasons he did so are far from clear. The sermon perfectly captured the religious and ethical themes Emerson had been developing throughout his ministry, albeit in a more traditional form than he had been accustomed to use. In "The Lord's Supper" more than in any sermon of his ministry, Emerson relied on arguments drawn from Scriptural exegesis to explain and validate his position.[46] Nevertheless, the most pungent parts of the sermon unequivocally stated Emerson's own belief about the practice of true religion: that it was the right and duty of Christians to judge truth on the basis of their own internal sentiment. The message was no different than that he had been preaching for over three years; it was, however, perhaps the first time where the implications of that message required of his listeners action clearly at odds with established practice.

Emerson told his congregation that his objections to the Lord's Supper were twofold. First, he did not believe that Christ meant the institution to be established in perpetuity. Simply because a rite had been celebrated for a long time was no reason to assume that it was supposed to last forever. In explaining his objections, Emerson developed for his listeners a hermeneutic for interpreting religious forms and symbols in the light of natural experience and of human sentiment, using the concrete symbol of the Lord's Supper as illustration. Where his listeners would be inclined to see the institution of an extraordinary event in Jesus' admonition, "This do in remembrance of me," Emerson saw "natural feeling and beauty in the use of such language from Jesus, a friend to his friends," as he merely urged them to remember him after his death.[47] Breaking down the distinction between extraordinary and familiar even as he had throughout his ministry blurred the distinction between natural and spiritual, Emerson explained the establishment of the rite in the context of Jewish and early Christian practice. The reason why we continue the practice today, Emerson argued, is not because we have found it an intrinsically valuable mode of commemorating the life and death of Jesus, but because we have "found it an established rite in our churches, on grounds of mere authority."

But even had Scripture sanctioned its celebration down through the ages, Emerson contended in the sermon's second and more potentially controversial part, the ceremony ought to be discarded if it no longer bred a religious attitude in people. The dictates of human nature overrode even the claims of Scripture. The ordinance was confusing to a generation that no longer understood its purpose. Its forms were "foreign and unsuited to us." More important, the rite no longer served its intended purpose. "This mode of commemorating Christ is not suitable to me," he maintained. "That is reason enough why I should abandon it." Where religious sentiment came into conflict with the traditional practices of institutions, individuals were obliged to follow the interior voice of true religion. "If I understand the distinction of Christianity, the reason why it is to be preferred over all other systems and is divine is this," Emerson told them, "that it is a moral system; that it presents men with truths which are their own reason, and enjoins practices that are their own justification." When the practices of the church interfered with the perception of moral truths, they were to be abandoned.

"The Lord's Supper" and Emerson's struggle to deal with the problems he thought the ordinance posed for Christians points clearly in the direction of themes he later developed in the Divinity School Address. There Emerson would make clear the extent to which the authority and tradition of the church stood at odds with spiritual practice as he conceived of it. In this sermon, however, Emerson only shadowed forth some of the objections to religious institutions he would later develop. Troubled by the controversies over religious practice in Boston and New England, Emerson tried to steer his congregation away from them by insisting that truth inhered in neither of the warring churches, but in the divine plan inscribed in the individual soul. Churches could become as corrupt as any other institution. It is important to note that during this era, evangelical Congregationalists and Unitarians were not the only religious groups proposing competing definitions of the nature of religious experience; they were only the most prominent. Methodists, Baptists, Universalists, Quakers, Episcopalians, and Roman Catholics among others had by this time become forces to be reckoned with as well. So evident was it to Massachusetts citizens that denominational pluralism had come to stay that in 1833 the state became the last in the Union to abandon an official religious establishment. The law in effect acknowledged what had been the state of affairs since the beginning of the century: churches now competed with each other for souls. In order to distinguish themselves in this spiritual marketplace, Congregationalists and Unitarians in particular had moved toward increasingly rigidified and exclusive definitions of sacred forms, symbols, and doctrines. Emerson's objection to the Lord's Supper represents a protest against that process. The practices of the churches seemed increasingly designed to sustain institutions, but at the expense of failing to accommodate human spiritual needs.

On 11 September, as planned, Emerson submitted his letter of resignation to the proprietors of Second Church. The sermon on the Lord's Supper seemed to have its desired effect. The congregation was moved by its pastor's sincerity and asked him to publish the sermon. He refused but eagerly awaited their response. Clearly a good portion of his parish desired him to stay, and his brother Charles reported on 13 September that "if any plan can be hit upon by which he can stay with them & not administer the ordinance, both parties will be pleased." On 26 September Charles told William that the parish was "to make arrangements so as to keep" Emerson. In another letter he informed William that the parish committee was still in session, hoping to find "means of keeping their minister, if that may be, without dismembering their church." They could not. On 28 October the proprietors voted thirty-four to twenty-five to dissolve the connection between the pastor and the church, with many persons staying at home "rather than vote to lose their minister." Resolutions were passed "expressive of their unabated regard for their late minister," but the deed was done. Emerson resigned his pastorate. The sincere minister had tried to lead in the paths of "experimental" religion, but his flock demurred, perhaps fearing that a schism within the congregation would result.[48]

"It is my desire, in the office of a Christian minister, to do nothing which I cannot do with my whole heart," the pastor had ardently told them in his September sermon. His conscience revealed the essence of true religion, and to violate it was to violate his calling. Everything in the ministry was pulling Emerson toward sectarian contention and formalistic complacency. Therefore, the old office, like the old rites, had to be abandoned to accomplish the true ends of religion, to make the individual aware of the unity of the human condition. "I have the same respect for the great objects of the Christian ministry & the same faith in their gradual accomplishments through the use of human means which, at first, led me to enter it," he wrote. "I should be unfaithful to myself if any change of circumstances could diminish my devotion to the cause of divine truth." But the office of the ministry, responding to changes in religious organization resulting from the sectarian controversy, no longer seemed the best way to accomplish those ends. "I am about to resign into your hands that office which you have confided to me," Emerson told his flock at the conclusion of his Lord's Supper sermon. Though sad, he was "consoled by the hope that no time and no change can deprive me of the satisfaction of pursuing and exercising its highest functions." Although he resigned his pulpit, Emerson would remain "essentially a preacher to the end of his days." The ministerial function might be best performed outside the sacred office, the ends of religion best attained beyond the walls of Second Church. Alone and dispirited but armed with his sincerity, the young minister set out from Second Church in search of a new career. He had already found his vocation.[49]

CHAPTER 6

The Calling

I think we must hold a man amenable to reason for the choice of his profession. It is not an excuse any longer for his deeds that they are the custom of his trade. What business has he with an evil trade? Has he not a Calling *in his character? Let him quit his foolish trade & embrace henceforward his Calling.*—Journals and Miscellaneous Notebooks, *May 1839*

ON CHRISTMAS DAY 1832, Emerson took the traditional course of Boston ministers when the cares and anxieties of the pastoral office broke their health: he set sail for Europe. The drawn-out controversy about the Lord's Supper had taken a toll on his digestive system. For several months he suffered from a diarrhea that incapacitated him for preaching during his final weeks in the pulpit of Second Church. "It has stripped me to bones," he wrote his Aunt Mary. "A wasted peevish invalid," Emerson left home hoping to recover his health, but the physical illness was the least of his worries. It in fact betrayed a more serious emotional malady for which he hoped Europe would provide a cure. His beloved wife, Ellen Tucker Emerson, had died less than two years before, and her death had been an emotional blow from which he had still not completely recovered. He had failed, moreover, to turn his people from the indolent formalism and rabid sectarianism that they seemed desirous of substituting for true religion. Certain of his duty but uncertain about what went wrong, Emerson sailed for the Continent in the dead of winter, alone and exhausted, in search of a new way to define his vocation.[1]

Over the course of the next few years, Emerson groped toward an entirely new place in the public arena. Wishing to combine the roles of orator and man of literature, he sought a way in which the private promptings of the heart might be brought into harmony with the responsibility to be a public actor and an influence for good in the community. He found, however, that he was imagining a profession that did not yet exist, at least not yet in any clearly articulated state. In response to the unavoidable pressure in the public sphere to accommodate himself to public opinion, Emerson came to propose as an antidote the role of scholar (or "Man Thinking"). A "representative man" peculiarly able to transcend the apparent conflict between public and private interests, he would act as a reminder to society of the wellsprings of moral behavior. During his European tour and its aftermath, Emerson came to reject categorically the intellectual roles available to him as too narrow and confining for conscience. With leisure to consider the possibilities, he began tentatively to fashion alternatives.

I

Early in 1833, Emerson traveled to Malta, Sicily, Italy, and France. It was not until he reached Paris in late June that he began to think in earnest about the rest of his life. Perhaps feeling his sojourn in Europe coming to a close, he thought it time to turn from his observations of the marvels of the Continent to the state of his soul. Perhaps because time had made the whole subject easier to handle, or perhaps because he had little liking for Paris, he had an opportunity to think about himself for the first time in a long while. Certainly his experience with the "great men" of the Continent had disappointed him. Whatever the reason, while in Paris Emerson began ruminating about his own role in life. "When will good work be found for great spirits?" he wrote sadly in his journal for 11 July.[2]

Though the isolated scholarly life of the litterateur appealed to Emerson, he remained committed to finding public work, and this work he continued to define in religious terms. His mission was to prophesy the good news of "the divine beauty of moral truth." "I feel myself pledged if health & opportunity be granted me [he wrote in his journal], to demonstrate that all necessary truth is its own evidence; that no doctrine of God need appeal to a book; that Christianity is wrongly received by all such as take it for a system of doctrines,—its stress being upon moral truth; it is a rule of life not a rule of faith." Even as Emerson reaffirmed his old vocation, however, doubts continued to plague him. Despite ringing declarations of virtuous independence, he found himself temperamentally "idle & too respectful to the opinions of others."[3] Remaining in the regular ministry offered the frightening prospect of continually battling the strong temptation to defer to the opinions of others.

In this pensive and in some ways desperate state of mind, Emerson arrived at the Jardin des Plantes during his stay in Paris. As he viewed the Cabinet of Natural History there, the same feeling that had dominated his ministry suddenly made itself felt in another area. The arrangement of objects in cases struck him strongly with a sense of the "occult relation between the very scorpions and man." All was related in the natural sphere as in the human and moral sphere. "Moved by strange sympathies," the sorely perplexed former pastor impulsively embraced a new career. "I will be a naturalist," he resolved. What that early impulse meant or how he should act on it Emerson had no idea at the time. In the languid Parisian summer, however, Emerson began to toy with the notion that he might make a place for himself outside the bounds of the institutional ministry.[4]

At sea off the coast of Ireland awaiting fair winds to hasten his journey home in September, Emerson still had no definite plans. "I know not, I have no call to expound," he admitted on 8 September, "but this is my charge plain & clear to act faithfully upon my own faith, to live by it myself, & see what a hearty obedience to it will do." Those high-toned words still did not answer the pragmatic question of what he would do next, however. While in Europe he had come into a substantial inheritance from his dead wife's estate, so the need to earn his living was not as pressing as it might otherwise have been. Upon his return to his native shores in October, he could afford to take his time in deciding a course of action, and he did so. He returned to Newton, the town in which he had sought refuge with his aunt and uncle Ladd during his illness in 1825, and there the religious and moral shortcomings of his age continued to rankle. His old complaints against the narrow focus of contemporary religion were renewed on his first Sabbath in the Calvinist church of Newton. The Reverend James Bates, "a plain, serious Calvinist. . .[,] one of the useful police which God makes out of the ignorance & superstition of the young of the world," preached the same outmoded doctrinal irrelevancies that Emerson had heard in evangelical Boston. "How long is society to be taught in this dramatic or allegorical style?" Emerson demanded with exasperation after witnessing the all-too-familiar spectacle. "When is religious truth to be distinctly uttered—what it is, not what it resembles?" Living in Newton during the fall of 1833, Emerson returned to the ministerial pulpit, preaching at Second Church on 27 October and supplying the pulpit of his cousin, Orville Dewey, in New Bedford for a month. Yet all the while, the fear that he might surrender principle in order to meet the expectations of the congregations he supplied bothered him. On the other hand, however, he saw around him "so many worthless lives" that it was apparent to him that he needed to continue to speak out.[5] A complete break with society was, under the circumstances, cowardly. The ministerial role chafed, but some kind of public role remained necessary for him.

Continuing to preach from the pulpit during the early part of 1834, Emerson returned to his cousin's New Bedford pulpit for most of February and March and wrote to his cousin Samuel Ripley from New Bedford that he was eager to talk with him about his recent sermonizing.[6] By April, however, the stint at New Bedford had come to an end, and Emerson returned to Newton, whence he bided his time by supplying "good mens' [sic] pulpits," in Cambridge, Boston, and Waltham. Events of the latter part of 1834, however, forced him to make some decisions about the nature of his vocation. In July the Unitarian church in Bangor, Maine, gave Emerson some indication that they and he might come to an agreement. "They are very anxious to have a minister of ability settled here," he wrote his friend and fellow minister, Frederic Henry Hedge, "& have got beyond the period when a violent Unitarian is wanted." The situation was tempting. "I am almost persuaded to sit down on the banks of this pleasant stream," he told Hedge on 12 July. By the fifteenth, however, he had successfully resisted the temptation. Though the people and the place seemed congenial, Emerson feared being trapped again by the forms and doctrines of sectarian religion. He confided his conflict to his journal: "In our plans of life an apparent confusion. We seem not to know what we want. Why, it is plain we can do best something which in the present form of society will be misconstrued & taken for another thing. I wish to be a true & free man, & therefore would not be a woman, or a king, or a clergyman, each of which classes in the present order of things is a slave." Again the best part of the man revolted against being the minister.[7]

While struggling with the dilemma of how to preach without making the enslaving formal commitment to the ministry, Emerson inadvertently stumbled upon a new organization that had sprung up in Boston to spread useful knowledge through lectures and demonstrations. The Boston Society for the Diffusion of Useful Knowledge, part of the lyceum movement founded by Josiah Holbrook in

1826, had been formed in 1828. George Bliss Emerson, Emerson's second cousin, served on its founding committee. By the time Emerson returned from Europe, the lyceum system had spread throughout New England and was firmly established in Boston. Lyceum lectures dealt with a variety of subjects for a "promiscuous" audience. The speaker was expected to treat of his subjects in "a plain, familiar way, fitted to the comprehension of all members."[8] The lectures served a threefold purpose that differentiated them from other forms of discourse such as the sermon: (1) they provided all classes of the community with useful knowledge in the common idiom; (2) they made their audience mindful (in Edward Everett's words) of "those views of our common nature, which belong to us as rational and immortal beings, and to those duties and relations which appertain to us as accountable agents"—that is, they couched their information in moral but nonsectarian terms; and (3) they drew together different portions of an increasingly fragmented community, particularly those alienated from the powerful elites, into a common public endeavor.[9]

Because clergymen were among those of the community most skilled in public oratory, they were frequently in demand as speakers during the early days of the lyceum movement. Thus when Emerson was asked to deliver a lecture on "The Uses of Natural History" for the Boston Natural History Society in November 1833, he accepted the engagement as he might have accepted a request to supply another's pulpit. When it became apparent that there would be a demand for further lectures, Emerson moved into the Washington Street residence of his brother Charles in Boston. There he had access to the libraries he needed to prepare lectures for the Natural History Society and the Mechanics Institute. Although his subject was assigned him by those who asked him to speak, it was not uncongenial to him after his experience in Paris. He was to deliver lectures on various aspects of science—to be, as he had vowed, "a naturalist." His concern, however, was not with the practical details of his subject, for he admitted only a "quite superficial knowledge" of the intricacies of the scientific endeavor. Rather, as preacher of the sacred to a secular age, he vowed to "treat this question not for the Natural Philosopher but for the Man, and offer you some thoughts upon the intellectual influences of Natural Science."[10] The lyceum lectern served as an extension of the pulpit for him. If all things were reflective of and had a bearing on the moral nature of man, what was to prevent him from carrying out a part of his moral ministry in a secular setting?

So encouraged was Emerson by the reception of his lectures that by the end of August 1834, he contemplated "being a popular speaker." His brother Charles thought it imprudent. Lecturing was not a full-time profession; it was an occasional responsibility for someone well-established in another profession. He should go back to the pulpit if he could see his way clear to do so, Charles urged. Emerson for his own part had clearly come to look upon his time in the ministry as a failure as well as an activity that lured its incumbents toward hypocrisy. Though he had to agree with Charles that his supply preaching in the country had stirred up interest there, the interest was not in his ideas. Rather, it was "founded on the false notion that here was a Boston preacher."[11] The country parishes were quite as hidebound as any he had seen in Boston. The lyceums, on the other hand, offered him a platform from which he could speak his mind. The audiences expected plain truth, not tradition. There the listeners came voluntarily and with open minds, not expecting to hear a defense of a partisan cause. There he might address an audience composed of all good people of the community without regard to religious persuasion.

In early September, Emerson was once more given an opportunity to follow his calling within the traditional ministry, and this chance was in many ways more attractive than any before it. A liberal parish in New Bedford needed assistance and unofficially offered Emerson a settlement there. He would not be required to celebrate the Lord's Supper, he was told. Emerson thought about the offer and returned the answer that if he accepted such a position, the congregation should not expect him to pray at stated times. The minister who prayed when he felt no impulse to do so violated the strictures of his own nature; he surrendered to formalism. Moreover, one could not be an effective minister to his people if he did so, for insincere prayer could never move a congregation to piety. The parish may have been liberal, but hardly that liberal. If a minister would not commemorate the Lord's Supper and would not pray at stated times, what function did he serve? From Emerson's point of view, such a minister could do a great deal—he would be a model and an inspiration to his people. The New Bedford congregation's definition of an appropriate ministerial role, however, differed. So Emerson wrote to his grandfather on 20 September that he had declined the position and added, "I return with pleasure to our former prospect of spending the winter at Concord."[12] In Concord he began to think systematically about what the modern substitute for the antiquated ministerial role might be.

II

The winter of 1834–35 at Concord was the turning point when Emerson began to carve out for himself a new professional territory. With his refusal of the Bangor and New Bedford settlements, he had finally rejected the settled ministry as too narrow a profession for the sincere and virtuous individual. Although he would continue to preach from the pulpit until 1838, he would never again consider a call to the permanent ministry. Yet the ministry was the traditional home of the public advocate of morality and of the scholar, both of which Emerson wished to continue to consider himself. In New England in the 1830s there were no other obvious career possibilities for such an individual. Emerson wished to assume a position of moral leadership in the community. But as the community had changed structurally, the church's function had changed as well. It was no longer an agent of social integration, and the minister no longer presided as a model of moral concern—as a "representative man"—over the community as a whole. What was the individual who wished to assume moral leadership to do now that the minister had abdicated that position? Emerson hibernated that winter in his clan's ancestral home to consider the question.[13]

The theme that recurs over and over in Emerson's journals for that winter is sincerity. "Insist on yourself. Never imitate," he wrote on 6 October, marking out the pathway to an essay he would publish some seven years later, "Self-Reliance." He began to cling ferociously to his right, indeed his duty as one who would pursue virtue, to follow the voice of nature. As he wrote lyceum lectures that winter, he continually reminded himself that he was to speak "not what they will expect to hear but what is fit for me to say." His duty, he now believed, was to remind those around him that virtue consisted in fidelity to the commands of human nature, not to the behests of a society that had distorted them. Against the temptation to easy conformity to public opinion, he affirmed the principle that "unto every mind is given one word to say & he should sacredly strive to utter that word & not another man's word; his own, without addition or abatement."[14]

The Quaker became Emerson's ideal of integrity that winter, for the Quaker enacted "his first thought however violent or ludicrous" without stopping "to consider whether the purport of his vision may not be expressed in more seemly & accustomed forms." Here was a model of the sincere man, the champion of moral truth. Emerson's interest in the Quakers was converted into a February 1835 lecture in his "Biography" series, given before Boston's Society for the Diffusion of Useful Knowledge, entitled "George Fox." In Fox's protest against Anglican formalism, Emerson recognized many parallels to his own experience with the Lord's Supper. "A consistent practical reformer," Fox "puts ever a thing for a hollow form," and he does so in a time when "the majority of society holding fast not to truths, not to things, but to usages, are keenly sensible when usages are invaded."[15]

As the winter wore on, it became thoroughly apparent to Emerson what different kinds of roles he needed to sort out if he were to maintain his integrity. Like Fox, he considered himself a "practical reformer." He aspired to be the firstborn of "a race of preachers" who would "take such hold of the omnipotence of truth that they will blow the old falsehoods to shreds with the breath of their mouth." In order to perform his role as moral reformer adequately, however, he had to have the freedom to follow his single thought as far as it would take him. He had to heed the voice of Nature within him, and that meant reserving himself from the crowd as a private individual, isolating himself from the pressures to conform to common usage. The dilemma was how to maintain the private virtue that the public man needed— how to transform the public sphere while standing at a distance from it.[16]

In addition, Emerson had always envisioned the great man as one possessed of "a unity of purpose" but a variety of talents. At regular intervals in his life he realized that he was attracted in varying degrees to all the different activities of mankind. Poet, novelist, scientist, farmer, mathematician, stagecoach driver, merchant, editor—all of these roles appealed to different parts of the man, and he expressed regret that he could not follow out all his inclinations. He had feared that if he did so, he would "die the last a forlorn bachelor jilted of them all," his life wasted in dilettantism. After trying out a single calling, however, Emerson was ready to admit that a profession that left out parts of the man was insufficient. The new vocation must allow sufficient scope to the varied impulses that made up an individual. Emerson had to find a calling that would permit of a variety of activities.[17]

The role that Emerson created for himself and held up to his age was that of the scholar. An individual who was free to follow wherever truth might lead and was called to deliver that truth to his contemporaries, the scholar was to recall for his age the eternal verities of nature that his own finely attuned nature perceived. In "The American Scholar," his famous Phi Beta Kappa address delivered at Harvard University in 1837, Emerson summed up for his age the conclusions to which his crisis of vocation had brought him. If "The American Scholar" is about Emerson, it is also about the relationship of self to work in the social order capitalism was shaping. When the inner man, the "true" self, begins to view his work as something apart from himself, something that does violence to his inner impulses, he feels the pressure of conflicting expectations and needs. He can neither surrender to his public role as constitutive of his "true" self, nor can he withdraw entirely from the world of works and men to dwell in solipsism with nature. Where work becomes a self-alienating activity rather than a part of self-definition, what is to be done? "The American Scholar" attempts to provide answers.[18]

The address begins with a passage that has frequently been interpreted as a plea for American literary nationalism. Phi Beta Kappa orations for years had patriotically addressed the lack of a true American literature. Although Emerson begins with a nod to the traditional theme that his audience would have expected, the remainder of the essay seems to have little to do with American literary nationalism. In fact, it was not just "our day of dependence, our long apprenticeship to the learning of other lands" which "[drew] to a close."[19] It was Emerson's own "day of dependence" on the opinions of others, and in his capacity as "representative man," the "day of dependence" of all conscientious individuals on anything other than their own natures. In the address, Emerson issues a call to his listeners to rely on their own internal promptings to tell them what they ought to do rather than on social custom. Nature tells us that we have many facets, Emerson says. "Man is not a farmer, or a professor, or an engineer, but he is all"; he is "priest, and scholar, and statesman, and producer, and soldier." Practicality necessitates a division of labor, but modern society has taken the principle too far: "The state of society is one in which the members have suffered amputation from the trunk, and strut about so many walking monsters,—a good finger, a neck, a stomach, an elbow, but never a man." Because man must diminish his human stature in order to fill the role society has prepared for him, "man is thus metamorphosed into a thing, into many things." In such a scheme of things, "the priest becomes a form," Emerson adds poignantly by way of illustration.

In this division of labor, according to Emerson, "the scholar is the delegated intellect." But as Emerson makes clear later in the essay, the office of scholar is not a mere profession; it is a way of life that potentially subsumes all professions. "Is not every man a student, and do not all things exist for the student's behoof?" Emerson asks. The true scholar—"*Man Thinking*"—would find his vocation to be a response to certain types of influences, influences to which he as representative man would respond as all men ought. First and foremost, the scholar would be aware of nature. Indeed, Emerson's scholar is defined not by traditional standards of learning, but by his peculiar willingness to heed the voice of nature. It would be "he of all men" whose calling would be to "settle [nature's] value" in its myriad aspect—physical, moral, and spiritual—"in his mind." The true scholar would learn the cardinal lesson that nature has to teach, that all things tend toward unity, and the corollary of that lesson, that his own nature mirrors the laws of the universe. Hence, the scholar would study nature as a guide to the laws that inform his own life. His vocation would be to know what it means to be a virtuous man and to act upon that knowledge.

The scholar as Emerson envisions him would also be influenced by "the mind of the Past," of which books are the best representatives. Literature communicates to the scholar the secrets of nature that others have discovered, and in a fresh way that speaks to the hearts of all men. Although Emerson cautions that "books are for the scholar's idle times," they are nonetheless an important way in which one individual communicates an insight derived from nature to another. The scholar must read and write, Emerson believes, not in order to define himself as a learned and distinguished professional, but in order to discover the "preestablished harmony" between minds dictated by nature. He comes to know the ways in which he is linked to his fellow. He discovers this relation through literature as well as through nature.

In addition to the contemplation of nature and literature, Emerson adds one more component to the scholar's vocation: he must use his knowledge to affect others. "Action is with the scholar subordinate, but it is essential," he insists. The temptation to withdraw into solitary contemplation of truth was strong for Emerson. Nevertheless, he affirms, the scholar who fails to find himself a public role is "not yet man," for cowardice deters him from putting his knowledge into action. Armed with the knowledge that nature provides him, however, the scholar could change the world. To do so, he would need only to apply to human nature in the abstract what he learns in solitude about his own nature. He could extrapolate from his private experience the facts about human nature and publish his conclusions to his age.

Here was the ideal, he told his listeners of the Phi Beta Kappa Society, but what was the reality? One could find out by looking at the clergy, "who are always, more universally than any other class, the scholars of their day." Disdained by "practical men" who believed that such men were content to speculate in abstruse issues because "they could do nothing," clergymen were "addressed as women." They were insulated from "the rough, spontaneous conversation of men" and consequently did not know the life that it was their duty to see and publish. They did not know the problems of their own age, nor did they care to know them. Therefore they could not act. They lacked "the heroic mind" without which there could be no scholar in the true sense of the word. Instead of providing an example to mankind of what men should be, they themselves lived an irrelevant life.

The problem that Emerson underlined in "The American Scholar" was in fact his own problem some two and a half years earlier. What was the appropriate course of action for a scholar? How might he influence the age rather than remain aloof and apart from it as current clerical practice seemed to dictate? If the minister and the scholar were at odds in this new social climate, what active role could a scholar take? Emerson explored the problem in the lecture series on "Biography," given before the Society for the Diffusion of Useful Knowledge in Boston in the winter of 1835. Although the topic was probably suggested to him by the Society, the particular figures he spoke about were of his own choosing. Emerson hoped to find in the biographies of those he admired "a Portraiture of Man which should be at once history & prophecy."[20] Here he might find models for his own life.

The men Emerson chose to lecture about came from different ages and circumstances, but they were all thinkers and artists who translated their thought into a reforming impulse. Michelangelo Buonaroti was the type of the artist who spurned the demands of popes and prelates to "express the Idea of Beauty." His life was extraordinary, Emerson found, because "he lived one life: he pursued one career." Martin Luther was the "scholar or spiritual man leading a great revolution, and from first to last faithful to his position." John Milton, the youthful Emerson's hero, combined for the more mature man the roles of reformer and poet. George Fox, the Quaker, transformed an inarticulate poetry of the mind into spiritual enthusiasm despite adversity and persecution. Edmund Burke, the man of affairs, brought philosophy to politics and was "a sort of artist or painter with words." Each measured the characteristics of his age against the standard of nature and found his own age wanting. Each insisted on nature. In a rotten age, Emerson implied in his "Biography" lectures, the scholar had to be reformer: the roles could not be separated. "In this age of seeming," the true scholar was obliged to speak out "to save the land."[21]

In Emerson's "American Scholar," it is easy to find strong parallels between his objections to the professional opportunities open to him and the widespread commodification of the entire social order taking place during his time. If ministers (among others) were strutting about like so many monstrously disconnected parts of the body of the community, amputated by their sectarian specializations from connection to the whole, they were only experiencing in their own way a process increasingly common to a number of different types of labor. For with the advent of merchant and industrial capitalism in New England, workers of all sorts experienced a transformation of their labor power into a commodity to be bought and sold in increasingly specialized markets. Ministers were first noticeably affected by this process around the turn of the century when the overt market for ministers emerged in the Boston area. With the development of that market, congregations more frequently had the power to define which services of a minister were to be valued and therefore purchased by the congregation. Ecclesiastics found their traditional power to act as intellectuals for the entire society eroded and their power to define their own roles and courses of action diminished.[22] Emerson, in looking to swim against this tide of specialization, hoped to recover through the role of scholar the function of the intellectual. Immersed in a culture where fragmentation of work experience was becoming the rule, it is not surprising that Emerson would note an increasing incapacity among his contemporaries, especially his brother ministers, to think of work in moral terms and in relation to the community in the abstract.

As the nature of community in Emerson's New England grew more and more elusive, the common theme that increasingly emerged in Emerson's search for a viable vocation was the relation of work to morality. What ways were available of contributing to a common good rather than a private or self-interested one? What work would help in overcoming the increasingly apparent conflicts of interest between factions, parties, sects, and classes of citizens? "The American Scholar" suggests that the specialization of roles inherent in the emergent social order of Emerson's day created three kinds of pernicious consequences. First, it encouraged individuals to see the worth of human functions as based entirely on their value as commodities, making persons more susceptible to the opinions and influences of others who could determine that value. Second, it obscured from individuals their larger moral responsibility to the public or common sphere, as they became immersed in the pursuit of a private good—whether it was personal, familial, or partisan. Third, with specialization of function came a divorce of thought from action, as the situation of the enslaved, effeminate ministers illustrated; no one retained responsibility for integrating the two.[23]

Emerson's solution was to build a vocation apart from the established institutions that, in buying out a man's labor, led him to fragmentation of self, paralysis and inefficacy, and moral blindness. Seeking a role that would allow him the freedom of thought possible only in the private sphere but which would empower him to act as public reformer as well, Emerson chose as his vehicles two areas still in the earliest stages of professionalization. As lyceum lecturer, he could take on the new role of secular intellectual. As a man of literature, he could legitimately publish his moral beliefs without allegiance to institutions. Through speaking and writing, a man morally impelled could publish the promptings of conscience, and he could do so while remaining clear of the deforming structures and institutions of society.

III

Ironically, what allowed Emerson to set out on a new path that circumvented the restrictions of his old ministerial role was the rise of a market for free-lance orators and writers. As long as intellectuals found themselves bound to specific local audiences, their ability to think and act was constrained by the expectations of their local clienteles. As Emerson had discovered in his experience with Second Church, the consequences of violating those expectations were simple and severe: loss of position and power. The same commercial labor market that hamstrung the minister, however, also provided the conditions under which a man such as Emerson could compete for the attention of the public in a translocal marketplace of ideas. In the new lyceums and in the profession of authorship, it seemed to Emerson, an individual might bring his moral mission to the attention of a general public not already bound up in partisan or sectarian causes and receive appropriate consideration.

Emerson found out early on in the life of the lecture system generated by the lyceums and mechanics' institutes that clerics or politicians could be much in demand as speakers. Nevertheless, these institutions differed from the others available to him in defining the knowledge they dispensed as strictly practical and pragmatic—explicitly non-ideological in character. They offered an escape from the opprobrium attached to the promotion of partisan causes precisely during the years when it became clear that both party politics and religious denominationalism would be permanent fixtures on the American scene. As Donald Scott has noted, the lecture system provided a forum for broadly conceived public discussion in an era in which the public arena had become notably fragmented among parties, sects, and classes. Although the lyceums in practice tended to provide a forum for the rising middle class of the region, they attempted to minimize class and occupational differences by spreading knowledge intended to level all distinctions.[24] It was just such a platform that Emerson sought as he looked to escape partisan restrictions in his own preaching. The lyceums were "as good a pulpit as any other," Emerson told his brother Charles during a November 1835 walk in the woods outside Concord. There one might preach whatever "Lay Sermons" one wanted. If the church seemed to endorse the divisions that were occurring within society as a whole, the lyceum, on the other hand, shared many of the features of the old church ideology. It was dedicated to the spread of a common culture. Though this common culture was now based on secular rather than sacred knowledge, Emerson's predisposition to imbue all knowledge with religious implication meant that he could look on this new cultural institution as a platform from which to preach a new sacred culture capable of replacing the defunct system of meanings. The lyceum was "freer," imposing few prescriptions on the speaker other than that he hold his listeners' attention. "It is the new pulpit," Emerson came to believe, and "the true church of today."[25]

The list of Emerson's earliest lyceum lectures provides a sense of the range of topics acceptable in the new public forum. Between 1833 and 1837 Emerson presented series on "Science," "Italy," "Biography," "English Literature," and "The Philosophy of History," and he also began a series on "Human Culture." Among the individual subjects included within these series were lectures on "The Uses of Natural History," "Water," "Edmund Burke," "Permanent Traits of the English National Genius," "Shakspear," and "Modern Aspects of Letters"; and general lectures on the subjects of science, history, art, literature, politics, religion, society, trades and professions, manners, and ethics. Though the breadth of learning necessary to talk about all these subjects seems staggering from a modern point of view, the admonition of the lyceum—that whatever knowledge presented be accessible to all and practical and useful in its orientation—freed Emerson from the responsibility of specialization and from assuming the role of the amputated, walking monster depicted in the "American Scholar" address. Despite their diversity of subject, the message of the early lectures is remarkably similar: the multiplicity of human experience, when seen from a moral perspective, points us toward the perception of the organic unity of human nature and of the real union of humanity with Nature itself. (Emerson's "Introductory" to "The Philosophy of History," for instance, begins with the familiar theme that history rightly written and understood "correspond[s] to the whole of the mind." The rest of the lecture is a gloss on the idea of the unity of the human mind.)[26] For Emerson, all knowledge had a moral character, and all moral knowledge was immediately accessible and practical to all persons.

Oratory itself had a high and honorable tradition as a public calling, further predisposing Emerson to see it as a possible solution to his problems. Hugh Blair had extolled the powers of speech in the following manner in Emerson's college textbook: "Speech is the great instrument by which man becomes beneficial to man: and it is to the intercourse and transmission of thought, by means of speech, that we are chiefly indebted for the improvement of thought itself. . . . What we call human reason, is not the effort or ability of one, so much as it is the result of the reason of many arising from lights mutually communicated, in consequence of discourse and writing." Thus, the individual who published his thoughts to others did the public a service. "He gives us to see with a new eye, to burn with a new fire," as William Ellery Channing put it. According to Edward Everett, the orator acted as "the public organ" of the highest sentiments of the community. Emerson, in sharing his contemporaries' good opinion of the possibilities of oratory, saw eloquence as "the voice of Virtue & Truth." A corrupt age was even more in need of it than a virtuous age. The orator as champion of truth under adverse circumstances spoke in behalf of the inmost nature of man: "Let him be the mere tongue of us all; no individual but a universal man, let him leave his nation, his party, his sect, his town-connexion, even his vanity & selflove at home & come hither to say what were equally fit at Paris, at Canton, and at Thebes." The orator "proceeds in the faith that . . . all have one fundamental nature which he knows how to address," Emerson believed. "This is to be eloquent." The audience would comprehend such speech.[27]

Moreover, theories of true eloquence in Federalist and Unitarian thought held that effective oratory nearly always proceeded from the virtue of the speaker. It belonged "only to towering souls, impressed with vast and strong conceptions, and glowing with great and generous emotions," the *Monthly Anthology* had proclaimed in Emerson's father's time. When those who thought seriously about the role of eloquence within society admitted the obvious, that artful men could sway by unscrupulous manipulation, they provided yet another reason to develop a model of virtuous oratory to combat such schemers. As in the ministry, in secular oratory too the sincerity of the man became the measure of the orator.[28]

As Emerson's sense that sincerity was at the heart of true eloquence grew, his tastes in oratory became more pronounced. Edward Everett, at whose feet the young Emerson had worshipped during his Harvard years, fell in Emerson's estimation, for "he is all art." "He is not content to be Edward Everett, but would be Daniel Webster. This is his mortal distemper," Emerson wrote in 1835. "He will not deliver himself up to dear Nature, but insists on making postures & sounds after his own taste, & like those he has heard of, & now he does not know there is any Nature *for him*. Neither has he any faith." Such posturing destroyed any hope one had of influencing people for the good, for it alienated the orator from the voice of his own nature. It was nature only, Emerson believed, that linked the orator's mind with that of his audience.[29]

Although Emerson expressed disappointment in his former mentor, he found a new model orator in Father Edward Thompson Taylor, pastor at the Seaman's Bethel in Boston. His preaching was eloquent enough to make him the "Poet of the Sailor & of Ann street." His secret? "He [was] profuse of himself[;] he never remember[ed] the looking-glass," and he therefore spoke a language that all could understand. "It is essential to eloquence that somewhere you let out all the reins," Emerson had concluded during his own ministry, and Father Taylor filled the bill. To eradicate personal idiosyncrasy, the result of calculation, from oratory, an orator had to abandon all sense of self, trusting to nature to speak through him. The result of such self-abnegation in public speech was that the sense of separation between self and others was erased: "The hearer would lose the sense of dualism; of hearing from another; would cease to distinguish between the orator and himself." The sincere orator could thus restore the community of thought and virtue so sorely missed in the fragmenting social milieu.[30]

The literary man through his own type of eloquence might do the same. In the public culture of New England during the early national period, writing itself most often derived from the models of oratory. Written discourse in effect was an extension of oratory whereby the orator was able to reach those out of earshot.[31] Although it provided the medium through which ideas could be extended through time and space to diverse audiences, the production of native literature for a time remained linked closely to local clienteles, at least until the growth of extensive communication networks that developed in tandem with commercial exchange. In the time of Emerson's parents, the most common type of reading available consisted of devotional materials, usually transcriptions of sermons by popular preachers. Parents often encouraged children to transcribe sermon notes themselves as a way of developing a sense of organization and style that would be equally transferable to oral or written discourse. Ruth Haskins Emerson urged her son Edward to "continue the exercise of writing sermon notes." His brother Waldo had done so and it seemed to have helped him, she prodded: "The practice will assist you in composition & give you more variety in style."[32]

The self-conscious growth of American literature and letters as something apart from oratory had begun to occur during Emerson's boyhood and young manhood. The rise of the American newspaper in the late eighteenth century opened up a new avenue of literary expression. To many of the educated elite, however, it was a medium that frequently seemed to lower the level of literary expression by its polemical concern with politics and commerce. Emerson's father made one of the number of the "Society of Gentlemen" who founded the genteel *Monthly Anthology* in Boston in 1803 "to apply caustic and lancet to the disorders of the American press." The *Anthology* took up literary topics in addition to the theological discussions characteristic of American church-related periodicals. Literature included not only poetry and belles lettres, but law, politics, and history, medicine and chemistry as well—in short, anything that the written word could be used to convey that the *Anthology's* authors deemed of value to its audience. Nevertheless, each work, no matter what its ostensible subject matter, was, like the sermon, to be looked upon as a way of examining questions that were ultimately of moral import. "The office of biography," for example, was "to teach by examples"; that of painting and sculpture, which were also criticized in the pages of the *Anthology*, was to "exemplify eternal rules of thought and action by which it is the duty of each individual . . . to model and perfect himself." In general, literature afforded the individual the opportunity to recollect in solitude the truths of religion and morality that the preacher rehearsed from a theological point of view from the pulpit.[33]

Imaginative literature in particular could be effective in leading its readers down the path to godliness. Its aim was to treat of the natural facts in the universe in such a way that the reader might perceive the harmony within the universe—the moral order—that was beauty. The perception of that order excited the emotions, enlisting them in behalf of virtue, beauty's counterpart in the realm of moral action.[34] Thus in literature as in oratory, the truly eloquent writer was the one who could touch the springs of human nature in another with a moral message. From Hugh Blair, Emerson learned that it was simplicity of style, "the very language of nature," that revealed best the writer's "own natural character." Nature spoke to nature, soul to soul. The harmonious unity of nature suggested the attributes of God and the contours of the moral order. According to the *North American Review*, a literary periodical founded by Unitarian Bostonians in 1815, "There is nothing lonely in nature, but each thing is connected with many others, by more ties than those which hold a tree in the ground." Such nature poetry as that of Washington Allston was especially laudable in that it "treats of us all in common, as creatures of like passions, sensible to like impressions, and capable of like thoughts." That is, like good oratory, it tapped the springs of human nature.[35]

Not surprisingly, then, in the Unitarian culture of Emerson's New England, literature had a social function. It was an instrument by which the community's moral sentiments and social cohesiveness might be fostered. Although literature was to be perused by the solitary individual, it was a public vehicle through which one's ties to others and to God might be reaffirmed. Theoreticians such as Hugh Blair praised good poetry and prose as a means of nourishing "publick spirit" and "of disposing the heart to virtue."[36] Levi Frisbie, Emerson's Professor of Natural Religion, Moral Philosophy, and Political Economy at Harvard, found the subject closely enough related to his own province to comment on it frequently.[37] Because literature served such a moral and social function for the community at large, a national American literature became not merely a luxury but a necessity. A national literature would sustain an indigenous moral social order as a foreign literature could not.[38]

Although this was the ideal, in reality literature was becoming something far different during Emerson's young adulthood. The tradition of moralism that had linked literature to the ministry was giving way on the strength of a growing market for print to a new type of mass-market literature. During the early nineteenth century, a popular literature centered on the novel arose to provide a challenge to the old, official literary model espoused by the class of persons represented by the *Monthly Anthology* authors. Written in a language accessible to the general public and represented by such works as Susanna Rowson's *Charlotte Temple* (1791) and James Fenimore Cooper's *The Spy* (1821), the new fiction broadened the potential reading audience beyond the professional elite of the community, who had heretofore been the primary consumers of print. In addition, this new genre threatened the ministerial monopoly on the interpretation of print, as it no longer required the intervention of the clergy as "mediating middlemen" to interpret the moral message thereby conveyed.

Though Emerson continued to rely on the old moralistic model of literature as the basis for his own writing, he did benefit from the professionalization of authorship that the new market for reading material encouraged. No longer was the minister the arbiter of letters; the author could write in a way that directly spoke to ordinary readers and expect now to find an audience for his or her writing. Moreover, the dissociation of the profession of letters from the profession of religion meant that literacy itself was freed from its predominantly religious framework. If, as Jack Goody and Ian Watt argue, literate cultures encourage the individual to make "his own more or less conscious, more or less personal selection, rejection and accommodation among the conflicting ideas and attitudes in his culture," the extention of popular literacy in spheres beyond the religious and the political opened the way for authors detached from local communities to shape public opinion in a variety of areas. Moreover, it encouraged readers to begin to think in terms of general and abstract conceptions of their lives and activities, obscuring the importance of "particularlistic" local conditions—precisely the sort of response Emerson sought to encourage.[39]

If religion had failed Emerson as an instrument of moral reform, then literature still held out hope to him. William Ellery Channing's important "Remarks on National Literature" in fact announced to his contemporaries that as politics became more corrupt, literature was destined to succeed it as the agent of progress and change in society. More and more, Channing found, "political life is less and less regarded as the only or chief sphere for superior minds, and that influence and honor are more and more accumulated in the hands of literary and thinking men." In his own age, as politics had been reduced to private influence and ambition, literature alone remained "to establish connections between the more or less gifted." "In a true time, I should never have written," Emerson would recall many years later. But as he believed the times to be false, Emerson found in literature a "Second Religion." There was no disjunction at all between the man of literature and the man of action. In the modern age, they were one and the same.[40]

In 1835, therefore, Emerson the orator turned to literature as another but closely related facet of his vocation. "When will you mend Montaigne?" he berated himself. "Where are your Essays?" It is significant that it was Montaigne, the powerful social critic and writer of moral essays, who first spurred Emerson on to try his hand at literature. We are best acquainted with Emerson's estimation of Montaigne through his role as "the Skeptic" in *Representative Men*. What Montaigne meant to Emerson in 1835 might be better suggested by this contemporary commentary on the essayist in the *North American Review* for April 1834: "The principal charm . . . of this work, is the complete freshness and truth of the observations on life and manners; and the secret of it appears to lie in the care with which the author studied the movements of his own heart and mind. He declares throughout his work, that he has made himself the exclusive object of his own study." Within a year and a half, Emerson would publish in *Nature* the first of his own moral essays.[41]

Thus would literature supply models of sincerity and rules of morality that would renovate society. But to imply that Emerson's interest in literature had its genesis in 1835 would be misleading. In fact, it went back to his boyhood. The fifteen-year-old Waldo dreamed of having "nothing to do but mount the heights of Parnassus & enjoy the feasts of polite literature." "But in this country where everyone is obliged to study his profession for assistance in living, & where so little encouragement is given to Poets &c it is a poor trade," he added in a letter to his brother Edward. "I have not the last thought of determination to follow it." Until 1835, most of the poetry that Emerson wrote was for his eyes only. His life and livelihood lay elsewhere. In his crisis of vocation, however, he began to reassess that renunciation of seventeen years before. Perhaps the poet was the best part of the man. Perhaps inner impulses had been stifled unwisely in an effort to fit into the professional structure of nineteenth-century society.[42]

In February 1835 Emerson clearly identified himself to his fiancée, Lydia (or, as he called her, Lidian) Jackson, as "a poet, of a low class without a doubt yet a poet." That, he told her, was his "nature & vocation." The statement has the sound of discovery rather than of long-standing surety. Emerson went on to explain how it was that he knew himself to be a poet. "My singing be sure is very 'husky,' & is for the most part in prose," he wrote to Lidian. "Still I am a poet in the sense of a perceiver & dear lover of the harmonies that are in the soul & in matter, & specially of the correspondence between these & those." To be a poet was not to be part of a profession, just as to be a scholar was not and to be a minister ought not to be. It was a designation for the lover of nature in a new guise. Emerson's serious poetry as well as most of his moral essays began to appear during this period of resolution.[43]

Poet, literary man, orator, scholar, naturalist—all were different names for the same thing, as far as Emerson was concerned. His vocation was to show his age how it ought to live by teaching and by example. He was called to be a "representative man." Within the bounds of traditional society, Emerson's position among the elite of a community would have accorded him that status. As the community outgrew an older, deferential pattern of integration and formed a new one clearly based on class and occupation, however, the positions of moral leadership in society seemed to have been vacated. In opposition to the tendency of the professions to narrow their roles to particular spheres or segments of the community, Emerson defined his own calling outside the professions. Literature was to be the new means through which men celebrated their common nature in a segmented society that gave them little else in common.

Emerson's definitions of the orator and the man of letters represent an attempt in the face of a widening distinction between public and private life to recombine the two—to obscure or eradicate the increasingly apparent distinction between personal and civic in the life of New Englanders.[44] The public sphere in Emerson's view was the realm of the impartial and universal point of view of normative reason. The private sphere, incorrectly taken by his contemporaries to be the legitimate domain of particularlistic individual interests, could be reconciled with the public sphere if particular phenomena were seen under their universal aspect. Emerson believed that the scholar, in defining his calling as advocacy of an impartial common good, would be a key figure in bringing about a new social harmony. Unlike the intellectuals tied to the interests of particular professions and clienteles, the scholar would be free and privileged to discover a universally applicable knowledge that would serve all. Neither technician nor manager, priest nor politician, this new "representative man" transcended the role of specialist, assuming the role of guardian of human culture in general.

Certainly in some ways Emerson's point of view must seem naive in retrospect. In order to escape the shortcomings of competition and conflict inherent in the new social order, he defined away any notion of difference. His response to the increasingly overt politicization of his world was to construct an apolitical moral universe. Emerson's philosophy, hinging on the ability to locate universal laws that transcend the context of their time and place, assumed as natural the forms of rationality on which it relied to construct its own cosmology. This moral calculus posited as an article of faith the ability of ideology to escape the exigencies of its time and place. The result was that Emerson, in assuming this new intellectual role, unwittingly came to play a crucial part in the rationalization of the new social order. By elaborating seemingly universal laws of human nature that in reality had their basis in the specific conditions of a particular social and economic order, he provided the new hegemonic culture with a language of morality that defined the nature of legitimate moral questions, and at the same time precluded certain other kinds of questions from being asked or even clearly articulated. Emerson's perspective sought to escape the moral dangers of economic individualism. In implying that the locus of moral decision making and the focus of moral questions ought legitimately to be limited to the individual, however, he provided unawares a moral rationale for reproducing the order to which he objected. The scholar in some ways could meliorate the effects of the new social order, but the very process by which that melioration took place ironically also reinforced it.

Many modern American professions can claim Emerson as forebear—he was the first professional intellectual, one of the first media heroes, the first modern American poet and writer, even a primitive ego psychologist of sorts. In fact, however, he intended to be none of these. He was antiprofessional in orientation. He wished to break down the boundaries between the various areas of human endeavor, to make his contemporaries mindful of the unity that underlay personality, society, nature. He meant to restore to society as best he could using the tools at hand an organic unity he believed to be slipping away. The world had failed, and it remained for the individual self-conscious of the nature of his own humanity to do something about it. Although no one could have foreseen it at the time, the most radical fruit of his struggle to cope with the transition between two different ways of life was neither his philosophy of nature nor his notion of vocation. Rather, it was his invention of a modern notion of the self that was destined to have the greatest impact in the new social order. That discovery of self was made not in the public sphere of his native Boston, but in the domestic sphere of Concord, to which he had looked for respite and protection.

PART 3

The
Discovery
of Self

CHAPTER 7

Uriel's Fall

To those who have been accustomed to lead, it is not quite indifferent to find their word or deed for the first time unimportant to society. Yet a human being always has the indemnity of acting religiously, & then he exchanges an eclat with the society of his town, for a reputation & weight with the society of the Universe.—Journals and Miscellaneous Notebooks, *December 1841*

WITH HIS REMOVAL to his ancestral village of Concord in 1834, the various facets of Emerson's life began to sort themselves out. After several years of litigation, Emerson finally received his legacy from Ellen's estate. In 1835, he remarried, taking Lydia Jackson of Plymouth as his second wife. The couple set up housekeeping in a frame house at the intersection of the Lexington and Old Boston roads in Concord. Concord was two and a half hours by stage from Boston; not until the coming of the railroad in 1844 would the commuting time to the metropolis be reduced to a manageable half hour. The town numbered only two thousand inhabitants and actually lost population between the time Emerson moved there and the 1840 census. In many ways, Concord seemed to offer the perfect environment for the reflection in solitude that Emerson had come to believe was a central prerequisite for an effective and virtuous public life. Though tied in through new transportation and commercial networks to Boston and the region it dominated, Concord also offered the opportunity for relative peace and privacy. Here Emerson might try whatever experiments he wanted as he worked out the new calling of scholar.[1]

Meanwhile, in Boston itself, far less tranquility prevailed. The challenges that had relentlessly dogged the city for several decades—rapid growth in population and demographic diversity, as well as a radically transformed economy and the metamorphosis of social mores that went with it—intensified in the years between 1834 and 1838. The country folk to whom Lyman Beecher's revivals had appealed so strongly continued to pour into the city at an unprecedented rate. Joining these newcomers in ever-increasing numbers were another group of migrants to Boston, equally strange to urban life and also alien to the Protestantism that the first group professed. These Irish Catholic immigrants combined with American-born migrants to Boston to swell the city's population by a third between 1830 and 1840. Boston and its four contiguous counties grew by nearly one hundred thousand persons during the same period.[2] Three railroads, completed in July 1835, joined the city and Worcester to the west, Providence to the south, and Lowell to the north.

While Emerson brooded in Concord over the violence that society did to conscience, Bostonians did physical violence to each other in the streets. Some of the riots that affected Boston in the 1830s originated in increasingly stark cultural differences. On a summer evening in 1834, working-class Charlestownians burned the Ursuline Convent to the ground. They had been stirred up in a series of sermons that pointed to Catholicism as the latest heretical menace to a cherished way of life.[3] These sermons had been delivered by none other than Lyman Beecher, back from Ohio where he had traveled in 1832 to launch a campaign against the forces of heresy and infidelity in the Ohio Valley. Little more than a year later, an unruly crowd drove abolitionist William Lloyd Garrison from Boston, believing him to be in league with the "intrigues" of foreign-born abolitionist agitator George Thompson, and in 1837, the dietary and sexual reformer, Sylvester Graham, was forcibly restrained from delivering his message to an all-female audience. In the late 1830s, violence increasingly sprang as well from severe economic dislocation. The international financial panic of 1837 precipitated a cruel economic depression; in its wake came suspension of specie payments, cuts in wages, increases in unemployment, and two more riots—this time clashes between working-class Bostonians and Irish immigrants. Violence and mob action, partisan and political activity, poverty, religious strife, and business failures rose sharply during the economic crisis.[4]

The Panic of 1837 and the desperation it bred were national, even international, news. Emerson was not so preoccupied with his vocational decision making that he failed to notice. The London *Age* told him of "loud cracks in the social edifice.—sixty thousand laborers . . . to be presently thrown out of work, and these make a formidable mob to break open banks & rob the rich & brave, the domestic government." Closer to home, the Exchange in New Orleans had been burned and the banks in New York ruined by a run on specie. "The land stinks with suicide," Emerson observed in May 1837. He could without effort find at his elbow "young men, young women at 30 and even earlier" who had "lost all spring and vivacity." People asked, "What shall I do? How shall I live?" and "their despondency and skepticism" seemed every day to spread a little further.[5]

Emerson suspected that the waves of protest washing over New England were not isolated phenomena. Everyone, it seemed, felt dissatisfied with something. Some found slavery representative of the moral bankruptcy of society, while others found problems with the church or with distribution of property or with marriage or with social convention. Though each would feel the ache in "a different part according to his circumstance," the wise man would find with time and insight that "his protest against a particular superficial falsehood" was only symptomatic of a more serious malady. Without making light of any of these individual complaints, Emerson contended that they were signs of a single disease—what he called the "lapse from the fair Ideal life."[6] The cluster of problems that troubled Emerson's contemporaries indeed had a common root: the heightened recognition of interest as legitimate ground for action, and a concomitant inability to agree on a common ground for maintaining social order. If people were at odds in the street and in the marketplace, Emerson suggested, it was because their understanding of the good differed according to their differing material circumstances. The dissonance of the age demanded more than piecemeal measures. It demanded a revolution in people's ways of thinking.

If Emerson believed that the times demanded a reevaluation of all aspects of social life, he hoped in his Concord retreat to be able to reflect upon the nature of the good society and of the new moral standards for which his age was searching. Planning to alternate periods of domestic solitude and contemplation with periodic forays into the public arena, Emerson hoped to sketch out for his age a new moral order to be based on the ideals of Nature. From 1834 until midway through 1838, he delivered lyceum lectures, preached occasional sermons, and oversaw the publication of Carlyle's work in the United States. He was trying, and with some success and contentment if his journals are to be believed, to live up to the image he had formulated of (in Stephen Whicher's words) "the hero-scholar, leading mankind to the promised land."[7] But as Whicher and other observers of Emerson's life have noted, this interlude in which society and solitude were set in perfect counterpoint was to be short-lived. On 15 July 1838, Emerson delivered an address before the senior class of the Divinity School of Harvard University, a sermon that symbolically addressed the crisis in the legitimacy of authority so evident around him. The reaction to it was so violent—and so unexpected—that Emerson was forced to rethink his position on the public role of the scholar-reformer.

I

Harvard, the setting for Emerson's address, had been the bastion of Massachusetts leadership since its founding in 1636. Nevertheless, in the turbulent 1830s, not even Harvard was completely safe territory for the merchants and professionals who set the tone of cultural life in Boston. As late as 1834, the college had seen a riot of its own, a disturbance that resulted in so many expulsions that the class of 1836 was the smallest save one since 1809. The incident began trivially enough. One of the freshman class, when asked by his Greek tutor to recite, refused. "I do not recognize your authority," he is reported to have said. The junior class "espoused his cause with great warmth, and proceeded, from one step to another, in a course of outrage and annoyance" that lasted several weeks. Rampaging students broke windows and furniture, assaulted officers of the college, and disrupted chapel services. The president of Harvard, former Boston mayor Josiah Quincy, threatened to call in civil authorities to quell the disturbance. Eventually, the whole sophomore class was dismissed, although most were later readmitted.[8]

Harvard had suffered through student rebellions before, but none had focused so explicitly on the nature of authority. Quincy, brought in as Harvard's president by its overseers in 1829, did much to consolidate the school's financial position, but as an authoritative paternal figure for his students, his tenure was an unmitigated disaster. A martinet, he believed in "thorough drilling" and law and order on campus.[9] The senior class of 1834 issued a circular imputing the intensity of the riot of that year to the fact that Quincy treated them in a legalistic, contractual way. In his zeal for efficiency and conformity to proper usage, he had contributed "to the

destruction of those feelings of kindness" which should exist between parent and child.[10] The distant president's emphasis on education as a ritual of self-discipline, coupled with his apparent indifference to the personal well-being of students, convinced many that
his authority was ineffective and illegitimate. One of a new breed
of administrators—neither teacher, scholar, nor minister—Quincy's
efficient, bureaucratic regime left him with little emotional connection to students.

President Quincy's failure to convince students of the legitimacy
of his authority is interesting in itself, but it becomes even more
intriguing when paralleled with both the pattern of disintegration of
authority in Boston itself and with Emerson's own rejection of Unitarian formalism. In fact, the question of who was in charge at Harvard and by what right had also been debated with increasing fervor
by the various constituencies that had arisen in Jacksonian Boston.
Since Lyman Beecher, evangelicals had been charging the state-sup-
ported institution with spreading sectarian—that is, Unitarian—
doctrine, and they demanded that the state support it no longer. The
lower and middle classes, who could not have afforded to send their
sons to Harvard even if they had wanted to, had no desire to see the
state subsidize the indoctrination of their future leaders in a religion of degeneracy. Their public funds were being used to support an
institution of "heretical" character and to perpetuate a scheme of
upper-class leadership at odds with their new conception of social
order. In 1834, Harvard clearly no longer stood as a representative of
agreed-upon communal cultural standards, and it could no longer
speak authoritatively to a broad constituency on the problem of
values. Hence, the door was now open to students to question the
authority of an institution incapable of providing the leadership in
society that it claimed to provide.[11]

In addition, large portions of Boston's population had become,
like the students, increasingly disenchanted with the tendency of
their own elite to refuse to deal with social disorder in any other
than a legal and contractual way. As society began to seem impersonal and inhumane as well as immoral, many responded with their
own rejection of the legitimacy of established authority in matters
religious as well as political. The Harvard riot of 1834, preceding
Emerson's Divinity School Address by four years, foreshadowed
some of the fundamental issues the address would raise. Of the six
members of the senior class in the Divinity School at Harvard in

1838, five had attended Harvard College during the tenure of President Quincy, and two had been members of the junior class during the 1834 rebellion.[12] The riot may not have been a turning point in their lives, but it certainly indicates that the legitimacy of the authority of institutions was an issue that would continue to be of grave concern to their generation. This was an issue that Emerson too was more than willing to address in his speech on the current state of religious sentiment in July 1838.

Emerson had long been preoccupied with the question of the proper duties of the Christian minister. In the winter and spring of 1838, he had looked with increasing disgust on the way Concord's minister, Barzillai Frost, had conducted himself as pastor. It was not that Frost was lacking in conscientiousness; he was in fact the picture of the proper Christian minister in observing the forms of the ministry. Nevertheless, he seemed notably lacking in imagination and had been remarkably unsuccessful in rousing his congregation to a spiritual knowledge of Christianity.[13] Emerson himself had recently determined to preach no more from the pulpit, partly in response to his strong negative reaction to Frost's ministry.[14] When the senior class of the Divinity School requested that he address them at their graduation, Emerson saw an opportunity to speak out. These aspiring ministers, attracted by his growing antiauthoritarian reputation, would enable him to use what he had learned to bring the clergy back to a true sense of their mission.

At first he was somewhat unsure of the kind of reception his jeremiad might meet.[15] On the first of April he went to talk with the Divinity School students on the topic of theism. "I went rather heavy-hearted for I always find that my views chill or shock people at the first opening," he wrote in his journal account of the day. But a surprise lay in store for him: "The conversation went well & I came away cheered. I told them that the preacher should be a poet smit with love of the harmonies of moral nature: and yet look at the Unitarian Association & see if its aspect is poetic. They all smiled No." He also presumably spoke with them on the designated topic of theism. Although he nowhere recounts what was actually discussed, a journal entry made one week prior to the meeting communicates the current state of his thought on the subject. "I deny Personality to God because it is too little not too much," he wrote. "Life, personal life is faint & cold to the energy of God. For Reason & Love & Beauty, or, that which is all these, is the life of life, the reason of reason, the love of love."[16] In other words, on 1 April Emerson probably outlined for the students of the Divinity School the sum and substance of the address he would deliver in three and a half months. They seemed to like it, and he was reassured.

II

It was, as it turned out, a false reassurance. Emerson's remarks on the nature of true religion provoked widespread controversy and violent disagreement. In his biography of Emerson, John McAleer summarizes the content of the Divinity School Address in this way:

> In strictly theological terms, the basic message of the Divinity address was that man by responding intuitively, through Nature, to the moral sentiment expresses his divinity. Christ taught that "God incarnates himself in man." Christian leaders have failed their fellowman because they have neglected to explore "the Moral Nature . . . as the fountain of the established teaching in society." They have fossilized Christianity by putting too much emphasis on formal ritual. True faith is attained only when a man experiences a personal awareness of the Supreme Spirit dwelling within him. These arguments led Emerson to two controversial conclusions. Endowing all men with divinity and the capacity to attain to a knowledge of moral truth without the aid of a mediator relegated Christ to a human condition. Insisting on the self-sufficiency of the soul repudiated the authority of the church and, consequently, ecclesiasticism as well.[17]

Emerson's theology obviously challenged standard Unitarian doctrine and it was open to dispute if only for that reason. Yet this controversy was not theological only. At a time when their right to rule was increasingly at issue on a number of fronts, Boston's elite heard in the Divinity School Address an attack on the very foundations of society as they knew it. Emerson's address seemed to question not only Unitarianism but Christianity and religion itself, at least as they understood them. To mount such an attack on the foundations of morality promised nothing less than complete social anarchy, for it deprived any social order of its legitimacy.

Exactly whom the Divinity School Address offended and why has been a matter of some critical discussion. It was, as Emerson himself observed, a sermon "which, I am told, none but very young men can like." It "offended the Faculty a good deal," he observed, and although some of the students found much in it with which to disagree, their reaction seems not to have approached the outrage of their elders.[18] The message itself, as one critic has noted, was not entirely new: William Ellery Channing had been implying such things for a long time, even if he had never been quite so blatant as Emerson in doing so.[19] Why the storm of outrage now?

First, some critics argue, it was the quality of Emerson's language in the address that was shocking.[20] It was "untactful," "irresponsible," inappropriate, according to the criticism of Andrews Norton, the Dexter Professor of Sacred Literature at Harvard, prominent Unitarian apologist, and one of Emerson's teachers while the latter attended Harvard. The address relies on exaggerated rhetoric and subversions of Biblical texts to make its point. Natural imagery instead of scriptural text illustrates the new spiritual "doctrine" of natural organicism. Nevertheless, it is important to note that Emerson in fact had long been using the natural fact as spiritual evidence, even tending during his ministry to leave out the scriptural evidence for his doctrine entirely. The Divinity School Address takes his earlier logic a step further, for he purposely illustrates traditional "spiritual" argument with natural fact and discusses traditional "spiritual" topics as if they were natural occurrences. He does so in order to point up graphically the unity between the two: the natural fact is spiritual, the spiritual natural. True religion was the realization that the two were one and the same, he believed, and he desperately wanted to get across that message to the aspiring young ministers. They were in a position to do something about the situation, as were the Unitarian clergy who sat before him.

That Emerson self-consciously played upon an inversion of his listeners' expectations to make a point in his address is undoubtedly true. That he intended to create a furor, however, is open to question. As he wrote Henry Ware, Jr., he sincerely believed that the doctrine he had spoken at the Divinity School was "not very new."[21] Clearly, before the address he had feared that what he would have to say would shock an audience immured in formalism. "We shun to say that which shocks the religious ear of the people & to take away titles even of false honor from Jesus," a journal entry for 8 July says. But Emerson continued in the passage to reassure himself that the truth, rightly spoken, never alienated, for all men must recognize what their own souls speak:

> But this fear is an impotency to commend the moral sentiment. For if I can so imbibe that wisdom as to utter it well, instantly love & awe take place. The reverence for Jesus is only reverence for this, & if you can carry this home to any man's heart[,] instantly he feels that all is made good & that God sits once more on the throne. But when I have as clear a sense as now that I am speaking simple truth without any bias, any foreign interest in the matter,—all railing, all unwillingness to hear, all danger of injury to the conscience, dwindles & disappears. I refer to the discourse now growing under my eye to the Divinity School.[22]

Though Emerson desired to get his point across and was willing to use unconventional language to do so, his rhetoric was meant to bring to the attention of a complacent audience an eternal truth that all sincere men must come to recognize upon reflection. The shock of innovation was perhaps unavoidable, but it was something to be overcome, not to be reveled in.

Another explanation offered for the howls of outrage following the address was the nature of the occasion at which Emerson chose to deliver his good tidings. Because the address was the valediction of the senior class at the Divinity School, the argument goes, it appeared to have official Unitarian sanction. The proclamation of such questionable theology provoked heated reaction from the Unitarian clergy because they feared that both the faithful and those less sympathetic to the cause of Unitarians might mistake it for approved doctrine.[23] This argument too is persuasive. The *Christian Examiner* itself took the address to task on two grounds. First, Emerson's speech, which subverted or rejected outright accepted Unitarian theology on miracles, the role of Jesus in human redemption, and the nature of good and evil, was "neither good divinity nor good sense," only unintelligible gibberish. Even worse, however, it was delivered under the auspices of the Divinity School. Although the *Examiner* did not presume to dispute Emerson's right to say whatever he wanted, it did complain of the impropriety of saying it from a Unitarian platform, thereby implying that what he spoke was Unitarianism.[24] In fact Unitarians had had enough trouble with evangelicals in recent years to want to avoid any renewal of the claims that they were unchristian, unbiblical, or indifferent to morality. On the face of it, Emerson's address might have provided ammunition for any of those charges. Hence, the Unitarian protest against Emerson was taken up to some degree in self-defense.

Moreover, Emerson had chosen a delicate situation in which to preach his sermon of renewal. He had stood before the assembled archangels of Massachusetts Unitarianism and told them that their ministries had been failures. "What a cruel injustice it is to that Law, the joy of the whole earth, which alone can make thought dear and rich; that Law whose fatal sureness the astronomical orbits poorly emulate;—that it is travestied and depreciated, that it is behooted and behowled, and not a trait, not a word of it articulated," he had told them. The implication was that those who travestied and depreciated, the hooters and the howlers, the unfaithful shepherds, were none other than those seated before him. Even worse, the decrepit moral state of the community could be traced directly to the Unitarian failure. "For want of this culture the soul of the community is sick and faithless," he had said. Lest the point be missed, Emerson repeated it for them a second time. The age was suffering from "a decaying church and a wasting unbelief," a "loss of worship," which was the direct cause of the decay of "all things" that the age was experiencing.[25] Emerson was intent on making the point that infinite possibilities for reform were open to the minister dedicated to living a life of the spirit and not of forms; the message that the assembled clergymen heard was that Unitarianism had failed to maintain morality in the new urban world. Emerson wrote Henry Ware that he "could not but feel pain in saying some things in that place & presence where I supposed they might . . . meet dissent—and . . . the dissent, I may say, of dear friends & benefactors of mine." Nevertheless, he continued, he had enough respect for those to whom he spoke to believe that they would not take personal offense at what he said.[26] He was, after all, sincere in his search for truth, and Unitarians had never flinched in allowing the Reason of Man its full play. From the perspective of the Unitarian clergy, however, Emerson's charge sounded only too familiar. They had been hearing the same thing for years from evangelicals. They were not disposed to let the matter pass.

Emerson's remarks also followed hot on the heels of a celebrated trial for "infidelity" that explicitly linked heretical religious doctrines to radical calls for economic and political change. It is entirely probable that many perceived some connection to the celebrated case of Abner Kneeland.[27] Kneeland, a former Baptist and later Universalist minister, claimed for the artisans, laborers, and mechanics the right to defy established authorities in both religion and politics, for he asserted that the logic of their religion and law merely supported the interests of a parasitic monied elite in society and kept it in power. In 1829 he had founded the Society of Free Enquirers, an organization based on the rationalist principles of Thomas Paine and Fanny Wright; at its height in the mid-1830s, Kneeland's society counted over a thousand dues-paying members and over two thousand men, women, and children present at weekly social gatherings. Calling upon his audience to throw off the superstition of religion altogether, Kneeland parodied the religious practices of the evangelicals with rationalist hymns and free-thought "revival" initiation ceremonies. Even more dangerously, in the eyes of the mercantile elite, he called for political and economic reforms that promised to shake the foundations of capitalist Boston. His "Working Men's Measures" included among them the establishment of a simpler and less expensive legal system; abolishment of all chartered monopolies; the abolition of private banking, which gave power to individuals to create monetary panic; a reform of the economic system giving each man all his own earnings that "the public good can spare"; abolition of imprisonment for debt; abolition of the "great Factories" as "great nuisances like a bad house as destructive to the well being of society and at variance with our free and equal institutions"; a channeling of profits to workers, not to capitalists, with the learned professions to be supported only for doing direct and tangible good; and Congressional purchase of the assets of "the lords of the spinning jennies," with subsequent division into small factories sold to "real manufacturers who will work and carry them on with their own families."[28] In response to the concentration of economic power in the hands of capitalists, Kneeland's followers demanded recognition of their own interests.

Kneeland was tried four times for blasphemy between 1834 and 1838. His prosecutor in his first two trials, County Attorney Samuel D. Parker, pointedly argued the dangers of Kneeland's religious stance in classic syllogism: "true religion" was the foundation and guarantee of civil government, Kneeland denied true religion, therefore Kneeland undermined "those salutary principles, morals and manners, which are the safety and security of the public peace, and of individual happiness."²⁹ Litigation reached its culmination in the spring of 1838, as the Massachusetts Supreme Court convicted Kneeland of the offenses of which he had been accused. The Kneeland trial above all was a test of Unitarianism's ability to check the development of heterogeneity in religious and political sentiment— or at least to keep it within safe limits. Just three and a half months before Emerson delivered the Divinity School Address, then, the issue of the limits of permissible religious sentiment in a republic led to the public condemnation of one freethinker and an atmosphere in which challenges to the dominant religious order could be read as challenges to the social order as well.

Perhaps the Unitarian clergy would have allowed Emerson his say with less uproar had they not already been under siege. The evangelicals had attacked them, the students had attacked them, the freethinkers had attacked them, and the abolitionists too had attacked them for indifference to moral issues. Now even one of their own was attacking them. John Gorham Palfrey, minister of Boston's Brattle Street Church, was very hurt. One young Bostonian wrote to a friend that Palfrey seemed to think that the class had chosen Emerson as a calculated insult to its elders. The seniors must have known what would come of it, Palfrey believed.³⁰ "It seems clear that it will be the distinction of the new age[,] the refusal of authority," Emerson had presciently written in June 1838, and that was precisely what Emerson's assembled audience had been afraid of.³¹ With the Divinity School Address, Emerson became the symbol of the refusal of authority. He was, to Unitarians, the incarnation of the threats to their hegemony that had proliferated over the previous few years.

Indeed many seemed to fear, both at the time of the speech and for months after, that Emerson was out to create a sect of his own. "The vulgar think he would found a sect & would be installed & made much of," Emerson wrote of himself in August. In October he warned Carlyle to put off a planned visit to New England because the local reaction to the Divinity School Address had made Emerson seem a partisan or sectarian religionist. "You should never come before our people as one of a clique," he advised him. As late as 1840, he reported reaping the fruit of this untoward speculation while on a lecture visit to Providence: "You must know I am reckoned here as a Transcendentalist, and what the beast is, all persons in Providence have a great appetite to know: so I am carried duly about from house to house, and all the young people ask me, when the Lecture is coming upon the Great Subject? In vain I disclaim all knowledge of that sect of Lidian's,—it is still expected that I shall break out with the New Light in the next discourse." The people expected in him a new Beecher. But Emerson vehemently denied that he had intended any new sectarian activity, any new Great Awakening. In a letter to his old friend and colleague, Henry Ware, Jr., he tried to put the latter at ease. "There was no scholar less willing or less able to be a polemic," he claimed. It disturbed him to see himself "suddenly raised into the importance of a heretic," as if he were expounding a doctrinal thesis he expected to defend rigorously. He realized, he told Ware, that his own perspective was somewhat alienated from the current "institutions & mind of society," yet he still retained the confidence and hope that his "better brothers who work with the sympathy of society & love it" might "unexpectedly confirm my perceptions, & find my nonsense is only their own thought in motley." Emerson continued to maintain throughout the storm that followed that he had spoken the truth as he had seen it, with "not the smallest personal or *partial* interest," as some of his critics had accused. He had no interest in or intention of reviving old sectarian antagonism.[32]

Henry Ware, Jr., replied to the Divinity School Address, in his sermon "On the Personality of the Deity," delivered in Cambridge in the fall of 1838. This sermon gives us an extended reading of what even the most liberal Unitarians found problematic in Emerson's address. Ware objected most overtly to Emerson's failure to account God a person. It was good, said Ware, to conform oneself to the wise and holy order of the universe; it was entirely appropriate that one try to discover therein the principles of righteousness. Nevertheless, none of these was God, as Emerson seemed to imply, for God was a person, not an abstraction. Ware clearly intended by his sermon to correct pernicious theology. Keeping in mind, however, that the way in which a people describes its God usually has a direct connection with the way in which they live their lives, we need to look beneath the surface of Ware's remarks to see what kind of social ideology was embedded in the theological disquisition. Of all the misappropriations of traditional Unitarian doctrine that Emerson made in the address—and there are several—why was his denial of personality to the Deity so offensive to Ware?

Ware hints at the answer in a mollifying letter to Emerson that accompanied a copy of the sermon. Ware's own address was not specifically directed at Emerson, he wrote to his former junior colleague, and Emerson must not take it that way:

It is a long time since I have been earnestly persuaded that men are suffering from want of sufficiently realizing the fact of the Divine Person. I used to perceive it, as I thought, when I was a minister in Boston, in talking with my people, and to refer to this cause much of the lifelessness of the religious character. I have seen evils from the same cause among young men, since I have been where I am [as Professor of Pastoral Theology and Pulpit Eloquence at the Harvard Divinity School], and have been prompted to think much of the question how they should be removed.[33]

In other words, Emerson was not alone in ignoring the personality of the Deity. Many, especially the rebellious young, were doing so, and it was their falling off that had resulted in the decline of religious character within the community.

What had neglect of the personal character of the Deity to do with the decline of moral sentiment? Ware's answer in his sermon provides an interesting commentary on the way in which Unitarians conceived of their social order. Both an abstract law of ethics and a personal God could require obedience to the dictates of virtue, Ware told his listeners. But which command was more likely to be obeyed, the abstract rule demanding conformity to virtue, or the statute of "a rightful Lawgiver"? Why the latter, of course, for "happiness [was] not the result merely of obedience to a command, but of affectionate subjection to a Parent." All true authority was personal authority. Let us put the matter in another light, Ware continued: What was the difference between a child who lived with his mother and one who lived in an institution? Both were provided for and governed, but one felt love and the other felt restraint. Now which, Ware asked his listeners, was more likely to obey? Surely not the child who lived in an impersonal environment.[34] The conclusion that Ware extrapolated from his thoughts on the personality of the Deity was that order and morality in the universe, as in the ideal Unitarian social order itself, had to be maintained by the personal government of a loving Father who ruled his family by the strength of his personality. Both religion and society properly conceived were, therefore, personal and paternalistic.

Now here had come Emerson, denying such divine paternalism, and by implication, the precarious social paternalism of Unitarian hegemony as well. And he was not alone, as Ware had observed in his letter to Emerson; there were many others who, because of the failure of Unitarian paternalism, could no longer conceive of ethics, morality, or the social order in paternalistic terms. Order could no longer be maintained by decree. What ruled the universe, according to these would-be innovators, was an abstract relationship that transcended all persons. God was more than a person, and by analogy, the social order more than the domain of an established hierarchy of persons. Religion, society, even nature itself existed not by virtue of the decree of a Great Clockmaker, but as a set of sacred relations that contained the reason for its own being. Persons, facts, and events were bound up into one inseparable whole, a unity of process, an abstract law that applied to all without distinction of personality or condition. Such a society did not need an external, personal God, for the God who was law transcended all persons.

On this issue, then, Emerson found himself for the first time explicitly aligned with the party of innovation, as he would later call it, against the entrenched conservative elite of Massachusetts. Henry Ware had put the matter succinctly: either one believed in a universe run on the basis of personality or one did not. The Unitarian hierarchy clearly did. They believed that to deny the force of personality was in religion atheism, in society anarchy. Emerson, on the other hand, had come to precisely the opposite conclusion: it was an overemphasis on the differences between persons—a factionalism based on personality—that had undermined the unity of spirit that was true religion. Therefore, the community was in moral disarray. The anthropomorphization of God as a personal lawgiver, to be obeyed because he commanded obedience and for no other reason, had produced formal and meaningless ritual and dogma. Religion was respected by his contemporaries not because it was conducive to creating religious sentiments, but because an inscrutable tyrant had commanded it. In society and government, such emphasis on personality had led to the glorification of demagogues instead of respect for true virtue, pursuit of private ends instead of dedication to a common good. Emerson believed that the personalism

Ware preached had cast his contemporaries into division, isolation, and fear. Was this the love of a parent of that Ware described?

In fact, despite Emerson's own mild protestations that what he was saying ought not to be terribly controversial, his critics were right in suspecting that the address posed a dangerous threat to established authority. For like Kneeland, Emerson provided (albeit more obliquely) a powerful though implicit critique of the social order in his criticism of its religious ideology. The Divinity School Address pointed to a religious system that the speaker believed left out the sacred. In addressing the problem, Emerson clearly expected to provide a substitute conception of sacred experience that would mend the "cracks in the social edifice" by addressing the problem at what he believed to be its most fundamental level. What perhaps was less clear to Emerson at the time of the address was the extent to which his new conception of the sacred implied an entirely new attitude toward all social structures. The Divinity School Address represents a claim via symbolic language that not only a new religious understanding but an entirely new conception of social reality had become necessary.

Not only "corpse cold" Unitarianism, but all the concrete religious expressions of Emerson's culture seemed to him to have been failing in some measure to explain people's experience in a coherent and emotionally energizing way, although the growth in evangelical belief during the period suggests that some alternatives did so for some people more successfully than did Unitarianism.[35] Nevertheless, for many individuals who saw neither a viable resolution of conflict, nor emotional commitment, nor social cohesion, nor personal integration in religious experience, the relation of religious failure to social failure must have seemed manifest. In the Divinity School Address Emerson reiterated in much stronger and clearer terms the argument he had first made in his "Lord's Supper" sermon six years earlier: that religious symbols and rituals had become so objectified as to stand in the way of commanding commitment, and a lack of emotional commitment to the sacred had led directly to a lack of social cohesion. In significant ways, Emerson responded directly here to conflicting, sometimes violent, contests over whose vision of society—the image and likeness of whose God—ought to rule.

The mechanisms by which the address approached the problem are familiar enough. Emerson began with a metaphor based in nature rather than in the theological symbol systems that embodied the sense of the sacred in his Christian culture. In so doing, he suggested a way to resolve conflicting claims: to find and to respond to the laws of Nature imprinted in all persons, he believed, allowed them to overcome in a very real way differences in expression of the sacred, which were merely symbolic. To recognize different theological arguments as symbolic representations of the unnamable ("tropes," he called them in the address), would allow all persons to move to a higher ground where they might recognize commonalities despite the different names they gave the experience of the sacred as a result of their differing cultural circumstances.

The subtext of the address throughout concerned the metaphorical nature of language, especially religious language. Both Charles Feidelson and Philip Gura have made the claim that Emerson's age—and in particular Emerson himself—were responsible for the emergence of a literature of symbolism in the United States. Feidelson sees Emerson as modifying schemes of typological interpretation handed down from his Puritan forebears; Gura claims that Emerson drew on a heritage of Continental scriptural exegesis.[36] Given the traditions out of which they write, their insights are useful ones. But to explore the issue a bit further, we might ask why this symbolic usage of language in both literature and religion emerged in *this* time and *this* place. Part of the answer may be that in a culture in which competing versions of reality mean that common names, taken literally, will inevitably produce contention, the only possible common ground for "transcending" conflict is to see all experience—even the most fundamental conception of experience that is religion—as something unnamable, ineffable, and self-consciously experienced in common only as symbol. ("These laws," says Emerson, "refuse to be adequately stated."[37]) In order to reconcile a multiplicity of conflicting points of view, we see them paradoxically as different metaphorical representations of the same experience, unless they have become empty metaphors, representing no experience at all.[38]

The world (and human experience, which for Emerson was practically the same thing) is one, not many, Emerson claimed, appearances to the contrary. Although he recognized conflicts in the interpretation of experience, he went on to deny both conflict and diversity in an ideal realm. In effect, he constructed a sacred order in which all conflict disappeared if one only attended to the experiential (or symbolic) rather than the objectified (or literal) aspect of the sacred. In social terms the metaphor also implicitly made the claim that all human conflict resulted from a literalist insistence that experience be described in the same terms. If individuals accepted the fundamental similarity of human experience as a given, they would be able to perceive truly that all conflict is epiphenomenal and thereby resolve it. If difficulties continued to persist, it was because all individuals had not yet found their way to this "higher ground." To transcend the different ways of naming with a transcendent theory of language, Emerson believed, was to resolve difficulties more apparent than real. Emerson trusted that conflict sprang not from real differences in power or experience, but rather from different ways of naming experience—that is, divergence in intellectual traditions.

As denominational pluralism transformed religion in New England into a commodity to be selected by different consumer markets, the sacred increasingly became a private matter, a way to survive the indignities of culture rather than to sustain or transform it.[39] In the Divinity School Address Emerson asked his listeners to remove the sacred from the province of those institutions whose role in a marketplace economy was not to harmonize the whole but to compete for individual souls by representing conflicting claims and views of reality. As he put the sacred in a realm available to individuals only apart from the institutions of the market economy, Emerson actively encouraged individuals to circumvent the narrowing and distortion of experience that institutions within this new order, churches among them, inevitably produced. Individuals would regain the power to speak of their own experiences as they reappropriated the power to interpret symbols from institutions who claimed them only for their own self-perpetuation.

The Divinity School Address implied a strong indictment of social relations within the new commercial culture, suggesting that *all* institutional representations of human experience in the new social order were apt to alienate persons from themselves. No wonder, then, that Emerson's critique of the situation of his contemporaries using the language of religious experience seemed so disturbing to those representing the authority of official Unitarianism. Yet despite the incipient radicalism of his message, Emerson personally seems to have generated little fear among Unitarians—or at least, he threatened Ware little. Ware said as much in what seems to be an oblique reference to Emerson at the end of "The Personality of the Deity": "To the pure all things are pure; and some men will dwell for ever in the midst of abstraction and falsehood without being injuriously affected. Express infidelity is not vice, and may exist together with great integrity and purity of life. Atheism is not immorality, and may consist with an unblemished character." There was more to think about than Emerson alone, however. More frightening was the use to which his anarchistic, antipaternalist theology might be put. Ware put the problem this way:

> But, however it may be with individuals, living in the midst of a believing and worshipping community, it is not to be doubted that a community, unbelieving and godless, would rush to evil unmitigated and hopeless. A philosopher here and there, by his science and skill, might perhaps live without the sun; but strike it out from the path of all men, and despair and death ensue.
>
> On this subject, then, we are first to look for the truth, and then at the consequences of denying it.[40]

Ware was right to have misgivings. Not even Emerson could foresee the extent to which his attack on formalism in religion would become a rallying cry for revolts against all forms of authority. The preacher who had wished to work to overcome division in society ironically became an overnight symbol of its polarization.

III

The response to the Divinity School Address knocked Emerson off balance. He had expected some disagreement with his point of view but nothing like the vitriol that poured out. Fall 1838 was time spent coming to terms with what the reaction to the address meant. In mid-August 1838, he still bravely clung to his belief that the true scholar would convince men immediately of the truth of his position. "He would utter opinions upon all passing affairs which being seen to be not private but eternal, would sink like darts into the ear of men & put men in fear," he wrote before the address was printed and reviewed. However, journal entries made as the fall progressed show a gradual decline in that faith. Here is the journal entry for 31 August: "Steady, steady. I am convinced that if a man will be a true scholar, he shall have perfect freedom. The young people & the mature hint at odium, & aversion of faces to be presently encountered in society. I say no: I fear it not. No scholar need fear it. For if it be true that he is merely an observer, a dispassionate reporter, no partisan, a singer merely for the love of music, his is a position of perfect immunity: to him no disgusts can attach; he is invulnerable." Those who attacked him were "men of no knowledge, & therefore no stability," their opinions "not worth dispersing." They were in the minority, Emerson steadfastly asserted, and their opposition would dissipate.[41]

He was wrong. The chorus of opposition grew. Emerson pretended to be indifferent to it, but clearly he was not. When even his friend George Bradford stopped by to tell him that "his intellect approves the doctrine of the Cambridge address, but his affections do not," he admitted to having been drawn "out of equilibrium" by "poor personal considerations." He began to speak of the value of revolutions and the "licence" that necessarily "attends reformation." Apparently, the displeasure of the educated elite had spread to the evangelical middle and lower classes, for several entries of the third week in September suggest that Emerson was suffering the brunt of popular displeasure as well: "It is easy enough for a firm man who knows the world to brook the rage of the cultivated classes. . . . But when to their feminine rage the indignation of the people is added, when the ignorant & the poor are aroused, when the unintelligent brute force that lies at the bottom of society is made to growl & mow, then it needs more than nerve, it needs the heights of magnanimity & religion to treat it godlike as a trifle of no concernment." Or again Emerson spoke of the "sour faces of the multitude," which rob one of sympathy and bring hatred along with them: "The state is so new & strange & unpleasing that a man will, maugre all his resolutions, lose his sweetness & his flesh, he will pine & fret." Finally he lambasted society for its refusal to respond to the scholar-hero in the proper fashion. "Society seem to have lost all remembrance of the irresponsibility of a writer on human and divine nature," he asserted defensively. "They forget that he is only a reporter, & not at all accountable for the fact he reports."[42]

By October the first sting of criticism had passed, and Emerson was able to admit to himself just how much pain the furor over the address had caused him. "I am sensitive as a leaf to impressions from abroad," he finally confessed. Although he had begun to forget the "threatening paragraphs & odious nicknames" that had "sable[d] his whole thoughts until bedtime" one night, the experience left him profoundly disillusioned. His trust in the power of sympathy to communicate the truths of human nature, for example, suffered a mortal blow. It would not be possible to bring the age back to the paths of virtue without creating dissension and strife. To a man whose life had been dedicated to counteracting the tendencies of his age to dissension and strife, the thought was disturbing, to say the least. Moreover, he confessed himself "not sure that the educated class ever ascend to the idea of virtue; or that they desire truth." They preferred merely to defend their own interests. Writing angrily, consciously in rebellion now, he threatened that he had "a great deal more to say that will shock you out of all patience." Emerson abruptly came to doubt the whole concept of vocation that he had been developing over the previous four years. The scholar could not speak his private thought to society without generating conflict. Some were not going to listen, others would intentionally misunderstand. The result in Emerson's mind was confusion. "When this fog of good & evil Affections falls," he mourned, "it is hard to see & walk straight."[43]

Emerson's confusion and subsequent bitterness emerge clearly in the famous parable of his Divinity School experience, "Uriel." Again, as in the address, he turns the expectations of the reader upside down. His allusion to Uriel, Milton's bright angel of the sun in *Paradise Lost*, leads the reader to expect a retelling of the story of the expulsion of the evil angels from heaven. Indeed, "Uriel" does describe a fall from grace, but in this topsy-turvy nineteenth-century paradise, it is the good angel who is expelled, the devils who remain in possession of the field. In "the lapse of Uriel,/Which in Paradise befell," Emerson reflected on the meaning of his own forcible expulsion from the ranks of the reigning social order, his own fall from society's graces into the sad knowledge of conflict and isolation. The poem is notable not only for what its narrative tells us about the way Emerson understood that July day in Cambridge, but also for what its tone conveys about the changes in his attitude toward society as a whole. It is important enough to quote here in its entirety.[44]

It fell in the ancient period
  Which the brooding soul surveys,
Or ever the wild Time coined itself
  Into calendar months and days.

This was the lapse of Uriel,
Which in Paradise befell.
Once, among the Pleiads walking,
Seyd overheard the young gods talking
And the treason, too long pent,
To his ears was evident.
The young deities discussed
Laws of form, and metre just,
Orb, quintessence, and sunbeams,
What subsisteth, and what seems.
One, with low tones that decide,
And doubt and reverend use defied,
With a look that solved the sphere,
And stirred the devils everywhere,

Gave his sentiment divine
Against the being of a line.
'Line in nature is not found;
Unit and universe are round;
In vain produced, all rays return;
Evil will bless, and ice will burn.'
As Uriel spoke with piercing eye,
A shudder ran around the sky;
The stern old war-gods shook their heads,
The seraphs frowned from myrtle-beds;
Seemed to the holy festival
The rash word boded ill to all;
The balance-beam of Fate was bent
The bounds of good and ill were rent;
Strong Hades could not keep his own,
But all slid to confusion.

A sad self-knowledge, withering, fell
On the beauty of Uriel
In heaven once eminent, the god
Withdrew, that hour, into his cloud;

Whether doomed to long gyration
In the sea of generation,
Or by knowledge grown too bright
To hit the nerve of feebler sight.
Straightway, a forgetting wind
Stole over the celestial kind,
And their lips the secret kept,
If in ashes the fire-seed slept.
But now and then, truth-speaking things
Shamed the angels' veiling wings;
And, shrilling from the solar course,
Or from fruit of chemic force,
Procession of a soul in matter,
Or the speeding change of water,
Or out of the good of evil born,
Came Uriel's voice of cherub scorn,
And a blush tinged the upper sky,
And the gods shook, they knew not why.

The first stanza, though brief, provides a frame for Emerson's poetic narrative. What will be described is an epic struggle, worthy to take its place with that other epic struggle of fall from grace, Milton's *Paradise Lost*. Though the poem grows out of a specific situation, what Emerson has learned from the situation has been profound enough to merit transmutation into the realm of eternal truth. Emerson signaled here that the Divinity School outcry was no isolated phenomenon, but a new and terrible revelation of the paradigmatic relationship between the seer and his age. Here was how society could be expected to react to the scholar-hero. There was to be no more assuming an automatic sympathy of perspective between the representative man and his contemporaries. This tale of "ancient periods" testifies to Emerson's sad discovery of the inescapability of conflict, even for the representative man.

The middle of the three stanzas describes allegorically the incident of the Fall itself. All the angels, including Uriel, were walking together in a Paradise of innocence. For Uriel, this Paradise consisted in the naive belief that all angels would be willing to listen when the truth was spoken. When Uriel repeated "his sentiment divine," he expected to strike a sympathetic chord in the hearts of his listeners. He resolved the argument of the "young deities" (or divines) in this spirit. Far from dismissing their discussions as trivial and unimportant, Uriel participated in them—in fact, answered them line for line. He furnished the "young gods" with the laws of form they sought ("Line in nature is not found"), as well as laws of orb ("Unit and universe are round"), quintessence, and sunbeams ("In vain produced, all rays return"). In response to their quest for a distinction between "What subsisteth, and what seems," he offered a concrete example of the law of compensation, which erases the distinction between the two ("Evil will bless, and ice will burn"). His willingness to defy "doubt and reverend use" "solved the sphere," giving the "young gods" the answers they sought. But it also "stirred the devils everywhere"—the older clerics who inhabited this Paradise, the fallen angels. And ironically enough, those in this world turned upside down evicted the good angel from heaven. In a perverted age, Emerson implies, what else can one expect? The representative man, who ought to rule, will himself be sent into exile.

Although Uriel spoke "with piercing eye"—the same inward eye that in *Nature* resolved the universe into abstract spiritual law—he was rejected by "stern old war-gods." Presumably these gods had been fighting similar theological battles in the name of a tyrant God for quite some time. They concerned themselves with victory in the battle, not with truth. When word of Uriel's "treason" reached them, they shuddered that "the rash word boded ill to all"; it seemed to them

> The bounds of good and ill were rent;
> Strong Hades could not keep his own,
> But all slid to confusion.

Here is Emerson's version of Henry Ware's argument on the personality of the Deity. Uriel's philosophy would subvert moral order; it would exacerbate the confusion of an age already gone crazy. It would release anarchy upon the community.

The final stanza, with its dominant notes of pain and self-doubt tempered by an undercurrent of righteous anger, captures the violent effect of the whole experience on Emerson. Suddenly aware of his own naiveté, a withering "sad self-knowledge" fell on Uriel. He had lost his faith both in the possibilities of society and in his power to move it. "Once eminent" in heaven, the defeated god "Withdrew, that hour, into his cloud," still not sure what had happened to him or what he was to do about it.

> Whether doomed to long gyration
> In the sea of generation,
> Or by knowledge grown too bright
> To hit the nerve of feebler sight,

he knew not. Emerson ends "Uriel" by reaffirming his faith that the message he has tried to bring to his contemporaries will one day be communicated to them, though he does not know where or how. He relies on Nature—whose messenger, after all, Uriel had been—to deliver his own message. Eternal truth will out despite the age's determination to suppress it. "Uriel's voice of cherub scorn" will speak again through some more impersonal means.

But what of Uriel himself? The end of the poem furnishes us no clue. His persona fades out of the poem entirely as he withdraws into his cloud, making his presence felt only through the universe whose spokesman he was. In the wake of the Divinity School Address, Emerson too felt inclined to withdraw entirely into the asylum of Concord. Never thick-skinned enough to endure criticism without self-doubt, he had been wounded deeply when his contemporaries impugned his good intentions.[45] It was deeply ironic that an individual so consumed by the desire to reconcile conflict should find himself irretrievably at the center of the conflict of his age. That one who had so concerned himself with restoring religious and humane qualities to his age should be attacked as a heretic and an atheist was doubly ironic. The irony was not lost on Emerson. "It is plain from all the noise that there is Atheism somewhere," he wrote bitterly. "The only question is now, which is the Atheist?"[46] To his aunt, Mary Moody Emerson, he rehearsed his doubts about his ability to bring about the ideal that he had envisioned: "Is the ideal society always to be only a dream, a song, a luxury of thought & never a step taken to realise the vision for living & indigent men without misgiving within & wildest ridicule abroad? Between poetry & prose must the great gulf yawn ever and they who try to bridge it over be lunatics or hypocrites?" Recalling the great reformers of the past, however, Emerson found in their stories not only a pattern of persecution, but also inspiration to continue in his vocation:

And yet the too dark ground of history is starred over with solitary heroes who dared to believe better of their brothers, & who prevailed by actually executing the Law (the high ideal) in their own life, & though a hissing & an offence to their cotemporaries yet they became a celestial sign to all succeeding souls as they journeyed through nature.... And now, in our turn, shall we esteem the elegant decorum of our world, & what is called greatness & splendor in it, of such a vast & outweighing worth, as to reckon all aspirations after the Better, fanciful or pitiable; & all aspirants pert & loathsome? There is a limit, and, (as in some hours, we fancy,) a pretty speedy limit to the value of what is called success in life.[47]

Though Emerson continued to pursue the calling he had chosen for himself during his fourth decade, the Divinity School controversy left its mark. Society in its current form seemed all the more corrupt—so bad, in fact, that any reform, however ill-conceived, was better than none. Emerson began to lean more and more, as his letter to his aunt indicates, to the notion that speech by itself would be unconvincing; it was the evidence of example that the age needed. He had to reexamine his own role as social reformer. "And I am to seek to solve for my fellows the problem of human Life, in words," he also mused in preparation for his winter 1838 lecture series on "Human Life." "Well, boy, what canst thou say?" What indeed? The response to the Divinity School Address had left him with doubts about how much he really knew about life. Was not the best course under the circumstances to retire to Concord to find out exactly how a man ought to live? "It seems as if the present age of words should naturally be followed by an age of silence when men shall speak only through facts & so to regain their health," he observed by September 1839. It was a time to take in sail, to withdraw to the New England countryside, to await a new definition of community, a new sense of the relationship between self and society. Though he continued to lecture as before, Emerson withdrew his energies from Boston and the public sphere there for a time. Whatever reform he could accomplish would be done in the private, sheltered atmosphere of Concord.[48]

In a significant gesture, Emerson went in mid-September 1838 "at sundown to the top of Dr. Ripley's hill & renewed [his] vows to the

Genius of that place." He read as "the dictate of the hour" a command "to forget all I have mislearned; to cease from man, & to cast myself again into the vast mould of nature."[49] He would withdraw himself from society as an intractable, uncomprehending entity and embosom himself in nature and what "natural" society Concord could afford. Uriel's successor appears in the poet of "Woodnotes I," published by Emerson in the *Dial* for 1840. This "Caesar of his leafy Rome" is at home only in the woods. His forest exile is not completely voluntary; Emerson indicates as much by the opening lines of the poem, lines that he later excised when the work was printed in the 1847 *Poems*:

> For this present hard
> Is the fortune of the bard
>   Born out of time;
> All his accomplishment
> From Nature's utmost treasure spent
>   Booteth not him.

The sense of an intense (and seemingly unsought) isolation—even abandonment—comes through even more poignantly in twelve more lines deleted from the revised poem:

> With none has he to do,
> And none seek him,
> Nor men below,
> Nor spirits dim.
> Sure some god his eye enchants:—
> What he knows nobody wants:
> In the world he travels glad
> Without better fortune had,
> Melancholy without bad.
> Planter of celestial plants,
> What he knows nobody wants;
> What he knows he hides, not vaunts.[50]

Emerson's aesthetic reasons for excising these lines from the poem's final version probably were sound: they contribute little to the overall moral lesson taught by the woods in the remainder of "Woodnotes I." Nevertheless, the change was made for more than the sake of aesthetics. As in his transformation of journal entries to sermons, lectures, and essays, Emerson obscures the particular "I" whose experience results in the moral wisdom gleaned. Though his attempt to objectify subjective feelings in the poem ultimately makes the experience seem a beneficial one, the first version indicates clearly that the solitude of Concord was not viewed by Emerson, at least not at first, as an unmixed blessing.

"Nature is the beautiful asylum to which we look in all the years of striving & conflict as the assured resource when we shall be driven out of society by ennui or chagrin or persecution or defect of character," he believed, so to nature he betook himself. There he would occupy himself asking new sorts of questions. For the next few years, he would turn his attention inward, to "things nearer, homelier" that might provide him with new ideas about how to overcome division. Not yet resigning himself to the status of an isolate, he would seek in the private sphere a substitute community for the public world that had failed him. It was time to turn to family and friends—"things wherein passion enters & hope & fear, [which] have not yet become too dangerous[,] too insipid for me to handle." Now, after the disillusionment of the Divinity School scandal, "how to spend a day nobly" was "the problem to be solved."[51]

CHAPTER 8

Concord
Experiments

Is this one of us, or is he a stranger?
is the enumeration of the ungener-
ous; but to those by whom liberality
is practiced, the whole world is but
as one family.—"Veeshnoo Sarma,"
July 1842

THE DIVINITY SCHOOL ADDRESS made Emerson a controversial figure. In its wake, he received few invitations to lecture, at least for a while, and for the first time he found himself on the fringes of public life by something other than his own choice. This experience left him less optimistic about his ability to make an impact on institutions and more skeptical about organized reform efforts. He began to speculate that "what was private and genuine" in relationships among a few people was "more real & so more public & universal than conventions for debate, and these weary speculations on reform." In an 1839 letter to Margaret Fuller, he summed up his current sense of the moral dilemma of his generation: "I see movement, I hear aspirations, but I see not how the great God prepares to satisfy the heart in a new order of things. . . . No church[,] no state will form itself to the eye of desire & hope. Even when we have extricated ourselves from all the embarrassments of the social problem it does not please the oracle to emit any light on the *mode* of individual life. A thousand negatives it utters clear & strong on all sides, but the sacred affirmative it hides in the deepest abyss."[1] For Emerson as it would be for Thoreau, the problem of the age was how to spend the day deliberately. He saw the institutional reforms of the day making little difference, and found it easier to identify those things that ought not be done than those that would lead to a rich and moral life.

In response to his alienation from the public life of Boston in the late 1830s and early 1840s, Emerson set out to see what fruits domestic life might yield. He hoped in Concord to find the privacy that he believed would enable him to live without encumbrance. By choosing as home a town that seemed free of the constraints of Boston, he expected to enjoy a natural community of family and friends who might share his vision. It was to the private sphere, not the public, that he now looked as the locus of the most significant moral reform of the age. And it was with like-minded family and friends that he now was determined to live out his philosophy of the unity of all in harmony with Nature. It would not be as easy as he hoped.

I

Emerson grappled with the most intimate challenge to his philosophy of the natural sympathy of sincere and principled souls in his second marriage. In September 1829, Emerson had wed his first wife, Ellen Tucker of Concord, New Hampshire.

Now am I stricken with the sympathy
That binds the whole world in electric tie,

he wrote after meeting Ellen in 1827. Marriage, he had felt, provided him a concrete spur to virtue in the person of Ellen. Indeed, his beliefs about the nature of matrimony echoed the old Puritan doctrine that spouses were joined together by God to encourage each other to spiritual growth and moral action. As husband and wife, he and Ellen were to be "yoked together by Heaven to provoke each other to good works so long as we lived." When Ellen died of tuberculosis in 1831, her loss was "a universal loss" to her husband. He had not only lost his life's companion; he had also been robbed of the beacon of "her beautiful character."[2]

Ellen did not live long enough for her relationship with Waldo Emerson to have assumed the overtones of domesticity that came with home and family. Tubercular at the time of her marriage, she remained an invalid until her death in 1831. She seemed to her husband an ethereal and saintly presence. His relationship to Lydia Jackson Emerson of Plymouth, whom he married in 1835, was a different matter altogether. As the realities of bourgeois domestic life quickly made themselves felt, marriage and family became pragmatic as well as ideal relations to Emerson. His life with Lidian was marked by a greater divergence of gender roles and a greater sense of ambivalence about the good that domestic life was capable of producing than his marriage to Ellen had been. The result was a relationship between spouses at once sustaining and beset by emotional tensions.

Lidian played the role Virginia Woolf has called "the angel of the house," although she considered herself such neither by choice nor temperament. Her role in the marriage reflected the influence of an ideology of domesticity that had begun to dominate middle-class life. As the work of production moved from the household to other sites of labor, a growing class of merchants, shopkeepers, entrepreneurs, and professionals came to define women's role as wholly peculiar to the family. Her responsibility was the private sphere and the affective welfare of those who did the work of production. If the circumstances of the public sphere forced men to give themselves over to passion, duplicity, and strategem, then women, freed of the necessity of negotiating life in a heartless world, could remain a sign to others of passionlessness, sincerity, and virtue. Because she lived apart from the pretense and artifice of the commercial world, woman could nurture in the home the virtuous tendencies and human sympathies of others. Her domestic influence provided the antidote to the unnatural world of public intercourse.[3]

Emerson believed, at least in theory, in the androgeny of the human soul. The unity of all persons in Nature meant that men had a feminine aspect, women a masculine one. On the basis of that belief, one might expect that he would have rejected the division of the world into separate spheres and the relegation of women to a domestic role. Moreover, he himself had criticized the public sphere as corrupt and destructive of virtuous individual impulses. His own philosophy supposed that men as well as women ought to oppose its tendencies in their beliefs and actions, and his own partial removal from the public sphere was testimony to his beliefs. Nevertheless, his attitudes toward marriage in practice, if not in theory, increasingly came to reflect the effects of the ideology of domesticity.[4]

Though Emerson's philosophy recognized the spiritual equality of women and men and looked to both to renovate the world, he readily admitted that in the present order of things women were particularly hard pressed to follow out their individual inclinations. At one point comparing their lot to that of slaves, Emerson noted in 1838, "Life is a pretty tragedy especially for women." As he thought particularly about "the fine women . . . who have had genius & cultivation who have not been wives but muses," he observed "something tragic in their lot" for which he found no ready explanation. Women frequently failed to fulfill their early promise of independence of mind and originality of thought. Emerson seemed to have no idea why this might be so, and thought force of will alone enough to overcome it.[5]

While women and men might share an essential unity in the realm of spirit, one might expect them to differ in their phenomenal aspects. Emerson seems to have believed that women are more emotional, more sensitive, closer to nature. Woman's "oracular nature" meant that what man expended great effort to discover, woman knew instinctively. Their natural qualities perfectly fitted women for home and family. Rather than challenging the expectation that women were by nature domestic creatures, Emerson instead implied that the best women sought to discover their true selves in the context of the home. "Woman should not be expected to write, or fight, or build, or compose scores," he wrote in 1841; "she does all by inspiring man to do all." Though women too were to be members of "a Congress of Sovereigns," Emerson seems not to have believed it necessary for them to leave the private domain in order to do so. For him, different individuals found a common identity when seen under their spiritual aspect; between the whole and the individual parts he saw no intermediating classes or groups that might make a difference in one's relationship to the whole. Thus, he could not go beyond urging individual determination and tenacity as a counterweight to women's tendency not to achieve spiritual self-reliance.[6]

In his marriages, Emerson looked above all for a common spiritual identification between spouses. With the philosophical and witty Lydia Jackson, he had expected to find "a community of sentiment & speculation" unlikely elsewhere. "This lady is a person of noble character whom to see is to respect," he wrote his brother William in February 1835; "in Plymouth she is dearly prized for her love and good works." Lidian in her turn was attracted to Emerson's spiritual qualities and showed a marked deference to him throughout their forty-seven years of marriage, refusing even to call him by his first name. Each agreed to postpone "what might seem even reasonable personal expectations" in "regard for truth & the universal love." Here was a marriage, they both believed, based on principle rather than on mere circumstance, expediency, or private passion. For Emerson, his wife was on occasion his "sibyl" and "dear friend." In fact, her aphorisms frequently found their way into Emerson's journals, lectures, and essays. Nevertheless, the harmony of sentiment they looked for in their relation became precarious as their roles, paths, and experiences diverged.[7]

Immediately upon their wedding, Lidian moved away from family and friends in Plymouth, quite against her inclination, to set up housekeeping in Concord at her husband's insistence. A son, Waldo, was born in 1836; two daughters, Ellen and Edith, followed in 1839 and 1841. A second son, Edward, arrived in 1844. Emerson's journals between 1836 and 1838 reveal vague undercurrents of dissatisfaction despite his affection for his wife and son. Between husband and wife Emerson noted a gap that seemed to grow with time. "People think that husbands & wives have no *present time*[,] that they have already established their mutual connexion, have nothing to learn of one another, & know beforehand each what the other will do," he wrote eight weeks after his marriage. The wise man could discern, however, that husband and wife were "chance-joined, little acquainted, & do observe each the other's carriage to the stranger as curiously as he doth." Almost a year later, he repeated the same sentiments. "If you go into a family where you supposed a perfect understanding & intimate bonds subsisted," he wrote, "you find with surprise that all are in a degree strangers to each other." By 1837, Emerson reflected ominously on the waning of the "community of sentiment" whose presence he had noted a few years earlier: "The lover on being accepted, misses the wildest charm of the maid he dared not hope to call his own. The husband loses the wife in the cares of the household. Later, he cannot rejoice with her in the babe for by becoming a mother she ceases yet more to be a wife. With the growth of children the relation of the pair becomes yet feebler from the demands children make, until at last nothing remains of the original passion out of which all these parricidal fruits proceeded."[8]

Both Lidian Jackson Emerson's letters and her daughter Ellen's biography of her mother reveal the extent to which the expectations of domesticity left her too feeling somewhat constricted and frustrated.[9] Lidian's letters are replete with the domestic challenges and frustrations inherent in the life of a wife with the responsibility for running a household, entertaining her husband's sometimes eccentric guests, giving birth to and raising four children, and keeping the family together during his periodic absences from Concord to lecture. Her situation was even more ironic in light of her reluctance to assume a domestic role in the first place. Well known in Plymouth as an engaging conversationalist and a deeply religious woman, Lydia married Emerson at the age of thirty-three with virtually no experience in running a household, and no great desire to learn. To Emerson's proposal of marriage she responded with a good deal of ambivalence, according to her daughter Ellen: "She shut her eyes while she told him that she foresaw that with her long life wholly aside from housekeeping she should not be a skillful mistress of a house and that it would be a load of care and labour from which she shrank and a giving up of an existence she thoroughly enjoyed and to which she had become exactly fitted, and she could not undertake it unless he was sure he loved her and needed her enough to justify her in doing it."[10]

While Lidian felt some misgivings about what the institution of marriage entailed, Emerson did not. The strict division of labor in the household provided Emerson the stability and sustenance to pursue a public career. Lidian filled a role that complemented Waldo's. But it did not result in intensely shared feelings. The cost was substantial: the difference in experience led, more than either perhaps would have liked, to a divergence of belief and sentiment.

Ellen Tucker Emerson, the Emersons' elder daughter, recounts that according to her mother, for five years the Emersons "were getting more & more married all the time. They were as happy as it was possible to be." Apparently what cut short this initial period of their marriage—at least for Lidian—was a sudden bitter realization sometime during 1840 or 1841 that her religious views differed substantially from those of her husband. She had "always felt as if Father's & her religious views were the same," she told her daughter; in fact, upon first hearing Emerson speak, she had taken the similarity in their spiritual thinking to be a portent of sorts. Now she decided that she had become " 'unconsciously warped' " by him, and she no longer believed he was a Christian, at least "not a Christian in her sense of the word." The realization pained her.[11]

Anger and a certain unsettledness appear in Emerson's views of marriage around this time, although specific comments about disagreements with Lidian are absent from his journals. "I marry you for better but not for *worse*," he wrote on one occasion in 1840, without bothering to elaborate at any length on what he meant. On another, he asserted that the perception of new truth by one person was capable of producing the equivalent of a spiritual divorce. "Heaven is the marriage of all souls," he concluded, affirming that earthly marriage was, at best, a partial relation. By 1842, the breach between the two was evident. When Lidian failed to write him about home and family during an out-of-town lecture trip, he wrote her asking, "Well is this to punish my philosophy?" Lidian denied that it was. Nevertheless, her letters to him contain pointed remarks about his unorthodoxy. On one occasion, for example, as she remarked on the Sunday weather, she chided that she hoped it would bring him inspirations—"not only of the Parnassian Muse—but of the Muse of Zion." In a marriage begun on the basis of common spiritual beliefs, the divergence of opinion between the two reflected not only theological differences, but also unspoken disagreements over values as well.[12]

Although Emerson loved his wife and family and continued to rely on them as the most basic source of stability in his life, he expressed more and more doubt about their ability to provide him the ideal spiritual community he sought. Domestic life, far from being the key to spiritual self-sufficiency, came to seem a mixed blessing—at the very least, a distraction from the higher things of life. Literary men ought to be released from all domestic responsibility, he began to claim, and thought that "the Roman Church with its celibate clergy & its monastic cells was right."[13] To engage successfully in the work of producing ideas, the claims of the private sphere had to be minimized. Apparently it never occurred to Emerson that a sharp bifurcation of marital roles might lead to divergence of sensibility between spouses, or that the domesticity that supported his work by its very nature deprived him of the ideal companion he sought. Lidian Emerson for her part did not object too strenuously to the demands of her life, except perhaps through frequent episodes of depression and illness.[14] If she found her role at times frustrating, she at the same time had opportunities for stimulating conversation with her husband's guests that other contemporaries would have envied. Even in a diminished and secondary role, she was far better off than she might have been.

Emerson's *Essays, First Series*, published in 1841, represents the first fruits of his Concord years. Many of the essays there reflect already familiar themes and mirror the content of lectures delivered earlier. "Spiritual Laws," "The Over-Soul," and "Circles" amplify Emerson's thoughts on what was, by 1841, an old theme for him—the all-encompassing laws of Nature that should instruct human conduct. The essays on "History," "Compensation," "Prudence," "Heroism," "Intellect," and "Art" elaborate in different ways the relation of moral laws to human nature. It is only in the essays clearly focused on human relationships—"Love," "Friendship," and

"Self-Reliance"—that Emerson begins to explore what is for him entirely new ground.

Emerson's ambivalent feelings toward marriage emerge clearly in the essay entitled "Love." "Love" examines the meaning of a specific love-relation, conjugal love, in hopes that the lessons learned might be generalized to include love of all types. The essay has frequently been offered as further evidence of Emerson's own coldness of temperament, for it contains little of the warmth that one has a right to expect from an essay on the topic. The speaker seems strangely distanced, as though he has had no direct experience with his subject. Emerson too found the essay inadequate, and in 1840, just after he had finished editing the lecture on which the essay is based for *Essays, First Series,* he tried to account for the coldness at its center: "I [am] cold because I am hot—cold at the surface only as a sort of guard & compensation for the fluid tenderness of the core,—have much more experience than I have written there, more than I will, more than I can write. In silence we must wrap much of our life, because it is too fine for speech, because also we cannot explain it to others, and because somewhat we cannot yet understand."[15] In the essay itself, he responds to charges that he has been "unjustly cold to the personal relations" in his public discourse by "shrink[ing] at the remembrance of such disparaging words."[16]

Emerson could not talk of his personal experiences—not because he lacked them, but because the intensity and confusion of his feelings forced him to put them at arm's length. Nevertheless, "Love" does translate his feelings about his own marriage into an impersonal language. The dissatisfaction with which critics have frequently read the essay stems directly from Emerson's own frustration with a marriage that had turned out to be, for reasons that lay beyond him, less than he had hoped. "Love" is an unsatisfying essay because it attempts to idealize conjugal love, as defined by the canon of domesticity, as a way of making the best of an intrinsically limited emotional relation.

Emerson's final version of the essay on "Love," published in 1847, begins on an unsettling note: when the soul receives what it thought it had wanted, the good fortune marks only the beginning of a new want. "Every promise of the soul has innumerable fulfillments: each of its joys ripens into a new want," he writes. No matter how much the individual receives, he craves more. The connection of this sentiment with connubial love is more apparent in the metaphor that opens the 1841 version of the essay: "Every soul is a celestial Venus to every other soul. The heart has its sabbaths and jubilees, in which the world appears as a hymeneal feast, and all natural sounds and the circle of the seasons are erotic odes and dances. Love is omnipresent in nature as motive and reward. Love is our highest word, and the synonym of God."[17] After observing how the fulfillment of the promise begets a new hunger, both versions of the essay continue in a vein that suggests the impermanence of the original attachment. "Nature, uncontainable, flowing, forelooking, in the first sentiment of kindness anticipates already a benevolence which shall lose all particular regards in its general light," Emerson says. The theme of the transience of particular love dominates the essay.

As nature represents truth on three levels—the physical, the moral, and the spiritual—so love manifests itself on three levels. The first type of love that one experiences in "the heyday of the blood" is what Emerson calls elsewhere the "initial" love of youth. Love seizes the young man "like a certain divine rage and enthusiasm" and "unites him to his race, pledges him to the domestic relations, carries him with new sympathy into nature, enhances the power of the senses, opens the imagination, adds to his character heroic and sacred attributes, establishes marriage, and gives permanence to human society." An attraction initially physical and private establishes the moral bonds between self and society, and on a higher level yet, urges the individual on to define the relationship between self and universe. Love begins in private, but its end is unity with "the universal heart of all." Here is Emerson's way both of explaining why marital love is insufficient and of reconciling himself to its insufficiency. "Every thing is beautiful seen from the point of the intellect, or as truth," he affirms. As truth, then, Emerson is determined to examine his own experience with the married state.

How does one experience love? First, Emerson finds, comes "a perfect equality" between the lovers. "The happy, affectionate nature of woman" flows out and establishes "the most agreeable, confiding relations" between persons. The lover gives himself over to visions of his beloved, but unbeknownst to himself, he is investing the maiden with "all select things and virtues." She becomes for him an incarnation of the true and the beautiful, although he cannot yet know that what he loves is the relationship to the universe that she represents, not what she is in particular. His mistress's beauty "suggests gleams and visions, and not earthly satisfactions." As he becomes more acquainted with his mate, he comes to a "warmer love of these nobilities." Hence he is ready to pass "from loving them in one, to loving them in all." Through his wife, he learns a sympathy with all others that he has before only known abstractly. "All men are good and wise," Emerson had told his lyceum audience in a lecture on "Home"; "we know it only of those nearest us."[18]

"But this dream of love, though beautiful, is only one scene in our play," he adds. Ellen Tucker Emerson had not lived long enough to ascend to love's second stage ("Daemonic" love, Emerson would call it in a poem on the subject), but Lidian Jackson Emerson did. Emerson's dalliance with Lidian in the first stage of love was brief, his day-to-day experience with her was more nearly reflected in his discourse on love's second stage. Though this species of love ranks higher in Nature's hierarchy than the private love of the first stage, it rings far less convincing as a satisfying way of life. In the second stage of love, Emerson says, one realizes that in the first stage the "rays of the soul" had only alighted on "things nearest." Soon, however, "neighborhoods, size, numbers, habits, persons" lose power over us. The individual longs for truth, and personalities become superfluous. "Thus even love, which is the deification of persons, must become more impersonal every day," he says. At first the lovers do not realize what must happen, as they revel in their feelings for each other. But they discover at the last, as they are "shut up in one house to spend in the nuptial society forty or fifty years," that real marriage does not exist for its own sake. Rather, "the purification of the intellect and the heart" is the third stage of love, the stage Emerson calls "Celestial" in his essay on Swedenborg in *Representative Men*. It is "a love which knows not sex, nor person, nor partiality, but which seeks virtue and wisdom everywhere, to the end of increasing virtue and wisdom."

Emerson's third stage of love sounds thin and unconvincing, and for good reason. He devotes the least discussion to it, for that stage is his realization of what *ought* to come after the second. "[O]ne to one, married & chained through the eternity of Ages," he wrote, was a frightful prospect. Emerson's celestial love was for him an abstraction that grew out of the organicism that had preoccupied him for some time. What he actually found in his search for intimacy through marriage fell far short of the ideal. He discovered without question the "perfect sincerity," the ability to be himself, that made comfortable his exile from society. In this sense, he took from the domestic arrangement of the Victorian family the best it had to offer. By 1842, however, even Emerson had come to despair of an ultimate spiritual communion between persons. "Marriage in what is called the spiritual world is impossible, because of the vast inequality between every subject & and every object," he concluded. "There will always be the same gulf between every me & thee as between the original and the picture."[19] Marriage became the metaphor for a relation that was finally unattainable.

II

Emerson's withdrawal in 1834 to the small town he made his home rendered problematic not only the nature of personal relationships within the family, but those outside it as well. Concord was no longer the village of the embattled farmers who fired the shot heard round the world in 1775. Now very much tied into a regional economy, Concord's farmers furnished cash crops such as oats, hay, and wood for the urban market. In 1830, the town supported a considerable variety of local endeavors, including nine stores, forty shops, four hotels and taverns, four doctors, four lawyers, and numerous county associations. By 1835, it also boasted an insurance company, a national bank, a savings bank, a town newspaper with a circulation of eleven hundred, an academy, a lyceum, and a library. On the verge of developing a suburban identity, it was, as Robert Gross has written, an "outpost of urban civilization in a largely rural countryside."[20]

Despite its gradual transformation in the half-century since the Revolution, however, Concord appealed to Emerson precisely because it was not the city. There one could enjoy the amenities of both rural and urban life without some of their obvious drawbacks. Like Emerson, the many Bostonians who eventually moved to suburbs dreamed of establishing (in the words of the urban planner Frederick Law Olmsted) "the harmonious association and cooperation of men in a community, and the intimate relationship and constant intercourse, and interdependence between families."[21] Like Emerson, they would attempt to substitute satisfying personal relationships for a public sphere that was beyond redemption as a humane environment.

Family had furnished Emerson most of the close friendships he had enjoyed before his removal to Concord. Brothers were natural friends: one might be sincere with them and be understood as with no one else. "I never read the treatises about friendship which ancients & moderns have written without thinking of our little brotherhood," Edward Bliss Emerson wrote his older brother Waldo in 1833. "When most feeble most threatened, least esteemed," he continued, "I feel strong if I can turn my thoughts homeward & assure myself of fraternal sympathy." An individual could expect kin to understand and sympathize with him, but friendship with those outside his family—at least for the Emersons—had heretofore been a rare and precious commodity.[22] Security in an unstable world depended on family, for family relations were stable if nothing else was.[23]

When his brothers Charles and Edward died, Emerson found himself without the friends that nature had provided him. Outside the pale of the ministry, he also found himself without a professional fraternity. With the "natural" sources of friendship lacking, he was forced to seek substitutes. His wife and children served as a partial solution. In order to maintain relations with society, however, he would have to seek out friends beyond the family. Such a course of action did not come easily for one so diffident and shy. "There are some public persons born not for privacy but for publicity who are dull & even silly in tete-a-tete," he observed, and clearly thought himself one of them.[24] Given over to the formulation of abstract laws to help guide his conduct in areas where he felt uncomfortable or where his own experience had failed him, Emerson in Concord set out self-consciously to define the role of friendship in his life.

Among the first of Emerson's attempts to replace the associations he had lost through his forfeiture of the settled ministry was his membership in the Hedge Club, or the Transcendental Club, as it later came to be known. Early members of the club were brought together by Emerson's friend and colleague in the Unitarian ministry, Frederic Henry Hedge, and included Unitarian ministers who, like Emerson, had come to object to conventional Unitarian doctrine. Present at the first meeting on 20 September 1836, in addition to Emerson and Hedge, were George Ripley, Convers Francis, Bronson Alcott, James Freeman Clarke, and Orestes Brownson. Of the number, only Alcott, whom Emerson had recently met, had not served in the active ministry. (He was admitted "over the professional limits," for Emerson found him "a God-made priest.") The purpose of Hedge's "symposium" was to form a class of supporters for reforms that had found little support among the most conservative of the Unitarian establishment. Within Hedge's club, those interested in new ideas—especially German romanticism—would be able to exchange notes. From the first, Emerson was skeptical that the club would satisfy his need for association with others. "I have never found that uplifting & enlargement from the conversation of many which I find in the society of one faithful person," he wrote Hedge. Confessing that "the experiment you propose has never been fairly tried by us," however, he looked forward to meeting with the group at the annual Harvard commencement.[25]

Though he participated actively in Transcendental Club discussions and maintained important quasi-professional contacts through it, it was never the bond to society that Emerson sought. The association seemed too artificial, too constrictive. He continued to attend the meetings faithfully, but he never felt that they provided the opportunity for much besides superficial discussion. Only "private, accidental conversation breeds thought," he still believed in 1838; "clubs produce oftener words." And again, more than a year after, he was still confiding to his journal that "all conversation among literary men is muddy."[26]

What he would have preferred, he wrote to Hedge in a letter before the latter's club ever met, was a more "natural" sort of society: "I will tell you what society would please me; that you should be the minister of Concord & George P. B[radford] its school master & Carlyle a resident whilst he lectured in Boston & Mrs. Ripley & Mr. Alcott should be visiters. But my castles that stood had fallen, and these will never stand." Again in an 1837 lecture on "Society," he outlined his vision of a natural community in which one lived with those with whom one shared a common view of culture: "A man should live among those people among whom he can act naturally, among those who permit and provoke the expression of all his thoughts and emotions. Among such only can there be one soul," he believed.[27] These words were very nearly the ones he had used to describe the benefits of home in an 1831 sermon. Slowly losing confidence in the ability of the family to purify society, however, Emerson converted what he took to be the redemptive values of home life and tried to project them outward onto a larger, semipublic sphere. If the isolated household could not sustain the individual, neither could one work directly with the unrepentant public sphere with its relentless demands for insincerity. In place of either, Emerson proposed a compromise circle of friends who would share, within the context of a community, in the intimacy of the family without the latter's awful isolation. Through such a group of likeminded intimates, the blessings of the private sphere might filter gradually into the public sphere. Emerson meant literally to duplicate within a larger social setting the brotherhood and sisterhood of private kinship networks.

If he had in mind such visions of an ideal society, however, what explains his curious reaction to the Brook Farm experiment? After all, this utopian scheme of some of his friends and acquaintances, conceived by George Ripley in 1840, was dedicated to providing people with the opportunity of "being wholly true to their natures as men and women." Intended as an exemplar to the age of what "Christ's idea of society" might be, the West Roxbury community was founded as a joint stock company whose social and economic organization was to create an atmosphere in which individuals were free to pursue an independent course of thought and action. Brook Farm's combination of fraternal/sororal living and manual labor would help individuals transcend "all the limitations that separate men from love and mutual trust" in the modern age.[28]

Why, then, did Emerson refuse to join either Ripley's Brook Farm or Bronson Alcott's later attempt "to initiate a Family in harmony with the primitive instincts in man" at Fruitlands, near Harvard, Massachusetts?[29] The answer is a complex one. His reasons have been interpreted unflatteringly by various observers as native coldness, inconsistency of character, or even as "a certain physical and mental inertness which the vulgar do not hesitate to call laziness."[30] He himself pleaded to Ripley that his own diffidence of character would make him an ineffectual member of such a community. He also had no need of the promise of financial security that Brook Farm held out to such as Nathaniel Hawthorne. Emerson grappled with the decision of whether to join the Brook Farm experiment for three months before deciding against it. He assured Ripley that he agreed with the goals of the utopian community. "Of all the philanthropic projects of which I have heard yours is the most pleasing to me," he wrote.[31] But even if he hoped that it would succeed, he still refused to join.

Emerson told Ripley that his reasons for not joining the community were wholly personal. He already had the resources and the opportunity, he believed, to pursue an independent course of thought and action within the context of the "natural" community of Concord. Without taking anything away from the value of the experiment, Emerson told Ripley that for himself it seemed "a circuitous & operose way of relieving myself of any irksome circumstances, to put upon your community the task of my emancipation which I ought to take on myself." Yet the pragmatics of the situation were also tied inextricably to his larger sense of how the laws of society operated. If the problem of individuals was at bottom a lack of virtue and fortitude, how would another complex social scheme right the matter? As he listened to George and Sophia Ripley, Margaret Fuller, and Bronson Alcott rehearse their plans, Emerson found himself wishing "to be convinced, to be thawed, to be made nobly mad by the kindlings before my eye of a new dawn of human piety." But he could not. The scheme sounded to him like the same old concern for "arithmetic & comfort." Beyond personal consideration, he could not get past the fact that the social and economic reforms proposed presumed an accompanying reform in moral outlook rather than providing for it.[32]

In "Fourierism and the Socialists," an 1842 essay in *The Dial*, Emerson sorts out his mixed feelings toward reform through social engineering in his reflections on Charles Fourier, the French socialist reformer who proposed a detailed blueprint for a utopian community. Fourier's plan for the establishment of "phalanxes" represented a mechanistic vision of society with which Emerson finally disagreed. However, he had praise for Fourier's scientific analysis of the roots of social evils, and a good bit of admiration for his plans for reforming them. For like Emerson, Fourier was concerned with universal and abstract laws of human organization. "The merit of [Fourier's] plan was that it was a system," Emerson wrote, "that it had not the partiality and hint-and-fragment character of most popular schemes, but was coherent and comprehensive of facts to a wonderful degree." Nevertheless, its weakness, Emerson believed, was "that Fourier had skipped no fact but one, namely, Life." Based on a positivistic, materialist view of the world, Fourier's phalanxes and other communitarian schemes like them seemed to Emerson to be seriously flawed as instruments of reform. Social structures did not maintain themselves by their own power, but rather through individual faith in their efficacy. Reform, he believed, had to begin with individual consciousness.[33]

Emerson rejected Brook Farm as he rejected all "artificial" constructs, preferring to trust the capabilities of the "natural": "What is true and good must not only be begun by life, but must be conducted to its issues by life." In the end, he simply seems to have been uncomfortable with reform schemes that would diminish the power of individuals. The troublesome doubt that acceptance of such a reform would subtly undermine the moral foundations of the philosophy he had been developing is evident in his thinking: "[T]o join this body would be to traverse all my long trumpeted theory, and the instinct which spoke from it, that one man is a counterpoise to a city,—that a man is stronger than a city, that his solitude is more prevalent & beneficent than the concert of crowds." Brook Farm seemed but one more crowd in danger of drawing him away from the beneficent instruction of Nature. He placed his hope for reform in a change in ideology, and as he did with his family, claimed the right as an intellectual to be free of all communal constraints that might interfere with his individual work.[34]

Nevertheless, the talk about Brook Farm ("to the point of ineffable weariness," he wrote his brother) led Emerson to resolve to make some changes in his own domestic situation. He intended, for example, to acquire habits of manual labor as a way of maintaining a balanced life, and to dispense in his household with hired help. In so doing, he hoped to "come one step nearer to nature than . . . usage permits." Moreover, he invited the Alcott family to try the experiment of living in his household for a year, in order to practice living plainly with like-minded individuals. At other times, both Margaret Fuller and Henry Thoreau resided with the Emersons for an extended period, as well as Emerson's mother and Mary Russell, the children's governess. "Those of us who do not believe in Communities, believe in neighborhoods & that the kingdom of heaven may consist of such," he affirmed in 1842.[35] Hence, he continued to seek his salvation in the neighborhood of Concord.

III

One important reason why Emerson refused to join the Brook Farm experiment was that by 1840, he seemed to have found among sundry newly made friends the "natural" companionship that he had been seeking. Sometime in mid-1835 he met the itinerant prophet-schoolmaster Bronson Alcott, and their friendship flourished. By 1837 Alcott appeared frequently in Emerson's journal entries. When Alcott's *Conversations with Children on the Gospels*, a volume of transcendental thought on pedagogy, was roundly attacked by the Boston press in March 1837, Emerson rushed to his defense in an article in the Boston *Courier*. Alcott spent time in the Emerson household and his host thought his vision "wonderful." To be sure, he was at times "monotonous," but in limited doses he was good company for one's visionary moments. In late 1837 or early 1838, Emerson had also met the son of a Concord pencil maker "who seems to have as free & erect a mind as any I have ever met." Henry Thoreau would later reside in the Emerson household for a time and would be recommended by Emerson as a tutor for William Emerson's children in New York.[36]

Emerson's friendships with Alcott and Thoreau were both overshadowed, however, by his relationship with the twenty-five-year-old daughter of Boston's upper caste, the exuberant Margaret Fuller. Emerson also met Fuller in 1835. Though she was "unattractive in person, and assuming in manners," her persistent interest in the preacher from whom she "first learned what is meant by an inward life" developed into a cordial, sometimes intense, relationship with the Concord hermit. Emerson, in turn, was attracted to her "sympathy with the artist in the protest which his work pronounced on the deformity of our daily manners." Moreover, Fuller made a conscious attempt to make her own large circle of intimates Emerson's own; the social connections with which she provided him, though unwelcome at times, gave the shy recluse opportunity to form friendships otherwise impossible for him. Caroline Sturgis, Anna Barker, and Samuel Ward, among others, would become close to Emerson through Margaret Fuller.[37]

As Fuller introduced her friends to Emerson one by one, he rejoiced in what was for him a new sensation. "Friends on any high footing are surely very noble possessions and make the earth & the starred night, as you walk alone, more divine," he wrote Fuller in

June 1838. "For a hermit I begin to think I know several very fine people." Again in September 1838, after reading a packet of letters from her friends that Fuller had forwarded him, Emerson excitedly expressed the hope that the intimacy he had dreamed might be possible in this new form of society: "I delight from my corner to know that such society is no fable, can & does organize itself in this country, & so near—out of elements I have seen with my own eyes. Such rare pictures as you paint, make me suspect my own habitual skepticism in respect to the stimulus of society to be merely mine & springing from want of organs which others have." When Alcott and Fuller visited him in October 1839, he could admit to an affection that before had alluded him. "Cold as I am," he wrote, "they are almost dear."[38]

Emerson's enthusiasm in his new friendships comes through clearly in his essay "Friendship." The work, most of which was written in 1839, reflects the first glow of Emerson's intimacy with Fuller's circle of friends. The extent to which he was especially pleased with his new outlet to society becomes particularly apparent if one compares the essay with "Love," its companion piece in *Essays, First Series.* "Love" seems subdued in mood, determined to make the best of a limited good. "Friendship," in contrast, contains as much overt emotion as the reserved Emerson is capable of mustering. "We have a great deal more kindness than is ever spoken," the essay begins. He seems pleasantly startled by unexpected warmth in his fellow humans: "Maugre all the selfishness that chills like east winds the world, the whole human family is bathed with an element of love like a fine ether. How many persons we meet in houses, whom we scarcely speak to, whom yet we honor, and who honor us!" The knowledge that the stranger who seems indifferent may not be, renews and revivifies him. He feels "cordial exhilaration," "the material effects of fire," "the sweetness of life" not apparent in "Love." His "intellectual and active powers increase." "What is so pleasant as these jets of affection which make a young world for me again?" he writes.[39] If marriage did not completely fulfill his need for relation, friendship—at least in 1839 and 1840— seemed to.

"Friendship" is more recognizably personal than many of Emerson's other essays. The persona of the essay is an "I" who deigns to acknowledge personal feelings. He admits to his shyness and to an extreme sensitivity that often manifest themselves to others as coldness or aloofness. As he speaks of the danger that his new friends may reject or leave him, he confesses "an extreme tenderness of nature on this point," and realizes, "It is almost dangerous to me to 'crush the sweet poison of misused wine' of the affections. A new person is to me a great event, and hinders me from sleep." He knows that he invests too much in his friends and expects too much of them, and he also admits in a more oblique way that his "bashfulness and apathy are a tough husk in which a delicate organization is protected from premature ripening." Here are excitement and fear and anticipation and candor and self-disclosure such as we seldom find in the representative public persona Emerson so self-consciously constructed. His friendship with Margaret Fuller and others had encouraged him to believe that he might feel comfortable in openly revealing himself.

"Friendship," therefore, is a particularly interesting essay because of its peculiar transparency in revealing Emerson's feelings about intimacy with others. Though he unquestionably is pleased with the new community nature has provided him, there is the feeling throughout that it cannot last. "Will these too separate themselves from me again, or some of them?" Emerson asks. Probably so, comes the answer. The fear that like everything else in life, friendship will prove "phenomenal" forces him to ascend to a spiritual plane from whence to view impersonally what his personal experiences signify. Friendship is important enough to him that he is determined to find the spiritual key that will make it last forever.

Seen from a social point of view, not from the personal point of view that counts the particular emotional benefits accruing from relationships, friendship becomes part of a dialectic between society and solitude finally resolved in the realm of spirit. Through friendship, the individual ferrets out the secrets of human nature. He does so first by attending to the voice of his own nature in solitude, then by comparing his experience to that of the others in society whom he loves, his friends. Friends call him back from the bane of preoccupation with his own personality. They provide him at a distance with images of other "selves," for in friendship the surface idiosyncrasies of personality are discounted, and what underlies personality is the same in all. He therefore comes to know, through others who in their sincerity become transparent to him, the laws of nature that self-preoccupation and egocentrism might hide from his vision in himself. Thus, friends provide a counterbalance for the solitude which is necessary but which might also prove distorting. In this way friendship illustrated concretely for Emerson how nature "[made] many one." It was only through revelation of self to others, Emerson now believed, that individuals could deal with each other as more than mere commodity. The community of friendship was based on this self-revelation. True community, Emerson had always contended, could only arise from mutual sincerity. Friendship could be defined as a concrete relationship based on such sincerity. Therefore, friendship could function as the model for true community that he looked for on a larger social scale. And because any person who was intent on being sincere would discover the laws of nature that constituted virtue within himself, such sincerity would prove the basis for a true social community founded on dedication to the common good. Friendship was the alternative to reform schemes such as Brook Farm. It was not an untried, utopian model; it grew out of the circumstances of daily life.

In "Friendship," Emerson found this "new web of relations" that was friendship "the solidest thing we know." A society without this kind of sincerity warped the individual. Nature sometimes seemed a distant and abstract notion, but friendship's "divine affinity of virtue with itself" concretely demonstrated how persons could relate to one another in a spiritual way. Friendship "demands a religious treatment," Emerson insisted, for it was here that he expected to find a substitute for the sacred community that the church had formerly provided. True friendship could be religion without dogma and rite, community without violation of the self. The sense of unity that the relation produced—the feeling that "the *not mine is mine*"—endured. Therefore, friendship took its place in a long line of institutions designed to overcome the gap between "the ME and the NOT ME" (as Emerson had put it in *Nature*), between self and something larger than self. The organic communities of an earlier age had suggested a way in which the individual could transcend himself; so had the sacred community that the church had provided. In *Nature* Emerson had tried to suggest substitutes for both. In "Friendship" he tried more specifically to define the relation between persons that would eradicate the awful feeling of detachment from others.

IV

"It has seemed to me lately more possible than I knew, to carry a friendship greatly, on one side, without due correspondence on the other," Emerson had noted with some ambiguity in the last paragraph of the essay on "Friendship." Only lately he had heard grumblings which, within a short period of time, would vastly change the character of his friendship with Fuller, the source of so much of the optimism that pervades "Friendship." The problem between the two surfaced in late 1839. Fuller told her friend that he "always seemed to be on stilts." He was holding back from the relationship, she told him, endeavoring to keep her and her friends at arm's length. She renewed the charge with more vehemence in August 1840. Here is how Emerson recorded the incident in his journal: "She taxed me[,] as often before[,] so now more explicitly with inhospitality of soul. She & C. [Caroline Sturgis] would gladly be my friends, yet our intercourse is not friendship, but literary gossip. I count & weigh but do not love. They make no progress with me, but however often we have met, we still meet as strangers. They feel wronged in such relation, & do not wish to be catechised & criticized."[40]

Emerson was stunned by the charge. He had assumed a perfect sincerity of feeling between himself and his friends, and they had come now to tell him that he had misunderstood totally. The incident set him to thinking with a new intensity on the true nature of friendship and marked the beginning of a remarkable correspondence between himself and Fuller and Sturgis on the topic. A few days after the devastating interview, he replied to the charges against him in a letter to Caroline Sturgis: "I heard the charge, I own, with great humility & sadness. I confess to the fact of cold & imperfect intercourse, but not to the impeachment of my will, and not to the deficiency of my affection. If I can count & weigh, I love also. I cannot tell you how warm & glad the naming of your names makes my solitude. You give me more joy than I could trust my tongue to tell you." Perhaps he did not understand how to express friendship, he admitted, but "if you will confide in me," he told her, "so far I will engage to be as true a brother to you as ever blood made." He would henceforth consider his friends as brothers and sisters, "*naturally* friends." "I shall never go quite back to my old arctic habits," he wrote Fuller. The prospect of this new kinship relation excited him. He had been "an exile so long from the social world," he told Fuller, that now that a new social world was "suddenly thrust on me," he was determined to "study to deserve my friends—I abandon myself to what is best in you all." Heaven had sent him friends to encourage him in his purpose to speak the truth to society. They made him feel, he told them, "that in speaking to you I may dismiss the consideration of *you*, may forget all persons, may speak the truth, & may love with the primary eternal heart."[41]

Yet the resolution was flawed from the beginning. Although Emerson did not realize it at first, his notions of friendship differed fundamentally from those held by Fuller and Sturgis—especially by Fuller. Emerson had hoped to find in the friendship of those "who live in the light of the same truth with ourselves" an ideal social relation. It became apparent, however, that even with close and sincere friends there could be no complete agreement. Fuller continued to tax him with his inability to understand her, even after his resolution to show her more openly the warmth of his feelings. "How often have I said, This light will never understand my fire; this clear eye will never discern the law by which I am filling my circle; this simple force will never interpret my need of manifold being," she berated him more than a month after his initial resolution. He had tried his best through his letters to display his innermost thoughts to her. It was not enough. In the journals he coupled his anxiety to please with a growing uneasiness at his inability to understand just what it was that Fuller wanted. On 24 October 1840, with obvious exasperation, he gave up the subject entirely. "There is a difference in our constitution," he wrote her. "We use a different rhetoric. It seems as if we had been born & bred in different nations." He slammed the door on their intense discussion of friendship with an abrupt, "Do not expect it of me again for a very long time."[42]

The incident has usually been explained as the result of either Fuller's overexacting temperament or Emerson's cold one. "Our moods were very different," Emerson remembered as he wrote of Fuller after her death. Or as Fuller put it, "We agreed that my God was love, his truth."[43] Certainly differences of personality and temperament were involved, but there may have been a larger gap as well: Fuller was in fact using a different rhetoric from his own, and it was indeed as if she has been bred in a different nation. Within the feminine sphere, definitions of friendship differed sharply from prevalent masculine notions of friendships. Male friends were to be as brothers to each other, with conversation "the first office of friendship." For men, ideas proved the focus of conversation, and emotion frequently went unspoken. In such a friendship, Emerson wrote Fuller, "a robust & total understanding grows up resembling nothing so much as the relation of brothers who are intimate & perfect friends without having ever spoken of the fact."[44] The cultural conventions surrounding women's friendships, however, differed. Female friendships were characterized by an intensity of emotion, often accompanied by physical expressions of love. In the private, feminine sphere, emphasis on emotion was legitimate, since the bonding power of feminine expressiveness was to act as the glue that would hold together a highly volatile society. Thus female friends frequently "assumed an emotional centrality in each others' lives" (in the words of Carroll Smith-Rosenberg) not present to as great an extent in male same-sex friendships.[45]

Both Fuller and Emerson believed that the antithesis between male and female cultural styles would be resolved in any good society. In "Woman in the Nineteenth Century," Fuller defended the thesis that each person has both male and female characteristics. Emerson came to the same conclusion in a roundabout way in an 1842 journal entry: "A highly endowed man with good intellect & good conscience is a Man-woman & does not so much need the complement of Woman to his being, as another. Hence his relations to the sex are somewhat dislocated & unsatisfactory. He asks in Woman, sometimes the Woman, sometimes the Man."[46] Both Fuller and Emerson shared in the Enlightenment heritage of radicals like Mary Wollstonecraft, who had held that beneath superficial differences of personality or character, men and women both obeyed identical laws of human nature. Despite their common intellectual position on the problem, however, both were bedeviled by the contrasting personality styles that the gender roles of nineteenth-century New England encouraged them to develop. Emerson hesitated to express emotion at all; Fuller's sometimes cloying emphasis on sentiment overshadowed all else.

The differences in behavior were thus as much constructed by culture as provided by nature or temperament. Because men were destined to take their places in the public sphere, male friendships centered around the concerns of the public sphere. Indulging one's own personal feelings was, except on rare occasions, illegitimate and dangerous in a world where to be vulnerable was to lose a competitive edge. Emerson himself found expressing emotion directly either uncomfortable or embarrassing. He frequently intellectualized his feelings, attempting to translate them into abstract and universal laws that explained human behavior. By doing so, he could address public concerns as befitted the incumbent of a position in society that demanded public consciousness. His feelings, even in his journals, lie hidden under a philosophical mask. Margaret Fuller, who by virtue of her sex was supposed to have inhabited only the private sphere, was under no such cultural constraints. Indeed, since women were the caretakers of the private sphere, it was entirely appropriate that they give far greater latitude to the expression of private emotion. Although Fuller was anxious for her own part to transcend the dichotomy between the public and private spheres into which she had been born—just as Emerson was bent in his own way on bridging that gap—she valued the patterns of friendship common to women of her age. When she tried to apply these feminine expectations about friendship to her relationship with her male friend, however, the results proved disastrous. Though the two intimates thought that they were speaking a common language when they spoke of friendship, time made it clear that such was not the case.

In retrospect, even Emerson could see that the friendship was troubled from the start. "I believed I fancied her too much interested in personal history," he remembered from the distance of more than a decade. Of Margaret's circle of friends, which she wore "as a necklace of diamonds about her neck," Emerson remarked, "She extorted the secret of life, which cannot be told without setting heart and mind in a glow; and thus had the best of those she saw." Giving herself to her friendships "with an entireness not possible to any but a woman," Fuller delighted in the private details of the interior life. Reports of her same-sex friendships, despite her attempt to bridge the chasm between gender roles, exhibit the intense, even passionate, relations common in Victorian female same-sex friendships. Writing in Fuller's *Memoirs*, Emerson recalled those friendships, and the subject produced in him evident discomfort: "Her friendships, as a girl with girls, as a woman with women, were not unmingled with passion, and had passages of romantic sacrifice and of ecstatic fusion, which I have heard with the ear, but could not trust my profane pen to report." When Fuller began her campaign to convert Emerson to her own feminine ideas of friendship, ideas that neither necessarily recognized as gender-based, he chafed. She expected overt emotion and disclosure of intimate feelings; he could not give them.[47]

Emerson noted a pattern of eroticism in Fuller's female friendships that certainly carried over to her relationship with him—or at least it played out differently in her connection with this male friend. Emerson seems to have suspected that Fuller wanted a sexual relationship with him, although she flatly denied it. Emerson hints at an exchange on the topic in a journal passage from September 1840: "You would have me love you. What shall I love? Your body? The supposition disgusts you. What you have thought & said? Well, whilst you were thinking & saying them, but not now. I see no possibility of loving any thing but what now is, & is becoming; your courage, your enterprize, your budding affection, your opening thought, your prayer I can love,—but what else?"[48] Bell Gale Chevigny speculates that in a world where only men were expected to experience sexual feelings, a woman such as Fuller might easily deny sexual feelings or interpret such feelings when they arose as something else.[49] Moreover, a woman such as Fuller, who aspired to something more than domesticity, was likely to have experienced the problem of vocation far more problematically than Emerson had. For her, friendships may have become virtually the only sources available of intellectual satisfaction, emotional support, and professional connection. Therefore, Fuller's search for meaning and purpose in her life came to center in a very personal way on her friends, especially on Emerson. Emerson was preoccupied, on the other hand, with establishing an appropriate relation to the public sphere. Their friendship began in their shared marginality and their desire to find an alternative to contemporary society. It withered because Emerson far more consciously chose his marginal role than did Fuller. Ultimately they were unable to transcend their differences.

Emerson's and Fuller's disagreements over the nature of friendship did not destroy their relationship, but it did dim Emerson's rosy vision of the institution. The ideal of friendship remained, but as he had expected in his essay on the subject, the fact would always fall far short of the expectation. "Who is fit for friendship? Not one," he wrote Caroline Sturgis in March 1841. Friends were temporary "expedients," he decided. "We are very cold, miserably cold: we build a fire & get warm: but the heat leaves us where it found us; it has not forwarded our affair a single step; and so the friend when he has come & gone." The community of friendship represented a more satisfactory sort of society than life in the public sphere or life in the household, but it too had its shortcomings.[50]

Fuller continued to express the hope to Emerson that experience would "yet correct your vocabulary and that you will not always answer the burst of frank affection by the use of such a word as 'flattery.'" Emerson, for his part, gave up trying to explain himself to Fuller. He began to find it "not strange that our love & our labor should ever be so disunited streams": "My love reacts on me like the recoiling gun: it is pain;—I was going to add something concerning the capacity to love of this reputed icicle, but the words would tell nothing, and we shall certainly pass at last with each other for what we are." He never explained again, never even hinted at it, in fact. The separation between souls was permanent, the isolation of the heart inescapable.[51]

Before mid-1838, Emerson had spoken of the sentiment that would restore individuals to unity with one another as "sympathy." Sympathy was a concept applicable to the whole of society. When it became apparent that sympathy in society was not forthcoming, Emerson turned to the private sphere in the hopes that there he would find a way of bridging the gap between self and other, the ME and the NOT ME. What he found in the private sphere might serve as a model for appropriate relationships in the public as well. Family and friendships as Emerson had envisioned them would be sites where individuals felt free and supported in living out an ideal counter to that of the dominant culture. Because they never directly challenged the principles on which the social order was based, however, his experiments in the private sphere can be classed as only partial successes. Despite appearances, Emerson's relationships in fact did not function in isolation from the social order of which they were a part. At home the division of labor he had objected to in the world of work resurfaced in the family, with husband devoted to the tasks of production, wife to the work of reproduction and social support. Similarly, from his experiment in friendship he had discovered that a common ideology could not necessarily overcome differences in lived experience. Individual alienation marked the private realm as well as the public.

In his final word on the relationship between self and society, his 1870 essay on "Society and Solitude," Emerson evaluated his Concord experiments in "natural community" during the period 1838–41. The judgment was first passed in an 1845 journal entry, but the sentiments endured a lifetime:

> Dear heart! take it sadly home to thee,—there is no coopera-
> tion. We begin with friendships, and all our youth is a recon-
> noitring and recruiting of the holy fraternity they shall com-
> bine for the salvation of men. But so the remote stars seem a
> nebula of united light, yet there is no group which a telescope
> will not resolve; and the dearest friends are separated by im-
> passable gulfs. The cooperation is involuntary, and is put upon
> us by the Genius of Life, who reserves this as a part of his
> prerogative. 'Tis fine for us to talk; we sit and muse and are
> serene and complete; but the moment we meet with anybody,
> each becomes a fraction.[52]

In the light of experience, Emerson found it necessary to qualify the optimistic theory of the unity of all he had extrapolated from an abstract model of Nature. "Sympathy is always partial," he was forced to admit by 1842. He was sobered by his knowledge of an inevitable gap that must exist between persons. With the death of his son Waldo in January 1842, he would come to question the benevolence of Nature itself.

CHAPTER 9

Experience

The years teach much which the days never know. The persons who compose our company converse, and come and go, and design and execute many things, and somewhat comes of it all, but an unlooked-for result. The individual is always mistaken. He designed many things, and drew in other persons as coadjutors, quarreled with some or all, blundered much, and something is done; all are a little advanced, but the individual is always mistaken. It turns out somewhat new and very unlike what he promised himself.
—"Experience," Essays: Second Series, October 1844

AT THE END OF 1841, Emerson still believed that the unity proceeding from virtue—or, as he had taken to calling it lately, love—could make of the fragmented universe a harmonious whole. His recent disappointments had severely tested his strong faith in his philosophy of nature, but they had not broken it. Society writ large had proven distant, unreachable, and confirmed in its error; marriage he was ready to regard as a brittle relationship, and he advanced the plea that it "should be a temporary relation."[1] Friendship, which was to have become "the solidest thing we know," had taught him that a gap must always come between persons, and the *Dial*, the literary journal born in July 1840, of "gems from the papers of love & friendship," proved unsatisfying. Insofar as it was "as much a journal of friendship as of literature and morals," Emerson's interest in it waned as he drew further away from his friends.[2]

Much of Emerson's world proved trying, but one aspect of his life in 1841 remained a source of surety. Like most parents, Emerson found hope in his children—Waldo, Ellen, and the infant Edith. Five-year-old Waldo in particular delighted him. In his only son (Edward was not born until 1844) Emerson felt the universe had reached out to him with a concrete pledge of its good will. The child's innocence and lack of self-consciousness seemed to Emerson personal emblems of the ideal harmony of the individual with self he sought. Moreover, Waldo represented in a tangible way a sympathy of affection realized in only partial ways elsewhere. "I feel how deathcold are all literary efforts by the side of this living child," Emerson wrote during the summer of 1841. "These are the touches that reanimate my defunct soul,—give it senses to grope in the dark of nature."[3]

In fact, Emerson's relationship with his son might have seemed no different from that of many another doting father with his child had not Waldo Emerson died on 27 January 1842. He had been ill with scarlet fever for only three days. His death shook Emerson, and, as it turned out, proved the catalyst for a substantial shift in his father's view of the world. Once able to say of himself, "I am nothing. I see all," Emerson wrote after his son's death,

The little captain innocent
Took the eye with him as he went[.][4]

Emerson had been discovering for some time the limitations of his philosophy of nature. With Waldo's death, his doubts about the beneficence of the universe crystallized in a new way that left his view of the individual's relation to nature transformed.

I

Nearly two months after his son's death, Emerson still could not understand how anything good might come of the event. "I comprehend nothing of this fact but its bitterness," he wrote. "Explanation I have none, consolation none that rises out of the fact itself; only diversion; only oblivion of this & pursuit of new objects." To his aunt, Mary Moody Emerson, he wrote a letter in which he mourned, "He adorned the world for me like a morning star, and every particular of my daily life." It was part of an epistolary outpouring of grief. "Shall I ever dare to love any thing again?" he wrote to Margaret Fuller; and to Elizabeth Peabody, "With him has departed all that is glad & festal & almost all that is social even, for me, from this world." Of everything in his life up until this point, Emerson had been able to make some sense; he had placed all facts into the context of the universal laws of nature and had insisted that the law of compensation provided "the deep remedial force that underlies all facts." But so deep was this loss that even after two years Emerson could still make no sense of it. "I have had no experiences, no progress to put me into better intelligence with my calamity than when it was new," he wrote Margaret Fuller in January 1844.[5]

The Emerson accustomed to translate all personal facts into abstract truths experienced his grief over Waldo's death as an affront to his long-standing trust in Nature. It had always seemed to him that the individual might find in Nature consolation in the face of loss and corruption. Indeed, Emerson had written in November 1838 that he believed his faith in Nature would keep him from grieving the loss of wife, child, or mother at all, and he wished he might communicate to them "the boundless resources of the soul,—remaining entire when particular threads of relation are snapped." He was thus unprepared for the new aspect nature put on as it turned unfeeling and uncaring. Waldo was dead, and nowhere was there explanation or comfort. "Meantime the sun rises & the winds blow nature seems to have forgotten that she has crushed her sweetest creation," he lamented.[6]

The first part of the poem "Threnody," written shortly after his son's death, conveys Emerson's sense of betrayal by nature. For the first time in his life, Emerson berates nature for its shortcomings. Before, it had always been man who fell short of nature's standards; now the tables were turned:

Perchance not he but Nature ailed,
The world and not the infant failed.[7]

With the solid reassurance that nature had formerly provided him removed, Emerson accelerated his reexamination of himself and his philosophy in 1842. "I have almost completed thirty nine years and I have not yet adjusted my relation to my fellows on the planet, or to my work," he agonized in April. On all fronts he was now troubled by the sense of his own inadequacy. Perhaps his secular preaching had failed as a result of shortsighted personal discontents—misgivings he had heretofore refused to admit to himself. "I do not satisfy myself; how can I satisfy others?" he wondered. "A man at peace would go through men & nature commanding all things by his eye alone." He came to doubt that he had much real faith in Nature or an adequate understanding of its workings. In fact, he was beginning to discover, his life had contained more than a touch of egocentrism itself. "Lidian sometimes taxes me at home with an egotism more virulent than any against which I rail," he wrote

Fuller in March 1842. Though it pained and confused him to consider the prospect, at the last he had to admit, "Perhaps she is right."[8]

In the second part of "Threnody," written over two years after his son's death, Emerson resolved his confusion over his own place in the plan of nature by reaffirming that it is the entire scheme that matters, not individuals. He wrote of the death and decay that is man's inevitable portion in life,

> House and tenant go to ground,
> Lost in God, in Godhead found.

Even his own innocent Waldo had only been a sign of something larger than himself. On the surface, Emerson's renunciation of the egocentrism of which he had recently become aware may seem only a variation on a theme that had long preoccupied him. Beneath the neat stoic resolution of the conflict between self and nature here, however, lay a fundamental change in attitude toward self, society, and the nature that underlay the two. "Threnody" glosses over the changes in Emerson's outlook, for the poem's purpose is to emphasize the continuities of life despite the pain of change. The essay on "Experience," however, published in *Essays, Second Series* (1845), indicates just how fundamentally altered was Emerson's emotional state. Especially when compared with his earlier essay on the self, "Self-Reliance" (1841), "Experience" reveals a startling new perspective on the process of self-definition. In "Self-Reliance," Emerson suggests ways in which individuals can reconstitute community through communion with nature; in "Experience," however, he explores the plight of the individual who knows that a community of shared beliefs and values is impossible. If "Self-Reliance" grew out of the social values of protocapitalist, postrevolutionary America, "Experience," in contrast, represents the full-blown conception of a social order where alienation is the inevitable fate of individuals. Emerson reluctantly affirms its insurmountability. "I find," he concluded, "a private fruit sufficient."[9]

II

"Self-Reliance" epitomizes the philosophy that Emerson had developed during the 1830s in response to the urbanization of his native

New England and its development of a commercial culture. If one looked around in society only to find corruption, one might find in one's own nature the springs of virtue, which, if followed to their source in nature, would restore to health one's own occluded vision. One would see beneath apparent confusion a unity of purpose within nature, and that vision in turn would enable one to overcome the contentiousness that a shortsighted society had permitted to flourish. Thus would a true community of purpose and values replace what had become the artificial community of geographical proximity. Through self, one could recover the sense of something larger and better than oneself.[10] "Lost in God, in Godhead found," was the way Emerson put the idea in "Threnody," but the notion was not new to him in 1845. In "Self-Reliance" he puts it another way in a passage that seems contradictory on the face of it but which in fact outlines the process of transcendence. "Nothing can bring you peace but yourself," he writes. "Nothing can bring you peace but the triumph of principles."[11] In principle, not in self, lay salvation, but principles were only discoverable through introspection, or self-reliance. All else was unreliable.

We have a right to ask how Emerson could genuinely believe that a commitment to self was anything more than a commitment to the very subjectivism and self-indulgent isolation that he claimed to be combatting. In fact, Emerson's philosophy of self-reliance represents a halfway house between two different ways of conceiving of individual identity: one which depended principally on social roles to describe the self, and another which claimed the existence of a self that transcended the social roles characterizing it. "It seems as if the effect of our increased knowledge had been to make men more contemplative, live less upon the public for excitement, feel the most deeply when alone, and suffer their imaginations to enter into and warm and illuminate their most serious thoughts," Edward Tyrrel Channing remarked in 1819 to his senior class in oratory at Harvard.[12] New England, as elsewhere, was beginning to assume that the inner man possessed an importance that overrode the claims of the public sphere. In the traditional culture of New England, the individual's primary responsibility had been to the community as a whole, whether community was defined as church, town, kin, or, as was most likely, as the conflation of all three. Self-definition, insofar as people thought it necessary to define themselves at all, stemmed from the ways in which the individual fit into the larger whole of which he or she was but a small part.[13] It was not until as late as the eighteenth century, for example, that the word "individual" came to mean anything other than a way of designating relation to a group of which the "individual" was the "ultimate indivisible division." This older usage of the word was still quite common in Emerson's youth. Likewise, "personality," until Emerson's own day, referred not to the unique and particular quality of an individual person, but rather to "the quality of being a person and not a thing."[14] The changes happening to the notion of selfhood in Emerson's times were drastic enough to result in permutations in the definitions of the basic words we use to speak of persons today.

It should not be surprising that Emerson, who grew up in a New England that continued to value the individual (at least rhetorically) according to his ability to submerge himself in the interests of a larger moral whole, would continue to try to define self with respect to an idealized community. His Puritan forebears had looked to the sanctified community of the saints as this source of identity; his republican fathers found self-definition as part of the virtuous community of civic-minded persons. Urbanization and the increasing reliance on a commercial exchange economy had produced a mobility and an anonymity inimical to communal "virtue." Widening class divisions and the advent of denominational pluralism, moreover, had made of the church a fragmented melange of institutions. As a result, Emerson found himself puzzled as to how to define the ideal moral community that would confer identity. "What is the aboriginal Self on which a universal reliance may be grounded?" Emerson asked in "Self-Reliance." The answer was what he called in an 1832 sermon "the Universal providence of God," rechristened "Nature" in his 1836 pamphlet. In a Nature defined as permanent, unchangeable, universal law, the individual found a context against which he could objectively define himself. There were absolute standards against which his life might be judged. If he was no longer part of a physical community that gave meaning to his life by establishing bounds, rhythms, responsibilities, and sacred precincts, he was still by implication part of a spiritual community whose laws he was bound to obey.

Despite his hypothetical membership in this idealized community, however, the individual more often than not found himself in practice a member of multiple communities whose cultures, values, and concerns it was up to him to integrate. As choice of conduct and setting of standards seemed to devolve increasingly on the individual, he became increasingly self-conscious of his own identity as someone unique, existing apart from any of the communities that conferred identity. "The key to the period appeared to be that the mind had become aware of itself," Emerson would later write. That self-consciousness was not always a pleasant sensation, as Emerson's description of "the young men . . . born with knives in their brain" reminds us.[15] "I resent this intrusion of *alterity*," Emerson wrote in his journal for 1841. "That which is done, & that which does, is somehow, I know not how, part of me."[16]

Emerson's painful sense of "alterity," or alienation, emerges throughout his earlier career as the force that pushed him toward the philosophy summed up in "Self-Reliance." Throughout the 1830s he expressed a sense of isolation from others that cannot be entirely accounted for by summoning up his repeated characterizations of himself as naturally diffident. "Few men communicate their highest thoughts to any person and this is not from a desire to withold them; by no means; but because they do not find persons proper to receive them," he preached in an 1832 sermon. And again in 1836, Emerson observed a disquieting self-consciousness that he saw as proper not just to himself, but also to his age: "At the age ludicrously called the age of discretion every hopeful young man is shipwrecked. The burdensome possession of himself he cannot dispose of." Cities in particular, Emerson suspected, produced this feeling of alienation from others. "I always seem to suffer from loss of faith on entering cities," he wrote his brother William. The crowds there seemed to be "all masquers who have taken mutual oaths of silence, not to betray each others secret, & each to keep the others madness in countenance." He wished to make emotional contact with "our passing fellows in the streets both male & female," but unfortunately, he noted, the things we want to say "we cannot say"; indeed we cannot even look at others "but for a moment." His brother Charles described the same feelings in an eloquent letter to his Aunt Mary: "The sights one sees in the city—the people one meets—the noises of civilization the atmosphere of a crowd—these things do not enter into the soul—they do not touch my being— but they lie like a frost or (homelier & truer simile) like a hot scurf on the outside of one's moral & intellectual nature, cramping all growth & suspending the living *action* of the powers."[17] In Emerson's Boston and in the regions beginning to be dominated by the new commercial culture, one encounters what must have been a painful paradox: in a society whose rhetoric preached the necessity of elevating the interests of the public sphere over private concerns, the individual seemed incapable of breaking out of his own private world. "We never touch but at points," Emerson told an audience in 1838.[18] There no longer seemed any escape from the prisonhouse of self.

If complaints about the introspective character of contemporary life were on the rise, perhaps it was because the heterogeneity and numbers of metropolitan areas precluded the sort of balance between public and private aims sustained in the earlier close-knit culture. The individual was now forced to reconcile inconsistent, sometimes conflicting roles. On the most basic level, personal relations now belonged to the private sphere, productivity to the public.[19] In "Self-Reliance," Emerson addresses the necessity for reconciling inconsistent parts of the self to each other. In the interest of preserving an undivided consciousness, Emerson directs his age back to an examination of the nature of self. The individual, he claims, is able to transcend any apparent division between public and private because character is rooted in an undivided aboriginal self. "Who shall define to me an Individual?" he wrote in his journal for May 1837. "I behold with awe & delight many illustrations of the Universal Mind. I see my being embedded in it."[20] Rather than a collection of parts, individuals were to see themselves as coherent wholes capable of resisting the corruption of the various individual cultures of which they were parts. It was only in maintaining an identity apart from the social roles comprising them that people could criticize and transform those roles into something worthy of whole men. For Emerson, the reform of the age meant a revolution in consciousness about the nature of the self. Through self-reliance, he sought to rid individuals of the burden of self-division and alienation.

III

As more than one critic has observed, the structure and repeating theme of Emerson's essay on "Self-Reliance" is paradox.[21] Inner and outer seem at odds, yet somehow Emerson manages to make them correspond. "Trust thyself," he says in one sentence and in the next,

"Accept the place the divine Providence has found you" (which includes "the society of your contemporaries" and "the connexion of events"). In fact, reconciliation of the inner and outer man is precisely the point of the essay. The true paradox, Emerson believed, was the existence of man at war with himself. "I must be myself. I cannot break myself any longer for you, or you," Emerson announces in the middle of the essay. Society demanded that he fragment his own consciousness to fill a constellation of implicitly contradictory roles; he answered by claiming, "Nothing is at last sacred but the integrity of your own mind."

"The virtue in most request is conformity," Emerson believed. Society seemed to be demanding allegiance to external standards that no longer bore much relationship to the thoughts and feelings of the inner man. Therefore, Emerson concluded, "we but half express ourselves." Under such a regime, a vital part of the person was stifled, and there could be no personal satisfaction or inner peace. Such self-division, which forced individuals to cater to external demands, even when these demands violated their "natural" impulses, was Emerson's notion of self-consciousness. This consciousness "clapped [man] into jail," as it were. He became trapped into continually meeting expectations that had nothing to do with the way in which he, the inner man, perceived himself. Forced to develop a public persona with which his private self could not come to terms, he became a constant spectator of himself.

In examining the reformers and the conformists of his age in "Self-Reliance," Emerson offers a pastiche of images of man divided against himself. The abolitionist, for example, promulgates a high standard of morality in public, but of the feelings he expresses self-righteously in public his private heart knows little. Emerson characterizes him as "an angry bigot" despite his "bountiful cause," and urges him to put his own house in order before he tries to deal with problems of which he has no personal knowledge: "Go love thy infant; love thy woodchopper: be good-natured and modest: have that grace; and never varnish your hard, uncharitable ambition with this incredible tenderness for black folk a thousand miles off. Thy love afar is spite at home." The journal passage from which this paragraph was originally taken offers a portrait of this "stiff, hard, proud, clenched Calvinist" who was typical of many who joined the abolitionist ranks.

Likewise, the "foolish philanthropist" comes in for criticism for his effort "to put all poor men in good situations." "Are they *my* poor?" Emerson responds on a seemingly callous note, but he rejects the benevolent and charitable relief societies not because he is indifferent to others, but because he thinks that they deserve more than dollars and cents. "I grudge the dollar, the dime, the cent I give to such man as do not belong to me and to whom I do not belong," he says. As with the abolitionist, the professional philanthropist attempts to reform the public sphere without any awareness of the evil that occurs when man becomes detached from the "virtuous" act he performs as if in penance for his inability to feel for the poor and the downtrodden. The Bible Society member, the party adherent, even the minister, uses his public acts to disguise and eventually to obliterate his own feelings. In so doing, each fails to shape society; each surrenders himself to be shaped by it. Each does such great violence to his true feelings in the process, moreover, that each is left without a self. A society that is a collection of such selfless men is no better than a mob, willing to be swayed by any demagogue who comes along. And "now," insists Emerson, "we are a mob."

The antidote to such self-annihilation was sincerity, or as Emerson called it, self-reliance. To understand how self-reliance was meant to come to grips with and overcome self-consciousness and self-division, it is helpful to glance briefly at its long cultural foreground. The literary critic Lionel Trilling has noted that the concern with sincerity arose (in English literature, at least) in the chaotic social milieu of the Elizabethan era. The rising tide of mobility in Shakespeare's England allowed individuals to pass themselves off as something they were not. A sincere person was one who admitted to the responsibilities of the social station to which he or she had been born, the insincere person one who wreaked havoc on the established order by masquerading as something he or she was not and by refusing to abide by the ascribed responsibilities of his or her social station. In the emerging social order, however, the individual (usually male), wrenched loose from stable social networks to assume his place in the market, experienced consciousness of a private self apart from the public order. It was all very well to advise the individual as Polonius had Laertes, "To thine own self be true," but when the self that one was supposed to be true to became fluid, the advice lost some of its pertinence.²² The revolutionary generation had attempted to solve the problem by conflating the public and private spheres. Although the individual might be aware of conflicts between private and public, the Federalist version of republicanism demanded that individuals forget the private self by voluntarily reimmersing themselves in an organic social order of their own creation. If only they would behave virtuously—that is, with concern for the whole rather than for themselves only—such a social order might be reconstructed. Here in the republican ideology, then, lies a definition of sincerity that supersedes the older concern with fidelity to ascribed role. Now the sincere individual became the one who consciously brought public and private feelings into accord, submerging the former in the latter.

Emerson grew to maturity with these republican exhortations to virtue ringing in his ears, yet he could not help but note that many of his contemporaries were discontented with their lives. His age tended to "insincerity," as private belief contradicted public pronouncement. Even more disturbing, however, Emerson began to see among his contemporaries a tendency to legitimize the split between public and private that republicanism in some measure had been designed to overcome. It seemed to him that the more people repressed their own feelings in order to produce "one of these communities of opinion," the wider the gap between private feelings and public acts became. Among men engaged in the market in particular, there now seemed to be a dangerous trend toward two selves, a public persona who was pledged to do what was right, and a private self who looked on such righteous public action with unfeeling detachment. The result was that "society everywhere" was "in conspiracy against the manhood of every one of its members." The individual was compelled to act insincerely as the only way of dealing with the conflict between the need for self-expression and the need for communal solidarity. In "Self-Reliance," therefore, Emerson is determined to make as bold a stand for sincerity as Luther had at the Wurtemburg Cathedral. "I will stand here for humanity," he announces, "and though I would make it kind, I would make it true." Only with the opening of the mind to the voice of nature could "the walls [be] taken down."²³

Emerson outlines in his essay a plan for restoring the individual to wholeness within a mass culture. The true self, Emerson claims, is not the self who artificially gives himself over to public opinion, but rather the private self, who is the locus of thought and feeling. Aware that the process of self-definition had become problematic for his contemporaries, however, Emerson had been careful throughout his career to specify exactly how the self he spoke of was to be defined. Faithfulness to the true self lay in obedience to the laws of nature that constituted the self on its most basic level. "Whilst you trust in self," the pastor Emerson had told Second Church, "*the origin of self must be perceived.*" Man did not make himself; the individual did not have the right to choose his own self-definition. He was bound to be true to the nature with which God, who had created him, had endowed him. "The moment he lets this truth go," Emerson affirmed, "he becomes a bundle of errors and sins." In another sermon, he addressed the problem of division between outer and inner man more explicitly:

There are two ways of speaking of self; one, when we speak of a man's low and partial self, as when he is said to be selfish; and the other when we speak of the whole self, that which comprehends a man's whole being, of that self of which Jesus said, What can a man give in exchange for his soul? And in that sense, when you say of a man that he thinks too much of himself, I say, No, that fault is that he does not think of himself at all. He has not got so far as to know himself. He thinks of his dress, he thinks of his money, he thinks of his comely person, and pleasant voice, he thinks of the pretty things he has got to say and do, but the eternal reason which shines within him, the immortal life that dwells at the bottom of his heart he knows not. He is not great enough—not good enough—not man enough to go in and converse with that celestial scene. Very likely he is so utterly unacquainted with himself, has lived so on the outside of his world, that he does not yet believe in its existence.[24]

Thus for Emerson sincerity again became a matter of conforming oneself to an ascribed position rather than a choice between different possible personae. This time, however, instead of conforming oneself to an explicit role within a social hierarchy, one was bound to conform to a position within a universal and divinely preestablished hierarchy. Nature, not the social order, taught one who one was and what one's responsibilities were. Sincerity became a matter merely of discovering nature's will and abiding by it.

Emerson anticipated that such an attitude might open him up to charges of antinomianism or subjectivism. "The populace think that your rejection of popular standards is a rejection of all standard, and mere antinomianism," he observed, but he assured them, "[T]he law of consciousness abides." He, not they, was keeping faith with nature; they, not he, gave themselves over to transgressions against the whole. They put themselves on display. "My life," he insisted, "is for itself and not a spectacle." Elsewhere, he refuted at greater length the charges that he had given himself over to subjectivism. "More genius does not increase the *individuality* but the *community* of each mind," he wrote in 1831. Or again in 1837, "I acknowledge that the mind is also a distorting medium so long as its aims are not pure." But so long as one conscientiously sought the truth in one's own nature, one was bound to find it. The distinction between subjectivity and self-reliance was meticulously drawn in this way in an 1839 journal entry: "We are misled by an ambiguity in the use of the term Subjective. It is made to cover two things, a good & a bad. The great always introduce us to facts; small men introduce us always to themselves. The great, even whilst he relates a private fact personal to him, is really leading us away from him to an universal experience. Their own interest is in Nature, & of course all their communication leads outward to it, starting from whatsoever point."[25]

"Self-reliance" in fact was the only way of avoiding the pitfalls of subjectivity and the pain of self-consciousness. The soul divided from itself felt illegitimate and unsure of itself; the conflicting demands of the inner and outer debilitated it. "A great step is made before the soul can feel itself not a charity boy, not a bastard, not an interloper in its own world," Emerson observed in a journal passage that found its way in an altered form into "Self-Reliance."[26] Until the individual discovered his center in a self defined by nature and not by contemporary opinion, he had no answer for the intimidating question that all of nature seemed to ask: "Who are you, sir?" Self-reliance provided him with the answer. In Nature he found his voice. His private self was everything and nothing—everything in that it was part of the divine order of nature, nothing in that it (along with his own self-consciousness) was absorbed into something bigger than itself. Emerson gloried in the knowledge. "All things are dissolved to their center by their cause, and in the universal miracle petty and particular miracles disappear."

Emerson's preoccupation with the conflict between inner and outer, public and private, placed him in distinguished company. Wordsworth, Rousseau, and Carlyle among European romantics also endeavored to deal with their own burdens of self-consciousness, while utopian reformers such as Robert Owen, John Humphrey Noyes, Adin Ballou, the Fourierists, and the Shakers addressed the problem by setting up model communities designed to minimize the conflict. Even the abolitionists, despite Emerson's indictment of them, were disturbed by the disparity between their private conviction and public practice. Today their efforts seem individualistic, sometimes self-indulgent, and always limited by their own subjectivism. However, in societies where a preindustrial social order was giving way under political, economic, and demographic pressures, older "objective" standards of action had been discredited. In nature and in an aboriginal self that partook of nature, such reformers hoped to find a substitute for sacred standards of value that no longer seemed self-evident.[27]

IV

The tone of "Self-Reliance" is confident and sure throughout. Through a communion with nature achieved through self-trust, self-division could be overcome. There seems to have been little doubt in Emerson's mind that the individual could be at peace if only he would conduct his life properly. Hence, the change in tone one encounters in "Experience," the essay on self published four years later, is startling. "Unspeakably sad and barren does life look to those who a few months ago were dazzled with the splendor of the promise of the times," Emerson writes there.[28] In "Self-Reliance" the individual could know all; in "Experience" he knows nothing. In "Self-Reliance" a union with others was potentially possible through Nature; in "Experience" the speaker acknowledges that human beings can never touch at more than a single point, and for no more than a moment. In the first essay Emerson urges the individual to dig beneath life's surfaces to find truth; in the second he insists that there is no truth that we can know—"We live amid surfaces, and the true art of life is to skate well on them." By 1844, Emerson saw the individual isolated from his fellows, trapped within his own consciousness, and condemned to an ignorance of nature's true aims. "Self-Reliance" holds out to the individual the hope that self and society can be reconciled so that the individual need no longer feel pitted against himself in an agony of self-consciousness. "Experience," in sharp contrast, offers no remedy for "the discovery we have made that we exist." We are forever left alone and ignorant in our subjectivity to "do what we must, and call it by the best names we can, and would fain have the praise of having intended the result which ensues." "Experience" thus represents the turning point in Emerson's evaluation of the relationship between self and others, society and solitude. He could find no consciously fabricated community in society.

"Experience" was published in *Essays, Second Series* in 1844, but unlike most of Emerson's essays, it had never been delivered as a lecture. Passages that would later be used in the essay begin to appear in the journals shortly after the death of Waldo, but the essay is somewhat less dependent on such passages than many of Emerson's other works. Apparently much of "Experience" was composed during a concentrated effort by Emerson to face up to the feelings that Waldo's death had brought to the surface. The subject seems to have been too painful to deal with in the isolated journal entries that Emerson usually used to develop his ideas on a subject. Thus, most of "Experience" appears for the first and only time in the essay itself.

Part of the reason that "Experience" is so startling is that this method of composition makes it difficult to trace the evolution of the idea in Emerson's mind. While Waldo's death obviously shocked Emerson, after the first few months following his death he made little overt mention of the tragedy in his journals. Instead, he apparently slowly and carefully reassessed internally what he knew of life in the light of his reaction to his son's death. During 1842 and 1843 he broadened his activity in the public sphere, assuming editorship of the *Dial* and lecturing at lyceums outside of New England. He attended to the friendships he had formed in Concord and supported discussion of reform whenever he could. None of this public activity, however, betrayed the profound changes taking place within. "Experience" is Emerson's admission of the deep-seated changes in himself that had taken place beneath the serene facade.

"Where do we find ourselves?" he begins, in an evident attempt to sort out his feelings. The answer is that we do not know. Even more discouraging, we realize in mid-life that we know as little of our situation as the day we were born: "The Genius which according to the old belief stands at the door by which we enter, and gives us the lethe to drink, that we may tell no tales, mixed the cup too strongly, and we cannot shake off the lethargy now at noonday," Emerson writes. "Sleep lingers all our lifetime about our eyes, as night hovers all day in the boughs of the fir-trees. . . . Ghostlike we glide through nature, and should not know our place again." The note of disillusionment in Emerson's voice is plain. Thinking he had set out on a course that would show him the true face of nature, he learned nothing. Believing that a true philosopher would change society, he had discovered that "we have enough to live and bring the year about, but not an ounce to impact or invest." "Experience," therefore, would be a studied attempt on Emerson's part to reflect on the philosophical lessons of his experiments thus far. In exploring the issue, he would come face to face with the dilemma of the individual in the transformed social milieu of New England: What was an individual life worth that seemed to count for so little in society, and indeed, in the scheme of nature itself?

Emerson uses the death of his son as the touchstone by which to judge the matter. Waldo's death, after all, had brought to a focus his nagging feelings that perhaps his natural philosophy was failing him. It was discouraging that action seemed so seldom to bear fruit, debilitating that no matter what we do "our life looks trivial, and we shun to record it." The knowledge that the family was merely "tragedy and moaning women and hard-eyed husbands and deluges of lethe," that most of life was preparation and routine, "custom and gross sense," was bad enough. But when even the most disastrous and horrifying of events left the individual untouched, what hope was there of diving below the surface of anything? At least in suffering, Emerson had expected, one might find the truth that he had found nowhere else. "Here at last," he wrote, "we shall find reality, sharp peaks and edges of truth." But he had not; "the only thing grief has taught me is to know how shallow it is." It was not that Emerson could not grieve; it is all too clear that he was still in agony over his son's death when he wrote "Experience." This numbing grief proceeded from the discovery that nothing raised the death of his son beyond mere phenomenal loss; it was a loss with no meaning for any but himself. How was his loss, when considered from a spiritual point of view, any worse or any different than the loss of a commodity—"a beautiful estate" or perhaps the "loss of my property"? The answer, Emerson grudgingly admitted, was that it was no different. The death of one particular person meant nothing.

Although grief could teach Emerson nothing, his reaction to grief can teach us something about his discovery, in the weeks and months following Waldo's death, of subjectivism. Before the loss of his son, Emerson looked to nature as a way of erasing the pain of self-consciousness. In the consciousness of the laws of human nature, a subset of natural law, the individual would ground himself in immutable, discoverable truth. He would no longer abandon himself to the relativism that resulted from subjecting himself to the whims of public opinion. In reward for such an attitude, the individual would know "reality." He would no longer be subject to the divided consciousness that was the hallmark of his generation, for to the extent to which he obeyed nature, he would be at one with himself. But in the death of his son Emerson had discovered a grief that, no matter how hard he tried to make it signify, meant nothing more profound to him than personal bereavement. Although he finally resolved the problem of meaning in Nature by reaffirming his faith that somehow it tended toward good, he could never know, after the experience of Waldo's death, how it did so. People could only know what events meant to themselves. "I take this evanescence and lubricity of all objects, which lets them slip through our fingers when we clutch the hardest, to be the most unhandsome part of our condition," he decided as he reflected on the meaning of his son's death.

If this were the case, however—if one could not know immediately what actions or events might signify in a larger scheme of things—how could one possibly reconstruct some sort of community of meaning among individuals? And if one could not, how was one to conduct one's own life? The groundwork for Emerson's later concerns with both evolutionary science and the advance of culture is laid in "Experience," as Emerson determined that life progressed without necessarily either the individual's knowledge or his cooperation. "The whole frame of things preaches indifference," he admitted in "Experience," marking an important departure from his earlier thinking. Before, it had seemed that Nature was a "beautiful mother" who enfolded within her comforting arms her unruly offspring. Now Emerson found himself cut off from knowledge and power, from the sense of possession of a true "self" (whatever that was), and from others. "Dream delivers us to dream, and there is no end to illusion," he now wrote. Though the impulse to recover community with others and integrity of soul remained as strong as ever, there remained to him no unimpeachable way of doing so. All plans for reform, though noble in their own ways, were doomed as partial and subjective in nature. "All our blows glance, all our hits are accidents," he finally acknowledged. "Our relations to each other are oblique and casual."

Through the lens of experience, Emerson viewed not only his son's death but also the whole gamut of his experiments in reforming self and society over the past decade. One's ability to shape society was decidedly limited. Emerson concluded his essay on "Experience" by declaring that "hankering after an overt or practical effect seems to me an apostasy." It had become clear to him through experience, he says in the course of the essay, that even the few original opinions proferred in society were subjective; they did not necessarily have anything to do with nature. Rather they were "organic in the speakers and do not disturb the universal necessity." Because he realized that these opinions were no longer legitimized by nature, good was not as contagious as he had hoped when he believed that the individual might respond naturally to the virtuous expression of human nature in another. Now that the plan of nature seemed opaque, the ability of the individual to communicate anything from one mind to another hung in doubt. "An innavigable sea washes with silent waves between us and the things we aim at and converse with," he observed.

For it seemed to him now that individuals were in a certain sense locked within their own private universes. Individual temperament "shuts us in a prison of glass which we cannot see." Therefore, society was not to be reformed by any amount of self-conscious attendance on nature. "The great gifts are not got by analysis," Emerson now asserted, for the individual could know very little of cause and effect by introspection. "Now skeptical or without unity," the good man was left with the faith that all parts "will one day be *members*, and obey one will." The depth of Emerson's disenchantment with his own earlier belief in the power of nature to reform emerges in one of the most haunting passages of "Experience": "But what help from these fineries and pedantries? What help from thought? Life is not dialectics. We, I think, in these times, have had lessons enough of the futility of criticism. Our young people have thought and written much on labor and reform, and for all that they have written, neither the world nor themselves have got on a step." Emerson's self-criticism here becomes even more apparent when one juxtaposes it with the picture he had offered less than a decade before in *Nature* of life advancing dialectically toward perfection. Now Nature tells him clearly, "You will not remember, and you will not expect." You will not understand and you cannot (consciously) change.

Where once Emerson had been able to write, "I am nothing. I see all," he now wrote, "As I am, so I see." Once he had asserted that "inward and outward senses" could be "truly adjusted to each other"; now he believed that "we do not see directly, but mediately, and that we have no means of correcting these colored and distorting lenses which we are, or of computing the amount of their errors." He had discovered to his chagrin that the conflicts between the ideal and the real, between society and self, were not as easily reconcilable as they seemed. Amid the "slippery sliding surfaces" of life, all that was left in this new moral world was faith in the inexorable progress of Nature. Nevertheless, that faith was no small consolation: by existing as the purposeful force behind the individual subjectivities from which there was no escape, Nature gave them order and meaning—even if that order was not readily apparent to individuals.

If Emerson devoted the early portion of his career to constructing a philosophy that both challenged the authority of the old order and critiqued the new, he spent his later career struggling with the implications of his lived experience for the theory he had proposed. He had been able, by removing himself from the direct influence of mainstream values and public discourse, to develop a powerful and coherent alternative conception of the world. He continued to see his philosophical efforts as reform in its most fundamental sense: to change the age's conception of the world was to change its norms of conduct and thereby its practical activity as a whole.[29] Increasingly skeptical, however, of the individual's ability to know enough of the workings of nature to effect any programmatic change, Emerson moved away from a critique of the social order as a whole and toward a working out of the transformative possibilities inherent in the individual moral vision. *Essays, Second Series* stands perfectly poised between the early efforts to formulate a philosophy and the later efforts to apply it. Other than "Experience," the most central and unifying piece in the collection is "Nominalist and Realist," an exploration of the relation between general, abstract ideas and the particulars that give them life. The topic proves the occasion for Emerson to have another go at the question of how we ought to live given the fact that our vision is and must remain partial. "If we cannot make voluntary and conscious steps in the admirable science of universals," he concludes, "let us see the parts wisely, and infer the genius of nature from the best particulars with a becoming charity."[30]

In coming to dwell more frequently in the realm of the quotidian as a way of understanding universal laws, Emerson later offered his audiences lectures and essays that seemed more accessible because more particular. The portraits of individual life in *Representative Men* (1850), for example, provide concrete examples of how the realization of genius by certain exemplary individuals leads to cooperation with Nature's laws, without the individual ever being completely conscious of the ways in which this process occurs. In addition, his courses of lectures reprinted in *The Conduct of Life* (1860) and *Society and Solitude* (1870) came to deal more frequently with limited or partial subjects, particularly those having to do with manners or aspects of the daily life of those likely to be listening. In his later work, he seems more aware than previously of the ways in which contexts, moods, and temperaments help to shape our understanding of the general laws of Nature we can never know directly. His central concern no longer addresses explicitly the nature of truth or spirit, so much as the pragmatic question he poses in "Fate" (1860): "How shall I live?" The answer he offers again and again is the same: "We are incompetent to solve the times. Our geometry cannot span the huge orbits of prevailing ideas, behold their nature and reconcile their opposition. We can only obey our own polarity."[31]

On 17 June 1844, society came to meet Emerson in the Concord forests in the guise of the railroad. The refugee who had come to his ancestral village to escape the moral pollution of urban society watched curiously as workmen constructed the medium that would make "Massachusetts Boston." While Emerson had never entirely removed himself from Boston, Concord had provided him with enough rural solitude to shield him from the evils of society. But the completion of the railroad, he had sensed one day in 1842, would put an end of sorts to his experiments in nature and in virtue in Concord. "I hear the whistle of the locomotive in the woods," he recorded in his journal. "Whenever the music comes it has a sequel. It is the voice of the Nineteenth Century saying 'Here I am.' " The conjunction of "Experience" with the coming of the railroad seems appropriate. With the passage of the Fugitive Slave Act in 1850, Emerson would discover in an even more immediate way how impossible it was to isolate himself from the evils of his age.[32]

Following the publication of *Essays, Second Series*, the pace of Emerson's public career picked up greatly. His fame spread, bringing in invitations to lecture from further and further away. Between October 1847 and July 1848, he toured Great Britain, speaking before crowds who saw him as something of an American curiosity.[33] In 1849 he published *Nature; Addresses and Lectures* and in 1850 his series on the power of men of genius, *Representative Men*. With the completion of an 1850 lecture swing through the Ohio and Mississippi valleys, Emerson had become a man of national stature. By the time of his death in 1882, he had published ten books, lectured all over the United States and the British Isles, and served as an overseer of Harvard University (which had for many years following the Divinity School Address barred his presence there). Admired throughout the United States and Europe as the very model of the wise and truthful man, the dissident in time became the most widely acclaimed American of his day.

Emerson died in 1882 at the age of seventy-nine. The last words of his long and distinguished career, uttered after a long period of mental deterioration and a short illness, were reported to have been, "The beautiful boy!" Lidian Emerson took them to be a reference to Waldo, dead now these forty years.[34]

Afterword   Emerson and the
Culture of Bourgeois
Individualism

EMERSON'S CAREER did not end in 1845. By about that time, however, the metamorphosis of his philosophy from one intent on
working out the implications of republicanism to another more reflective of the culture of bourgeois individualism had been completed. But despite the insights embodied in "Experience," Emerson
had not given up all hope of reforming public morality. With the
passage of the Fugitive Slave Law in 1850, Emerson the philosopher
had to confront a situation with immediate and pragmatic consequences. A law now compelled him to support as though it were a
positive good an institution he opposed as the embodiment of the
worst materialist tendencies of his age. As the contentious 1850s
wore on, he spoke out directly and with increasing heat against
slavery and those willing to make the compromises that allowed it
to flourish.

Nevertheless, this outpouring of effort in service of the antislavery cause was no new phase in the overall development of Emerson's philosophy. It was in fact of a piece with his earlier career. The
chief source of Emerson's opposition to slavery lay in his contention
that it was another example, particularly horrible, of the ways in
which the pursuit of commerce and the consumer goods now
readily available to large numbers of people led to a blindness to the
moral issues surrounding their production. In his "Address Delivered in Concord on the Anniversary of the Emancipation of the
Negroes in the British West Indies," Emerson outlined the crux of
his opposition to slavery. Slavery weighed in the balance for most,
he believed, as a question of costs and gains rather than one of
moral responsibility. "We found it very convenient to keep [the
slaves] at work, since by the aid of a little whipping, we could get
their work for nothing but their board and the cost of whips," he
told his Concord audience. "What if it cost a few unpleasant scenes

on the coast of Africa?" In this economy of exchange the exploitation that took place remained so remote that consumers never noted the human cost of the commodities they so matter-of-factly enjoyed. "The sugar they raised was excellent; nobody tasted the blood in it," Emerson noted. "The coffee was fragrant; the tobacco was incense; the brandy made nations happy; the cotton clothed the world. What! all raised by these men, and no wages? Excellent! What a convenience! They seemed created by Providence to bear the heat and the whipping and make these fine articles."[1] The slavery issue sharpened and focused Emerson's misgivings about the culture of economic individualism. In the antislavery cause and the Civil War itself, Emerson finally found a reform movement he could not refuse to support actively.

In "Egoism and the Freedom Movement: On the Anthropology of the Bourgeois Era," Max Horkheimer describes the basic contradiction of bourgeois society. An ethic of competition builds conflict between individuals into society, but at the same time, the culture's most important core value is widely taken to be the realization of individual happiness. What is left out is any conscious sense of the whole. The economic necessity of defining the individual as an isolated subject of interest leads to a social isolation, an alienation from others, which comes to seem the natural order of things.[2] In the United States, it was during Emerson's youth and early adulthood that this particular culture began to take shape. Emerson's distinction for his age lay in his ability to recognize many of the consequences of this contradiction in his own life, and to articulate them for his contemporaries in a peculiarly insightful way. His powerful moral critique encompassed many of the institutions most essential in shaping the discourse of the age—religion, politics, literature, philosophy. He has been instinctively recognized in many areas of discourse as the first to provide a liberal critique of American institutions, less perhaps because he embodied some ideal notion of the American character or his times than because he was one of the first to grapple seriously with some of the essential contradictions of the culture of commercial capitalism.

His moral vision, remarkable in the context of its own time and social circumstances, leaves out much of importance, as does American liberalism itself. Built on the presumption that a morality based on nature can release individuals from partisanship and self-interest, Emerson's philosophy does not deal with the implications of the fact that institutions and ideologies are constructed by individuals positioned in particular social and economic circumstances. Although Emerson acknowledged that the truths we discover must be partial, he saw individual temperament alone as the only mediating factor worthy of consideration as we think about differences in perspectives. His virtuous individual, the scholar, he believed to be free of the pervasive social and economic forces of his age by virtue of sincerity and the simple intent to remain virtuous. His critique of the common sense of his day was as vulnerable to appropriation by the new hegemonic order as was the old ideology of republicanism—and Emerson seemed not to have known or cared.

But if Emerson's language is limited, fraught with contradictions, and easily appropriated by others, such is the nature of language itself, and of intellectual discourse in particular. In the era of postmodern capitalism, Emerson's project of finding a solid basis for moral truth in the benevolent plan of nature can no longer be seen as a useful or viable one. Yet his assertion that we must be able to find a place from which to examine critically the common wisdom of the culture makes as much sense now as it did a century and a half ago. Unless we are able to find ways to think critically about the stock definitions of ourselves with which mass culture provides us, we are without the power to transform or to imagine things otherwise.

Although other nineteenth-century reformers may have had a more immediate impact on their contemporaries, Emerson's was long-lasting if subtle. As shifts in values inevitably accompany widespread social and economic change, the way in which people experiencing those shifts interpret them very much depends on the language available to them. By transforming the way many of his age were able to conceive of themselves, Emerson laid the groundwork for transformations of norms of conduct and of action. As the first philosopher of the mass culture of American capitalism, his career suggests the ways in which (in the words of Antonio Gramsci) "the choice and the criticism of a conception of the world is also a political matter."[3]

Notes

Abbreviations

For convenience, the following abbreviations are used in the notes.

CW	*The Collected Works of Ralph Waldo Emerson.* Edited by Robert E. Spiller, Alfred R. Ferguson, et al. 4 vols. to date. Cambridge, Mass.: Harvard University Press, 1971.
EL	*The Early Lectures of Ralph Waldo Emerson.* Edited by Stephen E. Whicher, Robert E. Spiller, and Wallace E. Williams. 3 vols. Cambridge, Mass.: Harvard University Press, 1959, 1964, 1972.
Emerson Family Papers	Houghton Library, Harvard University (bMS AM1280.226). By permission of the Houghton Library.
J	*The Journals of Ralph Waldo Emerson.* Edited by Edward Waldo Emerson and Waldo Emerson Forbes. 10 vols. Boston and New York: Houghton Mifflin, 1909–1914.
JMN	*The Journals and Miscellaneous Notebooks of Ralph Waldo Emerson.* Edited by William H. Gilman, Alfred R. Ferguson, George P. Clark, Merrell R. Davis, Merton M. Sealts, Harrison Hayford, Ralph H. Orth, J. E. Parsons, A. W. Plumstead, Linda Allardt, and Susan Sutton Smith. 16 vols. Cambridge, Mass.: Harvard University Press, 1960–1982.
L	*The Letters of Ralph Waldo Emerson.* Edited by Ralph L. Rusk. 6 vols. New York and London: Columbia University Press, 1939.

MS Sermon Houghton Library, Harvard University (bMS AM1280.215). By permission of the Houghton Library.

W *The Complete Works of Ralph Waldo Emerson.* Centenary Edition. Edited by Edward Waldo Emerson. 12 vols. Boston and New York: Houghton Mifflin, 1903–1904.

YES *Young Emerson Speaks, Unpublished Discourses on Many Subjects.* Edited by Arthur Cushman McGiffert, Jr. Boston: Houghton Mifflin, 1938.

Preface

1. Antonio Gramsci, *Selections from the Prison Notebooks*, ed. and trans. Quintin Hoare and Geoffrey Nowell Smith (London: Lawrence and Wishart, 1971), 323–77, 324, 344.

Chapter 1

1. For fuller descriptions of the economy of a preindustrial city in the initial stages of urbanization, a city such as William Emerson's Boston, see David T. Gilchrist, ed., *The Growth of the Seaport Cities, 1790–1825: Proceedings of a Conference Sponsored by the Eleutherian Mills-Hagley Foundation, March 17–19, 1966* (Charlottesville: The University Press of Virginia, 1967), and David Montgomery, "The Working Classes of the Pre-Industrial City, 1780–1830," *Labor History* 9 (1968): 3–22.

2. Mary Moody Emerson to William Emerson, [1795], Item 1051, Emerson Family Papers. For more information on Emerson's maternal family background, see David Greene Haskins, *Ralph Waldo Emerson: His Maternal Ancestors with Some Reminiscences of Him* (1887; reprint, Port Washington, N.Y.: Kennikat Press, 1971), 1–10.

3. Ruth Haskins Emerson to an unspecified sister, quoted in Haskins, *Ralph Waldo Emerson*, 48.

4. Henry Adams provides a description of the relationship between the Congregational clergy and the Federalist elite in his *History of the United States During the Administration of Thomas Jefferson* (New York: Albert and Charles Boni, 1930), 75–107. See also Conrad Wright's comments on the place of Boston's clergy in its cultural life in *The Beginnings of Unitarianism in America* (Boston: Starr King Press, 1955), 262–65.

5. Gordon S. Wood, *The Creation of the American Republic, 1776–1787* (New York: W. W. Norton, 1969), 426.

6. On Federalism, see James M. Banner, Jr., *To the Hartford Convention: The Federalists and the Origins of Party Politics in Massachusetts, 1789–1815* (New York: Alfred A. Knopf, 1970); Linda K. Kerber, *Federalists in Dissent: Imagery and Ideology in Jeffersonian America* (Ithaca: Cornell University Press, 1970); David Hackett Fischer, *The Revolution of American Conservatism: The Federalist Party in the Era of Jeffersonian Democracy* (New York: Harper and Row, 1965); and Wood, *Creation of the American Republic*, especially 46–90.

7. See Gordon S. Wood, ed., *The Rising Glory of America, 1760–1820* (New York: George Braziller, 1971), 1–22.

8. See Joyce Appleby, "Introduction: Republicanism and Ideology," *American Quarterly* 37 (1985): 461–73; "Republicanism in Old and New Contexts," *William and Mary Quarterly* 43 (1986): 3–19; and *Capitalism and a New Social Order: The Republican Vision of the 1790s* (New York: New York University Press, 1984). The concept of republicanism was hotly contested in the early republic and remains a source of controversy among historians. J. G. A. Pocock, in *The Machiavellian Moment: Florentine Republican Thought and the Atlantic Republican Tradition* (Princeton: Princeton University Press, 1975), describes a classical republican tradition on which the literature dealing with American republicanism builds. Robert E. Shalhope's articles "Toward a Republican Synthesis: The Emergence of an Understanding of Republicanism in American Historiography," *William and Mary Quarterly* 29 (1972): 49–80; and "Republicanism and Early American Historiography," *William and Mary Quarterly* 39 (1982): 334–56, provide a summary and overview of the relevant literature. On the liberal republican tradition, see (in addition to Appleby's works) Eric Foner, *Tom Paine and Revolutionary America* (New York: Oxford University Press, 1976), and John Patrick Diggins, *The Lost Soul of American Politics: Virtue, Self-Interest, and the Foundations of Liberalism* (New York: Basic Books, 1984). Explicit discussions of the tensions within the republican tradition, especially those attempting to explore the relationship between classical and liberal republicanism, include James T. Kloppenberg, "The Virtues of Liberalism: Christianity, Republicanism, and Ethics in Early American Political Discourse," *Journal of American History* 74 (1987): 9–33; Linda K. Kerber, "The Republican Ideology of the Revolutionary Generation," *American Quarterly* 37 (1985): 474–95; and Randolph A. Roth, *The Democratic Dilemma: Religion, Reform, and the Social Order in the Connecticut River Valley of Vermont, 1791–1850* (Cambridge, Eng.: Cambridge University Press, 1987).

9. Quoted in James Spear Loring, *The Hundred Boston Orators Appointed by the Municipal Authorities and Other Public Bodies, From 1770*

to *1852, Comprising Historical Gleanings, Illustrating the Principles and Progress of Our Republican Institutions,* 2d ed. (Boston: John P. Jewett, 1853), 313.

10. MS Letter, 24 December 1807, Item 2846, Emerson Family Papers.

11. On the ways in which a hegemonic ideology is created in times of transition, see Antonio Gramsci, *Selections from the Prison Notebooks,* ed. and trans. Quintin Hoare and Geoffrey Nowell Smith (London: Lawrence and Wishart, 1971); commentaries on Gramsci's model by Chantal Mouffe, "Hegemony and Ideology in Gramsci," in *Gramsci and Marxist Theory,* ed. Chantal Mouffe (London: Routledge and Kegan Paul, 1979), 168–204; and T. J. Jackson Lears, "The Concept of Cultural Hegemony: Problems and Possibilities," *American Historical Review* 90 (1985): 567–93.

On the traditional character of society in New England towns, see Kenneth Lockridge, *A New England Town: The First Hundred Years* (New York: W. W. Norton, 1970), and Michael Zuckerman, *Peaceable Kingdoms: New England Towns in the Eighteenth Century* (New York: W. W. Norton, 1970). On the dangers posed to that ethic by commercialization, mobility, and the social dislocations that intensified in the wake of the Revolution, see Robert A. Gross, *The Minutemen and Their World* (New York: Hill and Wang, 1976), and Richard L. Bushman, *From Puritan to Yankee: Character and Social Order in Connecticut, 1690–1765* (New York: W. W. Norton, 1967).

12. The sermon was Reuben Puffer's *A Sermon, delivered before His Excellency Caleb Strong, esq., Governour, His Honour Edward H. Robbins, esq., Lt. Gov., the Honourable the Council, Senate, and House of Representatives, of the Commonwealth of Massachusetts, May 25, 1803, Being the Day of General Election* (Boston: Young and Minns, 1803). For two views on the continuing uses of Puffer's literary form, the jeremiad, in preserving the semblance of communal solidarity in New England, see Perry Miller, "Errand into the Wilderness," in *Errand into the Wilderness* (Cambridge, Mass.: Harvard University Press, 1958), 1–15; and Sacvan Bercovitch, *The American Jeremiad* (Madison: The University of Wisconsin Press, 1978).

13. Puffer, *Sermon,* 6.

14. On the Federalist approach to the problem of historical change, see Kerber, *Federalists in Dissent,* 173–215, and Stow Persons, "The Cyclical Theory of History in Eighteenth-Century America," *American Quarterly* 6 (1954): 147–63.

15. Puffer, *Sermon,* 7, 12.

16. Ibid., 11–12. On the political stance of the old Federalists, see Fischer, *Revolution of American Conservatism.* On the Jeffersonian Republicans, see Paul Goodman, *The Democratic-Republicans of Massachusetts: Politics in a Young Republic* (Cambridge, Mass.: Harvard University Press, 1964).

17. Puffer, *Sermon*, 16.

18. Buckminster, "Sermon: He that hath no rule over his own spirit is like a city that is broken down, and without walls—Prov. xxv.28," *Sermons by the Late Rev. Joseph S. Buckminster with A Memoir of His Life and Character*, 2d ed. (Boston: Wells and Lilly, 1815), 221; Channing, *Dr. Channing's Note-Book: Passages from the Unpublished Manuscripts of William Ellery Channing*, ed. Grace Channing (Boston and New York: Houghton, Mifflin, 1887), 17. Such warnings against a slide into corruption through lust for wealth had become commonplace in New England since the Revolution, but they were on the rise in the early part of the nineteenth century. On this topic, see Perry Miller, "From the Covenant to the Revival," *Nature's Nation* (Cambridge, Mass.: Harvard University Press, 1967), 90–120.

19. Quoted in Kerber, *Federalists in Dissent*, 125. On the social significance of the classical education that Boston prescribed for its well-to-do sons, see Kerber, *Federalists in Dissent*, 95–134.

20. Emerson himself had certainly recited the piece in his own childhood. He makes a facetious reference to it in an 1816 letter to his brother William. See *L*, 1:17.

21. Edmund Quincy, *Life of Josiah Quincy of Massachusetts* (Boston: Ticknor and Fields, 1867), 308.

22. To Edward Bliss Emerson, Boston?, 20? January? 1816?, *L*, 1:18.

23. To William Emerson, Boston, 9 January 1816, *L*, 1:13; To Edward Bliss Emerson, Boston, c. 23 October 1816, *L*, 1:20; To Edward Bliss Emerson, Boston, 8 January 1817, *L*, 1:34; To Edward Bliss Emerson, Boston, 1 and 5 October 1817, *L*, 1:45.

24. Edward Waldo Emerson, *Emerson in Concord: A Memoir Written for the "Social Circle" in Concord, Massachusetts* (Boston: Houghton, Mifflin, 1889), 7.

25. To William Emerson, Waltham, Massachusetts, 6? February 1818, *L*, 1:57.

26. Edward Bliss Emerson to Mary Moody Emerson, 12 December 1817, Item 175, Emerson Family Papers.

27. Adams is quoted in "The Canal and Railroad Enterprise of Boston," in *The Memorial History of Boston, Including Suffolk County, Massachusetts, 1630–1880*, ed. Justin Winsor (Boston: James R. Osgood, 1882), 4:149.

28. The literature on modernization describes some of the dislocations accompanying the rise of urban, commercial economies. See, for example, Gino Germani, "Urbanization, Social Change, and the Great Transformation," in *Modernization, Urbanization, and the Urban Crisis* (Boston: Little, Brown, 1973), 3–58; Marion J. Levy, Jr., "Structural Features of Any Relatively Modernized Society," and "The Structure of Relatively Nonmodernized Societies," in *Modernization and the Structure of Societies: A Setting for International Affairs* (Princeton, N.J.: Princeton University Press,

1966), 1, 38–79, 85–129; and Horace Miner, "The Folk-Urban Continuum," *American Sociological Review* 17 (1952): 529–37. For discussions of the kinds of disruptions in social relations occasioned by such a transition, see Wolfram Fischer, "Social Tensions at Early Stages of Industrialization," *Comparative Studies in Society and History* 9 (1966): 64–83; and Alvin Boskoff, "Recent Theories of Social Change," in *Sociology and History: Theory and Research*, ed. Werner J. Cahnman and Alvin Boskoff (New York: Free Press of Glencoe, 1964), 140–57.

Historians have also noted the waning of "a nonabstract, direct, personal experience" in such societies and the rise of a "more abstract and formal conception of community." See especially Thomas Bender, *Toward an Urban Vision: Ideas and Institutions in Nineteenth-Century America* (Lexington: University Press of Kentucky, 1975), 129–57; and Rowland Berthoff, *An Unsettled People: Social Order and Disorder in American History* (New York: Harper and Row, 1971), 218–32. Richard Brown uses sociological criteria to locate the time of transition in New England in the last half of the eighteenth century in "The Emergence of Urban Society in Rural Massachusetts, 1760–1820," *Journal of American History* 61 (1974): 29–51.

29. Scholarship on the social structure of eighteenth-century Boston includes the following useful articles: James Henretta, "Economic Development and Social Structure in Colonial Boston," *William and Mary Quarterly* 22 (1965): 75–92; Allan Kulikoff, "The Progress of Inequality in Revolutionary Boston," *William and Mary Quarterly* 28 (1971): 375–412; and Gary B. Nash, "Wealth and Poverty in Three Colonial Cities: The Social Background to Revolution," *The Journal of Interdisciplinary History* 8 (1976): 545–84, and *The Urban Crucible: Social Change, Political Consciousness, and the Origins of the American Revolution* (Cambridge, Mass.: Harvard University Press, 1979).

30. Timothy Dwight, *Travels in New-England and New York* (New Haven, 1821), 1:507.

31. Joseph Buckminster to Joseph Stevens Buckminster, 27 December 1803, quoted in Eliza Buckminster Lee, *Memoirs of Rev. Joseph Buckminster, D.D., and of his Son, Rev. Joseph Stevens Buckminster* (Boston: Ticknor, Reed, and Fields, 1851), 139; *JMN*, 1:146; William Sullivan to Daniel Webster, 12 May 1828, *The Papers of Daniel Webster: Correspondence* (Hanover, N.H.: University Press of New England for Dartmouth College, 1976), 2:346.

32. *The By-Laws and Orders of the Town of Boston, Passed at Several Legal Town Meetings, and Duly Approved by the Court of Sessions: Together with the Rules and Orders Passed by the Selectmen* (Boston, 1818), 7.

33. Boston Record Commissioners, *A Volume of Records Relating to the*

Early History of Boston Containing Boston Town Records, 1796 to 1813 (Boston: Municipal Printing Office, 1905), 35:339.

34. Elias Boudinot, *Journey to Boston in 1809*, ed. Milton Halsey Thomas (Princeton: Princeton University Library, 1955), 52; Boston Record Commissioners, *A Volume of Records Relating to the Early History of Boston Containing Minutes of the Selectmen's Meetings, 1779 to, and including, 1810* (Boston: Municipal Printing Office, 1904), 33:150.

35. Boston Record Commissioners, *A Volume of Records Relating to the Early History of Boston Containing Minutes of the Selectmen's Meetings, 1811 to 1817, and Part of 1818* (Boston: Municipal Printing Office, 1908), 38:109, 216; Boston Record Commissioners, *A Volume of Records Relating to the Early History of Boston, Containing Minutes of the Selectmen's Meetings from September 1, 1818 to April 24, 1822* (Boston: Printing Department, 1909), 39:47.

36. Joseph F. Kett, *Rites of Passage: Adolescence in America, 1790 to the Present* (New York: Basic Books, 1977), 98–102. Paul E. Johnson finds a similar demographic situation existing in Rochester, New York, when the Sabbatarian movement emerged there. See especially his chapter on "Society" in *A Shopkeeper's Millennium: Society and Revivals in Rochester, New York, 1815–1837* (New York: Hill and Wang, 1978), 37–61.

37. *A Collection of the Miscellaneous Writings of Professor [Levi] Frisbie, With Some Notice of his Life and Character*, ed. Andrews Norton (Boston: Cummings, Hilliard, 1823), 113.

38. Ibid., 110.

39. "Report of the Boston Society for the Moral and Religious Instruction of the Poor," *Boston Recorder* 2, no. 44 (28 October 1817): 183; *Boston Recorder* 2, no. 18 (29 April 1817): 183; "Report of the Boston Society," 183.

40. Roger Lane, in his study of crime and the police in Boston, suggests that whether or not the level of crime and drunkenness-related crime was actually on the increase, such crimes had become more highly visible in the clogged city. The result was that people firmly believed that they were. See Lane, *Policing the City: Boston, 1822–1885* (Cambridge, Mass.: Harvard University Press, 1967), 6ff.

41. Josiah Quincy, *A Municipal History of the Town and City of Boston, During Two Centuries* (Boston: Charles C. Little and James Brown, 1852), 105.

42. Joshua Bates, "Reminiscences of the Late John Codman, D.D. with Brief Notices of the Prominent Traits of His Character," in William Allen, *Memoir of John Codman, D.D.* (Boston: T. R. Marvin and S. K. Whipple, 1853), 178; Parish Articles against Codman, 30 October 1811, quoted by Bates in Allen, *Memoir*, 204.

43. Preamble to "Subscriptions to New Church Lot, December 5, 1808,

Park Street Church," quoted in H. Crosby Englizian, *Brimstone Corner: Park Street Church, Boston* (Chicago: Moody Press, 1968), 26. That the source of the hostility of the other Boston churches to Park Street was less a theological response than a reaction to the church's exclusivity is witnessed by a letter of the Reverend Francis Parkman, Unitarian minister of Boston's New North Church and father of the historian. "I know not how this church flourishes at present," he says in an 1815 London periodical, "but it was opposed not because it was founded upon Calvinism; but on account of the intolerant spirit some of its first patrons displayed." [Quoted in Hamilton Andrews Hill, *History of the Old South Church (Third Church) Boston, 1669–1884* (Boston: Houghton, Mifflin, 1890), 369.] Accounts of the early days of the orthodox-Unitarian controversy include Earl Morse Wilbur's *A History of Unitarianism in Transylvania, England, and America* (Cambridge, Mass.: Harvard University Press, 1952); Wright, *Beginnings of Unitarianism in America;* and Charles C. Foreman's " 'Elected Now by Time': The Unitarian Controversy, 1805–1835," in *A Stream of Light: A Sesquicentennial History of American Unitarianism,* ed. Conrad Wright (Boston: Unitarian Universalist Association, 1975), 3–32.

44. To Edward Bliss Emerson, Boston, 1 and 5 October 1817, *L*, 1:47.

45. Ibid.

46. On the moral philosophy taught at Harvard during this period, see Daniel Walker Howe, *The Unitarian Conscience: Harvard Moral Philosophy, 1805–1861* (Cambridge, Mass.: Harvard University Press, 1970).

47. University in Cambridge, Order of Performances for Exhibition, 20 October 1818; 19 August 1819; 23 August 1821 (Cambridge, Mass.: University Press, 1818, 1819, 1821); and 30 October 1821 (Cambridge, Mass.: Hilliard and Metcalf, 1821).

48. On the character of Kirkland and his relationship with students, see Samuel Eliot Morison, "The Great Rebellion in Harvard College, and the Resignation of President Kirkland," *The Colonial Society of Massachusetts Transactions, 1927–1930, Publications of the Colonial Society of Massachusetts* (Boston: The Society, 1932), 27:54–112.

49. Preamble of the Pythologian Club, quoted in James Elliot Cabot, *A Memoir of Ralph Waldo Emerson* (Boston: Houghton, Mifflin, 1887), 1:65. For a contemporary description of student life at Harvard about the time of Emerson's matriculation there, see Benjamin Thomas Hill, "Life at Harvard a Century Ago As Illustrated by the Letters and Papers of Stephen Salisbury, Class of 1817," *Proceedings of the American Antiquarian Society* (Worcester: The Society, 1910), n.s. 20: 197–248.

50. Dwight, *Travels,* 1:487.

51. George Ticknor, quoted in Anna Ticknor, *Life, Letters, and Journals of George Ticknor* (Boston: James R. Osgood, 1876), 1:358–59.

52. To William Emerson, Cambridge, 23 July 1818, *L*, 1:68; To William

Emerson, Cambridge, 23 December 1817, *L*, 1:51–52; Josiah Quincy, *Figures of the Past from the Leaves of Old Journals* (Boston: Roberts Brothers, 1883), 20–21.

53. *JMN*, 1:244–45.

54. Faculty Records IX.263, 18 July 1821, quoted in Morison, "The Great Rebellion," 77n; N. A. Haven to George Ticknor, 15 September 1821, quoted in Ticknor, *Life*, 1:354n. For an account of the Rebellion of the Class of 1823 taken from the diary of a student participant, see Morison, "The Great Rebellion," 69–72.

55. The literature on antebellum college rebellions has tended to see them as motivated by the suppression of free thought on campus (see, for example, Steven J. Novak, *The Rights of Youth: American Colleges and Student Revolt, 1798–1815* [Cambridge, Mass.: Harvard University Press, 1977]) or as a result of the increasing reluctance of older students to acquiesce to severe parietal restraints (David F. Allmendinger, Jr., "The Dangers of Ante-Bellum Student Life," *Journal of Social History* 7 [1973]: 75–85, or Kett, *Rites of Passage*). In "Emersonian Genius and the American Democracy," *New England Quarterly* 26 (1953): 27–44, Perry Miller suggests that the malaise that was so widespread among the young men at Harvard during Emerson's generation had an ideological component as well. It seems to me that any adequate explanation of the riots must take into consideration the interplay of all of these factors. Nevertheless, since Kirkland's administration gave fairly wide latitude to students, at least extracurricularly, and since Harvard students at the time of the rebellions were still considerably younger than those whom Allmendinger's thesis anticipates, Miller's suggestion of a crisis of values remains the most intriguing of the explanations.

56. *JMN*, 1:39, 53.

57. Ibid., 237.

58. Ibid., 29–30.

Chapter 2

1. *JMN*, 1:94; To John Boynton Hill, Boston, 12 March 1822, *L*, 1:106.

2. To John Boynton Hill, 3 January 1823, *L*, 1:127.

3. "Union," *Boston Patriot*, 25 October 1820, p. 2, col. 1; "J," *Boston Daily Advertiser*, 23 October 1820, p. 2, col. 3.

4. For a brief history of attempts to reform town government, see James M. Bugbee, "Boston under the Mayors, 1820–1880," in *Memorial History of Boston, Including Suffolk County, Massachusetts, 1630–1880*, ed. Justin Winsor (Boston: James R. Osgood, 1882), 3:219–21.

5. Josiah Quincy, *A Municipal History of the Town and City of Boston, During Two Centuries* (Boston: Charles C. Little and James Brown, 1852),

28. On Josiah Quincy and his response to the town's transformation, see Robert A. McCaughey, *Josiah Quincy, 1772–1864: The Last Federalist* (Cambridge, Mass.: Harvard University Press, 1974).

6. Quoted by James Spear Loring, *The Hundred Boston Orators Appointed by the Municipal Authorities and Other Public Bodies, From 1770 to 1852, Comprising Historical Gleanings, Illustrating the Principles and Progress of our Republican Institutions*, 2d ed. (Boston: John P. Jewett, 1853), 378; Samuel Adams [mechanic], quoted in *A Full and Authentic Report of the Debates in Faneuil Hall, December 31, January 1, and 2, 1821–22, On Changing the Form of Government of the Town of Boston. Including the Speeches of Messrs. Clough, Emmons, etc., As Furnished by Themselves* (Boston, 1822), 18, 21; Loring, *Hundred Boston Orators*, 378; Josiah Quincy, quoted in *Report of the Debates*, 38. My discussion of the debates surrounding the change from town to city government is indebted to Andrew R. L. Cayton, "The Fragmentation of 'A Great Family': The Panic of 1819 and the Rise of a 'Middling Interest' in Boston, 1818–1822," *Journal of the Early Republic* 2 (1982): 143–68.

7. To John Boynton Hill, Boston, 11 May 1822, *L*, 1:110.

8. Ibid., 1:110–11.

9. Ibid., 1:111.

10. Ibid.

11. Ibid., 1:111, 112; To John Boynton Hill, Boston, 12 November 1822, *L*, 1:124.

12. To Mellish Irving Motte?, Concord, c. 16? April 1822, *L*, 1:109; To John Boynton Hill, Boston, 3 and 6 July 1822, *L*, 1:119–22.

13. *JMN*, 1:117–18, 119, 124–29. As Leonard N. Neufeldt points out in "Henry David Thoreau's Political Economy," *New England Quarterly* 57 (1984): 59–83, Thoreau too relied on the language of republicanism to describe his age.

14. RWE, "The Present State of Ethical Philosophy," in *Two Unpublished Essays: The Character of Socrates; The Present State of Ethical Philosophy*, ed. Edward Everett Hale (Boston and New York: Lamson, Wolffe, 1896), 72–73; *JMN*, 1:254.

15. RWE, "The Character of Socrates," in *Two Unpublished Essays*, 34–35.

16. Ibid., 19, 23–25.

17. RWE, "The Present State of Ethical Philosophy," 48.

18. *JMN*, 1:151.

19. Ibid., 1:96, 98; *JMN*, 2:8, 210. In "The Present State of Ethical Philosophy," Emerson had criticized Thomas Hobbes for claiming that social relations were "artificial and grotesque" (*JMN*, 1:56).

20. *JMN*, 1:106.

21. To John Boynton Hill, Roxbury, Massachusetts, 19 June and 2 July 1823, *L*, 1:133.

22. *JMN*, 2:202, 206.

23. Ibid., 254, 283.

24. Ibid., 321, 326–29.

25. Ibid., 326, 329.

26. For discussions of the ways in which individual freedom within capitalism masks a larger subjection to the economic process, see David Held's analysis of Max Horkheimer's "Authority and the Family," in *Introduction to Critical Theory: Horkheimer to Habermas* (London: Hutchinson, 1980), 194–97; and Georg Lukács, "Reification and the Consciousness of the Proletariat," in *History and Class Consciousness: Studies in Marxist Dialectics*, trans. Rodney Livingstone (Cambridge, Mass.: MIT Press, 1971), 83–222.

27. *JMN*, 2:332.

28. Sprague, quoted in Loring, *Hundred Boston Orators*, 416; Perkins, quoted in Samuel Eliot Morison, *The Life and Letters of Harrison Gray Otis, Federalist, 1765–1848* (Boston: Houghton, Mifflin, 1913), 2:251.

29. Quincy, "An Address Delivered at the Unanimous Request of Both Branches of the City Council on the Fourth of July, 1826, It Being the Fiftieth Anniversary of American Independence, by Josiah Quincy, Mayor of the City," quoted in Quincy, *Municipal History*, 432; C. C. Baldwin, *Diary . . . 1829–1835* (Worcester, 1901), quoted in Arthur M. Schlesinger, Jr., *The Age of Jackson* (Boston: Little, Brown, 1945), 146n; "R. J.," "Democratic Principles," *Boston Patriot*, 4 January 1824, p. 2. On the Massachusetts Jacksonians, see Schlesinger, *Age of Jackson*, 146–48; see also Richard P. McCormick, *The Second American Party System: Party Formation in the Jacksonian Era* (New York: W. W. Norton, 1966), 36–49; and Arthur B. Darling, *Political Changes in Massachusetts, 1824–1848: A Study of Liberal Movements in Politics* (Cos Cob, Conn.: John E. Edwards, 1968), 61–63.

30. *JMN*, 4:20.

31. "Circular to the Mechanics of the City of Boston and Vicinity" (Broadside), 11 February 1834, Boston Public Library; Judge Peter Oxenbridge Thacher, *Charge to the Grand Jury of the County of Suffolk* (1834), 16, quoted in Schlesinger, *Age of Jackson*, 165–66. On Antimasonry in Massachusetts, see McCormick, *Second American Party System*, 47–48; and Darling, *Political Changes in Massachusetts*, 85–129. On the Workingmen's party, see Schlesinger, *Age of Jackson*, 149–58, and Darling, *Political Changes in Massachusetts*, 98ff. For an intriguing discussion of the emergence of both groups in Massachusetts, see Ronald P. Formisano, *The Transformation of Political Culture: Massachusetts Parties, 1790s-1840s* (New York: Oxford University Press, 1983), 197–244.

32. Everett, "Lecture on the Working Men's Party, Delivered Before the Charlestown Lyceum, 6th October, 1830," in *Orations and Speeches on Various Occasions* (Boston: American Stationers' Company, 1836), 285, 271–72; Garrison, "Working Men," *The Liberator* 1, no. 1 (1 January 1831): 18.

33. John Warren James, quoted in Loring, *Hundred Boston Orators*, 463; Josiah Quincy to Sir Augustus Foster, Cambridge, Mass., 7 March 1834, quoted in Edmund Quincy, *Life of Josiah Quincy of Massachusetts* (Boston: Ticknor and Fields, 1867), 459.

34. See, for example, MS Sermon (57) "Thanksgiving," 25 November 1829; MS Sermon (61), [The year's end], 31 December 1829; "The Individual and the State," in *YES*, 78–80.

35. MS Sermon "Thanksgiving"; "The Individual and the State," 78.

36. MS Sermon (113), [Fasting, humiliation, and prayer], 7 April 1831.

37. MS Sermon (145), [Judging right for ourselves], 26 February 1832; see also MS Sermon (122A), [We are not our own], n.d.; MS Sermon (109A), [God in the soul], 5 March 1831; *JMN*, 3:277; "Politics," in "The Philosophy of History," *EL*, 2:81. Critics have traditionally focused on Emerson's democratic tendencies, sometimes confusing his belief in the republican rule of virtuous individuals with majority rule. For some typical appraisals of Emerson as "the Philosopher of Democracy," see John Dewey, "Ralph Waldo Emerson," in *Characters and Events*, ed. John Dewey and Joseph Ratner, vol. 1 (New York: Holt, Rinehart and Winston, 1929), reprinted in *Emerson: A Collection of Critical Essays*, ed. Milton R. Konvitz and Stephen E. Whicher (Englewood Cliffs, N.J.: Prentice-Hall, 1962), 24–30; Raymer McQuiston, "The Relation of Ralph Waldo Emerson to Public Affairs," *Bulletin of the University of Kansas Humanistic Studies* 3 (15 April 1923): 7–63; and F. O. Matthiessen, "Method and Scope," *American Renaissance: Art and Expression in the Age of Emerson and Whitman* (New York: Oxford University Press, 1941), vii–xvi.

38. *JMN*, 3:278.

39. MS Sermon (113), [Fasting, humiliation, and prayer].

40. *JMN*, 3:31. A number of scholars have pointed out that Emerson's belief in the intimate relation between public duty and private virtue traces back to the Puritan idea of the covenanted nation. Perry Miller points up Emerson's debt in general to the Puritan ethos in "Jonathan Edwards to Emerson," *New England Quarterly* 13 (1940): 589–617. Miller finds an antinomian streak in Emerson, a judgment that recent criticism has tempered. Sacvan Bercovitch, in *The Puritan Origins of the American Self* (New Haven: Yale University Press, 1975), contends that Emerson drew on New England's spiritual heritage to transform the self into an *exemplum fidei*. For Emerson as well as for his Puritan forebears, Bercovitch argues, the way through the self was ultimately meant to lead away from the self.

Far from being antinomian, Emerson saw the virtuous private self as microcosm of an orderly and virtuous whole. Wesley T. Mott, "Emerson and Antinomianism, The Legacy of the Sermons," *American Literature* 50 (1978): 369–97, lends support to Bercovitch's thesis. The Emerson of the sermons, Mott finds, distrusted antinomianism, and his concern with individual spiritual life was always linked to a concern for the communal and national welfare.

41. "Introductory," in "Human Culture," *EL*, 2:281; *JMN*, 3:104; MS Sermon (42), [True freedom], 4 July 1829; MS Sermon (38), [The Christian is free and solitary], 30 May 1829; MS Sermon (80), [Patriotism], 3 July 1830.

42. MS Sermon (154), [Duty], 6 May 1832.

43. Everett, "Address at the Erection of a Monument to John Harvard, September 26, 1828," in *Orations and Speeches*, 170; Mason, 4 July 1827, oration, quoted in Loring, *Hundred Boston Orators*, 447–48. Fred Somkin's *Unquiet Eagle: Memory and Desire in the Idea of American Freedom, 1815–1860* (Ithaca, N.Y.: Cornell University Press, 1967) provides an interesting discussion of Lafayette's visit to America in 1825. He believes the uproarious welcome accorded him was "an agonizing and finally unsuccessful attempt to retain the esprit of a sacred society, a family brotherhood, within a framework of conceptual and institutional constructs based upon freedom of contract"(6). The superheated patriotism of the day appears to have been an attempt to shore up the crumbling facade of social organicism in Boston as well as in the rest of an increasingly commercial and diversified nation.

44. MS Sermon (80), [Patriotism], 3 July 1830.

Chapter 3

1. *JMN*, 2:179; To Mary Moody Emerson, Boston, 10 June 1822, *L*, 1:115; Mary Moody Emerson to RWE, 1821, Item 824, Emerson Family Papers. On Emerson's failure throughout his life to appreciate greatly the sensual qualities of nature, see Joel Porte, *Emerson and Thoreau: Transcendentalists in Conflict* (Middletown, Conn.: Wesleyan University Press, 1966), 44–67.

2. *JMN*, 1:86; *JMN*, 2:33–34.

3. RWE, "The Present State of Ethical Philosophy," in *Two Unpublished Essays; The Character of Socrates; The Present State of Ethical Philosophy*, ed. Edward Everett Hale (Boston and New York: Lamson, Wolffe, 1896), 67; *JMN*, 2:5. On Emerson's definition of virtue, see Stephen E. Whicher, *Freedom and Fate: An Inner Life of Ralph Waldo Emerson* (Philadelphia: University of Pennsylvania Press, 1953), 41–44.

4. For an extended discussion of the Harvard moral philosophy to which Emerson was exposed, see Daniel Walker Howe, *The Unitarian Con-*

science: Harvard Moral Philosophy, 1805–1861 (Cambridge, Mass.: Harvard University Press, 1970), and D. H. Meyer, *The Instructed Conscience: The Shaping of the American National Ethic* (Philadelphia: University of Pennsylvania Press, 1972). See also George Ripley and George P. Bradford, "Philosophic Thought in Boston," in *The Memorial History of Boston, including Suffolk County, Massachusetts, 1630–1880,* ed. Justin Winsor (Boston: James R. Osgood, 1882), 4:295–330.

5. "Review: The Christian Philosopher; or the Connexion of Science and Philosophy with Religion. Thomas Dick," *Christian Examiner* 5, no. 1 (January–February 1828): 23; *Monthly Anthology* 1, no. 2 (December 1803): 61.

6. See Howe, *Unitarian Conscience,* 27–29, and Meyer, *Instructed Conscience.*

7. RWE, "The Present State of Ethical Philosophy," 68–69; Hannah Stevenson, one of Emerson's students, quoted in Edward Waldo Emerson, *Emerson in Concord: A Memoir Written for the "Social Circle" in Concord, Massachusetts* (Boston: Houghton, Mifflin, 1889), 31. Emerson mentions reading Stewart's moral philosophy in a letter to William and Edward Bliss Emerson, Brookline, Massachusetts, 30? July 1830, *L*, 1:306. He also highly praises the work of Scottish moral philosopher James Mackintosh in *JMN*, 4:7, and in a letter to William Emerson, Boston, 15 March 1832, *L*, 1:348. On the common sense philosophy, see Howe, *Unitarian Conscience,* and Ernest Lee Tuveson, "The Origin of the 'Moral Sense,'" *The Imagination as a Means of Grace: Locke and the Aesthetics of Romanticism* (Berkeley: University of California Press, 1960), 42–55. On Emerson's perception of the common sense philosophy, see Porte, *Emerson and Thoreau,* 68–92; J. Edward Schamberger, "The Influence of Dugald Stewart and Richard Price on Emerson's Concept of the 'Reason': A Reassessment," *ESQ* 18 (1972): 179–83; and Sheldon W. Liebman, "The Origins of Emerson's Early Poetics: His Reading in the Scottish Common Sense Critics," *American Literature* 45 (1972): 179–83.

8. *JMN,* 1:139; 2:161.

9. Ibid., 2:65.

10. On the hidden conservative bias of the common sense philosophy, see Meyer, *Instructed Conscience.*

11. *JMN,* 2:64–65.

12. Ibid., 1:107, 122, 86–87.

13. Ibid., 1:100, 82; 2:117.

14. See *J*, 2:98n, and *JMN*, 2:388n.

15. Ibid., 2:119–20, 312.

16. All quotations are taken from "Pray without Ceasing," in *YES*, 1–12.

17. *JMN*, 3:142, 127.

18. Ibid., 3:29; "Find Your Calling," in *YES*, 165.

19. RWE, "Right Hand of Fellowship at Ordination of Hersey Bradford Goodwin, 1830," in *Uncollected Writings: Essays, Addresses, Poems, Reviews and Letters* (New York: Lamb Publishing Company, 1912), 12; MS Sermon (26), [Affections for God can be cultivated, pt. 1], 13 November 1828; *JMN*, 3:213.

20. *JMN*, 3:212, 182.

21. Levi Frisbie, *Miscellaneous Writings*, ed. Andrews Norton (Boston, 1823), xxiv. On Emerson's Neoplatonism, see John S. Harrison, *The Teachers of Emerson* (New York: Sturgis and Walton, 1910), and Kenneth Walter Cameron, *Emerson the Essayist: An Outline of His Philosophical Development Through 1836 with Special Emphasis on the Sources and Interpretation of Nature*, vol. 1 (Hartford: Transcendental Books, 1945).

22. Emerson copied the following notes from his reading of de Gérando's *Histoire Comparée des Systemes de Philosophie*, a work that emphasized the spiritual unity of all things underlying the appearance of diversity that they presented to the senses:

Pythagoras.

—

taught that *Numbers were the principles of things*
the *monad* one, eternal, simple, perfect
dyad imperfect, matter, chaos.

"Beings are bound together by a chain of relations parallel or like to those which unite numbers. All of these relations converge to one center. World forms one whole. Symmetry presided over the systems of their dependance & their connexion.
The Pythagoreans first gave the name κόσμος [order] to the world— Beauty—"

[*JMN*, 3:366–67]

23. On Emerson's debt to Coleridge and Kant, see Cameron, *Emerson the Essayist*, 78–223; Harrison, *Teachers of Emerson*, 288–91; William R. Hutchinson, *The Transcendentalist Ministers: Church Reform in the New England Renaissance* (New Haven: Yale University Press, 1959); Frank T. Thompson, "Emerson's Indebtedness to Coleridge," *Studies in Philology* 23 (1926): 55–76.

24. Samuel Taylor Coleridge, *Aids to Reflection*, ed. James Marsh (Burlington, Vt.: C. Goodrich, 1829), notes, 371–72, reprinted in Cameron, *Emerson the Essayist*, 1:81; Coleridge, *The Complete Works*, ed. W. G. T. Shedd (New York, 1853), 2:176, reprinted in Cameron, *Emerson the Essayist*, 1:80.

25. *JMN*, 2:187.

26. Ibid., 3:214; "The Relation of Man to the Globe," in "Science," *EL*, 1:49; *JMN*, 4:287, 291.

27. "Shakespear [First Lecture]," in "English Literature," *EL*, 1:300; *JMN*, 5:222; To Thomas Carlyle, Concord, 17 September 1836, in *The Correspondence of Emerson and Carlyle*, ed. Joseph Slater (New York: Columbia University Press, 1964), 149–50; "Introductory," in "The Philosophy of History," *EL*, 2:17.

28. "The Heart," in "Human Culture," *EL*, 2:284; *JMN*, 3:190; "The Heart," in "Human Culture," *EL*, 2:284.

29. "Introductory," in "The Philosophy of History," *EL*, 2:11; *JMN*, 5:272; "Miracles," in *YES*, 122; "Introductory," in "The Philosophy of History," *EL*, 2:12.

30. *JMN*, 5:282; "The Head," in "Human Culture," *EL*, 2:248.

31. MS Sermon (43), [Christianity confirms natural religion], 11 July 1829; *JMN*, 1:335–36; MS Sermon (78), [Salvation, now], 12 June 1830.

32. *JMN*, 3:80; "Home," in "Human Life," *EL*, 3:28; *JMN*, 5:32; 3:258.

33. Georg Lukács, "Reification and the Consciousness of the Proletariat," in *History and Class Consciousness: Studies in Marxist Dialectics*, trans. Rodney Livingstone (Cambridge, Mass.: MIT Press, 1971), 136.

34. "Tragedy," in "Human Life," *EL*, 3:117.

Chapter 4

1. On Henry Ware, Jr., and Second Church, see John Ware, *Memoir of the Life of Henry Ware, Jr.* (Boston: James Munroe and Co., 1846), 91–93. Christ Episcopal Church in the North End was also commonly called "Old North," although the Second (Unitarian) Church claimed the original title of Old North.

2. To the Second Church and Society in Boston, Cambridge, 30 January 1829, *L*, 1:261.

3. Lyman Beecher to Dr. [Edward] Griffin, 1 March 1828, in *The Autobiography of Lyman Beecher*, ed. Barbara M. Cross (Cambridge, Mass.: Harvard University Press, 1961), 1:96. The literature on the social implications of the evangelical-Unitarian controversy is already extensive. For comments on revivalism as a response to social mobility, see Rowland Berthoff, *An Unsettled People: Social Order and Disorder in American History* (New York: Harper and Row, 1971), 235–74; on evangelicalism as a response to reorganization of social structures, see Donald G. Mathews, "The Second Great Awakening as an Organizing Process, 1780–1830: An Hypothesis," *American Quarterly* 21 (1969): 23–43; and Paul Boyer, *Urban Masses and Moral Order in America, 1820–1920* (Cambridge, Mass.: Harvard University Press, 1978), 3–33. On the rational impulse toward social reform in which the evangelicals played a part, see John L. Thomas, "Romantic Reform in America, 1815–1865," *American Quarterly* 17 (1965): 656–81.

Philip Greven provides an interesting commentary on the evangelical tendency to reject individual values in favor of communal ones in *The Protestant Temperament: Patterns of Child-Rearing, Religious Experience, and the Self in Early America* (New York: Alfred A. Knopf, 1977). For an important account of evangelicalism as an attempt to restructure society in an era when older structures were breaking down, see Donald M. Scott, *From Office to Profession: The New England Ministry, 1750–1850* (Philadelphia: University of Pennsylvania Press, 1978). My analysis of the religious controversy in Boston during the 1820s and 1830s draws on all these sources as well as on Clifford Geertz's assumption in *The Interpretation of Cultures* (New York: Basic Books, 1973) that religion represents symbolically a people's worldview—"the picture they have of the way things in sheer actuality are, their most comprehensive ideas of order" (89).

4. Beecher, *Autobiography*, 2:35; Beecher to Rev. E[lias] Cornelius, 16 February 1825, in Beecher, *Autobiography*, 2:12.

5. Accounts of the early days of the orthodox-Unitarian controversy include Earl Morse Wilbur's *A History of Unitarianism in Transylvania, England, and America* (Cambridge, Mass.: Harvard University Press, 1952); Conrad Wright, *The Beginnings of Unitarianism in America* (Boston: Starr King Press, 1955); and Charles C. Foreman's " 'Elected Now by Time': The Unitarian Controversy, 1805–1835," in *A Stream of Light: A Sesquicentennial History of American Unitarianism*, ed. Conrad Wright (Boston: Unitarian Universalist Association, 1975), 3–32.

6. Beecher to Dr. [Nathaniel] Taylor, Boston, 1 May 1823, in Beecher, *Autobiography*, 1:404.

7. Beecher to Edward Beecher, 5 September 1826, in Beecher, *Autobiography*, 2:48.

8. Beecher to Taylor, in Beecher, *Autobiography*, 1:402. In a letter to Edward Bliss Emerson dated Boston, 12 July 1831, Ruth Haskins Emerson lamented the fact that, of the city's three "elderly ministers," William Ellery Channing, John Gorham Palfrey, and Charles Lowell, only the latter was left in the city for the summer. She expressed some concern that in time of religious crisis there were so few experienced ministers around to combat the inroads of evangelicalism. See Item 2654, Emerson Family Papers.

9. Edward Griffin to the Reverend James Richards, Boston, 15 January 1810, quoted in William B. Sprague, *Memoir of the Rev. Edward D. Griffin, D.D.* (New York: Taylor and Dodd, 1839), 116.

10. "Preface," *Panoplist*, 13 (1817): iv; *Boston Recorder* 7, no. 25, 22 June 1822, p. 100, col. 1; Mathetes, "Unitarian Views Examined," *Boston Recorder and Telegraph* 11, no. 11, 17 March 1826, p. 41, col. 2. For some remarks from sixty years' distance on the "class distinction which was felt even in the sanctuary," see Oliver Wendell Holmes, *Ralph Waldo Emerson*

(Boston: Houghton, Mifflin, 1885), 34–35.

11. *Boston Recorder* 8, no. 15, 12 April 1823, col. 1.

12. Lyman Beecher, "The Faith Once Delivered to the Saints," delivered at Worcester, Massachusetts, 15 October 1823, at the ordination of Rev. Loammi Ives Hoadley, in *Sermons Delivered on Various Occasions*, vol. 2, *Works* (Boston: John P. Jewett, 1852), 259; Beecher to Taylor, Boston, 24 April 1823, in *Autobiography*, 1:401.

13. Buckminster, "Sermon: Whosoever Shall Confess Me Before Men, Him Will I Also Confess Before My Father, Which is in Heaven," *Sermons by the Late Rev. Joseph S. Buckminster with A Memoir of His Life and Character* (Boston: Wells and Lilly, 1815), 176.

14. William Henry Channing, *Memoir of William Ellery Channing, with Extracts from His Correspondence and Manuscripts* (London: John Chapman, 1848), 2:164–65; William Ellery Channing, "Unitarian Christianity Most Favorable to Piety: Discourse at the Dedication of the Second Congregational Unitarian Church, New York, 1826," in *The Works of William E. Channing, D.D.* (Boston: American Unitarian Association, 1877), 392; N. L. Frothingham, *A Plea Against Religious Controversy, Delivered on Sunday, February 8, 1829* (Boston: Munroe and Francis, 1829).

15. Pierce, quoted in William B. Sprague, *Annals of the American Pulpit* (New York: Robert Carter and Brothers, 1865), 8:96, 69; Samuel J. May, quoted in Sprague, *Annals of the American Pulpit*, 8:173; Sprague, *Annals of the American Pulpit*, 8:264; Joseph Tuckerman to unspecified friend, 1834, quoted in Sprague, *Annals of the American Pulpit*, 8:350. So practical was Emerson's preaching that he was reminded by his senior colleague twice not to forget the Scriptures in his sermons. "I have affected generally a mode of illustration rather bolder than the usage of our preaching warrants, on the principle that our religion is nothing limited or partial, but of universal application, & is interested in all that interest man," Emerson replied in a note to Ware dated 30 December 1828. "I can readily suppose I have erred in the way you mention, of failing to add to my positions the authority of scripture quotation—& am very much obliged to you for the particular improvement you have suggested, which I shall not fail to avail myself of when I shall have occasion to repeat that sermon" (*L*, 1:273).

16. "Christianity a Study for Intelligent Men," *Christian Examiner* 1, no. 1 (January–February 1824): 29.

17. Theodore Parker, *Theodore Parker's Experience as a Minister, with Some Account of His Early Life, and Education for the Ministry, Contained in a Letter from Him to the Members of the Twenty-Eighth Congregational Society of Boston* (Boston: Rufus Leighton, Jr., 1859), 30–31.

18. *JMN*, 3:259; MS Sermon (3), [Setting a good example], June 1827; MS Sermon (25), [The rights of others], November 1828; "Religious Liberalism and Rigidity," in *YES*, 88.

19. Beecher, *Autobiography*, 1:306.

20. Beecher, "The Bible a Code of Laws," in *Sermons Delivered on Various Occasions*, 154; *Lectures on Political Atheism and Kindred Subjects Together with Six Lectures on Intemperance*, in *Works*, 1:14; *Autobiography*, 1:296, 85; *Works*, 1:14; 1:3.

21. Beecher, *Spirit of the Pilgrims* 1, no. 1 (January 1828): 3, 14.

22. Joseph Stevens Buckminster to the Reverend Mr. [Thomas] Belsham, 5 December 1809, in Eliza Buckminster Lee, *Memoirs of Rev. Joseph Buckminster, D.D., and of His Son, Rev. Joseph Stevens Buckminster* (Boston: Ticknor, Reed, and Fields, 1851), 335, 340.

23. Beecher, *Spirit of the Pilgrims* 1, no. 1 (January 1828): 3, 6.

24. [Thomas Hamilton], *Men and Manners in America* (Philadelphia: Carey, Lea, and Blanchard, 1833), 94–95.

25. "Spirit of Orthodoxy," *Christian Examiner* 4, no. 5 (September–October 1827): 456, reprinted from the *Boston Recorder and Telegraph*.

26. John Ware, *Memoir*, 101; Second Church, Boston, MS Records, Vol. 9 (1816–1833), Massachusetts Historical Society, 20; Henry Ware, Jr., to Henry Ware, Sr., 30 May 1813, quoted in John Ware, *Memoir*, 48; Second Church Records, 21.

27. Second Church Records, 27.

28. On the new pietistic movement among some Unitarians in this era, see Anne C. Rose, *Transcendentalism as a Social Movement, 1830–1850* (New Haven: Yale University Press, 1981), 1–37.

29. Second Church Records, 27.

30. For the orthodox view of such meetings, see Beecher, *Autobiography*, 2:54, and H. Crosby Englizian, *Brimstone Corner: Park Street Church, Boston* (Chicago: Moody Press, 1968), 88–90.

31. Research on the demographic changes in nineteenth-century Boston reveals that at least during the middle third of the century, Boston was home to a highly mobile population. Peter R. Knights, in "Population Turnover, Persistence, and Residential Mobility in Boston, 1830–1860," in *Nineteenth-Century Cities: Essays in the New Urban History*, ed. Stephan Thernstrom and Richard Sennett (New Haven: Yale University Press, 1969), 258–74, estimates that during the era, the population turnover rate for any given year was 30 to 40 percent. Many of these people apparently alternated residence in the city with time in outlying rural areas, while others came to the city for only a short time and left never to return. On the nature of the population growth in Boston of which these highly mobile people were a part, see Peter R. Knights, *The Plain People of Boston, 1830–1860: A Study in City Growth* (New York: Oxford University Press, 1971); Everett S. Lee and Michael Lalli, "Population," in *The Growth of the Seaport Cities, 1790–1825: Proceedings of a Conference Sponsored by the Eleutherian Mills-Hagley Foundation, March 17–19, 1966*, ed. David T.

Gilchrist (Charlottesville: University Press of Virginia, 1967), 25–37; Allan Kulikoff, "The Progress of Inequality in Revolutionary Boston," *William and Mary Quarterly* 28 (1971): 375–412.

32. Anne C. Rose, "Social Sources of Denominationalism Reconsidered: Post-Revolutionary Boston as a Case Study," *American Quarterly* 38 (1986): 243–64, provides a valuable discussion of the social differences among the various Boston denominations in the period just prior to Emerson's pastorate.

33. Hamilton Andrews Hill, *History of the Old South Church (Third Church) Boston, 1669–1884* (Boston: Houghton, Mifflin, 1890), 341; Englizian, *Brimstone Corner*, 36–37.

34. Park Street Church, MS Church Records, 6 February 1809–February 1834, Congregational Library, 106.

35. The use of the Examining Committee to determine a candidate's fitness for membership contrasted sharply with Unitarian custom. In Second Church, for example, a certificate of membership from another church was criterion enough for transferring membership. Park Street also carefully noted the dismission of members who desired to remove themselves to another church for whatever reason; Second Church's records, in contrast, record only one case of dismission in the twenty-two year period from 1809 through 1831.

36. Significantly, in Unitarian churches the most furor over misconduct arose over public acts that seemed to affect the welfare of the community as a whole, while evangelical churches made little distinction between public and private misconduct. The most notorious suspension in First (Unitarian) Church records, for example, concerns James Thwing, who in his capacity as cashier of the Massachusetts Bank had lent bank money to a friend who failed shortly thereafter. Much attention was paid to his case but relatively little to routine cases of immorality. See *The Records of the First Church in Boston, 1630–1868*, vol. 2, in Publications of the Colonial Society of Massachusetts (Boston: The Society, 1961), 40:632–33.

37. See Englizian, *Brimstone Corner*, 68–69.

38. Beecher, *Autobiography*, 2:3; "On the Divisions in the Church," *Boston Recorder and Telegraph* 11, no. 2, 13 January 1826, p. 5, col. 3; Beecher to Edward Beecher, July 1826, in Beecher, *Autobiography*, 2:45; Reverend Richard S. Storrs, *Memoir of the Rev. Samuel Green, Late Pastor of Union Church, Boston* (Boston: Perkins and Marvin, 1836), 168; "Communications," *Spirit of the Pilgrims* 1, no. 2 (February 1828): 58.

39. See Paul E. Johnson, *A Shopkeeper's Millennium: Society and Revivals in Rochester, New York, 1815–1837* (New York: Hill and Wang, 1978), and Jill Siegel Dodd, "The Working Classes and the Temperance Movement in Ante-Bellum Boston," *Labor History* 19 (1978): 510–31. Mary Patricia Ryan's study of the rise of the middle class in Utica, New York, *Cradle of*

the Middle Class: The Family in Oneida County, New York, 1790–1865 (Cambridge, Eng.: Cambridge University Press, 1981) tends to confirm that the mobile sons and daughters of the mercantile class (those who no longer were involved in the household economy) were those involved in evangelical activity in the city. Moreover, in Utica young persons turned to evangelical-related voluntary organizations for peer group support in a strange environment. On the emergence of a class sensibility among the mechanics and skilled laborers of Boston, see David Montgomery, "The Working Classes of the Pre-Industrial American City, 1780–1830," *Labor History* 9 (1968): 3–22.

40. Beecher to William Beecher, Boston, 10 April 1826, in Beecher, *Autobiography*, 2:51.

41. Park Street Church—Membership Mobility, 1809–1834

Number received into church	831
Dismissed from church (did not die as members)	512
Dismissed 0–5 years from date of admission	182
Dismissed 6–10 years from date of admission	137
Dismissed 11–15 years from date of admission	84
Total dismissed 0–15 years from date of admission	403
Excommunicated	26

[Park Street Church, Index of Members, 1809–1850, MS, Congregational Library]

42. Apparently, the Unitarians who moved out of the North End and left their old haunts to the newcomers from the country maintained their old church affiliations from afar. John Nicholas Booth in *The Story of the Second Church in Boston (the Original Old North) Including the Old North Church Mystery* (Boston, n.p., 1959) states that by 1832, half of Emerson's parishioners lived in Boston's South End.

43. Mary P. Ryan, "A Woman's Awakening: Evangelical Religion and the Families of Utica, New York, 1800–1840," *American Quarterly* 30 (1978): 602–23, has found that in Utica, most of the converted in the 1820s and 1830s were the sons and daughters of women converted in the 1810s.

44. Salem Street Church, Boston, MS, Examining Committee Records No. 1 (1827–1837), Massachusetts Historical Society, 7–104; ibid., 15; Park Street Church, MS, Examining Committee Record Books, 1828–1834, Congregational Library, 29.

45. Beecher to William Beecher, in Beecher, *Autobiography*, 2:41.

46. On the connections between adolescence and revivalism, see Joseph F. Kett, "Adolescence and Youth in Nineteenth-Century America," in *The Family in History: Interdisciplinary Essays*, ed. Theodore K. Rabb and Robert I. Rotberg (New York: Harper and Row, 1971), 95–110; Whitney Cross, *The Burned-Over District: The Social and Intellectual History of Enthusi-*

astic *Religion in Western New York, 1800–1850* (New York: Harper and Row, 1950).

47. Park Street Church, Examining Committee Record Books, 151.

48. Ibid., 42.

49. Cleora, "An Address to Christians," *Panoplist* 11, no. 2 (February 1815): 68; Lyman Beecher, *The Memory of our Fathers. A Sermon Delivered at Plymouth, on the 22nd of December, 1827* (Boston: T. R. Marvin, 1828), 9; Beecher, *Lectures on Political Atheism*, 392. The literature on evangelical benevolence and reform is voluminous, that on Unitarian reform scarce. On evangelical reform, see Thomas, "Romantic Reform"; W. David Lewis, "The Reformer as Conservative: Protestant Counter-Subversion in the Early Republic," in *The Development of an American Culture*, ed. Stanley Cohen and Lorman Ratner (Englewood Cliffs, N.J.: Prentice-Hall, 1970), 64–91; Lois W. Banner, "Religious Benevolence as Social Control: A Critique of an Interpretation," *Journal of American History* 60 (1973): 23–41; John R. Bodo, *The Protestant Clergy and Public Issues, 1812–1848* (Princeton: Princeton University Press, 1954); Charles I. Foster, *An Errand of Mercy: The Evangelical United Front, 1790–1837* (Chapel Hill: University of North Carolina Press, 1960); and Clifford S. Griffin, *Their Brothers' Keepers: Moral Stewardship in the United States, 1800–1865* (New Brunswick, N.J.: Rutgers University Press, 1960). On Unitarian reform, see Rose, *Transcendentalism*, 1–37.

50. Joseph Tuckerman, quoted in William B. Sprague, *Annals of the American Pulpit*, 8:346; [Cyrus A. Bartol], *Influence of the Ministry at Large in the City of Boston* (Boston: James Munroe and Co., 1836), 50–52.

51. William Ellery Channing, "A Discourse on the Life and Character of the Rev. Joseph Tuckerman, D.D.," in *Works*, 580; *Second Semi-Annual Report of the Ministers-at-Large to the Benevolent Fraternity of Churches* (Boston: Tuttle and Weeks, 1835), 8, 12. The *Christian Examiner*, the official Unitarian organ, held forth in a similar vein: "There is an indissoluble connexion and mutual dependence among the classes of our society, and that the happiness of all, and in fact their existence, under free institutions, is mainly concerned in preserving a mutual confidence, respect, and esteem; so that it is a most unpatriotic, as well as unchristian effort, to attempt to separate these classes into opposite, conflicting, and irreconcilable parties" (42 [n.s. 12] [31 December 1830]:272). On Unitarian benevolence, see Maria Kleinburg Baghdadi, "Protestants, Poverty and Urban Growth: A Study of the Organization of Charity in Boston and New York, 1820–1865," Ph.D. dissertation, Brown University, 1975.

52. Beecher to Dr. [Benjamin] Wisner, 1825, in *Autobiography*, 2:11. The political arm of Beecher's "army" was the Hanover Association of Young Men. Eventually the Hanover Association blossomed into a number of young men's societies bent on wresting power from the Unitarian establish-

ment. See Beecher, *Autobiography*, 2:107–11; Review of Amasa Walker's "An Address delivered before the Young Men of Boston, associated for Moral and Intellectual Improvement, on the 55th Anniversary of American Independence," *Christian Examiner* 15 (n.s. 10) (September 1833): 125–26; Arthur B. Darling, *Political Changes in Massachusetts, 1824–1848: A Study of Liberal Movements in Politics* (Cos Cob, Conn.: John E. Edwards, 1968).

53. *The Liberator* 1, no. 1 (1 January 1831): 1.

54. Channing, *Works*, 139, 149, 148, 144.

55. *JMN*, 3:71; MS Sermon (92), [Reason and revelation], 24 October 1830; *JMN*, 4:75; *CW*, 2:30.

56. MS Sermon (77A), [Christian charity], June 1830; MS Sermon (40), [Charity], 14 June 1829.

57. MS Sermon (91), [Consolation in trouble], 10 October 1830. For comments in a similar vein, see MS Sermon (108), [Grief], 26 February 1831.

58. MS Sermon (19), [Actions derived from principles], 7 May 1828; MS Sermon (130), [Love thy neighbor], 1 October 1831; MS Sermon (38), [The Christian is free and solitary], 30 May 1829.

59. *JMN*, 3:259; MS Sermon (88), [The oracle within], 11 September 1830.

60. "Religious Liberalism and Rigidity," in *YES*, 83. Emerson amplified his remarks on the symbolic character of theological language in an entry in *JMN*, 4:14: "To be at perfect agreement with a man of most opposite conclusions you have only to translate your language into his. The same thought which you call *God* in his nomenclature is called *Christ*. In the Language of William Penn moral sentiment is called *Christ*."

61. MS Sermon (98), [Perfect love casteth out fear], 5 December 1830; To William Emerson, Brookline, Massachusetts, 27 May 1830, *L*, 1:303; MS Sermon (65), [Benevolence and selfishness], 6 February 1830; "Religious Liberalism and Rigidity," 86.

62. MS Sermon (43), [Christianity confirms natural religion], 11 July 1829; MS Sermon (133), [The reality and blessedness of religion], 30 October 1831; MS Sermon (111A), [The common basis of truth], 27 March 1831.

63. MS Sermon (105), [The imperfections of good men], 23 January 1831; MS Sermon (41), [Death levels varieties], 2 July 1829; MS Sermon (62A), [Love to Christ], 16 January 1830; "Religious Liberalism and Rigidity," 87; *JMN*, 3:301.

64. MS Sermon (56), [A true account of the soul], 21 November 1829.

65. In [Death levels varieties], Emerson speaks of the church's duty to gather together in common worship a "disparity of tastes, of ages, of success, & of expectations."

66. [Love thy neighbor].

Chapter 5

1. James Elliot Cabot, *A Memoir of Ralph Waldo Emerson* (Boston: Houghton, Mifflin, 1887), 1:13.

2. See, for example, To Edward Bliss Emerson, Boston, 1 and 5 October 1817, and To William Emerson, Cambridge, 14 and 15 February, and Boston, 20 February 1819, in *L*, 1:46–47, 77.

3. Mary Moody Emerson to RWE, 26 May 1818, Item 814, Emerson Family Papers. Edward Bliss Emerson mentions that his Aunt Mary has urged on him the same calling in EBE to Mary Moody Emerson, 3 May 1818, Item 176, Emerson Family Papers.

4. For some other assessments of Emerson's attitude toward the ministry and his decision leave it, see Henry Nash Smith, "Emerson's Problem of Vocation—A Note on 'The American Scholar,'" *New England Quarterly* 12 (1939): 52–67; Maurice Gonnaud, *Individu et société dans l'oeuvre de Ralph Waldo Emerson: Essai de biographie spirituelle* (Paris: Didier, 1964), 79–128; Joel Porte, *Representative Man: Ralph Waldo Emerson in His Time* (New York: Oxford University Press, 1979), 37–63; Stephen E. Whicher, *Freedom and Fate: An Inner Life of Ralph Waldo Emerson* (Philadelphia: University of Pennsylvania Press, 1953), 3–26.

5. See, for example, Eliza Buckminster Lee's discussion of the pastorate of the Reverend Joseph Buckminster, father of Joseph Stevens Buckminster, in Portsmouth, New Hampshire, in the late eighteenth and early nineteenth centuries, in *Memoirs of Rev. Joseph Buckminster, D.D., and of His Son, Rev. Joseph Stevens Buckminster* (Boston: Ticknor, Reed, and Fields, 1851), 156–61. For the New England clergy during the Revolution, political issues were frequently perceived as religious issues. On the clergy's role in the Revolution itself, see Alan E. Heimert, *Religion and the American Mind, From the Great Awakening to the Revolution* (Cambridge, Mass.: Harvard University Press, 1966).

6. Edward Waldo Emerson, *Emerson in Concord: A Memoir Written for the "Social Circle" in Concord, Massachusetts* (Boston: Houghton, Mifflin, 1889), 56. On Ezra Ripley, see also RWE's essay on his grandfather in *W*, 10:379–95. On the New England ministry and the changes that began to take place in the sacred office beginning in the late eighteenth century, see David D. Hall, *The Faithful Shepherd: A History of the New England Ministry in the Seventeenth Century* (Chapel Hill: University of North Carolina Press, 1972); Sidney Mead, "The Rise of the Evangelical Conception of the Ministry in America, 1607–1850," in *The Ministry in Historical Perspective*, ed. H. Richard Niebuhr and Daniel Williams (New York: Harper and Brothers, 1956), 207–49; Daniel H. Calhoun, *Professional Lives in America: Structure and Aspiration, 1750–1850* (Cambridge, Mass.: Harvard University Press, 1965); Donald M. Scott, *From Office to Profession: The*

New England Ministry, 1750–1850 (Philadelphia: University of Pennsylvania Press, 1978); and Daniel Walker Howe, *The Unitarian Conscience: Harvard Moral Philosophy, 1805–1861* (Cambridge, Mass.: Harvard University Press, 1970).

7. William Emerson to Ezra Ripley, 6 January 1796, Item 2892, Emerson Family Papers; William Emerson to Ezra Ripley, 8 March 1796, Item 2893, Emerson Family Papers. Emerson's situation was fairly typical of the plight of a growing number of the New England clergy in the postrevolutionary period. Another illustrious member of the Boston clergy, Henry Ware, Sr., came to Harvard in 1804 to assume the Hollis Professorship of Divinity because his Hingham parish provided him a salary inadequate to support his family. See John Ware, *Memoir of the Life of Henry Ware, Jr.* (Boston: James Munroe and Co., 1846), 16. On the subject of "translations" from country parishes to Boston pulpits, see William B. Sprague on the Reverend Samuel West of Boston in *Annals of the American Pulpit* (New York: Robert Carter and Brothers, 1865), 8:52–53; Calhoun, *Professional Lives in America*, 88–108; Evelyn Marie Walsh, "Effects of the Revolution upon the Town of Boston: Social, Economic, and Cultural," Ph.D. dissertation, Brown University, 1964, 204–7.

8. Lee, *Memoirs*, 69; *The Records of the First Church in Boston, 1630–1868*, vol. 2, Publications of the Colonial Society of Massachusetts (Boston: The Society, 1961), 40:591; Benjamin Austin, quoted in Cabot, *A Memoir of Ralph Waldo Emerson*, 1:7.

9. John Gorham Palfrey, quoted in Sprague, *Annals of the American Pulpit*, 8:403. On the meteoric rise of literary men such as Buckminster in the Boston clergy, see Lawrence Buell, "Joseph Stevens Buckminster: The Making of a New England Saint," *The Canadian Review of American Studies* 10 (1979): 1–29; Lewis P. Simpson, "Joseph Stevens Buckminster: The Rise of the New England Clerisy," in *The Man of Letters in New England and the South: Essays on the History of the Literary Vocation in America* (Baton Rouge: Louisiana State University Press, 1973), 3–31.

10. Henry Ware, Jr., to Mr. Allen, July 1818, in John Ware, *Memoir*, 124. On the trend toward a youthful clergy in the larger towns of New England, see Calhoun, *Professional Lives in America*, 151–52. The city's preference for young ministers was not the only reason the average ministerial age was so low: as discussed later in the chapter, the ambitious young ministers of Boston were dying of exhaustion and overexertion.

11. Joseph Stevens Buckminster, "Sermon: Take Heed How Ye Hear—Luke VIII.18," in *Sermons by the Late Rev. Joseph Stevens Buckminster with a Memoir of His Life and Character* (Boston: Wells and Lilly, 1815), 184; "On the Relation Between the Clergy and the People," *Christian Examiner* 2, no. 1 (1825): 5–6; Ruth (Haskins) Emerson to Mary Moody Emerson, 17 June 1818, Item 2682, Emerson Family Papers; Lee, *Memoirs*, 213;

Buckminster, "Take Heed How Ye Hear," 186.

12. [John Eliot], "Memoir of the Life and Character of the Late Rev. William Emerson," *Collections of the Massachusetts Historical Society*, 2d ser. (Boston, 1814), 1:257. On the literary and social interests of the Boston Unitarian clergy at the turn of the century, see Conrad Wright, *The Beginnings of Unitarianism in America* (Boston: Starr King Press, 1955), 259–61.

13. Joseph Stevens Buckminster, "Memoir of the Life and Character of the Reverend Joseph Stevens Buckminster," in *Sermons by the Late Rev. Joseph Stevens Buckminster*, xx; William Ellery Channing, "Theological Education: Being Extracts from Observations on the Proposition for Increasing the Means of Such Education at the University in Cambridge, 1816," in *Works* (Boston: American Unitarian Association, 1877), 279; Channing, "Letter on Catholicism. To the Editor of the 'Western Messenger,' Louisville, Kentucky," *Works*, 475.

14. Channing, 22 February 1840, quoted in William Henry Channing, *Memoir of William Ellery Channing, with Extracts from His Correspondence and Manuscripts* (London: John Chapman, 1848), 2:264; Henry Ware, Jr., *Works*, 2:194, quoted in Howe, *Unitarian Conscience*, 136. See also Henry Ware, Jr., *The Connection Between the Duties of the Pulpit and the Pastoral Office. An Introductory Address Delivered to the Members of the Theological School in Cambridge, October 18 and 25, 1830* (Cambridge, Mass.: Hilliard and Brown, 1830), 3–6; "Clerical Studies: Being the Substance of a Dissertation Read Before an Association of Ministers," *Christian Examiner*, 3d ser., 81, no. 12 (1837): 274–75. On the move toward experimental religion among the Unitarian clergy, see Howe, *Unitarian Conscience*, 162–69; Mead, "Evangelical Conception of the Ministry," 234–42; Conrad Wright, "The Early Period (1811–1840)," in *The Harvard Divinity School: Its Place in Harvard University and in American Culture*, ed. George Huntston Williams (Boston: Beacon Press, 1954), 21–77; and Anne C. Rose, *Transcendentalism as a Social Movement, 1830–1850* (New Haven: Yale University Press, 1981), 28–37.

Whether or not this change in clerical status was a result of a real loss of power in society on the part of the clergy has been a matter open to discussion. Lois W. Banner, in "Religious Benevolence as Social Control: A Critique of an Interpretation," *Journal of American History* 60 (1973): 23–41, maintains that the clergy were no worse off by the early nineteenth century than other classes of professionals. Ann Douglas in *The Feminization of American Culture* (New York: Avon Books, 1977), 17–49, provides a convincing counterargument.

15. Richard Sennett, in *The Fall of Public Man* (New York: Alfred A. Knopf, 1976), explores the process by which social intercourse in Western culture shifted increasingly in the eighteenth and nineteenth centuries from the public sphere to the private sphere. If the ministerial role seemed

ambiguous during the period, Sennett's analysis suggests that it was perhaps because the relationship of individuals to the social order as a whole during this period seemed to be particularly problematic.

16. *JMN*, 2:237, 231, 261.

17. Ibid., 2:238. Emerson's attitude toward the ministry is further revealed by the question he proposed for discussion at the second meeting of the Society for Improvement in Extemporaneous Speaking at the Harvard Divinity School: "Is it expedient, in consideration of the spirit of the age, that a minister should be a profound theologian?" (See "Regulations of the Society for Improvement in Extemporaneous Speaking," 23 March 1825, Harvard University Archives [HUD 3378–500], reprinted in Kenneth Walter Cameron, "A Glimpse of Young Emerson at Divinity College," *ESQ* 48 [1967]: 89–91.) On Channing as a powerful influence in Emerson's decision to enter the ministry, see Mary Edrich Redding, "Emerson's 'Instant Eternity': An Existential Approach," in *Emerson's Relevance Today: A Symposium*, ed. Eric W. Carlson and J. Lasley Damerson (Hartford: Transcendental Books, 1971), 43–52.

18. *JMN*, 2:238–42.

19. Ibid., 3:78. While on a brief vacation from his preaching in 1827 for reasons of health, Emerson decided again that although he was "cold & solitary," he was yet called to be "a moral agent of an indestructible nature & designed to stand in sublime relations to God & to my fellow men; to contribute in my proper enjoyments to the general welfare" (*JMN*, 3:72).

20. "The Miracle of Our Being," in *YES*, 210; *JMN*, 3:152–53. For another view of Emerson's decision to enter the ministry, see David Robinson, *Apostle of Culture: Emerson as Preacher and Lecturer* (Philadelphia: University of Pennsylvania Press, 1982), 30–47.

21. See Robinson, *Apostle of Culture*, 48–68.

22. To William Emerson, Hanover, New Hampshire, 16 August 1829, in *L*, 1:279; *JMN*, 6:129; "The Christian Minister: Part I," in *YES*, 27; Edward Bliss Emerson to RWE, 27 April 1827, Item 203, Emerson Family Papers; *JMN*, 3:130; "The Christian Minister: Part I," 28.

23. "The Christian Minister: Part I," 27; Frederick William Hedge on Emerson's preaching, quoted in Cabot, *A Memoir of Ralph Waldo Emerson*, 1:150. On the changes in the Unitarian sermon form during this period, see Lawrence Buell, *Literary Transcendentalism: Style and Vision in the American Renaissance* (Ithaca: Cornell University Press, 1973), 102–39.

24. "The Ministry: A Year's Retrospect," in *YES*, 72; "The Christian Minister: Part I," 28–30; "The Genuine Man," in *YES*, 186; *JMN*, 3:136, 185. For examples of the attitude of suggestion rather than of authority that Emerson took in his sermons, see MS Sermon (66), [Providence], 15 February 1830, and MS Sermon (86) [Prayer, the First Christian Duty], 28 August 1830. That Emerson's theory of preaching resembles that of the Puritan

plainstyle is, I think, no coincidence. Both were attempts to make religion the source of a renewed sense of community among people living in a situation of rapid and disorienting social change; the plainstyle did so by taking formal liturgical notions of piety and morality and transforming them into familiar and meaningful language.

25. MS Sermon (171), [The true priesthood], n.d.; *JMN*, 3:197; [The true priesthood].

26. Hugh Blair, *Lectures on Rhetoric and Belles Lettres*, ed. Harold F. Harding (Carbondale: Southern Illinois University Press, 1965), 2:106; Edward Tyrrel Channing, "The Orator and His Times," delivered 8 December 1819 at Harvard University in *Lectures Read to the Seniors in Harvard College* (Boston: Ticknor and Fields, 1856), 23; Captain Basil Hall, *Travels in North America in the Years 1827 and 1828* (Edinburgh, 1829), 2:112–13.

27. Joseph Tuckerman, MS Papers and Diaries (1803–1863), Massachusetts Historical Society; William Ellery Channing, quoted in Channing, *Memoir*, 2:155, 158; Henry Ware, Jr., *The Object and Means of the Christian Ministry: A Sermon, Preached at the Ordination of the Rev. Cyrus A. Bartol, as Junior Pastor of the West Church in Boston, Wednesday, March 1, 1837* (Cambridge, Mass.: Folsom, Wells, and Thurston, 1837), 25.

28. Ezra Stiles Gannett to Mr. Kent, Spring 1825, quoted in William C. Gannett, *Ezra Stiles Gannett, Unitarian Minister in Boston, 1824–1871. A Memoir* (Boston: Roberts Brothers, 1875), 144; *JMN*, 4:36–37.

29. "The Ministry: A Year's Retrospect," in *YES*, 70; To William Emerson, Concord, 30 April 1828, *L*, 1:234; To Ezra Ripley, Boston, 22 and 23 March 1829, *L*, 1:267.

30. To Ezra Ripley, Boston, 22 and 23 March 1829, *L*, 1:267.

31. On Emerson's various activities in the ministry, see Arthur Cushman McGiffert, Jr., "Introduction," in *YES*, xv–xvi.

32. Clericus, "On the Increase of Clerical Labours," *Christian Examiner* 3, no. 2 (March–April 1826): 94.

33. Robbins, quoted in Cabot, *A Memoir of Ralph Waldo Emerson*, 1:169.

34. *JMN*, 3:318.

35. MS Sermon (106), [Independence in faith], n.d.

36. "Religion and Society," in *YES*, 199.

37. MS Sermon 116B, [Keeping the Sabbath, I and II], 29 May 1831; "A Feast of Remembrance," in *YES*, 57–58.

38. One of the most powerful advocates of this point of view is Porte in *Representative Man*, 7–63.

39. See Edward Waldo Emerson, *Emerson in Concord*, 40–41.

40. Emerson, quoted in Edward Augustus Horton, *Ralph Waldo Emerson: His Services as Minister of the Second Church, and His Qualities as a Religious Teacher. A Discourse Preached in the Second Church, Boston, Sunday, April 30, 1882* (Boston: Beacon Press, 1882), 14.

John McAleer in *Ralph Waldo Emerson: Days of Encounter* (Boston: Little, Brown, 1984), 117–27, recounts the details of Emerson's decision. In his narrative, he quotes a letter Emerson wrote in later years to Cyrus Bartol expressing "his own pain in the rupture of the pastoral tie" (126; quotation from Cyrus Bartol, "Emerson's Religion," in *The Genius and Character of Emerson: Lectures at the Concord School of Philosophy*, ed. Franklin B. Sanborn [Boston, 1885], 110.)

41. [Keeping the Sabbath, I and II].

42. William Emerson to RWE, 17–22 January 1825, *L*, 1:352n; "The Christian Minister: Part II," in *YES*, 33; *JMN*, 4:30.

43. *JMN*, 4:27; Second Church, Boston, MS Records, Vol. 9 (1816–1833), Massachusetts Historical Society, 32–33; Second Church Records, MS Letter, Committee appointed to consider the question of the Lord's Supper to RWE, 15 June 1832.

44. *JMN*, 4:27.

45. Charles Chauncy Emerson to William Emerson, 6 July 1832 and 27 July 1832, *L*, 1:353n; RWE, "The Lord's Supper," *W*, 11:3.

46. McAleer, *Ralph Waldo Emerson*, 126–27, 120–21.

47. Quotations from the sermon are from "The Lord's Supper," *W*, 11:3–25.

48. Charles Chauncy Emerson to Mary Moody Emerson, 13 September 1832, Item 67, Emerson Family Papers; Charles Chauncy Emerson to William Emerson, 29 October 1832, in *L*, 1:356n; Charles Chauncy Emerson to Ezra Ripley, 30 October 1832, Item 164, Emerson Family Papers.

49. "The Lord's Supper," 24–25; To The Proprietors of the Second Church, Boston, 11 September 1832, in *L*, 1:357; James Freeman Clarke, *Memoir of Ralph Waldo Emerson*, reprinted from *The Proceedings of the Massachusetts Historical Society* (June, 1885), 4. No further information given.

Chapter 6

1. To Mary Moody Emerson, Boston, 19 August 1832, *L*, 1:353; To Mary Moody Emerson, Rome, 18 April 1833, *L*, 1:375.

2. *JMN*, 4:76–77. Emerson had seen Cranch and Landor in Italy and had found the latter particularly disappointing. His countryman Cranch, however, had been a pleasant surprise.

3. *JMN*, 4:77–78.

4. Ibid., 198–200.

5. Ibid., 83, 91, 252.

6. See RWE to Samuel Ripley, New Bedford, 28 March 1834, *L*, 1:407.

7. Charles Chauncy Emerson to Edward Bliss Emerson, Boston, 24 December 1833, Item 14, Emerson Family Papers; To Frederic Henry Hedge,

Bangor, Maine, 12 July 1834, *L*, 1:416; *JMN*, 4:306.

8. "American Lyceum," *Independent Chronicle and Boston Patriot*, 13 September 1828.

9. Edward Everett, "An Address Delivered as the Introduction to the Franklin Lectures, in Boston, November 14, 1831," *Orations and Speeches on Various Occasions* (Boston: American Stationers' Company, 1836), 288. On the lyceum movement and its significance as a cultural force in New England, see Donald M. Scott, "The Popular Lecture and the Creation of a Public in Mid-Nineteenth-Century America," *Journal of American History* 66 (1980): 791–809, and "Print and the Public Lecture System, 1840–1860," in *Printing and Society in Early America*, ed. William L. Joyce, et al. (Charlottesville: University Press of Virginia, 1983), 278–99. See also Carl Bode, *The American Lyceum: Town Meeting of the Mind* (New York: Oxford University Press, 1956).

10. "The Naturalist," in "Science," *EL*, 1:70.

11. *JMN*, 4:316.

12. To Ezra Ripley, Newton, 20 September 1834, *L*, 1:420.

13. A somewhat different perspective on Emerson's problem of vocation is taken by Leonard N. Neufeldt in " 'The Fields of My Fathers' and Emerson's Literary Vocation," *American Transcendental Quarterly* 31, supp. 1 (1976): 3–9. Neufeldt contends that it was Emerson's move to Concord that signalled the resolution of his problem.

14. *JMN*, 4:324, 317.

15. Ibid., 4:372, 348; 5:6; "George Fox," in "Biography," *EL*, 1:174, 180.

16. "George Fox," in "Biography," *EL*, 1:174; *JMN*, 4:313.

17. *J*, 2:7; To Mary Moody Emerson, Alexandria, D.C., 15 May 1827, *L*, 1:198. For a letter in a similar vein, see RWE to William Emerson, Boston, 25 December 1831, *L*, 1:343: "There is almost no walk of the muse & almost no way of life but at some time or other, I have caught the romance of it."

18. Other readings of "The American Scholar" as the resolution to Emerson's vocational crisis include Henry Nash Smith, "Emerson's Problem of Vocation: A Note on 'The American Scholar,' " *New England Quarterly* 12 (1939): 59–67; and Merton M. Sealts, Jr., "Emerson on the Scholar, 1833–1837," *PMLA* 85 (1970): 185–95.

19. All quotations from "The American Scholar" are taken from *CW*, 1:52–70.

20. *JMN*, 4:336.

21. "Michel Angelo Buonaroti," in "Biography," *EL*, 1:99; "Martin Luther," in "Biography," *EL*, 1:127; "Edmund Burke," in "Biography," *EL*, 1:200.

22. For discussions of the impact of the marketplace on the emergence of professionalism, see Lawrence Buell, *New England Literary Culture: From*

Revolution through Renaissance (Cambridge, Eng.: Cambridge University Press, 1986), 56–83; Ann Douglas, *The Feminization of American Culture* (New York: Alfred A. Knopf, 1977), 17–139; Burton J. Bledstein, *The Culture of Professionalism* (New York: Norton, 1976). On the erosion of the power of traditional intellectuals with the shift to capitalism, see Antonio Gramsci, *Selections from the Prison Notebooks*, ed. and trans. Quintin Hoare and Geoffrey Nowell Smith (London: Lawrence and Wishart, 1971), 5–14. On alienation, see Georg Lukács, "Reification and the Consciousness of the Proletariat," in *History and Class Consciousness: Studies in Marxist Dialectics*, trans. Rodney Livingstone (Cambridge, Mass.: MIT Press, 1971), 83–103.

23. For an illustration of parallel developments among the working class, see Sean Wilentz, *Chants Democratic: New York City and the Rise of the American Working Class, 1788–1850* (New York: Oxford University Press, 1984), 107–42. It should be noted that Emerson was concerned at this point with neither race nor gender, seeing the "enslavement" of those groups as a fact in which he had no interest or which he had no power to alter.

24. See Scott, "The Popular Lecture," 293; Bode, *American Lyceum*; and Mary Kupiec Cayton, "The Making of an American Prophet: Emerson, His Audiences, and the Rise of the Culture Industry in Nineteenth-Century America," *American Historical Review* 92 (1987): 597–620.

25. *JMN*, 5:109; Ralph Waldo Emerson to Thomas Carlyle, Concord, 30 April 1835, in *The Correspondence of Emerson and Carlyle*, ed. Joseph Slater (New York: Columbia University Press, 1964), 171; *JMN*, 7:277.

26. "Introductory," in "The Philosophy of History," *EL*, 2:7–21.

27. Hugh Blair, *Lectures on Rhetoric and Belles Lettres*, ed. Harold F. Harding (Carbondale: Southern Illinois University Press, 1965), 1:1; William Ellery Channing in *Dr. Channing's Note-Book: Passages from the Unpublished Manuscripts of William Ellery Channing*, comp. Grace Ellery Channing (Boston and New York: Houghton, Mifflin, 1887), 68; Edward Everett, "Oration Pronounced at Cambridge, Before the Society of Phi Beta Kappa, August 26, 1824," in *Orations and Speeches*, 9; *JMN*, 5:143, 102. On the orator as reformer, see Emerson on "Edmund Burke" in the "Biography" lecture series (*EL*, 1:183–201). The good orator, like Burke, "strives to put the subject into harmony with all particular and all general views and which draws arguments and illustrations from all regions of nature and art as if to show that all nature and all society are in unison with the view that is presented, which seeks to concentrate attention upon the facts but to consider them in accordance with the immense expansion in modern times of all powers of society" (200).

28. *Monthly Anthology* 1, no. 2 (December, 1803): 62. See also Henry Ware, Jr., *The Connection Between the Duties of the Pulpit and the Pastoral Office. An Introductory Address Delivered to the Members of the*

Theological School in Cambridge, October 18 and 25, 1830 (Cambridge, Mass.: Hilliard and Brown, 1830), 13.

29. *JMN,* 5:32–33.

30. Ibid., 6:134; 7:52. On New England oratory in this period, see Buell, *New England Literary Culture,* 137–65; "The Unitarian Movement and the Act of Preaching in 19th Century America," *American Quarterly* 24 (1972): 166–90; and David S. Reynolds, *Beneath the American Renaissance: The Subversive Imagination in the Age of Emerson and Melville* (New York: Alfred A. Knopf, 1988), 16–24.

31. On the relationship between speeches and literature in the rhetorical theory of early nineteenth-century New England, see Dorothy I. Anderson, "Edward T. Channing's Definition of Rhetoric," *Speech Monographs* 14, Research Annual (1947): 81–92.

32. Ruth (Haskins) Emerson to Edward Bliss Emerson, 13 April 1818, Item 2641, Emerson Family Papers. In family correspondence, Mary Moody Emerson and William Emerson, Sr., both mention exchanging books of sermons that they liked particularly well. See Mary Moody Emerson to Ruth (Haskins) Emerson, 26 March 1796, Item 965, and William Emerson, Sr. to Mary Moody Emerson, 24 December 1807, Item 2846, Emerson Family Papers. The enormous volume of the printed sermons circulated in New England also attests to the prominence of the spoken word in print in the New England of Emerson's boyhood. See also Robert A. Gross, "The Structure of Reading and the Dynamics of Print: Emerson's Concord and Emerson's America," Paper delivered at the seventy-eighth Annual Meeting of the Organization of American Historians, 19 April 1985.

33. James Elliot Cabot, *A Memoir of Ralph Waldo Emerson* (Boston: Houghton, Mifflin, 1887), 1:24; James Savage[?], "The Architecture of a Great Mind," *Monthly Anthology* 2 (July 1805): 370–71, reprinted in Lewis P. Simpson, ed., *The Federalist Literary Mind: Selections from the Monthly Anthology and Boston Review, 1803–1811, Including Documents Relating to the Boston Athenaeum* (Baton Rouge: Louisiana State University Press, 1962), 79–81. On literature as a source of moral tranquility and as an escape from party dissention, see Samuel Cooper Thacher, "Who Gave Up to Party: The Case of John Quincy Adams," *Monthly Anthology* 8 (April 1810): 249–68, reprinted in Simpson, *Federalist Literary Mind,* 88–93.

34. For fuller discussions of the moral uses of literature and aesthetics in early nineteenth-century New England literary criticism, see Daniel Walker Howe, *The Unitarian Conscience: Harvard Moral Philosophy, 1805–1861* (Cambridge, Mass.: Harvard University Press, 1970), 164–204; Ernest Lee Tuveson, *The Imagination as a Means of Grace: Locke and the Aesthetics of Romanticism* (Berkeley: University of California Press, 1960), 132–63; William Charvat, *The Origins of American Critical Thought, 1810–1835*

(New York: A. S. Barnes and Co., 1936); Lawrence I. Buell, "Unitarian Aesthetics and Emerson's Poet-Priest," *American Quarterly* 20 (1968): 3–20; Buell, *New England Literary Culture*, 30–44. For some contemporary assessments of the relationship of aesthetic beauty to a moral beauty inhering in nature, see, for example, "Article I.—Supplement to the Encyclopedia Britannica. Article, 'Beauty,'" *North American Review* 7 (May 1818): 14–24, and William Ellery Channing, "Remarks on the Character and Writings of Fenelon," *Works* (Boston: American Unitarian Association, 1877), 575–76.

35. Blair, *Lectures*, 1:390; "Article XVI. The Sylphs of the Seasons with Other Poems. By W. Allston," *North American Review* 5 (September 1817): 369. The conjunction of the emphases on feeling, nature, and social organicism resulted on the popular front in a literature of sentimentality that extolled the virtues of the home and of femininity, increasingly the loci of feeling and attachment as the social ideal no longer proved viable in public society. Thus a certain strain of literature came to be the province of a group Nathaniel Hawthorne would later label "that damned mobb of scribbling women."

36. Blair, *Lectures*, 1:13.

37. See, for example, Frisbie's "Extracts from MS Notes of Lectures," and "Inaugural Address, Delivered Upon the Author's Induction into the Office of Natural Religion, Moral Philosophy, and Civil Polity, in Harvard University, November 5, 1817," in *A Collection of the Miscellaneous Writings of Professor [Levi] Frisbie, with Some Notices of His Life and Character*, ed. Andrews Norton (Boston: Cummings, Hilliard, 1823).

38. On the connection between national literature and national virtue and morality, see Benjamin T. Spencer, *The Quest for Nationality: An American Literary Campaign* (Syracuse: Syracuse University Press, 1957); Linda K. Kerber, *Federalists in Dissent: Imagery and Ideology in Jeffersonian America* (Ithaca: Cornell University Press, 1970), 1–22; and Buell, *New England Literary Culture*, 23–55.

39. Jack Goody and Ian Watt, "The Consequences of Literacy," in *Literacy in Traditional Societies*, ed. Jack Goody (Cambridge, Eng.: Cambridge University Press, 1968), 63. On the emergence of the profession of authorship, see Buell, *New England Literary Culture*, 56–83; Michael T. Gilmore, *American Romanticism and the Marketplace* (Chicago: University of Chicago Press, 1985), 3–18. On the new mass-market literature and its audience, see Cathy Davidson, *Revolution and the Word: The Rise of the Novel in America* (New York: Oxford University Press, 1986), 38–54. On the spread of literacy, see Goody and Watt, "The Consequences of Literacy," 27–68; and Lee Soltow and Edward Stevens, *The Rise of Literacy and the Common School in the United States: A Socioeconomic Analysis to 1870* (Chi-

cago: University of Chicago Press, 1981).

40. William Ellery Channing, *Works*, 137, 126; *J*, 9:181; *JMN*, 12:49; *JMN*, 7:363; "Walter Savage Landor," *The Dial* (October 1841), in *W*, 12:341; "Literature," in "Philosophy of History," *EL*, 2:63; MS Sermon (134), [Words are things], 6 November 1831. See also Emerson's comments in "Literature," in *EL*, 2:56 ("Literature idealizes action"), and *JMN*, 5:417 ("Art seeks not nature but the idea which nature herself strives after").

41. *JMN*, 5:40; "Early Literature of France," *North American Review* 38, no.2 (April 1834): 363. On Emerson's attraction to Montaigne as literary model, see Charles Lowell Young, *Emerson's Montaigne* (New York: Macmillan Company, 1941).

42. To Edward Bliss Emerson, Cambridge, 12 June, and Boston, 17 June 1818, *L*, 1:63.

43. To Lydia Jackson, Concord, 1 February 1835, *L*, 1:435.

44. On the tendency of modern philosophers in general and those in the republican tradition in particular to see the public sphere falsely as the realm of the impartial and the universal, see Iris Marion Young, "Impartiality and the Civic Public: Some Implications of Feminist Critiques of Moral and Political Theory," in *Feminism as Critique: On the Politics of Gender*, ed. Seyla Benhabib and Drucilla Cornell (Minneapolis: University of Minnesota Press, 1987), 56–76.

Chapter 7

1. For contemporary descriptions of Concord, see John Warner Barber, *Massachusetts Historical Collections* (Worcester: Dorr, Howland, 1839), 379; and John Hayward, *Massachusetts Directory* (Boston, 1835), 81. See also Robert A. Gross, "Transcendentalism and Urbanism: Concord, Boston, and the Wider World," *Journal of American Studies* 18 (1984): 361–81; and "Culture and Cultivation: Agriculture and Society in Thoreau's Concord," *Journal of American History* 69 (1982): 42–61.

2. Figures are taken from Table 2, "Population of Boston and Its Environs," in Oscar Handlin, *Boston's Immigrants: A Study in Acculturation*, rev. ed. (New York: Atheneum, 1975), 239; and Leo F. Schnore and Peter R. Knights, "Residence and Social Structure: Boston in the Ante-Bellum Period," in *Nineteenth-Century Cities: Essays in the New Urban History*, ed. Stephan Thernstrom and Richard Sennett (New Haven: Yale University Press, 1969), 248.

3. The riot was not motivated by anti-Catholicism alone. A number of the daughters of Boston's Unitarian elite attended school at the Ursuline Convent, giving rise to fears that the Unitarians were now in league with Catholics against true morality and religion.

4. On the riots of the year 1834, see Carl E. Prince, "The Great 'Riot Year': Jacksonian Democracy and Patterns of Violence in 1834," *Journal of the Early Republic* 5 (1985): 1–19. On the Panic of 1837 in Boston, see William H. Pease and Jane H. Pease, *The Web of Progress: Private Values and Public Styles in Boston and Charleston, 1828–1843* (New York: Oxford University Press, 1985), 200–206.

5. *JMN*, 5:304, 334; "Tragedy," in "Human Life," *EL*, 3:104; *JMN*, 7:314; *JMN*, 7:256.

6. *JMN*, 7:155; "Reforms," in "The Present Age," *EL*, 3:260.

7. Stephen E. Whicher, *Freedom and Fate: An Inner Life of Ralph Waldo Emerson* (Philadelphia: University of Pennsylvania Press, 1953), 76.

8. E. S. Abdy, *Journal of a Residence and Tour in the United States of North America, from April, 1833, to October, 1834* (New York: Negro Universities Press, 1969), 3:253. For a narrative account of the Harvard riot and the precarious position of the university during this period, see Samuel Eliot Morison, *Three Centuries of Harvard, 1636–1936* (Cambridge, Mass.: Harvard University Press, 1936), 252–53.

9. The description is Morison's, *Three Centuries of Harvard*, 260. Student riots had been occurring every seven or eight years at Harvard for the past thirty years. The question of authority was certainly raised, but it was raised less explicitly than in the 1834 riot, with earlier riots usually beginning over food fights in the commons. In the 1819 riot in which Emerson's class participated, for example, the authority of President John Thornton Kirkland was never challenged directly, as was Quincy's in the 1834 riot. It was when the question of the nature of the relationship of the president to students was raised explicitly that the riot ceased to be an isolated incident and became a campus cause célèbre. For a comparison of student rioting at Harvard during this and earlier periods to that at other colleges, see Steven J. Novak, *The Rights of Youth: American Colleges and Student Revolt, 1798–1815* (Cambridge, Mass.: Harvard University Press, 1977), and David F. Allmendinger, Jr., "The Dangers of Ante-bellum Student Life," *Journal of Social History*, 7 (1973): 75–85. For a contemporary account of Harvard's troubles with the community and an assessment of Quincy's unpopularity with the students, see Harriet Martineau, *Retrospect of Western Travel* (New York: Harper and Brothers, 1838), 2:94–96. For Quincy's side of the story, see Edmund Quincy, *Life of Josiah Quincy of Massachusetts* (Boston: Ticknor and Fields, 1867), 464–66. For more modern assessments, see Morison, *Three Centuries of Harvard*, 257, and Robert A. McCaughey, *Josiah Quincy, 1772–1864: The Last Federalist* (Cambridge, Mass.: Harvard University Press, 1974), 144–45.

10. Harvard University, Senior Class of 1834, *Circular*, Metcalf Collection, vol. 504, John Hay Library, Brown University, 5. Apparently Quincy's zeal for discipline was not unique. In other American colleges of the period,

Novak finds a trend back to drilling in the classics as a means of creating not only mental discipline, but behavioral discipline as well. "With society seeming to come apart, academics tried to hold down their small part of the world by regulating student life," he notes (164).

11. Edward Everett Hale, a student at Harvard at the time of the riot, hints that students were probably aware, at least in some vague way, of the political repercussions of their actions. Of the political self-consciousness of his class he recalls, "We were crazily interested in politics. We were just at the beginning of the anti-slavery conflict, and we knew we were" (*A New England Boyhood and Other Bits of Autobiography* [Boston: Little, Brown, 1900], 351). The early antislavery campaign would focus, as did the Harvard riot, on the moral bankruptcy of established authority.

12. The senior class in the Harvard Divinity School in 1838 consisted of Harrison Gray Otis Blake (A.B., Harvard, 1835), Theodore Hasdell Door (A.B., Harvard, 1835), Crawford Nightingale (A.B., Brown, 1834; special student at Harvard, 1834–35), George Frederic Simmons (A.B., Harvard, 1832), as well as Benjamin Fisk Barrett (A.B., Bowdoin, 1832), and William Dexter Wilson. It is also interesting to note that Henry David Thoreau was a classmate of the freshman who repudiated the authority of the Greek tutor.

13. On this topic see Conrad Wright, "Emerson, Barzillai Frost, and the Divinity School Address," *The Liberal Christians: Essays on American Unitarian History* (Boston: Beacon Press, 1970), 41–61.

14. *JMN*, 7:21.

15. The term "jeremiad" is Joel Porte's, borrowed from Perry Miller, and is an appropriate characterization of the chastisement for past transgressions that is the Divinity School Address. See Porte, *Representative Man: Ralph Waldo Emerson in His Time* (New York: Oxford University Press, 1979), 120–23.

16. *JMN*, 5:471, 467.

17. John McAleer, *Ralph Waldo Emerson: Days of Encounter* (Boston: Little, Brown, 1984), 249.

18. RWE to George Bush, Concord, 2 September 1838, *L*, 2:156.

19. The observation is from Mary Worder Edrich, "The Rhetoric of Apostasy," *Texas Studies in Language and Literature* 8 (1967): 547–60.

20. Among the studies that attribute the violence of the reaction to the address to its shocking use of language are Edrich, "The Rhetoric of Apostasy," and Porte, *Representative Man*, 118–32.

21. To Henry Ware, Jr., Concord, 28 July 1838, *L*, 2:150.

22. *JMN*, 7:41–42. See also Stephen Railton, " 'Assume an Identity of Sentiment': Rhetoric and Audience in Emerson's 'Divinity School Address,' " *Prospects* 9 (1984): 31–47.

23. Such an argument is made by William R. Hutchinson in *The Tran-*

scendental Ministers: Church Reform in the New England Renaissance (New Haven: Yale University Press, 1959), 65–68.

24. Review of the Divinity School Address, *Christian Examiner* 25 (3d ser., vol. 7) (November 1837): 266.

25. *CW*, 1:88–89.

26. RWE to Ware, Concord, 28 July 1838, 2:149–50. Ellipses indicate instances where Emerson used the word "offend" and then crossed it out.

27. See Robert E. Burkholder, "Emerson, Kneeland, and the Divinity School Address," *American Literature* 58 (1986): 1–14; Roderick S. French, "Liberation from Man and God in Boston: Abner Kneeland's Free Thought Campaign, 1830–1839," *American Quarterly* 32 (1980): 202–21; and Henry Steele Commager, "The Blasphemy of Abner Kneeland," *New England Quarterly* 8 (1935): 29–41.

28. Boston *Investigator* 7, no. 12 (9 June 1837): 4.

29. *Report of the Arguments of the Attorney of the Commonwealth, at the Trials of Abner Kneeland, for Blasphemy, in The Municipal and Supreme Courts, in Boston, January and May, 1834* (Boston: Beals, Homer, 1834); reprinted in Leonard W. Levy, ed., *Blasphemy in Massachusetts: Freedom of Conscience and the Abner Kneeland Case* (New York: Da Capo Press, 1973), 188–89.

30. *L*, 2:147n.

31. *JMN*, 7:34.

32. Ibid., 7:60; To Thomas Carlyle, Concord, 17 October 1838, *The Correspondence of Emerson and Carlyle*, ed. Joseph Slater (New York: Columbia University Press, 1964), 197; To Ruth Haskins Emerson, Providence, 28 March 1840, *L*, 2:266; To Ware, Concord, 8 October 1838, *L*, 2:167; To Carlyle, Concord, 15 March 1839, *The Correspondence of Emerson and Carlyle*, 217.

33. Ware to RWE, Cambridge, 3 October 1838, quoted in George Willis Cooke, *Ralph Waldo Emerson: His Life, Writings, and Philosophy* (Boston: Houghton, Mifflin, 1881), 72.

34. Henry Ware, Jr., *The Personality of the Deity. A Sermon Preached in the Chapel of Harvard University, September 23, 1838* (Boston: James Munroe, 1838), 5–6.

35. See Clifford Geertz's definition of religion as a cultural system in *The Interpretation of Cultures* (New York: Basic Books, 1973), 87–125.

36. Charles Feidelson, Jr., *Symbolism and American Literature* (Chicago: University of Chicago Press, 1953); Philip F. Gura, *The Wisdom of Words: Language, Theology, and Literature in the New England Renaissance* (Middletown, Conn.: Wesleyan University Press, 1981).

37. "An Address Delivered Before the Senior Class in Divinity College, Cambridge, Sunday Evening, 15 July, 1838," *CW*, 1:77.

38. See Michael T. Gilmore, *American Romanticism and the Market-place* (Chicago: University of Chicago Press, 1985), 15–16.

39. Ann Douglas makes this case in *The Feminization of American Culture* (New York: Alfred A. Knopf, 1977), 17–309. "The key characteristic of all pluralistic situations," writes Peter Berger in *The Sacred Canopy: Elements of a Sociological Theory of Religion* (Garden City, N.Y.: Doubleday, 1967), " . . . is that the religious ex-monopolies can no longer take for granted the allegiance of their client populations" (138).

40. Henry Ware, Jr., *The Personality of the Deity*, 22.

41. *JMN*, 7:50, 60, 61.

42. Ibid., 63–71.

43. Ibid., 98, 105, 112.

44. *W*, 9:13–15.

45. The depth of Emerson's self-doubt, despite his occasional protestations to the contrary, emerges in full force in a journal entry for November 1838:

> I own, I am often inclined to take part with those who say I am bad or foolish, for I fear I am both. I believe & know there must be a perfect compensation. I know too well my own dark spots. Not having myself attained, not satisfied myself, far from a holy obedience,—how can I expect to satisfy others, to command their love? A few sour faces, a few biting paragraphs,—is but a cheap expiation for all these shortcomings of mine. [*JMN*, 7:140]

46. *JMN*, 7:112.

47. Transcription of a letter "To M.M.E.," in *JMN*, 7:114.

48. *JMN*, 7:124, 240.

49. Ibid., 74.

50. *W*, 9:43–48, 419–20.

51. *JMN*, 7:83–84, 237.

Chapter 8

1. *JMN*, 7:515; To Margaret Fuller, Concord, 6 September 1839, *L*, 2:220.

2. *JMN*, 2:411; To Charles Chauncy Emerson, Canterbury, New Hampshire, 7 August 1829, *L*, 1:276; To Edward Bliss Emerson, Boston, 20 and 23 April 1831, 1:321. Emerson insisted that their relationship was based not merely on conjugal ties but on friendship, a distinction he made in this inscription in Ellen's notebook during their courtship: "Love is Friendship without wings, and my affection, my beautiful queen, is a loving friendship, since it has all the fire of love, but it does not have wings; not a feather. Oh Ellen, it cannot move; it is a rock." (My translation from the French, in

which Emerson wrote to maintain a semblance of privacy.) (Quoted in Edith W. Gregg, ed., *One First Love: The Letters of Ellen Louisa Tucker to Ralph Waldo Emerson* [Cambridge, Mass.: Harvard University Press, 1962], iii.) On emerging patterns of courtship among middle-class Americans in the early nineteenth century, see Ellen Rothman, *Hands and Hearts: A History of Courtship in America* (Cambridge, Mass.: Harvard University Press, 1984), 17–84.

3. On the family as refuge from commercial society, see Richard Sennett, *Families against the City: Middle-Class Homes of Industrial Chicago, 1872–1890* (Cambridge, Mass.: Harvard University Press, 1970). Although Sennett deals with the subject in a later period, the trends he identifies were already apparent in Emerson's New England. On the domesticity that was at the heart of the conception of the family that emerged in the nineteenth-century, see Mary Patricia Ryan, *Cradle of the Middle Class: The Family in Oneida County, New York, 1790–1865* (Cambridge, Eng.: Cambridge University Press, 1981), 145–229; Mary Patricia Ryan, *Womanhood in America: From Colonial Times to the Present* (New York: New Viewpoints, 1975); Barbara Leslie Epstein, *The Politics of Domesticity: Women, Evangelicalism, and Temperance in Nineteenth-Century America* (Middletown, Conn.: Wesleyan University Press, 1981), 67–87; Barbara Welter, "The Cult of True Womanhood: 1820–1860," *American Quarterly* 18 (1966): 151–74; Carl N. Degler, *At Odds: Women and the Family in America from the Revolution to the Present* (New York: Oxford University Press, 1980); Daniel Scott Smith, "Family Limitation, Sexual Control, and Domestic Feminism in Victorian America," in *Clio's Consciousness Raised: New Perspectives on the History of Women*, ed. Mary S. Hartman and Lois Banner (New York: Harper and Row, 1974), 119–30.

4. On Emerson's sometimes contradictory attitudes toward marriage, and his marriage to Lidian in particular, see Anne C. Rose, *Transcendentalism as a Social Movement, 1830–1850* (New Haven: Yale University Press, 1981), 164–74.

5. *JMN*, 7:148; *JMN*, 5:410, 446. See *JMN*, 4:306.

6. *JMN*, 7:96; *J*, 6:134; *JMN*, 7:132. See also David Leverenz, "The Politics of Emerson's Man-Making Words," *PMLA* 101 (1986): 38–56. A September 1850 letter to Paulina W. Davis, who had asked Emerson to stand sponsor to a Women's Rights Convention to be held in Worcester, Massachusetts, in that year, summarizes his attitudes succinctly:

The fact of the political & civil wrongs of woman I deny not. If women feel wronged, then they are wronged. But the mode of obtaining a redress, namely, a public convention called by women is not very agreeable to me, and the things to be agitated for do not seem to me the best. Perhaps I am superstitious & traditional, but whilst I should vote for every franchise for women,—vote that they should hold property, and vote, yes & be eligible to all offices as men—whilst I should vote thus, if women asked, or if men denied these things, I should not wish women to wish political functions, nor, if granted assume them. I imagine that a woman whom all men would feel to be the best, would decline such privileges if offered, & feel them to be obstacles to her legitimate influence. Yet I confess lay no great stress on my opinion, since we are all liable to be deceived by the false position into which our bad politics throw elections & electors. If our politics were a little more rational we might not feel any unfitness in accompanying women to the polls. [*L*, 4:230]

7. To William Emerson, Boston, 5 February 1835, *L*, 1:436; To Lydia Jackson, Concord, 1 February 1835, *L*, 1:434.

8. *JMN*, 5:108–9, 193–94, 297.

9. Delores Bird Carpenter, ed., *The Selected Letters of Lidian Jackson Emerson* (Columbia: University of Missouri Press, 1987); Ellen Tucker Emerson, *The Life of Lidian Jackson Emerson* (Boston: Twayne Publishers, 1980).

10. Ellen Tucker Emerson, *Life*, 48.

11. Ibid., 79.

12. *JMN*, 7:336, 532; *L*, 3:12; *Selected Letters of Lidian Jackson Emerson*, 94.

13. *JMN*, 7:420.

14. See Carroll Smith-Rosenberg, "The Hysterical Woman: Sex Roles and Role Conflict in Nineteenth-Century America," in *Disorderly Conduct: Visions of Gender in Victorian America* (New York: Oxford University Press, 1985), 197–216.

15. *JMN*, 7:368.

16. All quotations from "Love" are taken from the version in *CW*, 2:99–110.

17. See the textual emendations in *CW*, 2:302.

18. "Home," in "Human Life," *EL*, 3:32.

19. *JMN*, 7:467.

20. Robert A. Gross, "Lonesome in Eden: Dickinson, Thoreau, and the Problem of Community in Nineteenth-Century New England," *Canadian Review of American Studies* 14 (1983): 1–17; "Transcendentalism and Urbanism: Concord, Boston, and the Wider World," *Journal of American Studies* 18 (1984): 361–81; "Culture and Cultivation: Agriculture and Society in Thoreau's Concord," *Journal of American History* 69 (1982): 42–61. On the increasingly suburban character of places such as Concord, see Ryan, *Cradle of the Middle Class*, 145–85; and Kenneth T. Jackson, *Crabgrass Fron-*

tier: The Suburbanization of the United States (New York: Oxford University Press, 1985), 47–52.

21. Frederick Law Olmsted, *Preliminary Report upon the Proposed Suburban Village at Riverside, near Chicago*, reprinted in *Landscape Architecture* 21 (1931): 275.

22. Edward Bliss Emerson to RWE, 20 January 1833, Item 218, Emerson Family Papers. Emerson acknowledges that the few close friends he did make outside his own family before 1838 were "like brothers" to him. See, for example, his letter to Thomas Carlyle, Concord, September 1836, *The Correspondence of Emerson and Carlyle*, ed. Joseph Slater (New York: Columbia University Press, 1964), 149, calling the latter "like a noble brother." After the death of George Sampson, another close friend of Emerson's, Charles Emerson wrote to his aunt that "Waldo will feel his loss deeply; Sampson loved him like a brother" (Charles Chauncy Emerson to Mary Moody Emerson, 26 July 1834, Item 85, Emerson Family Papers.)

23. Such kinship networks were particularly strong among Boston's elite, Paul Goodman finds in "Ethics and Enterprise: The Values of a Boston Elite, 1800–1860," *American Quarterly* 18 (1966): 437–51. Kinship webs increased the power of the family as a corporate entity as well as insuring the success of its individual members.

24. *JMN*, 8:36.

25. To Frederic Henry Hedge, Concord, 20 July 1836, *L*, 2:291. On the character of the Transcendental Club, see Daniel Walker Howe, " 'At Morning Blest and Golden Browed': Unitarians, Transcendentalists, and Reformers, 1835–1865," in *A Stream of Light: A Sesquicentennial History of American Unitarianism*, ed. Conrad Wright (Boston: Unitarian Universalist Association, 1975), 33–61.

26. *JMN*, 7:242.

27. To Frederic Henry Hedge, Concord, 20 July 1836, *L*, 2:30; "Society," in "Philosophy of History," *EL*, 2:104.

28. Quoted by John B. Wilson in "Emerson and the 'Communities,'" *ESQ*, 43 (1966): 57–62; Elizabeth P. Peabody, "Plan of the West Roxbury Community," *The Dial* 2 (1842): 361, 372. On Brook Farm and Emerson's thinking about that project, see Rose, *Transcendentalism*, 109–61.

29. Bronson Alcott and Charles Lane, "Fruitlands" (Letter dated 10 June 1843), *The Dial* 4 (1843): 135.

30. This assessment is Lindsay Swift's. Swift was a member at one time of the Brook Farm Community. He makes his judgment in *Brook Farm: Its Members, Scholars, and Visitors* (Secaucus, N.J.: Citadel Press, 1961), 10.

31. To George Ripley, 15 December 1840, in *L*, 2:371.

32. *L*, 2:369; *JMN*, 7:407.

33. Review of "Social Destiny of Man: or Association and Reorganization

of Industry. By Albert Brisbane," in *Uncollected Writings*, 154; RWE, "Fourierism and the Socialists," *The Dial* (1842), reprinted in *Uncollected Writings*, 72–74. He expresses similar sentiments on the neighborhood as the natural locus of reform in *JMN*, 7:401, and in a letter to William Emerson, Concord, 2 December 1840, *L*, 2:365.

34. RWE, "Fourierism and the Socialists," 74; *JMN*, 7:408.

35. *L*, 2: 372, 370; To Charles King Newcomb, Concord, 7 and 8 May 1842, *L*, 3:51.

36. *JMN*, 5:328, 452.

37. RWE, "Visits to Concord," in *Memoirs of Margaret Fuller Ossoli* (London: Richard Bentley, 1852), 2:66; Margaret Fuller, in *Memoirs of Margaret Fuller Ossoli*, 1:258; RWE, "Visits to Concord," 48.

38. To Margaret Fuller, Concord, 28 June 1838, *L*, 2:142; To Margaret Fuller, Concord, 28 and 29 September 1838, *L*, 2:163; *JMN*, 7:273.

39. Quotations from "Friendship" are from *CW*, 2:111–27.

40. Ibid., 2:127; *JMN*, 7:301, 509.

41. To Caroline Sturgis, Concord?, 16? August 1840, *L*, 2:325; To Margaret Fuller, 29 August 1840, *L*, 2:327; To Margaret Fuller, Concord, 13 September 1840, *L*, 2:332; To Caroline Sturgis, 13 September 1840, *L*, 2:334.

42. To Caroline Sturgis, Concord?, 25 September 1840, *L*, 337; Margaret Fuller to RWE, 29 September 1840, reprinted in *L*, 2:340n; To Margaret Fuller, Concord, 24 October 1840, *L*, 2:353.

43. RWE, "Visits to Concord," 77; MS Works of Sarah Margaret Fuller Ossoli (August 1842), 3:169, quoted in Henry F. Worfel, "Margaret Fuller and Ralph Waldo Emerson," *PMLA* 50 (1935): 593.

44. "The Heart," in "Human Culture," *EL*, 2:292; To Margaret Fuller, Concord, 24 October 1840, *L*, 2:353.

45. Carroll Smith-Rosenberg, "The Female World of Love and Ritual: Relations between Women in Nineteenth-Century America," *Disorderly Conduct*, 53–76. This essay is a particularly good description of conventions of female friendship in the nineteenth century. On the same subject, see also Degler, *At Odds*, 144–77.

46. *JMN*, 8:175.

47. RWE, "Visits to Concord," 269, 284, 286, 68; ibid., reprinted in Perry Miller, ed., *Margaret Fuller, American Romantic: A Selection from Her Writings and Correspondence* (Garden City, N.Y.: Doubleday, 1963), 49–50. Apparently Fuller began to develop a personal relationship with Emerson through his wife Lidian, or at least Emerson seems to have conceived the relationship as complementary to a more emotional one between Fuller and Lidian. The first letters from Emerson to Fuller and Elizabeth Peabody (the teacher, author, and educational reformer who counted herself a friend of Fuller and Emerson) mention Lidian frequently, as if Emerson were something of an intermediary for her. Lidian was pregnant at the time at which

the correspondence began and presumably was not feeling well enough to write herself. Even by 1838, Emerson, who was not admitting any emotional attachment, was closing his letters to Fuller expressing emotions that were legitimate within the conventions of female friendship. "Lidian, though not present, loves you," he wrote on 24 May 1838 (*L*, 2:136), or in another letter, "Lidian sends much love to you & depends on the visit" (4 May 1838, *L*, 2:130). Miller reprints a letter of Fuller's written in 1839 that shows the full intensity of emotion that she delivered and expected in her relationships with women (49–52).

48. *JMN*, 7:400. Carl I. Strauch in "Hatred's Swift Repulsions: Emerson, Margaret Fuller, and Others," *Studies in Romanticism* 7 (1968): 70–71, speculates that this passage refers to Fuller.

49. Bell Gale Chevigny, *The Woman and the Myth: Margaret Fuller's Life and Writings* (Old Westbury, N.Y.: Feminist Press, 1976), 70–71. For more on Fuller's friendship with Emerson, see Paula Blanchard, *Margaret Fuller: From Transcendentalism to Revolution* (New York: Delacorte Press, 1978), 98–117.

50. To Caroline Sturgis, Concord, 15 March 1841, *L*, 2:386; *JMN*, 7:522.

51. RWE, quoting Margaret Fuller to himself, 15 March 1842, in "Visits to Concord," 73; To Margaret Fuller, Concord, 31 July and 2 August 1841, *L*, 2:438.

52. *W*, 7:89–90.

Chapter 9

1. *JMN*, 8:95.

2. To Margaret Fuller, Concord, 21 June 1840, *L*, 2:305; "To Correspondents," *The Dial*, reprinted in *Uncollected Writings: Essays, Addresses, Poems, Reviews and Letters* (New York: Lamb Publishing Company, 1912), 179.

3. *JMN*, 8:5. The day after Waldo was born, Emerson reflected on the spiritual significance of his son's birth: "Blessed child! a lovely wonder to me, and which makes the Universe look friendly to me. How remote from my knowledge, how alien, yet how kind does it make the Cause of Causes appear! The stimulated curiosity of the father sees the graces & instincts which exist, indeed, in every babe, but unnoticed in others; the right to see all, know all, to examine nearly, distinguishes this relation, & endears this sweet child" (*JMN*, 5:234). See also "Self-Reliance," *CW*, 2:28.

4. "Threnody," *W*, 9:150, ll. 70–71.

5. *JMN*, 8:205; To Mary Moody Emerson, Concord, 28 January 1842, *L*, 3:7; To Margaret Fuller, Concord, 28 January 1842, *L*, 3:8; To Elizabeth Palmer Peabody, Concord, 28 January 1842, *L*, 3:8; "Compensation," *CW*,

2:73; To Margaret Fuller, Concord, 30 January 1844, L, 3:238.

6. JMN, 7:132; To Margaret Fuller, Concord, 2 February 1842, L, 3:9.

7. W, 9:153.

8. JMN, 7:458; L, 3:20.

9. "Experience," CW, 3:47.

10. Sacvan Bercovitch comes to a similar assessment of Emerson's notion of selfhood, although by a more circuitous route, in his The Puritan Origins of the American Self (New Haven: Yale University Press, 1975).

11. All quotations from "Self-Reliance" in this and the following section are taken from the text in CW, 2:25–51.

12. "The Orator and His Times," Lectures Read to the Seniors in Harvard College (Boston: Ticknor and Fields, 1856), 21.

13. For a description of such a public, preindustrial world, see Peter Laslett, The World We Have Lost: England Before the Industrial Age (New York: Charles Scribner's Sons, 1965).

14. On the changing meaning of the term "individual," see Raymond Williams, Keywords: A Vocabulary of Culture and Society (New York: Oxford University Press, 1976), 133–36, and Georg Simmel, excerpt from "Freedom and the Individual," reprinted in On Individuality and Social Forms, ed. Donald N. Levine (Chicago: University of Chicago Press, 1971), 224. On "personality," see Williams, Keywords, 194–97. Yehoshua Arieli, in Individualism and Nationalism in American Ideology (Baltimore: Penguin Books, 1964), notes that the word "individualism" itself was not coined until the nineteenth century, and it originally had negative connotations. It conveyed the idea of uprootedness, lack of ideals and common beliefs, social fragmentation, competitive and exploitative attitudes, and legitimized anarchy (207). On the changing nature of the public domain in Western culture in the eighteenth and nineteenth centuries, see Richard Sennett, The Fall of Public Man (New York: Alfred A. Knopf, 1976), 3–7.

15. "Historic Notes of Life and Letters in New England," W, 10:326, 329.

16. JMN, 8:10.

17. MS Sermon (140), [Friendship], 8 January 1832; JMN, 5:192; To Thomas Carlyle, The Correspondence of Emerson and Carlyle, ed. Joseph Slater (New York: Columbia University Press, 1964), 260–61; JMN, 5:247; Charles Chauncy Emerson to Mary Moody Emerson, Item 51, Emerson Family Papers.

18. "The Heart," in "Human Culture," EL, 2:279.

19. On the emergence of a sense of privacy at odds with the public sphere, see Sennett, Fall of Public Man; Joseph Bensman and Robert Lilienfeld, Between Public and Private: The Lost Boundaries of the Self (New York: Free Press, 1979); Burton J. Bledstein, The Culture of Professionalism: The Middle Class and the Development of Higher Education in America (New York: W. W. Norton, 1976), 56–57; Lionel Trilling, Sincerity and Authentic-

ity (Cambridge, Mass.: Harvard University Press, 1976); and Georg Simmel, in *The Sociology of Georg Simmel*, ed. Kurt H. Wolff (Glencoe, Ill.: Free Press, 1950), 67–81.

20. *JMN*, 5:336.

21. See, for example, Jonathan Bishop, *Emerson on the Soul* (Cambridge, Mass.: Harvard University Press, 1964), 92–97; and William K. Bottorff, "'Whatever Inly Rejoices Me': The Paradox of 'Self-Reliance,'" *ESQ* 69 (1972): 207–17.

22. Trilling's argument on the emergence of the modern personality is presented in *Sincerity and Authenticity*.

23. "Religion," in "Philosophy of History," *EL*, 2:85.

24. "The Limits of Self-Reliance," in *YES*, 238; "The Genuine Man," in *YES*, 182–83.

25. "Self-Reliance," *CW*, 2:42; *JMN*, 3:240; "Introduction," in "Human Culture," *EL*, 2:227; *JMN*, 7:320. Barry Wood in "The Growth of the Soul: Coleridge's Dialectical Method and the Strategy of Emerson's *Nature*," *PMLA* 91 (1976): 385–97, shows how Emerson's early concept of self-reliance differed from alienation, by tracing a dialectical process through which transcendence of self is achieved in *Nature*.

26. *JMN*, 5:404.

27. On the eighteenth-century attempt to submerge personality in nature, see Simmel, "Freedom and the Individual," 218–23. A good discussion of Hegel's attempt in particular can be found in John Torrance, *Estrangement, Alienation and Exploitation: A Sociological Approach to Historical Materialism* (New York: Columbia University Press, 1971). Morse Peckham, in "Emerson's Prose," introduction to *Essays, Second Series*, reprinted in Leonard Nick Neufeldt, ed., *Ralph Waldo Emerson: New Appraisals: A Symposium* (Hartford: Transcendental Books, 1973), 64–74, contends that Emerson's attempt to grapple with the problem of self-definition resembles that of both Marx and Kierkegaard.

28. All quotations from "Experience" are taken from the text in *CW*, 3:27–49.

29. See Antonio Gramsci, *Selections from the Prison Notebooks*, ed. and trans. Quintin Hoare and Geoffrey Nowell Smith (London: Lawrence and Wishart, 1971), 333, 344.

30. *CW*, 3:143. In both "The Poet" and "Character," for example, Emerson shifts away from his earlier focus on general laws for the reform of human life to examine the notion of "Genius"—the particular embodiment of some aspect of the law of nature in different individuals or types of individuals. The "representative man," one who "stands among partial men for the complete man," merits our attention because he can embody in a concrete way the general laws of nature that escape most of us most of the time. The contrast between the volume's essay on "Nature" and Emerson's

famous 1836 pamphlet on the same topic reveals the departure in approach and texture in this thought that *Essays, Second Series* represents. The later essay deals mainly with the restorative effects of the material and physical landscape, while *Nature* purported to outline the entire structure of the Universe and of spiritual knowledge.

31. *W*, 6:3.

32. To Margaret Fuller, Concord, 18 and 19 October 1843, *L*, 3:215; *JMN*, 7:482.

33. See Townsend Scudder, "Emerson's British Lecture Tour, 1847–1848," *American Literature* 7 (1935): 166–80; and Mary Kupiec Cayton, "The Making of an American Prophet: Emerson, His Audiences, and the Rise of the Culture Industry in Nineteenth-Century America," *American Historical Review* 92 (1987): 603–4.

34. Ellen Tucker Emerson, *The Life of Lidian Jackson Emerson*, ed. Delores Bird Carpenter (Boston: Twayne Publishers, 1980), 188.

Afterword

1. *W*, 11:123–24. For more on Emerson's attitude toward slavery, see also "The Fugitive Slave Law: Address to Citizens of Concord, 3 May, 1851," *W*, 11:177–214; "The Fugitive Slave Law: Lecture Read in the Tabernacle, New York City, March 7, 1854, on the Fourth Anniversary of Daniel Webster's Speech in Favor of the Bill," *W*, 11:215–44; "The Assault Upon Mr. Sumner: Speech at a Meeting of the Citizens in the Town Hall, in Concord, May 26, 1856," *W*, 11:245–52; "Speech at the Kansas Relief Meeting in Cambridge, Wednesday Evening, September 10, 1856," *W*, 11:253–63; "John Brown Speech at Salem, January 6, 1860," *W*, 11:275–81; To Oliver Wendell Holmes, Concord, March 1856, *L*, 5:17; *JMN*, 9:126–27, 430, 445–47; 13:110, 405; 14:429–30.

2. Max Horkheimer, "Egoism and the Freedom Movement: On the Anthropology of the Bourgeois Era," *Telos*, no. 54 (Winter 1982–83): 10–61.

3. Antonio Gramsci, "The Study of Philosophy," *Selections from the Prison Notebooks*, ed. and trans. Quintin Hoare and Geoffrey Nowell Smith (London: Lawrence and Wishart, 1971), 327.

Bibliographic
Essay

FORTUNATELY for Emerson scholars, much of what Emerson wrote has been published in well-edited standard editions. A new edition of the *Journals and Miscellaneous Notebooks of Ralph Waldo Emerson*, edited by William H. Gilman et al. and published by Harvard University Press, was completed in 1982. A new version of the *Collected Works*, edited by Robert E. Spiller et al., is currently being published, also by Harvard University Press. I have relied heavily on these volumes. I have also relied on Ralph L. Rusk's six-volume *The Letters of Ralph Waldo Emerson* (New York, 1939), the Riverside edition of *The Journals of Ralph Waldo Emerson*, edited by Edward Waldo Emerson and Waldo Emerson Forbes (Boston, 1909–14), and the Centenary edition of *The Complete Works of Ralph Waldo Emerson* (Boston, 1903). Other primary sources that have proved especially helpful in tracing the growth of Emerson's thought prior to 1836 include Emerson's 171 manuscript sermons in the Houghton Library of Harvard University, 25 of which have been published in *Young Emerson Speaks, Unpublished Discourses on Many Subjects*, edited by Arthur Cushman McGiffert, Jr. (Boston, 1938); the three-volume *Early Lectures of Ralph Waldo Emerson*, edited by Stephen E. Whicher, Robert E. Spiller, and Wallace E. Williams (Cambridge, Mass., 1959, 1964, 1972); and *Two Unpublished Essays: The Character of Socrates; The Present State of Ethical Philosophy*, edited by Edward Everett Hale (Boston, 1896). Joseph Slater's edition of *The Correspondence of Emerson and Carlyle* (New York, 1964) and Emerson's *Uncollected Writings: Essays, Addresses, Poems, Reviews and Letters* (New York, 1912) have also been useful to me. The Emerson Family Papers at the Houghton Library, Harvard University, include letters to Ralph Waldo Emerson from members of his family and others; they are an invaluable source of information on Emerson's family. David Greene Haskins's *Ralph Waldo Emerson: His Maternal Ancestors with Some Reminiscences of Him* (Port Washington, N.Y., 1887; reprint 1971), provides further information on Emerson's family, while James Elliot Cabot's two-volume *Memoir of Ralph Waldo Emerson* (Boston, 1887) supplies primary source material unavailable elsewhere. Kenneth Walter Cameron's various compilations of little-known material on Emerson are also useful tools.

Anyone who has had occasion to write about Emerson's life is indebted to two standard works of biography, Ralph L. Rusk's *The Life of Ralph Waldo Emerson* (New York, 1949) and Stephen E. Whicher's *Freedom and Fate: An Inner Life of Ralph Waldo Emerson* (Philadelphia, 1953). Each has shaped my thinking in important ways. I have not footnoted either extensively, but those who know Emerson scholarship will realize the extent of my debt to them. Two more recent biographies, John McAleer's *Ralph Waldo Emerson: Days of Encounter* (Boston, 1984) and Gay Wilson Allen's *Waldo Emerson* (New York, 1981), are encyclopedic in nature and extraordinarily valuable reference tools. Of the mass of criticism written about Emerson, I have found the work of two scholars in particular very stimulating. Although Perry Miller never wrote a book about Emerson, he wrote a number of articles full of significant observations on the relationship between literature and culture in Emerson's New England. Although I do not always find Miller's readings of nineteenth-century New England cultural developments entirely satisfying, his treatment of transcendentalism as the organic product of the New England environment is sensitive and suggestive. See especially such articles as "Jonathan Edwards to Emerson," *New England Quarterly* 13 (1940): 589–617; "Emersonian Genius and the American Democracy," *New England Quarterly* 26 (1953): 27–44; and "Transcendentalism: Native or Imported?" in *Literary Views: Critical and Historical Essays*, edited by Carroll Camden (Chicago, 1964). In addition, the work of Joel Porte, including *Emerson and Thoreau: Transcendentalists in Conflict* (Middletown, Conn., 1966) and *Representative Man: Ralph Waldo Emerson in His Time* (New York, 1979), has been among the most helpful to me of Emerson criticism. Like Miller, Porte has attempted to treat Emerson's thought and career in the intellectual and cultural contexts from which they sprang. Also particularly useful was Carolyn Porter's *Seeing and Being: The Plight of the Participant Observer in Emerson, James, Adams, and Faulkner* (Middletown, Conn., 1981). Other valuable studies of Emerson include Maurice Gonnaud, *Individu et société dans l'oeuvre de Ralph Waldo Emerson: Essai de biographie spirituelle* (Paris, 1964); Michael H. Cowan, *City of the West: Emerson, America, and Urban Metaphor* (New Haven, 1967); Jonathan Bishop, *Emerson on the Soul* (Cambridge, Mass., 1964); Sherman Paul, *Emerson's Angle of Vision: Man and Nature in American Experience* (Cambridge, Mass., 1952); Milton R. Konvitz and Stephen E. Whicher, eds., *Emerson: A Collection of Critical Essays* (Englewood Cliffs, N.J., 1962); and Hyatt H. Waggoner, *Emerson as Poet* (Princeton, 1974). Sacvan Bercovitch's section on Emerson in *The Puritan Origins of the American Self* (New Haven, 1975) is intriguing if at times opaquely written. Works such as F. O. Matthiessen's *American Renaissance: Art and Expression in the Age of Emerson and Whitman* (New York, 1941); Lawrence Buell's *New England Literary Culture: From Revolution through Re-*

naissance (Cambridge, Eng., 1986) and *Literary Transcendentalism: Style and Vision in the American Renaissance* (Ithaca, 1973); David S. Reynolds's *Beneath the American Renaissance: The Subversive Imagination in the Age of Emerson and Melville* (New York, 1988); and R. W. B. Lewis's *The American Adam: Innocence, Tragedy, and Tradition in the Nineteenth Century* (Chicago, 1955) all examine Emerson as part of a larger literary and social movement taking place in nineteenth-century New England. Both Cathy Davidson's *Revolution and the Word: The Rise of the Novel in America* (New York, 1986) and Michael T. Gilmore's *American Romanticism and the Marketplace* (Chicago, 1985) provide fascinating discussions of the impact of the rise of the marketplace on literature and literary expression.

The problem with writing the history of what has come to be called the Jacksonian period, especially in urban areas, is that there are as many views of what was happening as there were discrete social classes or interest groups. Because I have wished to focus on Emerson's social ideas, it has been necessary for me to limit myself to an exploration of one particular perspective on social change in Boston—that of a particular elite, conservative in political philosophy and liberal in religion. For a description of the Federalist philosophy of society and government in early nineteenth-century Boston, I have relied on Linda K. Kerber, *Federalists in Dissent: Imagery and Ideology in Jeffersonian America* (Ithaca, 1970); Gordon S. Wood, *The Creation of the American Republic, 1776–1787* (New York, 1969); James Banner, *To the Hartford Convention: The Federalists and the Origin of Party Politics in Massachusetts, 1789–1815* (New York, 1970); and David Hackett Fischer, *The Revolution of American Conservatism: The Federalist Party in the Era of Jeffersonian Democracy* (New York, 1965). Daniel Walker Howe, in his excellent study, *The Political Culture of the American Whigs* (Chicago, 1979), shows how Federalist ideas were preserved and adapted by the Whig party. Joyce Appleby's work, cited in the notes to Chapter 1, reminds us that the ideology of republicanism was contested terrain.

Because Emerson was a member of a learned and articulate social class, it is not difficult to find memoirs, diaries, letters, and documents by others who shared a Federalist perspective on society. I have drawn on primary materials from such important civic figures as Harrison Gray Otis, George Ticknor, Daniel Webster, and Josiah Quincy. James Spear Loring's *Hundred Boston Orators Appointed by the Municipal Authorities and Other Public Bodies, From 1770 to 1852, Comprising Historical Gleanings, Illustrating the Principles and Progress of Our Republican Institutions,* 2d ed.(Boston, 1853) is a collection of speeches delivered in Boston during that period and is a representative selection of the political rhetoric of the time. *The Reports of the Boston Record Commissioners,* vols. 22–39 (Boston, 1890–

1909) provide an official record of the transactions of the Boston town government from the late eighteenth century until 1822. Josiah Quincy's *Municipal History of the Town and City of Boston, During Two Centuries* (Boston, 1852) is a particularly good account by one of its first mayors of the changes surrounding Boston's transition from town to city. Quincy was an important figure in Boston during the 1820s and 1830s, and Robert A. McCaughey's portrait of him in *Josiah Quincy, 1772–1864: The Last Federalist* (Cambridge, Mass., 1974) provides an interesting description of how one old Federalist responded to the challenge posed by social change in the city. Roger Lane's *Policing the City: Boston, 1822–1885* (Cambridge, Mass., 1967) details some of the changes made in municipal services in the Quincy administration in response to Boston's growing size and heterogeneity.

The chief history of Boston remains the multivolume *Memorial History of Boston, Including Suffolk County, Massachusetts, 1630–1880,* edited by Justin Winsor (Boston, 1882). Oscar Handlin's *Boston's Immigrants: A Study in Acculturation,* rev. ed. (New York, 1975) provides some interesting background material, but was not very useful to me since he focuses particularly on the period following Emerson's departure for Concord. More helpful was William H. Pease and Jane H. Pease, *The Web of Progress: Private Values and Public Styles in Boston and Charleston, 1828–1843* (New York, 1985). Essays in *Nineteenth-Century Cities: Essays in the New Urban History,* edited by Stephan Thernstrom and Richard Sennett (New Haven, 1969), and in *The Growth of the Seaport Cities, 1790–1825: Proceedings of a Conference Sponsored by the Eleutherian Mills-Hagley Foundation, March 17–19, 1966,* edited by David T. Gilchrist (Charlottesville, 1967), also contain relevant material on urban growth in nineteenth-century Boston. Rowland Berthoff's *An Unsettled People: Social Order and Disorder in American History* (New York, 1971); Thomas Bender's *Toward an Urban Vision: Ideas and Institutions in Nineteenth-Century America* (Lexington, 1975); and Paul Boyer's *Urban Masses and Moral Order in America, 1820–1920* (Cambridge, Mass., 1978) provide information on urbanization that helps to locate the events occurring in Emerson's Boston in a larger social context—the attempt of Emerson's age to restructure social institutions in the face of rapid social change. On politics in Boston and in Massachusetts during the period from 1800 to 1840, see Ronald P. Formisano, *The Transformation of Political Culture: Massachusetts Parties, 1790s-1840s* (New York, 1983); Paul Goodman, *The Democratic-Republicans of Massachusetts: Politics in a Young Republic* (Cambridge, Mass., 1964); Arthur B. Darling, *Political Changes in Massachusetts, 1824–1848: A Study of Liberal Movements in Politics* (Cos Cob, Conn., 1968); Richard P. McCormick, *The Second American Party System: Party Formation in the Jacksonian Era* (New York, 1966); and Arthur M. Schlesinger, Jr., *The Age of*

Jackson (Boston, 1945). On Concord during this era, the work of Robert A. Gross, cited in the notes to Chapters 7 and 8, is of major importance. On the unsettlement at Harvard during Emerson's college years and during the 1830s, a good deal more remains to be said. The Harvard University Archives contain a fascinating collection of student diaries, class and club notes, faculty lecture notes, and records of official corporation actions. There is an abundance of excellent material there that promises to shed light on the reaction of Emerson's generation to the changes taking place within their society, and I regret that I did not have time to make better use of it. I have benefited from the Archives' collections on Henry Ware, Jr., Levi Frisbie, Edward Tyrrel Channing, and George Ticknor. Moreover, Daniel Walker Howe in *The Unitarian Conscience: Harvard Moral Philosophy, 1805–1861* (Cambridge, Mass., 1970) has done a thorough job of sifting through the Archives and has described in detail the Harvard curriculum during Emerson's years there. D. H. Meyer, in *The Instructed Conscience: The Shaping of the American National Ethic* (Philadelphia, 1972), draws out the implications of the Unitarian moral philosophy that Howe describes. Samuel Eliot Morison's *Three Centuries of Harvard, 1636–1936* (Cambridge, Mass., 1936) provides a helpful chronology of the major events that occurred at Harvard. Steven J. Novak's *The Rights of Youth: American Colleges and Student Revolt, 1798–1815* (Cambridge, Mass., 1977); Joseph Kett's *Rites of Passage: Adolescence in America, 1790 to the Present* (New York, 1977); and David F. Allmendinger, Jr.'s "The Dangers of Antebellum Student Life," *Journal of Social History* 7 (1973): 75–85, all provide valuable background on student rioting in the nineteenth century. Although I have not always found their generalizations about such riots directly applicable to those I have discussed at Harvard, these works have helped me to formulate my own ideas about the issues involved in such rioting.

Emerson came to terms with social change in Boston chiefly through the changes that it wrought in religious practice; therefore, I have thought it important to dwell on the interaction between religious ideas and social structure at some length. Boston offers a rich field for investigating such a relationship. Many manuscript church records are still extant. I have used those of the Park Street Church (in the Congregational Library, Boston), the Salem Street Church (in the Massachusetts Historical Society), and the Second Church in Boston (in the Massachusetts Historical Society). In addition, the records of the First Church in Boston have been published in *Publications of the Colonial Society of Massachusetts*, vol. 40 (Boston, 1961). Several histories of individual congregations have been published; these include H. Crosby Englizian's *Brimstone Corner: Park Street Church, Boston* (Chicago, 1968); Hamilton Andrews Hill's *History of the Old South Church (Third Church) Boston, 1669–1884* (Boston, 1890); and John Nicholas Booth's *The Story of the Second Church in Boston* (the *Original Old North) Including the Old North Church Mystery* (Boston, 1959). During the evangelical-Unitarian controversy, a large number of religious periodicals were published in Boston, papers that often treated of a wide variety of topics. Of these I have used the *Panoplist*, the *Boston Recorder and Telegraph*, the *Christian Examiner, The Spirit of the Pilgrims*, and the *New Jerusalem Magazine*. Pious Bostonians celebrated their ministers by publishing biographies and memoirs after their deaths. Memoirs of Henry Ware, Ezra Stiles Gannett, Samuel Green, William Ellery Channing, and Joseph Stevens Buckminster were particularly helpful in my research on sectarian controversy in Boston and on the ministerial role. William B. Sprague's *Annals of the American Pulpit*, vol. 8 (New York, 1865), a collection of biographies and excerpts from sermons of the Unitarian ministry, also provided primary source material on Boston's ministry. The records of the Unitarian Ministry-at-Large in Boston and the large volume of individual sermons published in pamphlet form have also been important primary sources.

Conrad Wright's *The Beginnings of Unitarianism in America* (Boston, 1955) is the definitive work on American Unitarianism. Other important works on Unitarianism include a collection of essays edited by Wright, *A Stream of Light: A Sesquicentennial History of American Unitarianism* (Boston, 1975), and Earl Morse Wilbur's *A History of Unitarianism in Transylvania, England, and America* (Cambridge, Mass., 1952). On evangelical Boston, there is no better source than Lyman Beecher himself; *The Autobiography of Lyman Beecher*, edited by Barbara M. Cross (Cambridge, Mass., 1961), and the three-volume *Works* (Boston, 1852) passionately describe the evangelical crusade in Boston during Emerson's time. Without question, Anne C. Rose's *Transcendentalism as a Social Movement, 1830–1850* (New Haven, 1981) provides the best single description of the changes that took place in Boston Unitarianism in response to the evangelical challenge. Donald Scott's *From Office to Profession: The New England Ministry, 1750–1850* (Philadelphia, 1978) delineates changes in the church's cultural role during the period. John L. Thomas's "Romantic Reform in America, 1815–1865," *American Quarterly* 17 (1965): 656–81; John R. Bodo's *The Protestant Clergy and Public Issues, 1812–1848* (Princeton, 1954); Charles I. Foster's *An Errand of Mercy: The Evangelical United Front, 1790–1837* (Chapel Hill, 1960); and Clifford S. Griffen's *Their Brothers' Keepers: Moral Stewardship in the United States, 1800–1865* (New Brunswick, 1960) discuss the evangelicals' banding together to become an important social force. Maria Kleinburg Baghdadi's unpublished Ph.D. dissertation, "Protestants, Poverty, and Urban Growth: A Study of the Organization of Charity in Boston and New York, 1820–1865" (Brown University, 1975) surveys Unitarian charity efforts during the same period. The most important works on the social aspects of revivalism are Paul Johnson's *A Shopkeeper's Millennium: Society and Revivals in Rochester, New York, 1815–1837* (New York, 1978) and Mary Patricia Ryan's *Cradle of the Middle Class: The Family in Oneida County, New York, 1790–1865* (Cambridge, Eng., 1981). Each links revivalism with the rise of the middle class, a distinctively urban group which no longer participated in a household economy. Although one must use caution in generalizing to Boston conclusions drawn from a different geographical area marked by different social conditions, their work on upstate New York has done the best job of exploring the interaction between religious change and social change.

My understanding of the changes taking place in the ministry as a profession derives mainly from accounts provided in the memoirs of the ministers who were Emerson's contemporaries, from charges delivered to ministers at installations, and from works written on the training of ministers and the cultivation of piety. The best secondary work on the changes the profession was undergoing is Scott's *From Office to Profession*. Other valuable studies include David D. Hall, *The Faithful Shepherd: A History of the New England Ministry in the Seventeenth Century* (Chapel Hill, 1972); Daniel H. Calhoun, *Professional Lives in America: Structure and Aspiration, 1750–1850* (Cambridge, Mass., 1965); Lewis P. Simpson, *The Man of Letters in New England and the South: Essays on the History of the Literary Vocation in America* (Baton Rouge, 1973); H. Richard Niebuhr and Daniel Williams, eds., *The Ministry in Historical Perspective* (New York, 1956); and Howe on the Unitarian strain of piety in *The Unitarian Conscience*. On the social uses of literature, I have benefited from reading the Unitarian *Monthly Anthology*, the *North American Review*, and *The Dial*. Hugh Blair's *Lectures on Rhetoric and Belles Lettres*, 2 vols., edited by Harold F. Harding (Carbondale, 1965), and the lectures of Edward Tyrrel Channing are also important as primary sources. In "Historic Notes of Life and Letters in New England," Emerson mentions that the other Channing, William Ellery, was also a potent force in shaping his ideas of literature. See especially Channing's essays on Milton and on Fenelon. Important secondary sources on the topic include Howe, *The Unitarian Conscience*; Ernest Lee Tuveson, *The Imagination as a Means of Grace: Locke and the Aesthetics of Romanticism* (Berkeley, 1960); William Charvat, *The Origins of American Critical Thought, 1810–1835* (New York, 1936); and Ann Douglas, *The Feminization of American Culture* (New York, 1977). Benjamin T. Spencer's excellent *Quest for Nationality: An American Literary Campaign* (Syracuse, 1957) puts the search for an American national literature into the context of republicanism. Donald Scott in "The Popular Lecture and the Creation of a Public in Mid-Nineteenth-Century America," *Journal of American History* 66 (1980): 791–809, and Carl Bode in *The American Lyceum: Town Meeting of the Mind* (New York, 1956) explore the rise of the lyceum as a new forum for the literary man. On Emerson's own problem of vocation, the most important commentaries include Henry Nash Smith, "Emerson's Problem of Vocation: A Note on 'The American Scholar,' " *New England Quarterly* 12 (1939): 59–67, and Merton M. Sealts, Jr., "Emerson on the Scholar, 1833–1837," *PMLA* 85 (1970): 185–95. On Emerson's time in the ministry, see David Robinson, *Apostle of Culture: Emerson as Preacher and Lecturer* (Philadelphia, 1982).

The problem of self-definition in a nontraditional, urban society is one that has not been discussed extensively. Nevertheless, I have found helpful several discussions of the conflict between public and private definitions of self that such a heterogeneous environment seems to produce. I found Richard Sennett's *The Fall of Public Man* (New York, 1976) especially stimulating, as well as Lionel Trilling's *Sincerity and Authenticity* (Cambridge, Mass., 1976). Also helpful on the topic are Raymond Williams, *Culture and Society, 1780–1950* (New York, 1958); Yehoshua Arieli, *Individualism and Nationalism in American Ideology* (Baltimore, 1964); Joseph Bensman and Robert Lilienfeld, *Between Public and Private: The Lost Boundaries of the Self* (New York, 1979); and Burton J. Bledstein, *The Culture of Professionalism: The Middle Class and the Development of Higher Education in America* (New York, 1976). On the domesticity that accompanied the rise of this conflict between public and private, I have relied on Mary Beth Norton, *Liberty's Daughters: The Revolutionary Experience of American Women, 1750–1800* (Boston, 1980); Nancy Cott, *The Bonds of Womanhood: "Woman's Sphere" in New England, 1780–1835* (New Haven, 1977); Carl N. Degler, *At Odds: Women and the Family in America from the Revolution to the Present* (New York, 1980); and Carroll Smith-Rosenberg, "The Female World of Love and Ritual: Relations between Women in Nineteenth-Century America," *Disorderly Conduct: Visions of Gender in Victorian America* (New York, 1985), 53–76. Primary works that have been helpful in my discussion of this aspect of Emerson's life have also included *One First Love: The Letters of Ellen Louisa Tucker to Ralph Waldo Emerson*, ed. Edith W. Gregg (Cambridge, Mass., 1962); Delores Bird Carpenter, ed., *The Selected Letters of Lidian Jackson Emerson* (Columbia, Mo., 1987); Ellen Tucker Emerson, *The Life of Lidian Jackson Emerson* (Boston, 1980); and *The Memoirs of Margaret Fuller Ossoli* (London, 1852). Perry Miller's *Margaret Fuller, American Romantic: A Selection from Her Writings and Correspondence* (Garden City, N.Y., 1963) was especially helpful on Fuller, as were biographies by Bell Gale Chevigny (*The Woman and the Myth: Margaret Fuller's Life and Writings* [Old Westbury N.Y., 1976]) and Paula Blanchard (*Margaret Fuller: From Transcendentalism to Revolution* [New York, 1978]).

Finally, a number of theoretical works suggested ways of exploring the implications of Emerson's life and philosophy. These include but are not limited to the following: Antonio Gramsci, *Selections from the Prison Notebooks*, edited and translated by Quintin Hoare and Geoffrey Nowell Smith (London, 1971); Georg Lukacs, *History and Class Consciousness: Studies in Marxist Dialectics*, translated by Rodney Livingstone (Cambridge, Mass., 1971); Clifford Geertz, *The Interpretation of Cultures* (New York, 1973); T. J. Jackson Lears, "The Concept of Cultural Hegemony: Problems and Possibilities," *American Historical Review* 90 (1985): 567–93; Lise Vogel, *Marxism and the Oppression of Women: Toward a Unitary Theory* (New Brunswick, 1983); and Seyla Benhabib, *Critique, Norm, and Utopia: A Study of the Foundations of Critical Theory* (New York, 1986). Two collections of essays were also helpful: *Gramsci and Marxist Theory*, edited by Chantal Mouffe (London, 1979), and *Marxism and the Interpretation of Culture*, edited by Cary Nelson and Lawrence Grossberg (Urbana, 1988).

Index

Adams, Charles Francis, 17
Alcott, Bronson, 202–7; *Conversations with Children on the Gospels*, 207
Alcott family, 206
Alienation, 224–25
American Society for Educating Pious Youth for the Gospel Ministry, 103
American Temperance Society, 103
American Unitarian Association, 86
Andover Theological Seminary, 14, 24, 25
Anglicanism, 5, 144. *See also* Episcopalians
Antimasonic party, 48
Antinomianism, 230. *See also* Subjectivism
Arminianism, 23, 89. *See also* Liberal religion; Unitarianism

Back Bay, 3–4
Ballou, Adin, 231
Bangor, Maine, 140, 143
Baptists, 25, 108, 134
Barker, Anna, 207
Bartol, Cyrus, 103
Bates, James, 139
Beacon Hill, 3, 46
Beattie, James, 61
Beecher, Edward, 86, 99–100

Beecher, Lyman, 64, 84–109 passim, 163, 164, 167
Beecher, William, 100
Belsham, Thomas, 23
Benevolent associations, 102–7
Berkeley, George, 61
Bible Society, 107
Blackwood's Edinburgh Magazine, 62
Blair, Hugh, 124, 152, 154–55
Bliss, Daniel, 112
Blood, Mary, 101
Boston, Mass., 26–29, 64, 112, 137, 153, 173, 201, 203; commercial development in, ix, 148–49; Emerson in, 3–4, 12–17, 30, 32–34, 36–39, 141–42, 147, 178–79; in Federalist period, 3–6, 11–12, 15; churches in, 17, 22–23, 24, 83, 115–18, 125, 127, 174, 176; expansion of, 17–25, 34, 43, 46–47, 163–64; social problems in, 19–22, 164; migration to, 20–21, 163–64; political parties in, 34–36, 48–49; Emerson on, 36–39, 50, 52–56, 57, 76–79, 106, 110–11, 160, 191, 237; religious controversy in, 83–111, 128, 134, 169; relation to Harvard University, 166–67; mobility in, 261 (n. 31). *See also* individual Boston churches

Boston Association, 23, 67
Boston Atheneum, 6
Boston *Courier*, 207
Boston *Intelligencer*, 20
Boston Latin School, 12–13, 25
Boston *Recorder [and Telegraph]*,
    21, 87, 88, 94
Boston Society for the Diffusion of
    Useful Knowledge, 140
Boston Society for the Moral and
    Religious Instruction of the Poor,
    21
Boudinot, Elias, 19
Bradford, George P., 182, 203
Brattle Street Church (Boston), 116,
    174
Brook Farm, 204–7, 210
Brown, Thomas, 61
Brownson, Orestes, 202
Brown University, 25
Buckminster, Joseph, 18
Buckminster, Joseph Stevens, 11,
    18, 93, 116–17; "Take Heed How
    Ye Hear," 116
Bulfinch-Street Chapel for the Poor,
    90
Bulkeley, Edward, 112
Bulkeley, Peter, 112
Burke, Edmund, 148
Butler, Joseph, 59

Calvinism, 5, 10, 22, 58, 84, 93,
    108–10, 139, 226. *See also* Con-
    gregationalism; Evangelicalism;
    Orthodoxy
Cambridge, Mass., 25, 27, 30, 58,
    140, 183
Cambridge Platonists, 72
Cambridgeport, Mass., 46
Campbell, George, 61
Capitalism, x–xi, 17, 48, 145, 148,
    159, 173, 221, 240–41. *See also*
    Commercialization

Carlyle, Thomas, 165, 203, 231
Channing, Edward Tyrrel, 124, 222
Channing, William Ellery, 118, 120,
    124, 130, 152, 170; on the times,
    11, 103–4; and Unitarian contro-
    versy, 23, 89, 105; as Emerson's
    teacher, 43, 62, 125; "Remarks on
    Associations," 105; "Remarks on
    Natural Literature," 156
Charles River, 3, 27, 46
Charles River Bridge, 46
Charlestown, Mass., 164
Cherokee Indians, 51
Christian Disciple, 23
Christian Examiner, 116, 119, 171
Clarke, James Freeman, 202
Cleora (*Panoplist*), 103
Codman, John, 23–24, 89
Coleridge, Samuel Taylor, 70; *The
    Friend*, 73; *Aids to Reflection*,
    73–74
Commercialization, 153, 193, 222–
    25; of Boston, 76; of literature,
    155–56
Concord, Mass., 69, 113; as Emer-
    son family home, 4, 15, 112; Em-
    erson moves to, 79, 143, 160,
    163–65, 195, 201; Emerson in,
    150, 187–91, 202–7, 217, 232,
    237–39
Congregationalism, 5, 22, 83, 97–
    98, 134–35. *See also* Calvinism;
    Evangelicalism; Orthodoxy
Conventicle Club, 28, 36
Cooper, James Fenimore: *The Spy*,
    155
Cragie's Bridge, 46
Cudworth, Ralph: *True Intellectual
    System of the Universe* and *Trea-
    tise Concerning Eternal and Im-
    mutable Morality*, 72

Dedham decision, 85
De Gérando, Marie Joseph, 70, 72
Democracy, 7–8, 39, 63
Democratic party, 38. *See also* Jacksonian Democrats; Jeffersonian Republicans
Dewey, Orville, 140
Dial, The, 205, 218, 231
Domesticity, 192–97
Dorchester Neck Bridge, 46
Dwight, Timothy, 18, 27

Edinburgh Review, 62, 73
Eliot, John, 90
Emerson, Charles Chauncy, 12, 15, 132–33, 135, 141–42, 150, 202, 224, 283 (n. 22)
Emerson, Edith, 195, 218
Emerson, Edward Bliss, 12, 14, 15, 24, 154, 157, 202
Emerson, Edward Waldo, 195, 219
Emerson, Elizabeth Bulkeley, 112
Emerson, Ellen Louisa Tucker, 50, 130, 137, 139, 163, 192, 200, 280 (n. 2)
Emerson, Ellen Tucker, 195, 196, 218
Emerson, George Bliss, 141
Emerson, John Clarke, 12
Emerson, Joseph (great-great-great-grandfather), 112
Emerson, Joseph (great-grandfather), 112
Emerson, Lydia (Lidian) Jackson, 157, 163, 175, 192–97, 200, 220, 238
Emerson, Mary Caroline, 12
Emerson, Mary Moody, 8, 16, 113, 137, 187, 219, 224; Calvinism of, 5, 24, 57, 58
Emerson, Phebe Bliss, 4, 112
Emerson, Phebe Ripley, 12
Emerson, Ralph Waldo, ix–xi, 4, 34, 79, 117, 152, 154, 155, 159–60, 166, 241; birth of, 3, 12; Federalist education of, 12–17; attends Harvard College, 25–31; as poet, 28–29, 31, 157–58; early attempts at literature, 31–32, 157; on Boston municipal reform, 36–39; on social problems, 36–39, 43–46, 50–55, 66, 76–78, 164–65, 221–23; Federalist tendencies of, 36–41, 43, 45, 50, 53, 57; on political parties, 37–38, 51; on reform, 39–42, 164–65, 191–92, 205–6, 239–40; development of ethical philosophy, 39–46; philosophical influences on, 40–41, 70–74; on nature, 41–42, 44–45, 58–64, 76–77, 153; on moral economy, 42, 44–45, 66–70, 75–78, 151, 168, 186; moves to Roxbury, 43–44, 46; on natural law, 44, 55–56, 58–59, 66–69; on sympathy, 44–45, 216–17; enters into ministry, 49–50, 112, 119–21; marriage to Ellen Louisa Tucker, 50, 130, 137, 192, 200; on virtue, 50–55; pastorate of, 50–55, 83–85, 104–11, 128–36, 260 (n. 15); republicanism of, 50–56, 228; on Nature, 62, 64, 69, 74, 76–78, 145, 153, 165, 179, 180, 193, 210, 217, 219–21, 231–37; on natural religion, 64–70, 76–78, 134–35, 170, 178–79; on character of God, 70, 77, 168–69, 176–78; on benevolent organizations, 105–7; on sectarianism, 105–11, 128–35, 139–40; on abolitionism, 106, 226–27, 231; on ministry, 121–27, 168, 171–72, 178–80; on eloquence, 122–24, 152–53; on Unitarianism, 128, 131–32, 167, 169, 171–72, 178–80; and Lord's Supper contro-

versy, 129–36; travels to Europe, 137–39, 237; on the scholar, 138, 145–49; lyceum lecturing of, 140–45, 150–51, 165, 191; on moral value of literature, 156–58; moves to Concord, 163, 188–91, 201; marriage to Lydia Jackson, 163, 192–97, 200–201; and symbolic language, 179–81; and domesticity, 192, 197, 206; on marriage, 192–97, 200–201; on women, 193–94, 199, 213; on love, 198–200, 218, 280 (n. 2); friendships of, 202–3, 207–8, 211–17; on friendship, 202–3, 207–11, 218; on Brook Farm, 204–7; and death of son Waldo, 217, 219–21, 232–34; on sincerity, 227–29; death of, 238; later career of, 238–40; on slavery, 239–40; on genius, 287 (n. 30)
—Works: "Address Delivered in Concord on the Anniversary of the Emancipation of the Negroes in the British West Indies," 239; "The American Scholar," 145–49, 151; "Art," 197; "Biography," 144, 147–48, 151; "Character," 287 (n. 30); "The Character of Socrates," 40–42; "Circles," 42, 197; "Compensation," 197; *The Conduct of Life*, 237; Divinity School Address, 166–91, 238; "Edmund Burke," 151; "English Literature," 151; *Essays, First Series*, 197–98, 208; *Essays, Second Series*, 221, 232, 236, 238, 288 (n. 30); "Experience," 221, 231–36, 238, 239; "Fate," 237; "Fourierism and the Socialists," 205–6; "Friendship," 197, 208–11; "George Fox," 144; "Heroism," 197; "History," 197; "Home," 200; "Human Culture,"

151; "Human Life," 188; "Intellect," 197; "Italy," 151; "The Lord's Supper," 133–36, 178; "Love," 197–201, 208; *Memoirs of Margaret Fuller Ossoli*, 214; "Modern Aspects of Letters," 151; *Nature*, 157, 186, 210, 223, 236, 288 (n. 30); "Nature," 287 (n. 30); *Nature; Addresses and Lectures*, 238; "Nominalist and Realist," 237; "The Over-Soul," 197; "Permanent Traits of the English National Genius," 151; "The Philosophy of History," 151; *Poems*, 189; "The Poet," 287 (n. 30); "Pray Without Ceasing," 66–68; "Prudence," 197; *Representative Men*, 157, 200, 237, 238; "Science," 151; "Self-Reliance," 42, 106, 143, 198, 221–32; "Shakspear," 151; "Society," 203; *Society and Solitude*, 237; "Society and Solitude," 217; "Spiritual Laws," 197; "Threnody," 220–22; "Uriel," 183–87; "The Uses of Natural History," 141, 151; "Water," 151; "Woodnotes I," 189
Emerson, Robert Bulkeley, 12, 15
Emerson, Ruth Haskins, 5, 12, 15, 16, 24, 116, 154, 206
Emerson, Thomas, 112
Emerson, Waldo, 195, 217, 218–21, 232–34, 285 (n. 3)
Emerson, William (grandfather), 4, 112
Emerson, William (father), 152; as member of Federalist elite, 3–15 passim, 39, 57; as minister, 4–6, 112–15, 117
Emerson, William (brother), 12, 15, 16, 30, 43, 113, 126, 131–33, 135, 194, 207, 224

Enlightenment, 26, 213
Episcopalians, 134
Evangelicalism, 107, 134; and Lyman Beecher, 84–85, 86, 88, 91–94, 96, 97; separation from Unitarians, 85–86; criticisms of Unitarianism, 86–87, 88, 89, 91–94; church organization, 97–99; church membership, 99–102; reform efforts of, 102–5; Emerson on, 107, 110, 111, 128–29, 131. *See also* Calvinism; Congregationalism; Orthodoxy
Evarts, Jeremiah, 23
Everett, David: "Lines Spoken at a School-exhibition, by a Little Boy Seven Years Old," 13
Everett, Edward, 48, 55, 130, 141, 152
"Experimental Religion," 66, 77, 109, 135

Federalism, 26, 33, 43, 45, 47; as a political party, 6, 25; ideology of, 6–19, 50, 57, 62, 152, 228; and Boston civic reform, 34–39
Federal Street Church (Boston), 43, 125
First Church (Boston), 89, 99, 262 (n. 36); and William Emerson, 3, 5, 15, 83, 115, 117
First Church (Charlestown), 22
Fourier, Charles, 205
Fourierists, 205, 231
Fox, George, 144, 148
Francis, Convers, 202
Freeman, James, 90
Frisbie, Levi, 20–21, 59, 60, 72, 155
Frost, Barzillai, 168
Frothingham, Nathaniel, 89
Fruitlands, 204
Fugitive Slave Act, 238, 239
Fuller, Margaret, 191, 206–9, 211–16, 219–21; "Woman in the Nineteenth Century," 213

Gannett, Ezra Stiles, 125
Garrison, William Lloyd, 48–49, 105, 164
Goodwin, Hersey Bradford, 69
Gorham, Benjamin, 34
Graham, Sylvester, 164
Green, Mr. (Lynn, Mass., minister), 125
Green, Samuel, 104–5
Green Street Church (Boston), 97
Greenwood, Elizabeth, 101–2
Griffin, Edward, 87

Hale, Edward Everett, 278 (n. 11)
Half-Way Covenant, 88
Hanover Association of Young Men, 264 (n. 52)
Hanover Street Church (Boston), 84–85, 86, 92, 97, 100, 104, 108
Harvard, Mass., 5, 114–15, 204
Harvard College, 5, 13, 22, 25, 33, 62, 113, 124, 170, 222; in 1817, 26–30; student rebellions at, 27–30, 166–68, 251 (n. 55), 277 (n. 5), 278 (n. 11); moral philosophy of, 59–61
Harvard Divinity School, 73, 118, 176; Emerson enters, 46, 66; and Emerson's address, 166, 168, 171–72; class of 1838, 167–68
Harvard University, 238
Haskins, John, 5
Hasty Pudding Club, 26
Hawthorne, Nathaniel, 204
Hedge, Frederic Henry, 140, 202–3
Hedge Club, 202–3
Henshaw, David, 47
Hill, John Boynton, 36–39, 43
Holbrook, Josiah, 140

Howard Benevolent Society, 107
Hume, David, 61, 120

Idealism, 61, 71
Individual, conceptions of, 222–25
Individualism, 45, 59, 239, 286
(n. 14)
Intellectuals, ix–x, 148–50, 158–59

Jackson, Andrew, 47, 49, 51
Jacksonian Democrats, 47, 51
Jeffersonian Republicans, 8
Jeremiad, 9–11, 32, 50, 52, 168
Johnson, Joseph, 101

Kant, Immanuel, 73
King's Chapel (Boston), 90
Kirkland, James Thornton, 26, 30,
90, 251 (n. 55), 277 (n. 9)
Kneeland, Abner, 173–74, 178

Ladd, Elizabeth Haskins, 25, 139
Ladd, William, 66, 139
Lathrop, John, 90
Liberalism, 8, 240–41
Liberal religion, 6, 10, 22–24, 26,
90–91, 108. *See also* Arminian-
ism; Unitarianism
Liberator, 48, 105
Literature, 154–58; Emerson's early
attempts at, 31–32, 43; Emerson
on, 146–47
Locke, John, 60–61, 72, 120; *Essay
on the Human Understanding*,
61
London Age, 264
Lord's Supper, 54, 89, 111, 129–36,
142, 144
Lowell, Charles, 20
Lowell, Mass., 164
Luther, Martin, 148
Lyceums, 140–41, 150–51

Market, 116, 155–56, 180
Mason, William Powell, 55
Massachusetts Historical Society, 6,
117
Massachusetts Missionary Society,
102
Massachusetts Society for Suppress-
ing Intemperance, 22
Mechanics Institute (Boston), 141
Methodists, 66–67, 109, 134
Michelangelo Buonaroti, 148
Middling Interest, 37, 47, 87, 99
Milton, John, 148, 183, 185
Ministry, 22; in Federalist Boston,
6–7; and Emerson family, 112–13;
changes in, 113–19, 124–25; im-
portance of character in, 124–25
Ministry-at-Large to the Poor of
Boston, 90, 103–4
Missionary Society, 107
Montaigne, Michel Eyquem de, 157
Monthly Anthology, 6, 23, 60, 152,
154, 155
Moral law, 59, 69–74
Morse, Jedediah, 22, 23, 85, 86

Natural aristocracy, 7, 8, 54
Natural History Society (Boston),
141
Natural law, 219, 234; of human
ethics, 40–41, 44, 54–55, 57, 66–
69, 75–78, 179, 229–31, 240; and
human nature, 42, 44–46, 105,
108, 110, 125, 155; and liberal
theology, 59–64; and the scholar,
143, 147, 159. *See also* Nature
Nature: Emerson's interest in, 41–
42, 58–59, 64–69, 139; as system
of spiritual laws, 56, 74–79, 145,
153, 165, 169, 179, 192, 193, 197,
199, 200, 206, 210, 217, 229–31;
romantic ideas of, 72–74; changes
in Emerson's understanding of,

220–23, 234–37. *See also* Natural law

Neoplatonism, 71–74

New Bedford, Mass., 140, 142, 143

New England Association of Farmers, Mechanics, and Other Workingmen, 48

New England Quarterly Magazine, 12

New North Church (Boston), 90

New South Church (Boston) 26, 90

North American Review, 155, 157

North End (Boston), 79, 83–85, 96–97, 100

Norton, Andrews, 170

Noyes, John Humphrey, 231

Old South Church (Boston), 14, 24, 84, 86

Olmsted, Frederick Law, 201

Oratory, 158; Federalist, 13, 152; ministerial, 116–18; Emerson's views on, 123–25; and lyceums, 141, 151–52

Organicism, 72, 159; social, 12–14, 16, 36, 57, 63–64, 85, 93, 275 (n. 35); natural, 63–64

Orthodoxy, 10; controversies with liberals, 22–25, 83–85, 87, 91, 93–94, 95, 101, 107–9

Otis, Harrison Gray, 47

Owen, Robert, 231

Paine, Thomas, 173

Paley, William, 59, 72; *Natural Theology*, 59

Palfrey, John Gorham, 117, 174

Panic of 1837, 164

Panoplist, 23, 87, 94, 103

Parker, Samuel D., 173

Parker, Theodore, 90

Parkman, Francis, 250 (n. 43)

Park Street Church (Boston), 24, 84, 86, 87, 97–102, 250 (n. 43), 262 (n. 35)

Peabody, Elizabeth, 219

Peace Society, 107

Perkins, Thomas Handasyd, 47

Phi Beta Kappa, 26, 145, 147

Phillips Church (South Boston), 97

Pierce, John, 90

Pine Street Church, 97

Prescott, William, 39

Providence, R.I., 25, 164

Puffer, Reuben, 9–12, 57, 88

Pythagorean School of Platonism, 72

Pythologian Club, 26

Quakers, 134, 144, 148

Quarterly Review, 62

Quincy, Josiah, 28, 35, 47, 49, 166–68, 277 (n. 9)

Railroads, 164, 237–38

Rationalism, 58, 59, 77, 173

Reason, 73–74, 123

Reid, Thomas, 61

Republicanism, 26, 228, 239, 241; and Federalism, 7–8, 10, 12, 47; Emerson and, 31–32, 52–53, 57

Rioting, 29, 164, 166–68

Ripley, Ezra, 4, 15, 69, 112–14, 126, 188

Ripley, George, 202, 204–5

Ripley, Samuel, 140

Ripley, Sophia, 203, 205

Robbins, Chandler, 127

Roman Catholics, 134, 164

Romanticism, 70–74, 203, 231

Rousseau, Jean-Jacques, 231

Rowson, Susanna: *Charlotte Temple*, 155

Roxbury, Mass., 43–44, 46

Russell, Mary, 206

Salem Street Church (Boston), 97, 100, 101

Sampson, George, 283 (n. 22)

Schelling, Friedrich Wilhelm Joseph von: *Naturphilosophie*, 73

Scottish Common Sense Philosophy, 61–62, 70–72

Seaman's Bethel (Boston), 153

Second Church (Boston), 57, 86, 88, 90, 99, 106, 118, 123, 137, 139, 150, 229, 262 (n. 35); and Emerson's call to pastorate, 50, 83–85, 126; and Unitarian pietism, 95–97; and Lord's Supper controversy, 111, 132–36

Second Church (Dorchester), 23–24

Sectarianism, 91, 110, 137, 140

Sensationalism, 60–61, 70–74

Shakers, 231

Sincerity, 227–29

Skepticism, 61

Society for Propagating the Gospel among the Indians and Others in North America, 102

Society for Suppressing Intemperance, 107

Society for the Diffusion of Useful Knowledge, 144, 147

Society of Free Enquirers, 173

Socrates, 40–41, 55

South Boston, 46

Speaking Club (Harvard), 26

Spirit of the Pilgrims, 92–93, 94

Spiritual law(s), 67–69, 70, 73–74

Sprague, Charles, 47

Staël, Anne-Louise-Germaine de, 73

Stewart, Dugald, 61, 71

Strong, Caleb, 6

Sturgis, Caroline, 207, 211–12, 215

Subjectivism, 230, 234–36. *See also* Antinomianism

Sullivan, William, 8, 18, 39

Sunday schools, 21–22

Swedenborg, Emanuel, 200

Sympathy, 44–46, 216

Taylor, Edward Thompson, 153

Taylor, Nathaniel, 86

Thompson, George, 164

Thoreau, Henry David, 191, 206–7

Thwing, James, 262 (n. 36)

Ticknor, George, 27, 29

Transcendental Club, 202–3

Transcendentalism, 73, 174

Tuckerman, Joseph, 90, 103, 125

Understanding, 73

Union Church (Boston), 97

Unitarian Association, 168

Unitarianism, 21, 50, 134–35, 140, 202; controversy with orthodoxy, 23–24, 83–94, 97–107, 128–31, 167; natural and moral philosophies of, 59–64, 65, 67; pietistic reform of, 94–96, 124–25; Emerson on, 107–11, 128–31, 169; ministry within, 114, 117–19, 127; philosophy of letters, 152, 155; and Divinity School controversy, 169–78, 180. *See also* Arminianism; Liberal religion

Universalists, 134

University at Cambridge, 25–26. *See also* Harvard College

Ursuline Convent (Charlestown), 164

Ward, Samuel, 207

Ware, Henry, Sr., 22, 59

Ware, Henry, Jr., 116, 118, 123, 126, 186, 260 (n. 15); as pastor of Second Church, 83–85, 95–96, 102; reaction to Divinity School Address, 170–72, 175–78, 180–81; "On the Personality of the Deity," 175–78, 181

Washington Benevolent Society, 13
Webster, Daniel, 39, 152–53
Wells, Samuel A., 34–35
West Boston, 46
West Boston Bridge, 27

Wollstonecraft, Mary, 213
Worcester, Samuel, 23
Worcester, Mass., 164
Wordsworth, William, 73, 231
Wright, Fanny, 173